ELSEWHERE, CANADA:

MUSINGS OF A KATIMAVIKER

by Devon Flynn

Thanks so much for the support Cori! Hope you enjoy the story and all the Devonisms! - Devon

ISBN-13: 9781738255610
First Edition

This story is based on a true story of my lived experience. Some names and details have been changed to protect the privacy of individuals involved. I have re-created events, locales, people, and organizations from my memories to the best of my ability. In some cases, I have edited conversations for brevity. Otherwise, I have made the effort to be faithful to my experience while acknowledging that same experience may have been different for others.

DEDICATION:

This story goes out to all the Katimavikers and anyone else who stepped outside their comfort zone during that unnerving period of time in your life when you both feared the world and were ready to take it on.

I extend my deepest appreciation to my friends who put up with my incessant questions and rants regarding writing and publishing, as well as my excited bouts of sharing my own progress.

And finally, I want to thank everyone who waited patiently for my story to come to fruition. I can't think of a single person who didn't believe I would make this happen.

TABLE OF CONTENTS

CHAPTER 1

November 2005. Sault Ste. Marie.

"How many of you come from a small town and just needed to get out and do something different?"

In a large room where thirty or so young bodies stood, plenty of hands shot up in answer to this question. Mine was included. I was surprised at how accurately that question seemed to hit home, to see how many people felt the same way I did. People began shouting their explanations.

"My parents signed me up."

"It was my school counsellor's idea."

"My brother did it and said I should."

There were several older people in the room, a small handful of women who looked to be in their late twenties or perhaps early thirties. "I've heard every single one of those reasons before. Now, how many of you actually *knew* what Katimavik was before you joined?" Fewer hands rose to answer this question. One girl even admitted she didn't even know how to pronounce it when she signed up! Still, there was comfort in knowing that there were others who were just as clueless and nervous as the person beside them. I, on the other hand, had a pretty good idea of what I was getting into; that's why I was there.

I'd known about Katimavik for several years. It was a volunteer program for youth between 17-21 years old, but it mostly appealed to recent high school graduates like myself. It was at my school where I first heard of Katimavik. One of the program's volunteers gave a presentation during a Career and Personal Planning class. He was only a few years older than me and my friends, making him more relatable than some of the other, older guest speakers we occasionally had in our classes. As much as I respected them, this young man wasn't an authority figure like a nurse preaching safe sex in health class or a police officer warning us about the dangers of drugs. Rather than boring us with facts and stats, his presentation was animated with enthusiasm yet sincere as he told us more about the program that had him living in a house with people his age from different provinces, with whom he lived and worked with daily. His arms flailed wildly as he described his "Project Leader," or PL, a head figure who oversaw the group. He emphasized how it was the participants themselves, however, who drove their experience. They were the ones ultimately responsible for planning all sorts of trips and activities while also volunteering in their communities, which could be anywhere across Canada.

Katimavik was touted as an excellent alternative to working or attending college or university after high school. Frankly, I couldn't believe it was free, considering the travel to your new community and subsequent living expenses were covered. And after completing the nine-month program, you were even awarded a $1000 bursary, which only sweetened the deal as far as I was concerned. Besides, I definitely wasn't ready for university. Despite having been an "A" Honour Roll student my entire life, I didn't have a burning desire to pursue a post-secondary education. I wanted a break from books and tests. I also didn't know what I wanted to study, so it seemed pointless to spend tens of thousands of dollars to attend school when I didn't even know what subject I wanted to major in. Some people thought Katimavik was just another way of stalling the pursuit of an obligatory bachelor's degree, but for me, it was exactly what I wanted to do.

The following summer, I found myself involved with Katimavik participants once again, only this time, I was working alongside two of them. I was hired as a landscaper for the town while they did it as part of their volunteer work. We were closer in age than the participants who had presented in my class, but I still felt they had their own wealth of knowledge to impart from the travel and the communities they lived and volunteered in so far. Katimavik groups lived in communities for three months trimesters at a time before rotating to a new one. That particular group found themselves stationed and living in Hazelton, a community nestled away in the Bulkley Valley region of north-western British Columbia. Each participant shared the same opinion: The mountains and rivers here were beautiful and the people were friendly. Every participant in Hazelton absolutely loved the place I called home. Regardless of how brief their stay of three months was, they saw something in the place I grew up that I intrinsically knew was there, but didn't quite see or appreciate like they did. Still, it was a nice change from the general attitude of my peers who all wanted to get out of town as soon as they could.

As we worked together landscaping different properties and helping out on various projects around the town, these "Katimavikers" told me more about the volunteer program which I was growing increasingly fascinated by, answering questions I didn't get to ask the previous Katimaviker who spoke in my class. The young man and woman were several years my senior but with plenty of worldly experience as far as I was concerned. The two of them obliged my curiosity, describing similar experiences that I'd heard from other Katimavikers placed in Hazelton. They also shared off-the-record stories, anecdotes that weren't exactly appropriate for a guest speaker to talk about during a classroom presentation. It sounded like when participants weren't volunteering or adhering to a busy schedule of planned activities, they got into some ridiculous situations, especially on their days off.

Whether it was the structure around things that interested me, or the fun spontaneity of the people involved, Katimavik sounded right up my alley—just a bunch of silly people volunteering, helping out the community they lived in, while occasionally goofing off and having a laugh. The more I learned about Katimavik, the more appealing it became, until I finally signed up in my graduating year.

As excited as I was to have flown thousands of kilometres away from home to be find myself in rural Ontario—now a new Katimaviker myself—I was not listening to the leaders explain rules and expectations of the volunteer as part of our "Mass Orientation," or Mass-O as we started calling it. I was preoccupied with looking around the room, studying the faces of my peers. We had all come from across the country to be joined in this room, myself included. In addition to being the furthest I had ever travelled, it was also my first time travelling alone. I put home out of my mind though. I could deal with being homesick later. For the moment, I felt like I was right where I needed to be.

I continued scanning the room, looking for the participants who would be in my group. In one of the last orientation emails we'd received before we all left for Katimavik, everyone was given the contact information of the participants in their group. We were encouraged to reach out to each other before the start of the program to get to know those we'd be living with ahead of time. Most of us immediately began messaging each other online, sharing what we were bringing, our thoughts about the communities we'd be living in, and what we expected Katimavik to be like. Now that we were there in person, I was trying to put faces to names.

One member of my group was a petite francophone named Bethany. When she and I chatted online, she admitted her English wasn't great and that she was nervous about how well she would adapt. I promised to help her practise her second language in exchange for her helping me learn mine. I wasn't sure if our online messages might have come off as flirtatious, with my confidence bolstered by speaking with someone who was unsure of themselves in comparison to my unbound excitement. I would have to see for myself if she would take me up on my offer to help her.

I tried to spot Bethany among the group, but there were a lot of us standing around. It wasn't just members of my group at orientation after all. Everyone there belonged to one of three groups, named after the community they'd be living in: Sault Ste. Marie, Blind River, and Thessalon. Together we were a "cluster" and were told that we would sometimes do activities together but otherwise most of our time during the program would be spent with our respective group. Still, it meant new people to meet.

I continued looking around, observing the diverse group of individuals: a tall, freckled redhead standing in the back; a round, bearded guy, wearing a Nintendo shirt; a cute blonde girl with highlights and wearing a green Rough Riders jacket.

Wait... did she just smile at me?

The woman at the front of the room finished speaking.

"Don't worry too much about remembering everything. For now, let's eat!"

Lunch consisted of an obnoxious amount of hummus and more varieties of salad than I had ever seen before. The food had been prepared for us ahead of time by our own Project Leaders, or PLs as we were soon calling them. For the first week of Katimavik, these heads of the house would take care of duties, like shopping and cooking, until they were eventually taken on by their participants once we'd settled into our homes and become familiar with a routine. It was a good thing they'd cooked for us in advance. The small buffet was devoured by the large pack of hungry teenagers. I tried a little bit of everything and found all of it delectable. I had never even heard of kale before, but apparently there was a whole type of salad devoted to the leafy green.

That was the routine for how the rest of Mass-O went. Each day was structured and dense with new information. Plenty of questions were asked and answered. Numerous pages of chart paper were written on, flipped, and started anew. There were lots of terms and acronyms thrown at us, very few of which I retained. In between workshops, someone would start up some sort of camp game or activity that kept us mobile and out of lunchtime food comas. Some participants were still catching up on their sleep from the long day(s) of travel needed to get to where we were. Those in my group were no exception.

Each morning over the three days of Mass-O, our PL, Linda, would call on us all to wake up from the bottom of the stairs. She had to make sure that the group of ten kids in the house didn't sleep in and got up, showered, ate breakfast, and were out the door. If she was successful (she usually was), we would all pile into a large white van with the Katimavik logo on its side at a decent time which Linda would drive to Thessalon for the all-day workshops.

Everyone hit the ground running with the sudden shift from our regular lives, but I was impressed with the positive vibes that seemed to prevail. As Mass-O progressed, every participant began coalescing, smiling as we ate and went through the long workshops. We were in this crazy new thing together, so we would figure it out together as well.

During an extended lunch break on our last day of Mass-O, a girl named Ashley suggested a walk down to the waterfront. She was the blonde who had smiled at me on day one. A few of us took her up on the idea. We wanted to get away from the building we had been cooped up in for the last few days, but also to explore downtown Thessalon. The lake was close enough that we could be back before we missed the last part of Mass-O.

When we arrived at the shore of Lake Huron, I could barely see land across from where we stood. A crisp, late November wind pushed waves that crashed upon shore. The sound was unusual to me. I was so used to rivers and small lakes nestled in the bottom of valleys between mountains. It was hard to believe there was a body of water this big, smack dab in the middle of Canada. It felt more like an ocean.

"Wow. I've never seen a lake this big!" Ashley said, sharing my awe.

Once we had taken in the view of one of Canada's Great Lakes, Ashley pulled out a small foam football which we began to toss around on the grassy lawn next to the shore. In between catches, she told me more about how things were different back in Saskatchewan.

Even though she seemed comfortable enough talking, Ashley struck me as shy. Her eyes glinted with excitement as she spoke about farms and barns and cows back home. She always seemed to have a story or small anecdote to tell in response whenever she learned something new about someone else. I sensed how some people might find her habit of comparing everything with her life back home annoying, but I found it endearing, relatable almost. It had only been a few days since we started, but Katimavik seemed to mean a lot to Ashley. Like most of us, it was a chance to get out of our own province and see more of the country, something Ashley revealed she had done so little of. Coming to Ontario was an even bigger change for her than it was for me.

By then, the small group of us were walking and passing Ashley's football between each other while chatting idly, although Carlos was quieter than the rest of us. He was in my group, but I hadn't learned much about him. All I knew was that he grew up in Kitchener, Ontario, but originally came from Columbia, which was hinted at by his mild accent, dark hair, and olive skin.

Someone had passed the ball to him which he aimed at me, but I shook my head. We were now walking by a rock jetty. One wrong bounce and the game of toss would quickly be over. Despite my warnings not to throw the football near the water, Carlos' next pass came up short. The red football was just out of my reach and took two bounces before it plopped into the water, bobbing like a buoy before it ebbed away from the shore. I contemplated walking into the frigid water after it, but the drop was too deep and I had no spare change of clothes. We weren't far from the building where orientation was being held, but the blustery winds coming off the lake would have ensured I succumbed to pneumonia by the time we returned. I didn't want the PLs going out of their way to prevent a participant getting sick in the first few days. My laments weren't as loud as Carlos's loud Colombian accent berating me.

"Ee-diot! Aye aye aye!"

Ashley assured me it was no big deal and laughed it off.

"It's okay. Easy come, easy go."

I still felt terrible at the loss of her football. More accurately, I was upset at Carlos for having lost it. I thought about whether I could have actually saved Ashley's football from its watery fate if I acted fast enough. It could have been a heroic gesture, but alas, the moment had passed.

"So, what do you guys think about Linda?"

We were back in Sault Ste. Marie in what would be our home for the next three months. I suspected a few of us might have given the whole volunteer thing a second thought if we were told they were going to cram nearly a dozen of us into one side of a duplex, but somehow we managed. There was something about living on Pine Street that I found adorable. The name seemed generic and archetypal, yet quaint, like hearing someone say they lived on Broadway or Main Street. A group of youth volunteers living in the duplex on Pine Street—it sounded like it was pulled from a young adult novel. The premise certainly had a cozy charm to it.

No one had a room to themselves except for Linda which was still quite small itself. The boys all shared the bedroom next to hers while the girls took the large bedroom downstairs for themselves. Both sexes had to sleep in separate rooms for obvious reasons. Given the limited space for everyone, bunk beds were necessary. Having grown up with two older brothers, I was used to the concepts of leftovers, hand me downs, and utilizing whatever space was left for me to cram my belongings into. They got the big rooms while the youngest got the smallest. At least here, we were all on a level playing field. It was going to take some of us longer to get used to the cramped arrangements, but I wasn't too bothered by it. The close quarters meant we were going to get to know each other whether we wanted to or not. That, and there were no other rooms available. The sooner we got used to it, the better.

It had been a long couple of days of being fed information, expectations, and salad from Mass-O. Being even more spacious than the living room, we gathered in the girls' room to decompress. With orientation behind us, we were finally able to settle in, to have a minor release of the mad energy that came from meeting so many vibrant people, playing games, yelling, laughing, and running around in between workshops. Erica, a curly-haired girl from Fort McMurray, was quietly strumming her guitar while the rest of us shared our thoughts about our own Project Leader.

"She seems pretty cool," said Jess. "Very relaxed. But not someone I'd want to upset."

"Like a mom," Luke chimed in. "In that, if we fucked up or broke the rules, she'd be more disappointed than upset."

There was a mumbled consensus there. Linda was a slender blonde woman in her late twenties. Her tender attitude did come off as motherly at first, but without an overbearing attitude. Then again, we had only known her for a few days. In that time, she had shared how she had been influenced and inspired by Japanese culture from having travelled and lived in the country for a short while. Even her boyfriend was Japanese, and she hoped to introduce us to him one day. Linda was also vegetarian, a characteristic that left a few of us a little nervous, but mostly the guys. The group had agreed to step outside our comfort zone and try the vegetarian meals she promised to cook for us.

"So long as there is the occasional plate of burgers, ribs, or steak, I'm fine with some vegetarian meals," Luke pointed out. He and I were in agreement, though it might have been more difficult for Luke. With the focus on healthy eating that Katimavik encouraged, he hoped to come out of the program with a few pounds less than when he went in. Luke wasn't what I would consider fat, but he was one of the more rotund of us there.

Our conversation felt like a scene from the Breakfast Club. There was no doubt we'd find even more similarities—and likely differences—the longer we all lived together. My friends back home and I joked around, of course, but rarely did we ever have situations like what was taking place, an intimate setting to see raw, blossoming people. I was content to be an observer of what I felt was something special taking place.

Carlos spoke up. "And what about you, Devon?" He tipped his head up at me. "You haven't said much. Why are you so quiet?"

He was right. I suddenly realized that I hadn't spoken for quite some time.

"Just … taking it all in. Pretty much on the same page as you guys. I think Linda is great and don't mind trying some new foods." It was true. I shared more or less the same opinions everyone else had expressed. I had been content to nod and smiled in agreement with them as I listened to them talk. After admitting that I felt the same way as most people, it didn't seem necessary to rehash what had already said.

Carlos harrumphed at my answer and went back to a private conversation with Rosalie who lay on the bed next to him.

The conversation had transitioned from talking about Mass-O and Linda to talking about ourselves, leading our late night into the early hours of the morning. It was a casual chat, but it felt like the end of an interview, the part where you could speak more freely about yourself rather than just trying to impress the other people in the room. We shared where we grew up, likes and dislikes, impressions of Sault Ste. Marie, why we joined Katimavik, future goals, etc. Everyone was eager to learn more about the others we'd be living with for the next nine months, myself included. Even though we were all roughly the same age, I wanted to hear about their lives, how different they were from mine, and how they might have led them to the opinions and thoughts they willingly divulged late that night.

"Ooh, I got a good one," said Rosalie. "What were everyone's first impressions of each other?"

Victor spoke up first. "I actually thought Devon was some sort of obnoxious punk kid. The blue hair, all the bracelets. I didn't think we'd get along." Victor was one of the first Katimavikers I met when I left Hazelton. He was sitting at a food court table in the Vancouver Airport along with members of both the Blind River and Thessalon group. "But now that I've got to know you, you're just ... well, not like I expected."

I shot him a look of light-hearted disbelief.

"Don't worry, it's a good thing," Victor chuckled. "You're cool."

I appreciated Victor's sincerity and knew he meant no harm in his comment. I was aware that my freshly dyed blue hair and wrist full of colourful bracelets would catch people's attention. In fact, I expected it.

Before I left home, I wanted to do something special, something crazy. I had dyed my hair before on whims, but nothing as outlandish as a vibrant ultramarine blue. Even the hairdresser had to ask if I was sure it was what I wanted. It was. A lot of people asked why I decided to dye my hair such an outrageous colour. "Why not?" I would respond. It could have been blue, red, hell, it could have been green and orange. Whatever colour it was, I wanted it to be part of the first impression people had of me, something that told them I wasn't some boring, small-town kid.

Victor's comment reminded me of the first time all three groups were brought together. It had only been a few days ago. Technically it hadn't been at the start of Mass-O, but at the Greater Sudbury Airport. Outside was a chartered bus hired to drop us off at our new homes where our new PLs eagerly waited for us to arrive. Most participants on the bus were already tired from travelling when we left the airport that evening and soon fell asleep. Others, like myself, stayed up for the remainder of the bus ride, chatting with the other participants with a restrained buzz so as not to wake up those who slept. We couldn't wait until the orientation the next morning to answer our burning questions. Where was everyone from? Which group did they belong to? And what in the hell did we just sign up for? With only the dim light from the console of the bus driver to illuminate faces, first impressions were made by people's voices and opinions. Daniel, who I later learned was in my group, made his known by speaking the loudest.

"That's what I love about this program. I can be anyone I want," he said. "For all you guys know, I'm just a big asshole, but in Katimavik, I can be a completely *different* kind of asshole!"

While Daniel's boisterous comment on the bus made us laugh, he had a point. No one on this side of the country knew me, who I was related to, or any embarrassing stories from my past. I didn't have to be a shy, small-town boy. I didn't even have to be the Devon Flynn people knew back home. I could be whoever I wanted to be, someone who wasn't a loser, but rebellious, nerdy, outgoing, charismatic, obnoxious, adventurous, flirtatious, brave, whatever I wanted. I could be any one of those things to people who didn't know who I was or where I came from.

I had a while to figure out who I wanted to be, but I knew I didn't have to decide right away.

CHAPTER 2

November 2005. Sault Ste. Marie.

We piled into the large white van. Four of us in the back seat, three more in the next seat up, then another three, and finally one riding shotgun with Linda. It was a ritual we were getting used to already. I enjoyed the drives. It always seemed like an adventure, a bunch of young weirdos in a van ready to joke and laugh and make the best of wherever we were off to.

Linda was taking us all over the city that day. We were touring the different workplaces we would be volunteering at. These work placements were the core foundation of Katimavik. Participants were required to work five days of the week, just like a regular job, only we didn't get paid. Katimavik "paid" participants a spending allowance of $3.00 a day. With the incentive of a regular paycheque out of the equation, most of our decisions on where we wanted to work were contingent on how much fun that place would be.

"I want you guys to choose where you think you'll fit in well. Not just where you'll have the most fun," Linda said to all of us. I was sitting in the back seat, but somehow she managed to make undeniable eye contact with me in the rearview mirror. I swear she read my damn mind.

The van turned a corner and pulled into our first stop—Community Living Algoma.

As soon as we walked through the front doors of the facility, we were met with a loud and frightening squawking noise. I was embarrassed with how much it made me jump, not expecting the piercing sound to be made in such a quiet place. Around the corner was the source—a drooling man swaddled in a large blanket. He lay in a basket suspended from a giant metal frame. It almost looked like it might be soothing had it not been for the squawks and moaning screams of the man hanging there. He watched the equally confused group of youth who tried hard not to stare at him or the other patients wandering the living room. I was instantly a stressful blend of nervous, anxious, and depressed at seeing the people walking by us.

Everyone looked to have some form of mental or physical disability, possibly both. Linda had barely given us any information about Community Living Algoma, just that it was a facility for those with disabilities. I didn't know what to expect, but I immediately felt ashamed of how uneasy I felt.

A care worker finally came out from one of the doorways. "You must be the Katimavik group," she apologized. "I'm sorry no one was able to greet you at the door. We had a small emergency with one of our clients. Follow me." She led us away, past the swaddled man who squawked loudly again. "Don't mind him, he's just excited."

The rest of our morning tour followed a similar format as we visited very different workplaces, including: a daycare facility, a forestry office, the Canadian Red Cross, the United Way, a bush plane museum, a learning disability centre, an animal shelter, and of course Community Living Algoma, which our tour guide explained was a facility that supported people with intellectual disabilities. At each workplace we visited, we were given a tour by an employee who shared what it was they and their co-workers did and how it contributed to the community, all while inserting cute little anecdotes here and there. Almost all the workplaces had typical nine-to-five jobs for us, although some of our guides hinted at the occasional odd days when we could potentially leave early. All the placements entailed some degree of office work, data entry, or helping clean up and organize.

Much to our disappointment, the most appealing facets of each job were dismissed as something we either weren't trained for or something that was rarely done. Needless to say, whoever volunteered at the animal shelter wouldn't be playing with cute puppies and kittens all day, but instead cleaning up after them. I could appreciate hearing an honest account of the pros and cons. It gave us a better idea as to what we could expect, good and bad. Wherever I ended up working, I'd make the most of it. As far as my own preference was concerned, it could be at any one of the places we toured, with the exception of perhaps Community Living Algoma.

Our workplace tour concluded with United Way. The organization had graciously provided us with lunch which Luke suspected was a bribe, a way to entice a plucky new volunteer. United Way had also provided us with a spare meeting room where we met the representatives from all the workplaces again for a short interview. Linda insisted that we shouldn't feel the same pressure as a job interview, but we should treat them as such regardless.

"Yeah, there's no pressure because we're not *getting hired*—we're volunteers," Daniel whispered. Linda shot him a brief, but disappointed glance. She was right though. It was now our turn to sell ourselves.

I felt perfectly at ease during each interview. I had no problem sharing my strengths, though my weaknesses always seemed so generic and bland:

"I work too hard and don't always know when to stop."

"Sometimes I get distracted."

"I crave variety and dislike the same old task."

All the interviewers listened and nodded at my sincerity, particularly the woman from Community Living Algoma. When she asked what I thought about their facility, I took a deep breath before politely admitting how I didn't see myself working there.

"But I really respect the work you do! I think it takes a certain kind of person to work with those types of people," I said, choosing my words carefully. "I just don't think I'd be comfortable working there. I ... I'm sorry." She appreciated my honesty, insisting that my observation was correct; as rewarding as it was, working with individuals with disabilities did indeed require a unique set of people skills.

After dinner later that evening, Linda announced where we'd be working. She had been busy the majority of the afternoon on the phone speaking with the representatives from the work placements, hammering out which participants would go where. We were excited to hear where we'd be placed for the next three months. Bethany was the first one announced. She would be working at Community Living Algoma.

"Sure, give 'em the French girl. I don't think she'll be speaking much to them anyway," said Daniel.

He had a point. English wasn't her strong suit. Maybe Bethany was a good fit there where she wouldn't be required to communicate much.

Linda continued: Victor was going to the learning disability centre; everyone was jealous of Luke *potentially* working with fuzzy kitties at the SPCA; Rosalie would help out at United Way; Carlos, the Red Cross; and Simone, the forestry office. Apparently, she was going to need a special security access card. We joked how she was going to have to ninja her way into work until her card arrived next week.

"As for Devon, Daniel, you two will be going to the Bush Plane Museum," Linda finished.

This surprised me, but not because I didn't like the place. I felt like I had nailed the job interview with Demmy, the coordinator of marketing and promotion at the museum. She did, however, admit there wasn't much work to be done in the upcoming winter though, something I didn't mind. It seemed like a neat place to work, very different from a regular office. I thought I might be able to help out with the exhibits or the planes. Hell, maybe I'd even get to fly in one, although I knew that hope was a stretch.

When I pressed for why the museum wanted two volunteers after learning there wasn't enough work for one, Linda's answer left us in the dark.

"You know... I'm not sure," Linda said, having to think about my question. "They just asked if they could have two of you."

With our new placements at the forefront of our thoughts, Linda excused us for the rest of the night. I went up to the guys' room and saw a large package on my bed. It had arrived earlier that morning, but with our work tours occupying most of the day I had completely forgotten about it. I brought the cardboard box down to the living room to open where most of the group was still sitting around.

"Is that the package from your friends back home, Devon?" Victor asked.

"Mmmhmm. And I have *no idea* what they put in here."

I had already talked a lot about my two friends, Bailey and Courtney. I met the pair of sisters when I became involved with a historical acting group one summer. They were homeschooled, which meant instead of spending time with them during class like my other friends, we bonded over other things, like our time spent acting, something most of my other friends had no interest in doing. My friendship with Bailey and Courtney was rooted in ridiculousness; whether it was laughing at the most asinine things while rehearsing plays we had written ourselves or hanging out indoors on a rainy weekend quoting *Monty Python* or *Family Guy* for the thousandth time, we never took things too seriously regardless of the stares we got.

I wrote my friends an email any time the house computer was available. I'd tell them about where we our group was off to that day and what we were up to, even though my friends admit they never knew what the hell I was talking about half the time. They had only responded to every other email, usually confused about who was who any time I referred to someone by name. Their emails were about as unapologetically rant-filled as my friends were in person, even occasionally dropping a movie quote randomly into the midst of their message, although it didn't have quite the same effect in text as in person. It made me miss them.

But if I couldn't share my group with my friends as well as I'd hoped, maybe I could share my friends with my group. I gathered everyone in the living room as I opened the box to see what Bailey and Courtney had sent me.

The box was filled with an assortment of goodies: strips of paper containing random *Family Guy* and *South Park* quotes, a handful of dinner mints the girls stole from the restaurant we went to as part of our last dinner before I left, and other silly reminders of inside jokes we had. I grabbed a letter from Bailey which I began to read aloud to everyone in the room. Most of the contents of the box didn't make sense without context anyway. I assumed Bailey's letter would be the same.

In it, Bailey asked how the program was so far, whether the people in my group were a bunch of weirdos or if I had that role covered, and if I had hit on the "French chick" yet. I bit my tongue hard as soon as the words came out of my mouth.

Whoops. God damn it, Bailey!

She was obviously referring to Bethany, who just happened to be sitting in front of me as I regrettably read that letter. I wasn't sure whether or not she understood the comment that was about her, but I avoided making eye contact for confirmation. Rather than stopping, I continued reading the remainder of the letter, believing a sudden silence would only draw more attention to me. I was convinced I was blushing and hoped no one would notice.

"Make sure you don't do anything stupid while there, like read this letter in front of everyone," read the last sentence.

Everyone in the room laughed at the excruciating irony, including Bethany. *Too little, too late. I'm definitely going to have to remember that for the next package.*

"Devon, it's a *volunteer* job. What are they going to do, fire us?" Daniel reminded me.

It was our first day of work. Linda had left bagged lunches on the kitchen table with each of our names written on them. We all thought it was adorable, but we knew it wasn't going to be part of our regular routine. In the next week, house managers would be decided. These were pairs of participants who would be in charge of cooking meals and cleaning up after participants for a week at a time. In the meanwhile, Linda had laid out precise bus fare in front of the bagged lunches for us to catch public transit to our workplaces, most of which were located downtown. The City of Sault Ste. Marie was planning on donating bus passes to us so we wouldn't have to pay to use the bus every time. Those kinds of donations were paramount for Katimavik groups as it was unfeasible for Linda to drive us everywhere like some overworked soccer mom. It would have also been detrimental to our house budget to pay for twice-a-day bus fare for ten young adults. And with our $3.00 a day allowance we sure as hell couldn't pay for bus passes ourselves. Until we received our complimentary passes, Linda had us covered and made our transition into a volunteer routine much simpler.

Daniel and I both agreed a perk of working at the Bush Plane Museum was that we started the latest and finished the earliest out of everyone. The two of us couldn't figure out the bus schedule unfortunately and decided to walk to the Bush Plane Museum for our first day of work. I had never ridden a city bus before. Hazelton had a small public transit bus, but it had a very limited and therefore inconvenient schedule. It was simpler to either bike where you needed to go or just ask someone for a ride. The pamphlet indicating Sault Ste. Marie's bus schedule were confusing columns depicting times, routes, and bus numbers which I had no idea how to decipher. I was surprised Daniel couldn't make sense of it either considering he was born and raised in Calgary. I assumed he would have had more experience with riding city buses, but he insisted he just walked everywhere and was amenable to that solution once again.

I was used to having to drive long distances to get anywhere back home and erroneously thought walking the densely packed city suburbs might somehow take less time. We expected it to take about twenty minutes if we kept a good pace, but we had sorely underestimated the true distance. On account of my badgering to make a good first impression for our first day of work, Daniel and I ran the last stretch so as not to be exceptionally late.

Though we had already been to the museum during our initial workplace tour, our new boss Demmy showed us around again. This time, she delved further into what programs and services the museum offered. Daniel and I were allowed to wander the museum freely, check out the displays, and even try the flight simulator whenever we felt like it. We could read the books in the gift shop and were allowed one free pop from the staff fridge. Work hours were 10–4 p.m., and lunch was an hour.

"Your first job is to help me out with our raffle," Demmy told us. The museum's raffle was one of their larger fundraisers for the year. "And your job over the next two weeks is to sell, sell, sell!"

And that was precisely what we did for the rest of the afternoon on our first day of work. Demmy gave us a book of raffle tickets and dropped Daniel and me off at the Sault Ste. Marie Station Mall. I still wondered why two of us were needed as volunteers for the museum, but sitting behind a table in a quiet mall for five hours may have answered my own question: two volunteers sold tickets better than one and it also kept the other from getting lonely and bored. Daniel might have been opinionated and even a bit obnoxious, but he kept things fun and was otherwise good company during a very dull job.

"So? How'd we do on day one?" Demmy asked when she swung by at the end of the day. She was moderately pleased with how many we sold. Even I was surprised with how Daniel managed to cajole people into purchasing raffle tickets. He hadn't exactly been an enthusiastic seller and was more concerned with making small talk with people in order to stave off his own boredom.

We packed up the signs, folding table, and raffle tickets into Demmy's vehicle. Once we dropped everything off at the museum, she offered Daniel and me a ride home, saving the two of us a very long walk. I swore to study the bus schedule and figure it out so we wouldn't be late again in the morning or have to rely on being given rides.

Daniel and I might have started work the latest that morning, but we also happen to be the first to arrive back at the house. We dropped off our bags and relaxed as the rest of the group began to trickle in. One by one, everyone returned from work and settled into the living room couches, sharing stories about our first day at our work placements.

"Dey made me do laundry all day. Who do dat?" Bethany bemoaned. From what she described, she would rarely ever be interacting with the Community Living Algoma patients. Doing so required specific training Bethany most definitely did not have and wasn't likely to receive over the next three months. I suspected her complaint might have been first day jitters, that laundry might have just been a task that simply needed to be done. I tried to explain how things would likely change down the road, but Bethany was not fully convinced.

"Yeah, well, it better not be all da time!" she huffed and heaved.

Erica and Carlos were the only two who really seemed to like their jobs. Erica was working at a daycare. She loved children and made a gleeful noise in telling us about their shenanigans under her care. Both the noise Erica made and the kids she described sounded adorable which surprised me. Erica didn't strike me as the maternal type.

"But seriously you guys, as cute as they are, kids are dumb!" she emphasized. "They are utterly oblivious to the liquids that are constantly dripping out at least one of their orifices at all times."

We wondered if Erica would last at the daycare. Even though she was convinced the children and their drippy noses would get her sick in no time, Erica assured us that she loved working there.

Carlos, on the other hand, seemed to have the most spiritually satisfying job at the Red Cross. He was currently learning how to repair wheelchairs and other mobility aids, but down the road he would be providing assistance to medical programs and putting together kits to be donated and shipped to villages around the world that needed them.

"I'm glad I'll be doing some good. I mean, don't get me wrong, Devon. Someone needs to… do whatever the hell it is you and Daniel are supposed to be doing," he said condescendingly. "I'm just happy to be helping those in other countries."

Having been born and raised in Columbia, Carlos had learned a lot about the socio-economic gaps that existed in developing countries. Anytime someone brought up the topic of social issues like homelessness, war, or drugs, Carlos was quick to jump in and state how well Canada had it in comparison to his home country.

I envied Carlos. He was passionate in his desire to help those who needed it, and his position at the Red Cross afforded him that opportunity. I wanted to do the same, but hey, we couldn't all change the world. Someone needed to sell raffle tickets.

"Yo Devon," Victor said from the kitchen. "I'm going to get started if you want to give me a hand."

As house managers were yet to be decided, we were paired up for single-meal cooking duties. Victor and I were partners that night. We were just about to cook the burgers (including veggie) that had been thawing in the sink until Linda came into the living room.

"Hey gang. I just got off the phone with Rosalie's supervisor at the United Way. She asked if we could help them sell raffle tickets tonight. Their draw is tomorrow, but they haven't sold nearly as many as they'd hoped. Feel free to say no, as it is a last-minute thing, but I know they'd love it if we could go door-to-door and help out with one last push."

Everyone hummed and hawed at the request. We might have been volunteers, but we had also just got home.

"She's also willing to buy the house pizzaaaaaa," Linda said with a tempting tone.

Burgers were nice, but pizza was better, especially when we didn't have to cook. I was oddly proud that everyone agreed to help, especially so close to supper time.

Granted, it was only going to be for an hour. Our hunger could hold off for sixty minutes.

We quickly split into pairs—again—and coordinated who would go where in the neighbourhood and quickly got to work. I went with Simone, a tall and soft-spoken girl from Fredericton.

"Devon, I have to admit, I'm a little nervous about knocking on doors and requesting money from strangers," Simone admitted. She kept her hands tucked in her coat pockets as we made our way to our first house. I didn't know Simone well, but I didn't think it was necessary to make her do something she wasn't comfortable with just to split the workload fairly. I offered to do most of the talking. It seemed appropriate if I was going to sell raffle tickets for the Bush Plane Museum over the next two weeks.

"Are you sure?" she said, second guessing herself.

"I'll consider it extra practice," I told her with a wink.

Simone tucked a sweet smile into the collar of her jacket. It might have softened me up to the idea as well, but I wasn't about to tell her that.

In between houses, Simone described how much like the rest of us, she had been nervous about leaving her hometown to join Katimavik. She didn't know what she wanted to do after school and when the opportunity came up, she went with it. It was only our first week, but she was already missing her friends dearly. I tried to put her worries at ease.

"I miss my friends too. But the great thing about the program is meeting new people. I know it hasn't been long, but… I like to think *we're* your friends now," I suggested kindly.

"You guys are," she said with humble embarrassment.

Simone and I finished our last house on the street before our expected end time. We started to make our way back when she spoke up.

"Thanks for listening to me about my problems, Devon," Simone told me. It seemed like an unnecessary comment. Of course I'd hear her out. I knew it was a hard transition for most people to leave their home to commit to a nine-month program. I wasn't sure whether the others felt the same way. I wondered if I was adapting the best out of my group.

When everyone returned to the Katimavik house, Linda helped tally up the remaining raffle books. Rosalie's supervisor was with her. She was ecstatic. Not only did she gush with appreciation for our willingness to take on her last minute request, but was amazed at how many we had sold in such a short time. True to her word, she bought us dinner. Participants didn't make much money in Katimavik, but damn if we weren't rich in pizza that night.

The delivery guy came by, and the pizzas were quickly wolfed down by hungry Katimavikers. I gathered everyone's plates to put in the sink when I realized Victor and I hadn't put the now-thawed burger patties back into the freezer. I didn't want to waste them or risk subjecting my group to food poisoning, so I decided to cook them to be used for lunch the next day. I had never cooked burgers before, least of all for other people, and it dawned on me how little cooking experience I had. I was confident I could cook them to a visibly 'done' state, but I started to feel nervous about making my group sick and decided to use a meat thermometer to ensure they were fully cooked. The process took forever. An hour in, Jess came up behind me and rested her head on my shoulder. Being the tallest and stockiest out of everyone in the group, it felt heavy and uncomfortable.

"So ... what are you going to do about Bethany?"

Of course the girls had been talking. What did I expect? Even if Bethany didn't understand what that stupid note meant, everyone else did! This wasn't high school damn it. It was our first week for fuck's sake! I wasn't about to launch into any drama, especially when I didn't know what was already inferred, discussed, or rumoured. Without looking up from the frying pan, I replied calmly to Jess.

"Absolutely nothing."

Jess lifted her head and walked away. "Okay. Just be caaaaaaaareful," she chimed quietly.

Her annoying intrusiveness aside, she wasn't wrong. We had all been warned and heard stories of "exclusive relationships" in Katimavik. They seemed as much a cornerstone to the program as PLs, volunteering, or salads. An exclusive relationship was just as it sounded: spending personal time with another individual to the point at which it began to affect group dynamics. This was the main concern that Katimavik had with them and why PLs were prone to warning against them. Having a personal and intimate relationship with a fellow group member or even one from another group excluded others. They were prone to distract you from program responsibilities, adding emotional drama to a group that had to live together. The thought of a "break-up" where the ex-couple had to continue living under one roof left me feeling queasy. Besides, I had no intention of rocking the boat. I liked where I was, the people I was with, and what I was doing. I didn't want to fuck that up. I understood why the rules were in place. I wasn't normally one to break the rules, but if I did, it would be done with subtlety and aloofness. It was too early in the program to even think about getting involved with anyone, especially if it was going to be everyone's business.

CHAPTER 3

November 2005. Sault Ste. Marie.

Daniel and I were back to selling raffle tickets, only this time we had company. The mall was hosting a community fair. Along the corridors of the mall were tables from other non-profit organizations, including the SPCA which Luke tabled for, and the United Way that had Rosalie working on their behalf. By this point, Daniel and I had been experimenting with different tactics to garner attention to our own raffle, including adding balloons to our table, wearing a large sandwich board sign, and holding a promotional sign upside down. The latter usually resulted in someone pointing out our mistake.

"Ah yes, but you *noticed* it though, didn't you?" Daniel and I would tell them. We felt it was effective.

The number of ticket sales wasn't particularly improved by our antics, but they worked well in attracting attention and staving off boredom. At least we had creative freedom with our lack of supervision. When my arms got tired from holding signs, I visited with Rosalie or Luke, while Daniel was content to read whatever book he fancied that week. Daniel was convinced that anyone who wanted to buy a ticket would likely do so of their own accord regardless of how we held a sign. It became very clear that he was more interested in keeping himself entertained than in the success of the raffle or even our job.

Daniel's cavalier attitude toward work started to paint a picture for me as to what he was like when he was younger. I imagined him handing in assignments to his teachers, complete with childish doodles and made-up information, just to see if they were paying attention. Of course, I knew it wouldn't be the end of the world if we didn't sell all the raffle tickets, but I wanted to at least make an effort. Daniel would likely just shrug his shoulders regardless of how many we sold. Maybe it was appropriate that he and I were partnered together at work.

I explained our different work styles to Rosalie, sitting with her at her table. She couldn't help but roll her eyes. She was neither fond of Daniel nor shy about voicing it. Even if Daniel heard what she thought of him, he would lap up her derision like sweet milk. Rosalie took a noticeable pause, clearly ready to change the subject to something more to her liking.

"So, what's going on with you and Beth?"

I wasn't surprised she wanted to know. Rosalie struck me as one of the more "girly girls," the type interested in make-up, gossip, dressing up for dates, and of course, boys. Then again, I didn't want to be presumptuous. After all, we had only been living together for a few weeks. There was still lots to learn about people. I knew how naïve it was to jump to conclusions and assumptions about people, although I was still waiting for Daniel to surprise me. I played the situation down between me and Bethany, mostly because I didn't know what to make of it myself.

"The letter kind of gave it away, Devon," she smirked. "English isn't her first language, remember, but it might be nice if you took more of an interest in learning French." Rosalie didn't need to tell me. Doing so wouldn't even be for Bethany's sake.

As a means of embracing the French culture that was so embedded into Canada's history, part of Katimavik's programming required participants to practise the country's official second language. This was done in several ways, one of which was through the second language committee where members planned activities to practise French. This could include inviting francophone guest speakers to the house, watching movies in French—with subtitles of course—or visiting French historical sites.

Katimavik also had one rotation where participants would live in a French-speaking community where they could focus more extensively on these language studies. This typically took place somewhere in Quebec, but sometimes these rotations were francophone communities in other provinces. I had average grades in my basic high school French classes that would be put to the test, but I didn't want to wait until our French rotation for me to begin practising. As I poorly explained to Rosalie, my French was, *"pas très bien."* Still, I agreed with her; getting an early jump on my French was a good idea.

Before supper that night, I perused a bookshelf in the living room. I skipped my index finger past cheesy Harlequin romance novels, how-to guides for living off the land, and boring history books until I found what might work—a thin French children's book. It was about a small bear and his family, exactly what I needed.

I walked down to the girls' bedroom and found Rosalie and Bethany on their beds.

"Can… can you two help me read this book?" I asked. I could feel my ego beginning to bristle, but I shoved it down for the time being. "I haven't practised for a long time, so I thought I'd start small."

They agreed.

I felt like a child as I read the book aloud, "*en français*," but it was satisfactory to finally make it to the end. It was particularly frustrating however to have to repeat the French word for bear—"*ours*"—over and over. It was a soft word, a throaty pronunciation somewhere between saying "whores," "ours," and "horse" that I just couldn't seem to get. Bethany and Rosalie found my struggle adorable, almost comedic, but stifled their giggles when they saw the frustration grow on my face. It was hard not to feel somewhat patronized, even though they appreciated my attempt. It might have been a different kind of "cute" than what I was going for, but the effort seemed to put a smile on Bethany's face.

There had been a growing discussion almost every evening about going to a local bar. Anyone of legal age was allowed to drink, but Katimavik had zero tolerance for underage drinking, and it was never allowed in the house. Linda must have sensed our dedication to the idea and suggested we visit the bar at the local university just down the road. She was hesitant about bending the rules, but was willing to turn a blind eye to our attempts to sneak those of us who were underage *into* the bar, a leniency we found more than fair.

"But I'm not taking responsibility if anyone gets turned away or into trouble," she warned us.

"You guys heard Mom, no bailouts from jail," I said. Linda smirked just a little at my comment.

With our PL's soft and distant approval, we chose a night to make our inaugural bar visit happen, one on which Lyndsey, our guide to Sault Ste. Marie's nightlife, would be free to join us. Lyndsey was a local Katimavik alumna whom we met at a welcome party the Bush Plane Museum had hosted for us in our first week. Now in her mid-twenties, she was still familiar with the day-to-day life of Katimavikers, having been one herself elsewhere, as well as the burning desire to escape the house and explore the local watering holes. Lyndsey agreed that the bar at the university campus might work. It was one of the more relaxed drinking establishments in town, one we might all get in under the guise of students. After a bean-and-salad-rich supper one evening, we gussied ourselves up and met up with Lyndsey before making our way to the bar.

Much to our disappointment, Jess and Simone weren't feeling up for it the night of and decided to stay in. Those of us who were underage—Bethany, Rosalie, and myself—were still willing to try. Our plan was to walk in with our heads high and full of confidence, and immediately find a place to sit. If we were asked for ID, we would complacently show them but insist the underage drinkers weren't drinking. The worst-case scenario was being refused entry or being booted out.

No one asked.

Lyndsey bought a pitcher of beer for the first round. Everyone drank with quiet joy.

"You sure you don't want any more, Devon?" Lyndsey asked me. I politely declined.

Most of the parties I had attended in high school ended with friends getting obnoxiously drunk and acting like asinine morons. I wasn't oblivious to what alcohol did to people, and while I knew it took more than a single beer to get to that level of intoxication, I didn't want to act like that, especially in front of my group. But for that night, I was content with nursing a small portion of the bitter beer in my glass to play the role and avoid suspicion from the bartender. I was enjoying the camaraderie of my group though. Looking around the table tucked in the back corner of the bar, I listened as Victor and Erica got into a noticeably louder debate about politics, Daniel and Luke discussed video games, and Carlos chatted inaudibly with Bethany. Rosalie was bored and asked me to join her in a game of pool still racked up by previous players. We blocked the balls from falling into the pockets on someone's shot and set them aside so we could play again. Each game of pool cost a loonie and a little bit of fun added up fast, especially when you only made $3.00 a day. We had to save money where we could.

A DJ set up his equipment and started playing music. Everyone got out from the booth and moved to the dance floor. The girls were impressed that I could breakdance. Seeing an attractive redhead in the corner, I asked her if she wanted to join us. She looked nervous but obliged. After the brief but enjoyable song together, she went back to her seat and the rest of us returned to our table. Rosalie and Bethany thought it was cute that I asked a complete stranger to dance. I shrugged it off. That's what you did, wasn't it? When the two of them went back to talking amongst themselves, Daniel leaned over. He had to shout over the loud music the DJ played.

"What's your technique?" he asked.

"Technique?"

"For picking up girls!"

I told him there was no "technique." All I did was ask if the girl wanted to dance. But soon the table's conversation turned into a discussion on pick-up lines and attracting the opposite sex. Daniel was very vocal about his own bravado, but we unanimously called bullshit on his claim. Everyone was soon throwing in their own opinion on confidence, respect, and intention when it came to wooing the opposite sex. I kept quiet and listened, occasionally looking to see if the redhead was still around. She was gone.

In our heated discussion, no one had noticed the bartender walk over.

"Can I see your IDs?"

The jig was up. After we showed our cards, the attentive bartender saw three of us weren't supposed to be there and we were politely asked to leave. We didn't mind. Everyone had some drinks and some fun and agreed to leave quietly. Lyndsey offered to call up some friends and buy more booze for an impromptu house party, but we declined and thanked her for joining us. Daniel, Bethany, and Rosalie decided to return home, but the rest of us were still energetic and caught the bus to the nearest Tim Hortons.

Over hot chocolates and honey crullers, our previous discussion on the opposite sex turned into gossip around who was already bonding with who in the group and the relationships that were budding, intimate or otherwise. Victor and Carlos soon cornered Erica, the only female present, and jokingly pressed her for details we weren't privy to. Erica stood her ground though.

"Nope, sorry boi-yos!" she said, crossing her arms. "I'm a brick wall and I ain't about to crack."

It was easy to see Erica was stubborn and wouldn't spill the beans. While I was intrigued, I didn't have a burning desire to probe her with further questions. Figuring out who liked who seemed like something we did in high school, not afterwards. My memories of friends dealing with it made it sound emotionally draining for those involved. Though Erica gave us little reason to believe there were any concrete romances already blooming, I had no doubt the topic would come up again.

House meetings were a weekly norm for every Katimavik group. They were intended to address any group matters, upcoming events and activities, and otherwise check in with participants to get a feel for how everyone was doing. They usually lasted an hour or two and normally took place after supper, although we'd heard some groups chose to have them in the morning. Our upcoming meeting that Sunday was moved to the afternoon to give us time to tackle a growing list of things that needed attending to. It was going to be a doozy.

There were several we had apparently been putting off for a while. Linda brought us up to speed on what needed to be done. We still had to decide committee members so activities within those groups could get started, and we had to write out our planned group activities.

"That includes a mandatory reflection workshop that needs to happen sooner than later," Linda explained. "I'm sorry gang. I feel like this is my fault for letting some of these slip by."

None of us held Linda in any contempt. We knew she had a role and responsibilities as a PL. It wasn't as though we'd been avoiding the required activities. Our house meetings so far had merely gone on longer than we wished to tolerate those nights, postponing agenda items until later. It was catching up with us though, and Linda politely but firmly wanted to nip it in the bud before everything got out of hand.

We all agreed to squeeze in the required reflection workshop that afternoon to get it done and out of the way. With so much for us to get done, that afternoon seemed as good a time as any. Linda suggested we multitask so we could finish the day a little sooner. While she elaborated on the purpose of Katimavik committees, we listened and cut out coloured puzzle pieces. They were intended to be part of the reflection workshop which Linda commenced after the committee talk. Now that we knew what they were all about, she gave us a deadline in the next few days to choose which committee we wanted to be part of.

"With that out of the way, we can jump right into the reflection workshop," Linda said, catching her breath after so much talking. "These puzzle pieces are intended to represent your role in the group: the piece you bring to the bigger picture and how you all fit together."

"Subtle," Daniel said under his breath. Linda ignored him.

"You can fill them in any way you'd like," she continued. "But while you do, I want you to think about what you expect to gain from the program, any fears and doubts you might have or goals you hope to accomplish."

Linda insisted it was an open-ended and unrestricted activity, that we could draw whatever we wanted on our personalized puzzle pieces so long as we kept those questions in mind. On my piece, a vivid scene started to emerge of a valiant knight facing a dark dragon across a pit of lava. Someone was using the black crayon so I used the next darkest colour I could find, a deep violet. As I watched the illustration on paper take shape, I thought about how I might justify it should anyone ask. I rehearsed an explanation in my head, how it was a metaphorical depiction of the expected ordeals and conflicts we could expect during the program and the anticipated overcoming of them. In reality, I simply drew the first thing that came to my mind. I didn't want to waste time overthinking the task.

"I see most of you are done or almost done. You can finish it later if you'd like, because I still need to have one-on-one meetings with everyone," Linda told us. These were brief follow-ups on our new work placements and the initial job interviews, another Katimavik requirement we agreed to knock out that day.

As Linda organized herself with an assortment of notes at the kitchen table, some of us went to our rooms while a few of us stayed in the living room to put the finishing touches on our puzzle pieces. Unsurprisingly, Daniel didn't care to finish his and was content with the minimalist approach he took to the project. With a bored curiosity, he randomly grabbed a binder of Katimavik guidelines from a nearby shelf and plopped himself onto the couch to begin nonchalantly flipping through the pages. Daniel read several sections aloud, commenting on how he thought they were more 'suggestions'.

"Hey, according to this, if we time our 48 hours off with a holiday, we can get three days off!"

Every rotation, participants were given two consecutive days off, 48 hours to be exempt from Katimavik commitments. They were effectively vacation days, time when participants could do whatever they pleased, including prohibited activities, so long as they were not in the house. Otherwise, participants still had to abide by Katimavik rules if they remained at the house during that time. Essentially, it was two days of unbridled freedom, the opportunity to get into the type of shenanigans that would either result in participants getting kicked out or become stories of

Katimavik legends. It was always an interesting topic of discussion. Some participants were content with using this time to relax, read, or maybe watch videos, which was a treat in a place that otherwise discouraged televisions and DVD players. Others had an itching desire to use this time to travel, take taxis, hitchhike, drink, smoke, have sex, and simply do everything that was difficult or not allowed while under the confines of Katimavik rules. I still hadn't made up my mind what I wanted to do with my 48 hours, but I wanted to do something cool, and preferably with some of the group.

"Devon?" Linda called from the kitchen. I sat down across the corner of the table from her as she reviewed her notes. She looked pleased.

"All the interviewers said more or less the same thing, that you were a very thoughtful and considerate young man," Linda said with a praising smile. "You certainly have a voice, but you don't express it like everyone else."

"Like Daniel, you mean?" I pointed out with a hint of sarcasm.

"Yes, I know what you mean," she smiled to herself, reluctant to comment any more on him. "But it's something I've noticed at house meetings too. You're kind of a ... silent leader," Linda said, carefully trying to find the right description. "From what I've seen, you speak up when you have to. And I think it resonates with people a lot more."

A silent leader? What did that mean? Linda's tact was appreciated, but her comment caught me off guard. It felt more like an insult, like I was being put on the spot or challenged. Obviously, that wasn't her intention. Linda was merely giving feedback and most of it positive. The more I thought about it, the more it bothered me though. I struggled to unravel why.

Having heard that term for the first time, I realized I didn't like it. A silent leader sounded more like a deficit rather than a strength. Why would anyone take you seriously if you weren't willing to speak up, defend your stance, and stand up for what you believe in? I knew being heard didn't necessarily mean having to be the loudest—again, Daniel came to mind—but it just seemed like a silent leader would be ... *ineffective.*

Linda's comment left me in a ponderous funk for the rest of the day. The evening gained a quiet lull after everyone had been debriefed by Linda. Most of the group attended a local hockey game that the Red Cross had donated tickets to us for, but Victor, Jess and I stayed behind. I didn't care much for watching sports. Once I finished my personal chores, I decided to go for a run at the YMCA which had also granted us free passes. Victor was too tired and declined, and Jess was nowhere to be found, so I went alone. As much as I enjoyed spending time with the group, I was content to work out alone.

The YMCA gym was wide and open. There were few people present which left the machines abundantly available. This included the treadmills and elliptical machines lined up against a wall of large windows that faced one of the city's main streets. Lamps lit the snowy sidewalks, but it was still dark enough outside that the bright interior lights turned the large windows into vivid mirrors. I stepped onto a treadmill, put in my ear buds, turned on my MP3 player, and started the machine. It wasn't long before my brisk walk turned into a steady jog. Ten minutes in, a slight itch spread across my body as my heart rate increased and I started to sweat. I knew it would go away soon enough and kept jogging. As I let my mind wander, I found myself staring not out the window, but at it. There in my reflection was my doppelganger, keeping pace with my movements. He smiled. I smiled back. We were both happy with where we were.

I never had much of an interest in sports growing up. Any time spent on an organized sports team was usually out of necessity. In elementary school, our classes were so small that teams consisted of anyone our teacher could convince to participate in order to make the minimum size team needed to play games against students from the next town over. The tournaments were fun, but I was never overcome with that burning competitive spirit to become a star athlete.

I might not have been picked first for sports, but I was still an active child. After school, I would often explore the outdoors, climbing trees, and building forts out of whatever logs, sticks, and branches my friends and I could find lying around. Once I started high school, I focused more on extracurricular activities instead of sports. I became the editor of our school newspaper, the Spartan Gazette. It was a hassle to encourage other students to write and submit articles, sometimes leaving it up to me to whip something up to fill the empty pages. There were times it seemed like the newspaper would fall to the wayside if I didn't spend most of my free time cobbling together the monthly editions as best I could in between classes. With the exception of the occasional lunchtime intramural volleyball and softball games on the days when I didn't have five places to be during my lunch hour, I wasn't left a lot of time for consistent, structured athletics.

While I was content with where I focused my time, I still aspired to be more fit as a teenager. I wanted to be bigger and bulkier, to have the traditional male physique I was convinced every female desired. I was small and nimble but nowhere near the same level of fitness as some of the larger boys in my gym classes. I wasn't exactly a 100lb weakling though. I could throw a mean dodgeball if it was one of the small rubber ones and I could run pretty fast, but not for long. I didn't have asthma. I wasn't chubby. By most accounts, I was far from unhealthy, but I wasn't happy with myself physically.

While some people found Katimavik's focus on healthy lifestyles challenging, I welcomed it. As much as we joked about the vegetarian-focused meals and the copious amounts of beans, tofu, or salad that filled our plates, these robust foods were simply new to most of us and took some getting used to. Many of the meals were delicious and well prepared, their diversity appreciated. Linda made most of them. She was an amazing cook, something else she had picked up from her time spent abroad. Linda insisted she found cooking therapeutic and would occasionally offer to take a meal off the hands of the pairs of participants who were in charge of cooking that day. No one ever objected. We knew that the treat of Linda cooking for us would be coming to an end once house managers were decided. After that, meals would be dependent on them and their whims as to what balanced recipes they wanted to cook and what the budget allowed, so long as they accommodated the vegetarians, Jess and Victor.

Katimavik presented a significant change to most of our diets, but old habits die hard. There had been the occasional late night slushie runs when a few of us wanted to slip out of the house to satisfy our craving for an icy, sugary beverage. The healthy meals must have made a difference, because I no longer had the stomach for large-sized slushies and gladly opted for smaller cups, another means of stretching out our $3.00 a day allowance. In the back of my mind though, I knew better.

When I was thirteen, I attended a workshop for teenagers that focused on rural community health, specifically diabetes and heart disease. It was eye opening, even if it didn't seem directly relevant to me. I didn't run the risk of cardiovascular disease any time soon, but I also didn't want to slip into a lethargic lifestyle that the presentation seemed to indicate was a big part of the problem. I didn't want to be a statistic, another sick person from some small town who only took control of his life after it was too late.

And here I was, enrolled in a volunteer program that just so happened to provide us with a free gym pass and nutritious meals. If I couldn't change my habits now in order to be healthier and more active, it likely wasn't going to happen anywhere else.

I continued my staring contest with my dark doppelganger. It kept me from glancing down at the treadmill's display of the time passed and calories burned. I knew the digits wouldn't be what I wanted them to be. Thankfully, a familiar song played from my MP3 player which reminded me of home, a welcome distraction.

When I was old enough to stay up late, my parents would occasionally go to bed early, leaving me alone in the living room. When the TV shows currently playing didn't interest me, I would flip through the other channels, occasionally finding myself listening to the music channels to see what was playing. This was mindless procrastination, but there would usually be one or two songs that would make me stop and have a listen. They tended to be popular songs that would float between the pop, rock, or alternative genres, songs with catchy beats and picturesque lyrics, satisfying whatever criteria the music industry needed to ensure it was a chart topper. It must have worked because I would stop and listen to those songs all the way to the end.

Whether it was a spur-of-the-moment effort to burn off some excessive energy from my restlessness before finally committing myself to going to bed or if the music stirred something inside of me, I couldn't sit still when those songs came on. I was compelled to get off the couch and do push-ups, sit-ups, some sort of simple physical activity that I could do along with the beat. And while doing so, I'd squeeze in a few more reps to dull the feelings of inadequacy I was soon left with. As I brushed my teeth and readied myself for bed, I'd make empty promises to myself. I'd tell myself that I just needed a bit more exercise, and that with a bit more dedication, those feelings would go away.

I didn't want to be popular per se, but I wanted to be more liked. I wanted to be a better version of myself, more than what I was naturally dealt. I could be more like my athletic friends, the ones I heard rumoured to be dating the attractive girls. Pushups weren't going to get women to fawn over me, but maybe I would feel a little more confident. If I did, maybe I would have been able to eat my lunch in the cafeteria rather than hiding in the school bathroom because I was worried about being bullied for sitting by myself; I would have been relieved for the rare days when I didn't have any lunchtime commitments during school instead of becoming overwhelmed by anxiety and a crushing insecurity that I was alienating myself with my overachieving personality; and maybe I would have remembered the school dances more fondly rather than finding myself suddenly lonely when the last slow song came at the end of them, terrified at the notion of graduating from high school single and without someone to share that milestone with.

On those nights with only the light from the TV illuminating the dark living room, I'd turn the volume up just loud enough for me to hear and feel the song playing. The last thing I wanted was to wake my parents up and have them question why the hell I was randomly doing a workout at 1 a.m. I wouldn't know how to explain the sudden surge of energy that came over me, how I secretly hoped it would push me towards becoming someone better than who I was, that if I didn't exert it somehow, I'd find myself restless and unable to sleep those nights. Aching muscles were much more preferable than whispering voices reminding me that I wasn't good enough.

I started to increase my stride on the machine now, breathing hard but steadily. I stared intensely out the window, desperately seeking out anything to distract me from my heart and lungs that screamed at me to look down at the display, to see that I had somehow ran longer than expected and that I could stop putting my body through such a painful ordeal. As I focused harder and harder, I found myself locking eyes with the other Devon. Stride for stride, pump for pump, the dark image in the mirror matched me physically. I imagined he was thinking the same things: memories of pathetic push-ups late at night in front of the TV; naïve hopes that his talents might be highlighted in Katimavik while his failures and social ineptitude could be swept under the rug or ignored; deep-seated fears that nothing would change no matter how hard he pushed himself; and that the reason he did was because he didn't want to be the same person when he went home.

I increased the volume on my music player and increased the speed of the treadmill, pushing myself into a faster sprint. My breathing grew deeper as I now swung my arms harder with flat palms. As I stared intensely out the window at my own face, daring it to flinch, the treadmills beside me disappeared from my peripheral vision and the streetlights outside faded. My legs and chest screamed louder in pain, demanding that I stop, but I refused to yield to their weakness, just like I refused to break eye contact with the man in the window.

I let my imagination flow, toying with the idea of somehow running faster than my reflection, watching him struggle to keep up. He certainly seemed to be showing some form of exasperation and exhaustion, but every time I blinked, my twin's facial features appeared to darken and blend into something different. The lights behind me embellished the shadows on deepening cheekbones. His blue hair bounced into tapered ears. Eyes once hidden behind glasses now glowed with a fierce luster below menacingly narrowed brows that held back a fury.

I jabbed the speed button several more times, bracing for the added cries my body was sure to produce. And sure enough, they came, but I swung my arms harder and harder to silence them, booming jackhammers that pierced the air in front of me with every pump. Spittle beat past my lips and teeth and onto my chin as my heartbeat faster and harder inside my chest. I felt drops of sweat drip on my brow collect and finally roll down past my eyes, thankfully missing them and avoiding stinging them. When I sensed them fall off my face and onto the track that rotated furiously below me, I focused my vision and looked back in the window.

Where my reflection once ran, there now gazed a dark dragon. And he was looking right at me.

I slammed the stop button with the palm of my hand and somehow found the dexterity to grab the safety rails of the machine and jumped, firmly landing my feet on the outer edges of the treadmill while the track beneath me braked to a slow roll. I continued to pant heavily, a stony fire bashing my chest with every beat of my heart. I yanked my headphones out of my ears. They continued blaring music, much louder than I thought had been playing. I looked around the gym to see if anyone had watched the scene unfold, but there was no one.

There was only me.

CHAPTER 4

November 2005. Sault Ste. Marie.

I didn't think two weeks were enough to get close to someone, but the disappointment and sadness told me otherwise.

Simone was leaving.

Her decision to quit the program didn't come out of the blue. Simone had mentioned a desire to go back to school during some of our late-night hangouts in the girls' bedroom. Attending college or university had been one of the many things we talked about, but as far as I could tell, most of us were still cultivating our interests before making that commitment to jump back into formal education. I know that was my stance, which tended to keep me quiet during those discussions. The thought of looming student loans, stressful exams, hell, just the paperwork in order to enroll alone felt overwhelming. I realized in hindsight that Simone seemed to wear a mask of glumness whenever the topic came up. It must have been on her mind more than I realized.

No one tried to change Simone's mind when she informed us of her decision at the next house meeting. That didn't stop me from sarcastically threatening to tie her up or suggesting we have Daniel leave in her place, something he was not entirely opposed to.

I was happy she had not only decided on a path but wanted to start walking down it now and not later. Simone and I were not particularly close, but she had a large smile that warmed the room whenever someone—usually me—could make her laugh. The person behind that smile was leaving and already I could feel that in her place there was going to be a void in the crazy Katima-family I thought we were creating.

Simone had some things to take care of before she officially left, but she assured us she would still participate in the few activities we had planned over the next two days before her departure. It didn't leave me a lot of time for the plans I had brewing as soon as she broke the news to us. The next day, I made sure to bring my camera for the few outings we had. I tried to take as many candid pictures of Simone as I could without her noticing. When some free time opened up after our tour of the local recycling plant, I snuck off to Walmart and had photos developed. It had only been two weeks, but I had already amassed a good selection of photos of the participants in our group: crowded meals with two long wooden folding tables that acted as our dinner table, hijinks on the bus rides downtown to the movie theatre, numerous workshops and games from Mass-O. I chose the most entertaining or memorable photos, those that told a story, or at least hinted that something funny had happened. Armed with a healthy selection of prints, I pasted them onto a poster board and had everyone sign it as an oversized going away card for Simone.

Despite still needing to pack, Simone remained present with the group, including our mandatory physical activity night. Our busy schedule might have given us some fun final memories with her, but it also kept us from zeroing in on our friend's impending departure. That night we all walked to the YMCA and played a short four-on-four game of basketball. No one had any concrete understanding of the rules, aside from the goal of getting the ball through the hoop. The only one who had any skills on the basketball court was Erica, which we jested was only due to her height. The game left us sweaty and eager to use the pool facilities afterwards. While the guys swam, the girls watched from the lounge chairs on the pool deck, no doubt pressing Simone for what her plans were and how she was feeling about going back home.

We made it back to the house a half hour shy of our 11:00 p.m. curfew. It wasn't something Linda was keen on strictly upholding. She instead trusted us to understand *why* the rule was in place. Participants weren't children, but PLs still didn't want to be hunting us down after midnight, our whereabouts unknown. Linda must have understood our desire to spend one last night with our friend. Our almost-tardiness was an exception.

"Good game?" Linda asked as we piled in through the crowded entrance of the house.

"I'll say," said Luke. "For a bunch of people who didn't know what we were doing, I'd say we put on a pretty good sweat."

"Glow, Luke," Rosalie corrected him. "Women don't sweat, we glow!"

"Hey Ro, I think you were dripping 'glow' all over the court when we whooped your ass," I said, eliciting a scowling snake tongue from the Ottawa girl.

"Perfect," said Linda with a mischievous smile. "Then you all earned some well-deserved calories tonight!"

To celebrate Simone's leaving—or "her affirmation of life goals" as Linda put it—our beloved PL bought an ice cream cake. She must have waited until we were out of the house to buy it. An ice cream cake in a fridge in a house filled with ten young adults wouldn't have remained a secret for long. The unexpected reveal created an enthusiastic ruckus amongst everyone as Linda began to cut into the

Dairy Queen staple. There was a bittersweetness to the cake. After two weeks of salads, beans, and tofu, the sugary rush from the ice cream and chocolate-crumble filling was balanced out by the realization of why we were having cake in the first place. Our general volume tended to decrease during meals anyway (hard to be loud with a mouth full of food), but there was an extra quietness during that dessert. It was only broken up by the occasional clink of spoons and forks against the bowls in our hands.

Exhausted from our earlier physical activity and now with bellies full of cake, we eased into a well-deserved late-night lull. Half of us were lazily strewn about the three second-hand couches that occupied the L-shaped living room. Two of the couches were Chesterfields, one of which had a spring missing. Every so often someone would sit too far back and sink into the rear crevasses of the ugly brown floral-patterned couch. It was the only empty seat in the living room as we tossed a foam football around.

After making a perfect spiral to Bethany, Linda leaned down to me and whispered in my ear.

"I think that now would be a good time to pull out the surprise for Simone."

She was right. Simone was catching a cab to the airport the next morning. We would likely be struggling to wake up before we saw her off, making this the most opportune time. From behind the broken couch, I pulled out Simone's going away card which I had hidden earlier. I presented it to her along with a sneaky kiss on the cheek which left her incredibly touched and near tears. I wasn't sure which gesture she was reacting the most to, but I wasn't about to spoil the moment.

CHAPTER 5

November 2005. Sault Ste. Marie.

Daniel and I proved to be surprisingly productive that week, both as volunteers at the Bush Plane Museum and at home. The raffle we had been selling tickets for was finally finished. They hadn't sold out like Demmy hoped for, but we sold enough of them to feel it had been worth our time trying. Our work at the house felt like more of an achievement, for Daniel and I had finally cleaned and organized the boys' room. The task had long been overdue.

One thing every participant could agree on was that personal bubbles shrank in Katimavik houses. The issues with the lack of storage and space tended to happen when there were far fewer rooms than people. Even large houses were quick to feel cramped when filled with a large group of participants. Our one side of the Pine Street duplex was no exception, but we did the best we could with the space we had.

The girls' bedroom was slightly larger than the guys' upstairs. Linda had designated the bedrooms in advance prior to our arrival. Seeing how much more luggage the girls brought in comparison to the other half of the group, I could see why she made that decision. Still, both rooms were small given how many people were crammed into them. Storage space for one's belongings was a luxury; closets, drawers, and shelves usually went to those who filled them up first. These were constant points of contention in Katimavik. Given we had less room upstairs than the girls—and even fewer beds—their complaints of storage fell on deaf ears.

When our group first arrived, there had only been two bunk beds. Linda ordered a third, but it didn't arrive until a week after our arrival. The group had become busy so quickly that we hadn't had the chance to put it together and so it sat in the basement, still in its box. Daniel had graciously volunteered to sleep on the floor until we assembled it, which unfortunately meant he slept in the middle of our small, shared bedroom. Getting to know Daniel as I did, I expected his decision was less for altruistic reasons and more just to be different and eschew any sort of conventional setup. As careful as we tried to be, someone would occasionally accidentally step on him or jar him awake late at night or early in the morning. Our guilt quickly faded when we realized how stubborn Daniel was in refusing to get up anyway. Even he eventually started to miss a soft bed.

After moving a large chair from the corner of our bedroom to downstairs, there was now just enough space for the third assembled bunk bed. We might as well have torn down a wall with how much more space we now had. Victor and Carlos had already stored their belongings in the walk-in closet while Luke and Daniel used the second closet and door organizer, so no one objected to my using the bottom of the new bunk as my own personal shelf.

As we lay down in our beds, appreciating the improvement to our storage situation, we could hear another argument between the girls through the floor, this time over the use of a nightstand.

No problem like that up here, I thought. *Hell, we don't even have a nightstand!*

I was glad for the ample space. Nowhere else could I put the bulky green duffle bag my parents bought me for a high school graduation gift. It would have been obtrusive and bothersome anywhere else in the room. Having it on the lower bunk allowed me to root through my "closet" with ease and find a dress shirt for later that night.

Community Living Algoma was throwing a Christmas party for its clients. A few of us had helped set up tables and hang decorations, but with the abundant staff and volunteers available it took no time at all. We were soon told to relax and enjoy ourselves and we did, watching guests arrive dressed to the nines, some of them wearing actual suits and gowns. Compared to them, I felt underdressed in my generic dress shirt and black corduroy pants. Formal events were a deviation from our normal Katimavik affairs. Before long, the music began playing.

I was oddly captivated by the dancing. I was curious and tried to distinguish Community Living staff from clients, although I knew people with cognitive disabilities didn't always show them physically. I took notice of a male and female pair. The man clearly had the tell-tale visible signs of Down Syndrome while the woman had a mild sag in her face. What really caught my eye, however, were the big grins they both wore on their faces. They staggered awkwardly across from each other and danced noticeably off-beat from the music, but neither seemed to be aware or care. It made me smile and, yet at the same time, it also made me feel somewhat jealous. The two of them had an envious immunity to critical judgement which was a far cry from whenever I found myself at a dance. My self-consciousness could at times be debilitating and had on occasion robbed me of the beautiful moments I was a part of.

As the next song came on, another gentleman I recognized as a client waltzed over and tried to squeeze in a dance from the woman. The first man smiled and appeared to play off the stealing of "his girl" albeit in a calm and collected manner.

He gently pushed his competition away to make space for himself and demonstrated some striking dance moves to impress his lady dance partner. The woman swooned and the competition was on.

Bethany came over to see what had captured my attention. I pointed the trio out and we watched the playful scene together. It wasn't long before our group decided enough was enough and we joined in.

The dance was fun, but it ended earlier than I expected and left me missing the participants from the Blind River and Thessalon groups. We hadn't seen any of them since Mass-O. Our separate Katimavik groups lived and volunteered in different communities and wouldn't cross paths regularly unless we shared a workshop or event together. These didn't happen often though, so in lieu of those, I would occasionally call the other groups' Katimavik houses to catch up.

I liked keeping that link between the three groups. Sometimes the conversations would spark ideas for excursions to plan later or partnerships to help reduce our respective budgets. I was curious in which ways the groups were different from each other and which ways we were similar, whether we were dealing with the same struggles or with things that were completely different for all of us. We had all been put into the same program with the same rules, albeit in different places and with different people. Sault Ste. Marie was larger and more urban than Thessalon, which presented different opportunities but also different challenges, like my situation with the city bus. Many of us joked that Katimavik was just one big social experiment, to see if you could put kids from different parts of Canada in a house and see if they could avoid killing each other and perhaps even thrive. I was determined to find that out myself, but I thought I might get a leg up by seeing how the others did things on their end. Ashley shared my curiosity.

I never knew who would pick up the house phone when I called. Whoever was on the other end was usually eager to talk to me and catch me up on the latest gossip. Whenever I called Blind River, though, I always hoped it was Ashley who'd pick up. If it wasn't, she would eventually be handed the receiver anyway with someone screaming into the house that the guy with the blue hair was on the other end of the line.

That night, a girl named Hélène handed the phone to Ashley. She had a thick Québécoise accent which I could hear as she yelled for Ashley.

"You are *très* cute Devon! Ashley wants your sex!" she hollered in the background, followed by audible kissing noises, clearly trying to embarrass Ashley. She and I ignored the badgering comments of the French girl. Once she had successfully ejected Hélène from the room she was in, I told Ashley about the Community Living dance I had come from earlier that night.

"Awww, I want to dance with you!" she said.

Everyone in our group was glad our phone was cordless and not limited by a springy cord like when we were younger. Participants could take the phone into rooms or even downstairs for private conversations, a luxury when making calls with our calling cards that most of us were equipped with. That night, I happened to find a comfortable seat on the living room couch. I casually looked around in case anyone might have seen me blushing from Ashley's words, but remarkably no one was.

"I'd like that," I told her. I suggested that we would one day, even though I had no idea when.

CHAPTER 6

December 2005. Sault Ste. Marie.

"I think Daniel is perfect for a mascot," Erica said as Victor guided him carefully around the room.

"Why's that?" I asked.

"Because you're not supposed to talk while wearing the suit. It's the easiest way to get him to shut up for a while."

I couldn't disagree.

We were volunteering at the Children's Development Centre, or as Daniel put it, "volun-told." One of the staff had reached out to Linda and requested our assistance. Linda knew we had already been quite busy the past week, which was why she put on her sweetest mom-voice when she asked us if we'd be willing to use the little free time we had to help out. We thought it was low when she asked us to "do it for the children," but damn if it wasn't effective.

As much as we resented being recruited at the last minute to volunteer, we knew the Development Centre could use it. Most of their staff and volunteers were unable to attend because of a seasonal flu that was making its rounds. Our help would make a huge difference and also make a lot of kids happy. Whether it was because it was a deserving and charitable place to lend our services to or because no one wanted to say no—to a cause for children, no less—we agreed to help out. It was Christmas time after all.

We were quickly put to work at different stations around the centre. Some of us assisted other volunteers in leading the children through Christmas-themed games while the rest of us manned craft stations where kids could make Christmas decorations. Some of the decorations were the same ones I had made when I was a child, likely stuffed in a ratty cardboard box shoved somewhere in the back of our garage back home.

One of the highlights of the event was the appearance of Hoopie, the owl mascot for the Sault Ste. Marie Learning Disability Association. When we were asked if anyone was willing to wear the costume, Daniel of all people had offered to don the heavy suit and walk around, interacting with everyone. The kids went nuts for Hoopie. I couldn't fathom why they felt the urge to blindly scream adoration for the giant mute bespectacled bird. It certainly helped that Daniel had the silent gestures down pat that made Hoopie friendly and approachable. Victor and Erica continued to guide him around, occasionally stopping for parents so they could take pictures of their kids with him or let them hug Hoopie. It was adorable.

When the event was done, decorations had been made, candies eaten, games played, and holiday cheer successfully spread. Daniel miraculously remained silent during his time as Hoopie, no children behaved like brats, and everyone had done a great job at their stations. Many parents saw how I interacted with the children and were impressed with how well I had carefully explained to them how to make the crafts or play games afterwards. Their comments were flattering, but I felt like I hadn't done anything exceptional. I just did what I was told to do.

Feeling pretty good about ourselves, Victor suggested rather than calling it a night, we reward ourselves for a job well done by trying out another bar. He had learned there was one called Madison's tucked in the plaza beside the grocery store down the road from our house, well within walking distance.

Jess was hesitant about going and needed extra coaxing to join us. By the time we had made the short walk and arrived outside the inconspicuous pub though, she had made up her mind.

"I'm just going to go home guys," she moaned.

Daniel and Bethany had graciously offered to skip the bar and walk back to the house with Jess, but the rest of us remained committed.

Inside, we found a booth tucked in a dark corner. Having yet to be asked for IDs, everyone quickly ordered food and beer. We played pool and listened to a local band play, but the highlight of the bar adventure was the food itself. I didn't want to drink but was more than happy to join in on the fries and onion rings. They may have been common menu items of bars and fast-food joints everywhere, but that night they were elevated to a much higher status of deliciousness. Once we realized we could cover the greasy deep-fried potatoes and onions with ketchup, we attacked them with an even more voracious zeal.

In working towards Katimavik goals of healthy eating, houses were sometimes discouraged from buying store made condiments or anything that could easily be made from scratch, but no one bothered to take up the task. I had tried to make homemade mayonnaise once, but it didn't emulsify properly. The result was an oily mess that tasted nothing remotely like mayonnaise. I doubted ketchup would be that much easier to make, so we reveled in the sweet, sugary red paste that drowned the crunchy vegetables.

Satiated with loud music and deliciously bad food, we returned home. Daniel and Bethany were quietly chatting in the living room when we walked in.

"Hey guys. Did you find out what was bothering Jess on the walk back?" Luke asked.

Daniel sighed with a noticeable lack of compassion and rolled his eyes.

"She says she feels left out from the group."

"What a crock of shit!" I was the first to speak up. Normally tactful, even I was surprised at how sudden I was to argue. "We've invited her out everywhere. We invite *everyone* out everywhere." I said with unabashed frustration. I kept my volume low so Jess wouldn't overhear me from the girls' room in case the door was open, but I did not temper my words.

Looking back at all our off-the-clock outings over the past few weeks—the trips to the mall, the slushie runs, the gym—we had always ensured everyone was invited. Unless we explicitly wanted to be alone, it seemed we were spending more time together than by ourselves. It was very clear that in Katimavik, group activities were the norm. Nowhere, however, was it mandated that everyone had to hang out together all the time. I knew it wasn't everyone's cup of tea, but I preferred it. The conversations were lively and interesting, the jokes ongoing and entertaining, and I simply enjoyed the company. We were still getting to know everyone, and while I could respect if Jess simply didn't want to join us that night, saying she felt unwelcome was ludicrous.

Social cues were not Jess' forte, something others in the group had noticed as well. She had a habit of pointing out the obvious, especially for unnecessary situations. If someone mentioned we had done an activity in the morning, Jess would correct them by stating that it had actually been at 12:02 p.m., making it the *afternoon*. As we had observed that night, Jess would isolate when we were inclusive, but she also did the opposite. In situations when people wanted to be alone, she would intrude. There had been times when she would put her head on someone's shoulder when they clearly didn't want that kind of physical affection. When you lived in a house with so many people, it helped to clue in to how everyone was feeling, even if people were joking. One example came to mind.

Though sex in the Katimavik house was prohibited for obvious reasons, the people at Katimavik Head Office must have recognized the futility in upholding a rule based on strict abstinence, especially when the program was specifically for hyper-sexualized 17–21-year-olds. As such, every Katimavik house was stocked with a supply of condoms. When Linda first gave us a tour of the house, she pointed out a package of rubbers underneath the bathroom sink. The premise was that if someone *were* to have sex, she wanted it to be done safely. "Emergency condoms," she dubbed them. Motherly as she was, we appreciated Linda's honesty and candor in upholding PL law. Even so, we made sure to never understate the importance of the prophylactics in an emergency situation.

"The house is on fire! Get the emergency condoms!"

"The kitchen is flooding! Quick, someone get me a condom!"

"Linda, can we buy another box of emergency condoms next time we go to the store, we're out!"

Hilarity often ensued whenever the condoms were brought up, even if they were never touched. Well, with one exception. One night while Linda stepped out, someone had decided to open one of the condoms, inflating it to a ridiculous size before tying it off. Finding ourselves pleasantly bored, we pawed at the condom like lazy cats, passing it between the living room couches like a party balloon. Luke grabbed it and with a permanent marker drew some anatomical details on the condom to make it look more like a penis.

"It's a big one, make it a veiny fucker!"

"Don't forget the pubes!"

Luke added a few more squiggles with the marker before the condom burst, leaving us all in a fit of laughter. Just as our childish giggles began to subside, Jess spoke up.

"Do you guys know why the condom popped?" she asked. We stifled a few residual laughs and waited for her answer.

"No, why?" someone asked, still snickering.

"Because the chemicals in the marker ate the latex and caused it to blow," she said expressionless.

Silence took over. Everyone remained deadpan until Luke broke the awkward silence.

"Remind me not to write on my dick with a marker next time!"

We burst out laughing once more. Jess huffed and walked out of the room. Maybe it was a poor attempt at a joke, but maybe Jess simply wasn't adjusting to group living like I assumed we all had been. If her reaction the night we went to the bar was any indication, Jess' behaviour and mannerisms hadn't coalesced, but instead grew noticeably more abrasive. I was not the only one who noticed, nor was I the only one who felt uncomfortable around her. This made her claim of not feeling included even more frustrating to me. Despite her awkwardness, we still encouraged her to spend time with us. Did she think our offers were disingenuous? How did we address something like that?

Her sulkiness left a sour taste on an otherwise fun night. I was convinced it was a problem that was only going to get worse.

CHAPTER 7

December 2005. Sault Ste. Marie.

In following the program's foundation for healthy lifestyles, our group soon found ourselves taking part in another Katimavik tradition: we learned how to make bread.

It was considered an important skill for participants to have and fit most of the criteria for our personal achievement goals: trying new things, cooking new foods, hands-on learning, etc. Bread also had a lot of versatility in being added to various meals and snacks. With house managing duties just around the corner, it also happened to be another workshop that was long overdue for our group. Only a few of us had ever made bread before, but those who hadn't were eager to learn.

The group was chipper and chatty the day of our bread-making workshop. Fortunately, our instructor was very patient with the overzealous bunch of youth she was working with. Whether it was instructing us on how to improve the globby dough that we stretched between our hands or the horrible bread/*pain* puns we couldn't help but make, our teacher remained cheery amid our distracting Katimavik-isms. As I kneaded my dough one last time before leaving it to rise, I felt Jess rest her chin on my shoulder.

"I was just talking to Linda. She's made up the list of house managers. She told me you and I are going to be the first pair of house managers."

I cringed. Not just because Jess had been bothersome the last few days, but because being the first house managers meant a lot of expected trial and error, bumps, and hiccups. I had never shopped, cooked for, or cleaned up after such a large group of people and was nervous to do so. Furthermore, it was with someone I was finding increasingly difficult to spend an afternoon with, least of all an entire week. It seemed the harder I tried to get along with Jess, the more bothered I was by the things she did. The problem was they weren't really all that bothersome. She wasn't rude or did anything discernible that made her unlikeable, but something left me uncomfortable, withdrawn, and usually silent around her. I realized I was acting on that old adage: if I couldn't say anything nice, I shouldn't say anything at all. So I didn't, and considered the news she had given me with stoic quiet. I had no doubt that Jess would be helpful and attentive and, despite my attitude towards her, would make a great house manager partner. Whether house managing was a success or not, I was convinced that it was going to be a very quiet week for me.

"Cool," I responded to her without looking up and continued kneading my dough in silence.

Everyone's carb-laden creations turned out amazing. We made challah bread, cinnamon buns, and pizza for supper. We were proud of ourselves and returned home in high spirits that night. It made the deterioration of the house meeting that much more unexpected.

"Things are going to get busy, so we need to stay organized." Linda pulled out three coloured poster boards with grids on them. "Which is why we need these!"

The main goal of the house meeting that night was to create calendars for the next two and a half months. Calendars were one of the main organizational tools that Katimavik groups used to help keep track of most day-to-day activities and events: upcoming volunteer gigs, workshops, holidays, special events, and committee meetings; even the house managers were noted for that week. The more things Linda listed, the more I could see how visual aids were necessary.

As Carlos wrote in each daily square, Rosalie and Bethany added spirally doodles and random stickers along the border. The calendars served a practical purpose, but there was no reason we couldn't add some creative flair. Just when we thought we were done filling up a week, someone would chime in with another commitment that needed to be penned in. It was impressive to see the range of activities Katimavikers planned for themselves, but it made me wonder whether participants ever slept in. There wasn't a single day of the week on any of the three month-long calendars that didn't have something written on it. It was a bit overwhelming, but also exciting to know we had so much in store for us. There was no room for apathy or boredom.

"Oh right, we should put in the days I'll be gone as well," said Linda. Although PLs seemed like an omnipresent part of Katimavik life, they were entitled to—and no doubt deserved—time away from the participants. We, however, also had days off. 48 hours, actually.

Although Linda didn't need to know what our plans for our 48 hours were, she did need to know when we were taking them off. We could spend that time together or on our own if we wanted, but we had to agree on the same date. Linda insisted that if we didn't choose the days for our 48 hours that night, we would have to choose very soon to solidify the calendar. It wasn't an easy decision to make. We didn't want to use our 48 hours on dates we were tentatively expecting to plan excursions or trips.

Linda had made it clear when we started the meeting that it would be another long one. A quick glance at the clock above the dining table told us she wasn't kidding. Despite having stayed mostly on task, planning the calendars ate up most of our evening. We agreed it was better to finish the calendars and get them done with and out of the way instead of postponing the decision about our 48 hours until later. This didn't make it any easier to choose. It wasn't long before the volume of disagreement began to shake the tiny duplex living room.

"We should take our 48 hours off that weekend!"

"Why? We don't even know what we're doing then!"

"What about a trip during that week?"

"We can't, they need me at work then!"

"Well, we're not going plan everything around *your* workplace!"

I tried to avoid adding my voice to the mass confusion, as I could tell Carlos was already having a tough time clarifying between what days were confirmed and what was still being discussed, a task made more difficult with everyone trying to get their two cents in. I was indifferent to what dates were chosen; I had no plans to do anything on our 48 hours off, so when we took them off was irrelevant. I had talked to Ashley about potentially visiting her in Blind River during those days off, but it was pointless as her group was also in the process of planning their calendar that same night, possibly at that same moment. Neither of us knew when their 48 hours off would be. If she and I were to plan anything together, it would have to wait until after our house meetings.

With the way Carlos was starting to shout over people, it didn't seem like our meeting was going to end any time soon. Linda struggled to steer us in a cohesive direction, but even she was having difficulty. Jess had been sitting next to me and tried to speak up several times, but was ultimately ignored or not heard. Linda noticed this and managed to finally get everyone's attention.

"Guys, guys!" she said, not quite yelling but raising her voice to a level I'd never heard from her. "I'd like to hear from Jess who's been trying to say something for the past few minutes."

Jess looked up with a disgruntled face. "Why bother? No one listens to me. Everyone can just fuck off!" She stood up and stormed away from the living room.

An unsettling silence took over. Linda spoke up.

"I think that now would be a good time to take a break and pause the meeting. We'll have everyone come back in an hour, because we *do* need to finish this tonight." We were not off the hook.

All the girls quickly ran off, some rushing off to use the bathrooms, while others went to see what was up with Jess. It was just the boys in the living room, reluctant to wait in line for the bathroom and just dumbfounded as to what just happened. The living room had become quite hot and since we were already planning around holidays, Daniel took it as a good sign to declare the following day, "No Pants Day". The decree was unanimously accepted by those present. The spontaneous humour helped release some of the recent tension, but we weren't done. Linda pleaded for Daniel to put his pants back on. When he finally did, she called us back.

"Everyone, time to finish the meeting," Linda shouted from the living room a short while later. "I'd like to politely remind everyone that, we don't just have to choose our 48 hours, we *also* have the rest of the house agenda to discuss."

Frustrated sighs were swallowed as we reconvened to our previous spots on the couches. Before Linda spoke again, Jess pulled out a stick covered in bits of string and a few stick-on jewels.

"First of all, I want to apologize for my outburst earlier."

No one said anything.

"So, as you guys know, I'm part Cherokee…"

Again, nothing. I don't think any of us knew this. Had she ever shared this with us? Should we have asked? Was this something we should have learned by now? Or did Jess not feel comfortable revealing that to us?

"My grandma used to have a tradition of using a talking stick in meetings. I thought maybe it would be helpful to use during our house meeting so we don't *speak over everyone*," she said with crude emphasis.

"Can I use, *s'il vous plaît?*" Bethany asked quietly. Jess handed her the stick. "I would like to point out how rude it eez to *read* during a meeting, Dan'hiel!" she glared across the room. I tried not to snicker at her Québécoise pronunciation of his name.

Daniel looked up calmly from the book he was reading, something I hadn't even noticed he'd been doing that whole time. "What does it matter? I don't really care what decisions everyone makes in this meeting, and if that's the case, why shouldn't I read and be productive if I'm going to be bored?"

Erica grabbed the stick from Bethany. "Because it makes you an asshole, that's why," she scoffed. I nodded in agreement. It didn't matter if he was indifferent to the decisions made that night. Being present at the meeting wasn't a matter of convenience, it was a matter of respect.

"Why are we even using a stupid talking stick anyway?" he retorted. "If we're going to use a stick, why don't we just raise our hands?" Alas, Daniel might have been an asshole, but he had a point. Were props necessary if they served the exact same purpose?

Jess, however, did not take his comment well, and soon the group erupted into a mess of frustrated callouts and demands to finish the house meeting.

"I know it's been a long night," Linda said, acknowledging our frustrations. "And looking at the time, we're not going to finish everything we needed to. But starting with the calendars, let's see what we can get done, okay?"

Linda somehow miraculously managed to have us complete our calendars with some sense of decorum. We managed to choose a pair of days to spend our 48 hours with minimal compromise between participants. Linda allowed us to postpone the remainder of the house agenda until the following week, reminding us that it would also be a long meeting, though not as bad as the one we had just endured.

It was nearing midnight by the time we finished. Everyone was tired, frustrated, and simply wanted to go to bed. Even so, I spoke up before everyone lurched away.

"It was a hell of a night. And obviously there's stuff left unresolved," I said, carefully gauging reactions for any renewed volatility. I knew I had to keep what I had to say short and sweet. "I want to end the house meeting on a positive note. Can we bring it in for a group hug before we hit the sack?" I hoped that the gesture would remind us that we were capable of overcoming disagreement and could still get along afterwards. We had to if we were to survive the nine-month program.

I was relieved when everyone obliged, even Daniel, allowing a well-needed calm to take us over. When everyone broke away, Jess spoke up.

"Devon, can I have the talking stick?" I forgot I had been holding it when I suggested the group hug and handed it back to her. She snapped it in half. "I don't think we need this."

Things were at ease now, but the cat was out of the bag. The warm, fuzzy picture so many people had of Katimavikers—myself included—now had dark clouds brewing overhead. Behind the smiles of bubbly youth volunteers who joked and laughed and had a good time were gritted teeth, held tongues, and a mounting pile of insecurities. These hadn't come from nowhere. This had been brewing for quite some time, something inevitable which we couldn't avoid, or perhaps had avoided up until now. True to Linda's warning, it had indeed been a long meeting that night. I doubted sleep would put to rest some of the issues that had reared their ugly little heads. This was a temporary peace, a calm before the storm.

The honeymoon period was over.

CHAPTER 8

December 2005. Sault Ste. Marie.

Once the raffle was over, Daniel and I were more bored than ever at the Bush Plane Museum. Demmy even allowed us to come in later some mornings due to how slow the museum had become, an option that Daniel was eager to take advantage of. With winter holidays coming soon, we expected things to slow down even further at our workplace. The Bush Plane Museum was an interesting place, but I just couldn't see it being a destination tourists wanted to visit during Christmas time. Even purchasing bush plane related gifts or knick-knacks seemed like something only diehard enthusiasts would consider. It wasn't our place to think about those things, nor did we have the experience to justify our opinions. We were there as volunteers; that meant being there when asked, even if there were days where we wouldn't see a single visitor. Since our time then became mostly dedicated to occupying the front desk, Daniel and I were taught how to work the cashier's till, take phone calls, make sales from the gift shop, and other tasks. It was so rare we had to do any of those things that I sometimes forgot how to do them when we finally did get a visitor, prompting me to occasionally reach for the instruction manual. To combat our boredom, we read books from the gift shop or that we brought from home ourselves. I was tempted to bring in my Game Boy, but thought that might make the visual to our slacking off look even worse.

The Ontario winter cold also brought mice indoors. It was a recurring problem to find some of the exhibits either chewed on or littered with rodent droppings. One of our jobs was to check and reset the mouse traps as needed. Catching a mouse became an oddly exciting highlight of the work placement as Daniel and I debated on what techniques and bait worked best for catching mice. Peanut butter was the consensus, as we acknowledged that cheese just didn't stand up to the stereotype portrayed in popular media. When we weren't working the front desk or hunting mice, Daniel and I whittled away the afternoons in a hidden corner of the archives.

The archives were easy to miss. The majority of the museum was actually inside an immense hangar. The planes and exhibits covered most of the floor with a workshop and storage area at the far end of the building, but through an inconspicuous pair of swinging doors on the left side of the hangar were the archives.

That section of the museum was part library and part office. It was technically open to the public, but very few people knew that. Even some staff didn't know about it whenever we were asked where we kept disappearing to. One of the small rooms was crowded with several tall metal bookshelves that held texts, documents, reports, and books containing history and information on everything related to bush planes. There was even a little bit of history of Sault Ste. Marie itself in some of the books. As curious a reader as he was, even Daniel never bothered to read anything off these shelves. We didn't know how the books were catalogued, if they were at all, and were reluctant to find out.

There was a vague notion that we weren't supposed to be in that room to begin with. It was actually Demmy who let us in there in the first place. She knew our Katimavik group had events and activities to plan and that we needed internet access to do so, so Daniel and I were given permission to use the computer tucked in the corner. I suspected Demmy felt somewhat guilty at our usual boredom and turned a blind eye to the amount of time we spent in the archives, out of trouble. Upon hearing where we were spending our afternoons, some museum employees would raise an eyebrow or shake their heads nervously.

"You guys shouldn't really be in there. There's a lot of old books you shouldn't touch."

We confidently informed them that we weren't touching the books at all and were using the computer for "research." But more often, we simply told them: "Demmy said we could." Our supervisor didn't seem like a particularly high authority in the museum, but no one bothered us or cared to raise a stink. I felt our time was better spent there than at the front desk. There, we were just reading whatever dusty book was available from the gift shop, but in the archives, we were learning about the city we lived in and utilizing time and internet on Katimavik-related things that we'd end up having to do anyway. I was much happier putting our time to practical use.

"—happy birthday dear Linda, happy birthday to you ..."

It wasn't the most energetic rendition of "Happy Birthday," but Linda smiled all the same.

In order to celebrate Linda's birthday, everyone had to wake up early before the madness of our morning routine began. Tired Katimavikers were still wiping the sleep out of our eyes when we sang her the traditional song, but it was the only time we were able to do it. Linda had a meeting in Thessalon later that day that would keep her away overnight. For the brief time before we began to get ready for work, we gave Linda the attention and praise she so deserved.

"Oh, what's this?" she asked as I handed her a small box.

Earlier that week, my parents had sent me a package which included a simple watch. Part of the packaging included a soft piece of thin white leather-like material. I didn't want to throw it out because it felt far too fancy for how basic the watch it came with was, plus I knew I would be able to make use of it somehow. When we learned of Linda's upcoming birthday, I was glad I'd kept it. I spelled her name out with Japanese kanji characters with the characters for peace on one side and love on the other. Rosalie had seen me meticulously working on the bracelet the night before. When she asked what I was working on, I refused to tell her. I loved surprising the group, keeping my secrets until the last minute.

"Devon, this is incredibly thoughtful and creative, thank you," Linda said, giving me a hug. "Oh, look at the time. You better all get ready for work."

We all returned home to an empty Katimavik house that evening. Linda would be away until the following day. For the first time in what seemed like a long while, we were in the house unsupervised. And while the PL is away, the participants will play.

No one explicitly wanted to stir trouble or break the rules, but we all acknowledged we had an opportunity that shouldn't be wasted, even at the risk of a CTI.

A CTI—commitment to improve—was part of Katimavik's punitive policy for unacceptable behaviour. They were dished out for acts that were considered extremely disrespectful or dangerous, like smoking indoors, theft, physical fighting, or even simply refusing to participate or do your fair share of help around the house. Beyond these, some violations got you an immediate expulsion from Katimavik. These were big no-nos, like hitchhiking, using illegal drugs, or leaving the country. If breaking one of the big rules didn't buy you a one-way ticket back home, three CTIs would. Three strikes and you were out, sent home packing.

It took some effort to get formally written up by a PL, however. As the language of the concept would suggest, the idea was that you learned from your mistakes rather than continuing to make them. As Linda described it to us one day, Project Leaders didn't want to act like jail guards. Nobody wanted participants to be treated like children. We wanted Linda to return home and know that we could be trusted in her absence—even if we bent the rules, just a little.

Victor and Erica pulled out bottles of alcohol from out of nowhere and a drinking game began in the living room. Drinking in the house typically netted you a CTI, but it was something everyone was willing to risk for a good time that night. I stuck with my glass of ginger ale. Even though I wasn't partaking, I promised to remain silent about the events that took place that night. Just because I wasn't drinking didn't mean I had to ruin it for everyone else.

"When Linda comes back, we should tell her that we drank and that we hid booze in the furnace room," suggested Luke. "She'll think it's a joke, but she'll look anyway and wonder where the hell we hid it." There was nothing in the small furnace room whatsoever except for the appliance itself, surrounded by several feet of empty space. It was surprisingly devoid of any sort of clutter or boxes one might expect to see stored there. Given how difficult it was to hide anything larger than a golf ball in or around the furnace without it sticking out like a sore thumb, the idea of Linda actually searching the room for signs of hidden contraband was funny and left a few of us giggling.

"I know. When you think about it, we're better off hiding shit in our own bags in our rooms," Victor said, pouring himself another drink. His observation was astute. Space was limited in most of the rooms in the duplex, especially shared space. House rules and common courtesy dictated you didn't touch something that didn't belong to you. This was tricky if belongings were in a shared space, like the bathroom or living room. Bags, bedroom shelves, and underneath beds, however, were considered explicitly private. The only condition in which PLs were allowed to go through your belongings was if there was an immediate danger. This made our bags ideal for hiding alcohol. Linda was sweet and trusting. We never imagined she would resort to such an extreme breach of privacy. This didn't make these hiding spots perfectly safe though. We had all heard stories of theft within Katimavik houses, but these were rare occurrences. I wasn't concerned. I had nothing to hide, and I trusted everyone in front of me.

The drinking continued. It was a quiet night. Everyone seemed content to relax rather than get hammered. Except Daniel.

"Ugh, you people are boring. If no one's going to get wasted, then I might as well!" he said, cheering himself on.

Daniel did exactly what he set out to do and quickly became drunk, irritating, and somehow more immature. It was a stark difference to Victor whom I noticed had drank as much as Daniel. In contrast to Daniel's buffoonery, Victor was instead quiet, clever, and witty, an inebriated behaviour we appreciated much more in comparison, especially when we began to worry that Daniel might damage or break something which would leave evidence to our deviant behaviour. Erica and Bethany offered to take him to the guys' room and babysit him until he sobered up or fell asleep. Someone had suggested everyone sleep in the living room that night—another rule to break—but the idea was quickly scrapped. People were getting tired and most of us were ready to call it a night, including Daniel thankfully. Rosalie and I weren't quite ready to call it quits and sat on the couch. We ended up talking later than expected.

We continued the conversation from the night of our first arrival, when everyone had been hanging out in the girls' bedroom late in the morning. Rosalie elaborated on why she joined and what she expected things to be like, both before and after we left the program. Katimavik seemed to mean as much to her as it did to me. She thought of it as an opportunity for change, to break away from the image she thought people had of her when she was younger. She had been chubby as a young girl but had recently developed an interest in dancing, a hobby she was growing fond of. Fortunately for Rosalie, there were plenty of opportunities for dancing back home in Ottawa.

"Especially salsa and merengue," she shared were her favourites. "I love the passion, the energy shared between two people expressed through rhythm between their bodies." As Rosalie told me more about different kinds of dances that I had never even heard of, she stirred next to me. Once we realized how tired we were, we moved from sitting to lying next to each other on the couch. Everyone else was already fast asleep in their own beds on the other side of the house.

"What's your passion, Devon?" she asked, turning the question to me.

My first reaction was to say video games. They were something I enjoyed growing up and continued to appreciate. Much like a good book, many of the memories I had of early video games were the stories within, albeit with less developed characters and plots that were a little more on the nose than the best-selling young adult novels. But that's what I liked about them; your mind could fill in the blanks with the motivations of the protagonists you played, the struggles they sought to overcome. Unlike a book, you had to earn a game's story through skill, a reward for the increasingly challenging levels that demanded hand-eye coordination, puzzle solving, and strategy. Video games had a unique web of sub-cultures that you could share with people equally as passionate and eager to discuss them. I tried to explain to Rosalie that that was one of the reasons I got along with Daniel and Luke; we simply had a shared enthusiasm for gaming.

"No, what's a passion you want to share with people?" she urged.

I wanted to argue that it *was* something you could share, but I knew it wasn't the answer she was looking for. Rosalie enjoyed dancing because of how expressive and emotional it was. I struggled to think of whether I had any kind of passion like that, but nothing came to mind. I didn't have anything that offered the same sort of intimacy and closeness that Rosalie felt dancing had, something you could share uniquely with another person and not someone else. I had energy, enthusiasm, and humour to give, but those were gifts I gave to everyone. It didn't seem right to limit them to one person.

Or maybe I just hadn't met the right person yet.

CHAPTER 9

December 2005. Sault Ste. Marie.

Dishes. They never seemed to end.

This was one of the first things Jess and I learned as our group's first pair of house managers. It was no surprise that cooking and cleaning for ten people was a lot of work. Even without the endless dishes to clean, a lot of time was spent in the kitchen. House managers were required to make breakfast for all the participants. Before Jess and I had started, everyone had been responsible for making their own breakfasts which usually consisted of fruit, cereal, or granola and yogurt, because those were the easiest morning meals to make. Linda had occasionally treated us to a hot breakfast of pancakes or French toast in that time, a treat we knew we should savour. The same yogurt containers that we emptied from breakfast quickly became the same containers we used to pack lunches, which were usually leftovers from dinner the night before. It took some time to get used to having to cook meals that were also large enough to accommodate leftovers for such a large group, but Jess and I were starting to figure it out.

The two of us wanted to start house managing off with a positive reception and had planned for a simple but delicious meal for our first dinner: Caesar salad, noodles Alfredo, and sautéed shrimp on the side for the non-vegetarians to add. While everyone agreed the meal was delicious, the compliments were undermined by the complaints about it being served later than expected, which caused our weekly house meeting that Sunday night to start late. Shopping had taken much longer than Jess and I originally expected that afternoon. We wanted to avoid time-consuming second trips to the store and decided to purchase all the ingredients for the whole week's menu. Fortunately, the grocery store was just down the street, although it made for some hefty pushing of the shopping cart which we vowed to return the next day.

After preparing that first night's meal, Jess and I realized how difficult it was to both cook and keep things reasonably clean. People coming and going in and out of the kitchen slowed both of those chores down dramatically. Everyone would deposit their dirty lunch containers into the sink upon returning home, right around the time we were preparing supper. This forced either Jess or I to eventually stop what we were doing and wash a load of dishes in order to use the sink. It was rare that Katimavik houses ever had dishwashers. I suspected that if we had one, we likely would have been encouraged to wash dishes the old-fashioned way—slow and laboriously.

It was a massive relief when those hot meals hit the table. When the group sat down to supper, stresses melted away as people talked about things that happened at work, a joke someone had, or upcoming events. Linda had politely asked if we might humour her in saying "*itadakimasu*" before every meal, insisting it wasn't a prayer so much as simply thanking whatever people or sources from which the food came. We were happy to indulge her in this custom.

It never took long for dinner talk to get loud and difficult to hear, making it uncanny when there weren't any conversations taking place over the table. Hearing nothing but the satisfied noises of people munching away was sometimes unnerving, but I considered chewing mouths a satisfying compliment to the chefs' work. More importantly, supper time meant Jess and I were relieved of cooking and cleaning up for the rest of the night. In the house meeting earlier that week, everyone came to a unanimous agreement on a rotating schedule for a pair of participants to wash the supper dishes, exempting house managers from that duty for the night. This was a fantastic arrangement as Jess and I were sick of doing them after day two.

Having everyone gone for work left the house eerily quiet during the day. It was incredibly easier to get work done when people were out of the house and out of the way. With only the remainder of my house managing week to take advantage of that opportunity, I used my limited free time to pursue different projects. One of my first self-imposed tasks as the solo member of the environmental committee—Simone had been the other person before she left—was to post energy-saving tips or advice on how to be more environmentally friendly around the different rooms of the house. These were written underneath the French and Spanish translations of random household objects and appliances, the Spanish having been strongly encouraged by Carlos. A sign taped above the toilet read, "Toilette/inodoro/yellow let it mellow, brown flush it down." Below a ceiling fan were sticky notes stating "Ventilateur/ventilador/turn on to push hot air downwards in winter." I figured if we didn't learn something intentionally, we might learn it through subliminal repetition.

A mostly empty Katimavik house also meant a readily available computer. Between the living room and the kitchen sat our aged computer tower beneath a scratched-up office desk. While we were all thankful the internet wasn't dial up, it was still relatively slow. The slower speed was a mixed blessing, as it kept me from wasting time buffering YouTube videos and focused more on researching more environmental tips and tricks. In between reading about vermicomposting and the drastic impacts of climate change for the umpteenth time, I emailed family and friends back home as well as Ashley. She wasn't going to be house manager for the Blind River group for a few more weeks, but I thought I could give her a leg up with some advice on what she could expect from my few days' experience. We had been communicating regularly since exchanging emails at Mass-O. Seeing new emails from her in my inbox put a smile on my face. They were usually full of spelling errors and flighty to read as Ashley zipped from topic to topic, talking about her group, how she missed her family back home, or just asking me random questions on life. Normally this erratic sort of dialogue would bother me, but it felt genuine, much like I was talking to her in person, an animated and cheery girl who brightened the day of those around her.

Three of us were lazily tossing a foam football around. The dinner dishes were done, lunches for the next day prepared, and the house relatively clean. I was tired, but relieved that dinner went well that night. I had never made meatloaf before, but wanted to try my hand at making it. Only while making it did I realize Jess and I were missing some key ingredients from the recipe.

"No garlic salt? Chop up garlic and throw in extra salt!"

"We don't have basil. I like the smell of cumin though, let's use that!"

"Shit, is a cup the same as a pound? Let's find out!"

Our improvisation made it more surprising when the final result was edible, let alone well received. Just when I felt Jess and I were hitting our stride as house managers, details like those tripped us up. We were keeping our heads above water, but still ready for our turn as house managers to be done.

Not wanting to think about the next morning's breakfast, I loafed in the living room with Luke and Erica. It was one of the rare evenings where we didn't have anything planned. I was grateful when no one objected to the idea of doing nothing to fill that void. Even though my body was slowly moulding to the oblique shape of the couch I still managed to catch Luke's errant football throws with ease. Our discussion turned onto the topic of Simone and the hole she left in the group, among other things.

Several days after Simone left, the guys had been hanging out in our room upstairs. Victor was organizing his belongings, Carlos was writing something, Daniel was reading on his bed, Luke was playing his Game Boy, and I was putting away a batch of laundry fresh out of the dryer. When I pulled out my last shirt, something black and stringy was attached. I peeled off a pair of woman's panties which crackled from the static cling.

"Didn't peg you as the lacy type," Luke said, ignoring my protests the undergarments weren't mine. The boys thus began a deep investigation, chiming in with our own faux expertise as to which girl in the group we thought the panties belonged to. We considered personalities, tastes in clothes, and any other factors we thought might provide us with a decisive answer. In the end we ended up just asking the girls if it belonged to them, but none of them claimed to be the owner. We decided they must have been accidentally left behind by Simone. We hung them on our ceiling fan as a testament to our now-gone sister. Erica insisted we were disgusting.

"Hey, they came out of the laundry, so at least we know they were clean!" I said tossing the ball to Erica who rolled her eyes at the past event. "It's the only thing we have left of her. She's gone, Erica, she's gone and she's never coming back," I pretended to cry, wondering if I could force tears on command. Erica lobbed the ball to Luke.

"Hey, it's early in the program. We could still get another participant."

Erica was right. After a certain time, it was considered too late for a new participant to join a Katimavik group. We suspected this was because newbies wouldn't gain the full experience and might have trouble adjusting, but I was sure there were other factors to consider besides a belated start. We hadn't even passed the month mark yet, so I urged Head Office in silent prayer to make it happen. Even when Simone had been with us, we had not been a full house. The maximum size for a Katimavik group was twelve, so with Erica, Bethany, Jess, Rosalie, Luke, Daniel, Victor, Carlos and me, there was still space for three more participants, plenty of room to add to our little collection of misfits.

"I just want the next one to be a girl," I said. Another boy in the house meant I would have to sacrifice my bunk bed shelf so he had a place to sleep. Aside from that, I also genuinely wanted another girl in the group.

The more Luke and I discussed the pros and cons of male vs. female company, the more I thought about my friends back home. I realized Bailey and Courtney struck an excellent balance between the two genders. Courtney eschewed any sort of traditional femininity, foregoing make up and anything resembling a dress, and tended to wear androgynous clothes. In fact, she was fond of occasionally dawning pirate costumes, regardless of whether it was Halloween or not. As tomboyish as Bailey could be, she would sometimes indulge in a dress and grew adept at the makeup skills her older sister refused to learn. Despite their differences, both were fun to be around. Whereas Courtney would throw entertaining, almost childish tantrums at even the hint of flirtation (which I only ever did because I knew how much it irritated her), Bailey would double-down on her sarcastic retorts if I gave her the same kind of attention. I could be more of myself around them then I could with some of my male friends. With that in my mind, I told Luke how I thought we had enough testosterone in the group. Luke disagreed.

"Dude, they already outnumber us!" he argued, whipping the football at me hard. I snapped it out of the air with a firm one-armed grip. "I once heard a story of a guy in Katimavik who ended up being the only male in his group. It did not end well."

"What happened?" That scenario would definitely make for some interesting group dynamics.

"He *died!*" Luke laughed maniacally. "But no, for serious, it sucked ass. I heard he mostly hid in his room."

"I would too," Erica chimed in, snagging the ball out of the air mid-throw. "Especially when the girls sync."

"What do you mean, 'sync'?" I asked, catching her toss.

Erica smirked in disbelief of my ignorance, but gladly enlightened Luke and I. "Women tend to sync periods when they live in groups for a long time. If you don't believe me, look it up!"

Luke and I looked at each other in disbelief. "No they don't! Why would God allow such a horrible, horrible thing to happen?" he said sarcastically. I couldn't tell if Erica was joking. I was far from an expert on women. Everyone knew the stereotype of the emotional woman going through her period. I suddenly realized I had always missed that with Bailey and Courtney back home. *Or perhaps I just never noticed.* My two female friends never shared such personal information with me. It wasn't as though I'd ever ask them that kind of question directly. To do so would risk facing the sister's combined fury. It dawned on me that I might have been present for their monthly occurrences and simply been oblivious to the real reason behind their targeted frustration with me some days, thinking I might have inadvertently rubbed them the wrong way. Still, the thought of a small duplex filled with young women menstruating together horrified me and Luke.

"I bet it's like when you have a stroke. Except instead of smelling burnt toast, you'll smell blood, acid, and contempt!" I joked. "And when it does, Luke, that's our cue to leave the house for the rest of the day."

He agreed. "So, back to Simone's replacement. I want Simone 2.0 to be tall, funny, love video games and guys with curly hair…"

"Maybe I can jump in." Linda walked into the living room, holding her hands out for a catch. I tossed it to her. "I can't promise she's cute, but her name is Tiffany and she's from New Brunswick." Linda could see the excitement light up in our eyes. "And she should be here after the holidays."

Linda called the rest of the group to share the details of the exciting news. When everyone assembled in the living room, we quickly began to discuss ways of "welcoming" Tiffany to the group. We wanted to do something more original than a banner or a cake. Someone floated the idea of pretending Katimavik was secretly a volunteer cult. We would call the new participant "New Simone," and everyone would take on some quirky identity or trait. I volunteered to be a deaf mute, Rosalie offered to act like a spoiled brat, Carlos would only speak in Spanish, and Daniel would be a blathering idiot.

"Yeah, that won't be much of a stretch," piped Jess, a zinger coming from the last person we expected. Daniel was still onboard with the idea though.

"Maybe I can pretend to be some hard-ass boot camp sergeant, threatening everyone with push-ups and drills!" Linda suggested, getting in on the excitement. The idea was entertaining, but we all knew that in the end Linda would cave and request we be civil to our new groupmate. The conversation and zany ideas carried on into the night. I just hoped the new girl was cute.

It was nearing the end of house managing. Jess and I had survived each other's company, but I was ready for it to be done and pass the torch onto someone else. We had been so busy cooking or washing dishes that I had little time to be bothered by her. Any downtime I did have I put to use on other projects. The week we spent paired as house managers was more practical than anything. Aside from appreciating her work ethic, my affability toward Jess hadn't changed. She and I lived together, though; if we were going to bond, we would have plenty of time for that to happen, whether intentionally or not. I tried not to give it much thought. I had other things on my mind.

New Year's Day was fast approaching. It was a unanimous decision between the three groups to have a joint New Year's party and that it should be held in Sault Ste. Marie. The Soo was bigger than Thessalon and Blind River combined and had more options for food, things to do, and places to stay. With our group effectively hosting the other two, someone in our group needed to spearhead the organizing. Knowing things needed to be planned soon and having more free time during the day than the others who were at work, I volunteered. In between the shopping, cooking, and cleaning of house managing, I was either on the computer or phone planning the big event. The most challenging part was finding a venue to host us. Our Katimavik house was barely big enough for one group, let alone three, and was definitely not an option, even if only for a few days. I contacted service clubs, community halls, even churches. All politely refused.

I called Ashley later that night to update her. She had more or less become the unofficial liaison of Blind River with our group through me, and vice versa. Her group was anxious about the plan for New Years and was eager for details. They needed to know where everyone would be staying, which groups would be buying/bringing what food, and other important details that were necessary for the long, drawn-out excursion plan.

Excursion plans were the bane of every Katimavik group, even if they were an essential part of the whole program. If any activity took longer than two hours to do, required funding from one of the committees, or took you out of town, it likely warranted an excursion plan. These lengthy, detailed plans had to be reviewed and approved by Katimavik Head Office to ensure that the activities and purpose of the trip fit within the learning goals of the program. On one hand, we had the opportunity to go on trips to national parks, museums, river-rafting, horseback-riding, mountain hikes, or whatever adventure our group could justify on paper. On the other hand, doing so required the inclusion of painfully specific details:

itineraries of where you were going, how the activities served the purposes of one or more of your five committees, who was in charge of those activities, how long it would take to drive to the destination, how much would everything cost, what committee's budget would pay for them, when and where we would stop to pee and whose damn hand we would hold while doing so. These reports seemed exceptionally unnecessary when some of the activities were so simple. For those ones, Linda encouraged us to fluff up the answers a little bit. We could justify a simple hike by including expectations of team-building and physical activity, learning about local flora and fauna, and getting in touch with nature. We needed to back these up with some sort of proof that those goals had been met, but we'd usually figure out a way to do it.

A New Year's party was a bit more difficult to sell on an excursion plan, however. There weren't exactly lessons to learn or goals to achieve. It was a party, plain and simple. Blind River and Thessalon were able to dress up their excursion plan by including other activities to do while visiting Sault Ste. Marie. But in order to do that, they needed to know what was happening on my end so they could include those details in their reports, information I didn't have and was increasingly stressing over. If the event didn't happen, it was going to be my fault and a huge failure on my behalf.

Ashley was supportive though and appreciated how much time and energy I had been putting into the event.

"I know you've been working hard at this, Devon. Everyone here is excited to go to Sault Ste. Marie." Her voice gasped with anticipation. "Especially me! I can't wait to see you again!" A sickly nervousness grew in my throat.

I needed to find a venue, and I needed to find one *soon.*

"Were you talking to Aaaaaaaaaaaashley?" said Luke as I placed the cordless phone back on its charger. "Dude, you know she's got a thing for you, right?"

I wanted Luke to be right. I didn't want to get fixated on something only to find out I was barking up the wrong tree. But if Ashley did like me back, what then? Was I supposed to act differently or just play it cool? I didn't want to suddenly change the way I behaved and scare her off.

The reality was, I liked Ashley. Talking with her was easy. There was something about hearing her stories about growing up on the Prairies to which I could relate. Maybe it was because she was the only other person who came with us to the lakeshore in Thessalon during Mass-O that made her stand out. Maybe it was because during Mass-O, I picked her up and threw her over my shoulder during an impromptu game of tag and when we tripped and she fell on top of me, everyone else seemed to disappear for a moment. Maybe it was that we both didn't know what to do about that feeling or how to take it beyond late phone calls and daily emails. I sure didn't, which was a problem that left me restless some nights. More recently, I toyed with pleasant thoughts and scenarios about what might happen on New Year's, making it even more imperative that the event happen.

As Luke continued to pester me about Ashley, Carlos walked into the kitchen. "How could he? He likes Bethany!"

I cursed at Carlos in my head. He had recently made a habit of stating that more often, especially when Bethany was present in the room. I couldn't understand why he was so standoffish, particularly to me, but it was becoming increasingly annoying. I placated Luke by playing dumb and ignored Carlos, merely admitting Bethany was cute and left it at that, a statement which was not untrue. She was very sweet, with a cherubic face that would get animated in her pronunciations in both languages. Bethany and I got along well when we were alone. We spoke about home, our families, work placements, though never in exceptionally great depth. There didn't seem to be a burning desire to get to know her more intimately. I didn't know if it was part of the language barrier that created this hesitance or a latent guilt from not following up my pre-Katimavik flirtations with her. Now that we had met and gotten to know each other, it wasn't quite the same. Whatever Carlos thought he knew, he was wrong. And I didn't need to explain myself to him when he was being such a dick about it.

Carlos walked away in a huff muttering. "Pft, whatever."

It was a relief to hear that it wasn't just me who noticed Carlos' snarky attitude. I asked if Luke knew why Carlos seemed to have a stick up his ass all the time.

"It's ... complicated. Look, just be careful. People think you like Bethany and apparently Ashley has a thing for you. You might have some tough decisions to make in the future," he advised poignantly. I suspected he was right, but his comment left me with childish rage.

Tough decisions? What the hell does that mean? I'm the one involved here, not you guys. How about I do what I think is right? I couldn't outright ignore what Luke had said though. This was new territory for me. I could barely handle one girl liking me, let alone two. I had no intention of deceptively leading on two people I was fond of. In fact, I loathed the idea of hurting either. For the time being, it seemed like the best option was to wait and see what happened.

CHAPTER 10

December 2005. Sault Ste. Marie.

It was over. Thank God it was finally over.

I was no longer house manager.

Jess and I had survived house managing and each other's company. It was a time to celebrate, not only because of the end of mountains worth of dishes, a snow-melt puddle near the front entrance that refused to dry no matter how many times we mopped it, and hit-or-miss meals that seemed more miss than hits, but it was also Jess' birthday. And birthdays meant cake.

Every week, Linda would dole out our $21.00 a week, giving us a $20 bill and a loose loonie. One house meeting, everyone had come to a unanimous decision to use the leftover dollar and put it towards a group slush fund which we would use for birthdays or any events that would warrant gifts or cake. Almost everyone was celebrating a birthday during the nine-month program, so most were content with this arrangement.

The promise of baked desserts was made extra sweet with the other news I received that day. The pastor from the Willowgrove United Church had called and agreed to let us use their hall for our New Year's celebration, free of charge. The icing on this metaphorical cake was that it was within walking distance of our house which kept the groups' gas budgets low. With plans being confirmed for the three groups, it felt like holiday cheer was starting to set in, especially with Christmas only a week away. Even our worries about the holiday tradition of having a Christmas tree had been alleviated. Linda surprised us one evening with a real evergreen set up in the living room. It was yet to be decorated, but I could see the creative individuals in the group already planning things in their head to cut, colour, and glue to help decorate the tree with.

At this point, everyone had time off from their work placements for the holidays, but it didn't leave our group with as much free time as we expected. We had to put one day aside for not only one but two of the big workshops that

Katimavik required groups to do. These mandatory workshops were intended to help participants set goals, reflect, and otherwise solidify as a group. Linda gave us the option of tackling them back-to-back but warned us it would make for a long and exhausting day. We agreed as a group to suck it up and get them out of the way. Planning them any other day would have conflicted with other workshops and activities, none of which we could or wanted to rearrange any further.

The first was a nutrition workshop, knowledge most of us thought would have been more helpful near the beginning of the program. By that point, though, we felt we had a decent grasp of basic nutrition. Linda was very knowledgeable as a long-time vegetarian and had done well at casually introducing new foods to us, explaining key points to balanced meals. There was naturally a degree of educational osmosis that went on in the house, usually around the dinner table. Everyone had some knowledge to impart, anecdotes or little tidbits of info picked up at some time or another in our lives. We might hear about a delicious recipe someone had made once and wanted to make again, a perilous kitchen story, or just valuable tips someone knew that were themed around food or cooking. Our nutrition workshop facilitator helped us fill in the gaps, almost making me excited to be house manager again.

Almost.

Our second workshop was less delicious. It was about group development where the goal was to improve, well, group development.

"I know this workshop probably won't be as fun as the one you had earlier, but I assure you it's an important one," our facilitator said, failing early to get us excited.

Kristie was our Project Coordinator. We had met her once during Mass-O. Whereas Project Leaders were in charge of a group of Katimavik participants and the houses they lived in, Project Coordinators oversaw all three groups in their entirety. They coordinated and supported PLs in their own responsibilities, but also facilitated other aspects of the program, including certain workshops, like group development. This particular one had to be done without the PL present. My guess is that having them around would stifle the development process, something we needed to do with a neutral person in charge. We watched quietly as Kristie drew a cross in the middle of a flipchart, labelling each quadrant: Forming, Storming, Norming, and Performing.

"This is the typical progression of Katimavik groups," Kristie explained as she wrote. "Orientation and the first few weeks are typically about 'forming.' This is the excitement about being in a new place, making friends, you know, the fun stuff. 'Storming' is exactly like it sounds. You settle into your work placements and house managing a bit more, and you'll find there's a lot of friction and people disagreeing." Some people shuffled in their seats. "Then comes 'norming' where you start realizing you're all in the same boat, and participants—hopefully—start to be a bit more understanding. And when you are and you better understand how Katimavik works, how to write excursions, and get a good routine going, the group can peak and really start 'performing.' That's what we want to strive for—for everyone to perform."

Kristie looked around at us, ruminating and digesting those four words. "I've been doing this with countless groups, and I can tell you that these stages may happen at different times, and you may get through them at a different pace than other groups, but they almost *always* happen this way."

She uncapped the marker in her hand and added more to the flipchart paper.

1) Forming - something you appreciate about the group
2) Storming - something you wish for the group to improve upon
3) Norming - what you bring to the group, and
4) Performing - what role you play.

We were about to start shouting examples for Kristie to write down, but she held up her hands in pause.

"We're actually going to do this for each participant. We're going to tape your sheets to your back with the stages I just told you about and people are going to fill in these answers for you as an individual." She gave us tape to begin taping our sheets. This shift from what we expected left a few of us uneasy, but still willing. For the next ten minutes over fits of giggling caused by the pen scratches that tickled our backs through the paper and our shirts, we wrote what we thought of the person we were scribbling on. Afterwards the papers were removed and the comments read in silence. Mine had surprising themes.

I expected most of the comments on my sheet to say something like I didn't take things seriously in the group or that I joked too much. Much to my surprise, everyone claimed to enjoy my sense of humour. Whereas I sometimes felt my lame jokes and silly stories were a source of exasperation, they had actually served to break tension and relieved a lot of stress in group settings.

"We also know you've been busting your ass planning the New Year's party," said Erica. And just when I started to believe it had gone unnoticed.

But almost all the scribbles in my storming section, the suggestions for my own personal improvements, paraphrased themselves to one thing: Open up.

"We never know what you're thinking or how you feel about things going on in the group," Rosalie explained when we were given an opportunity to ask questions about our papers.

You mean like personal relationships? I assumed she was referring to that. I could already feel myself growing defensive, words to justify my actions. I thought I had been open as of late, that I *had* been sharing. I guess talking about the weird little adventures I had with my friends back home or what it was like growing up and attending school in a small town where everyone knew each other's business wasn't enough. It was hard to argue with a clear consensus, both written and verbal. I knew I had been exceptionally closed around Jess, although I was still trying to understand why she seemed to rub me the wrong way no matter what she did. To hear everyone else demand I open up more was surprising. What more did they want from me? I wasn't very well going to start talking about who liked who in front of Linda. I was confident our PL turned a blind eye to a lot of louder-than-we-realized conversations that took place in the house, but substantiating exclusive relationships might require her intervention, something none of us wanted. I couldn't and wasn't going to explain myself to the group when I was still trying to understand those feelings myself and with whom they were about. My group was going to have to bloody well be content with the existing gossip that seemed invisible, yet undeniably present. I didn't need to jump into matters that didn't require my input, even if people thought it did.

But again, my silence did me no justice. Not knowing what else to do with everyone staring at me, I promised I would try to speak up more about group decisions and how I felt about them. I could tell that wasn't what some people were hoping for. Too bad.

The two back-to-back workshops had been as draining as Linda warned us they would be. It had been a lot of information to take in and reflect on. When all was done, someone suggested a night out.

"I heard there's an all-ages event or something at a place called The Canadian," Linda suggested during dinner. "You wouldn't need to worry about anyone being unable to get in." I wondered if Linda knew about our other outings. "Besides, it sounds like you all could use a break from tonight."

Our beloved PL wasn't wrong on several accounts. A quick look online confirmed there was indeed some sort of alcohol-free youth night going on that evening. While we didn't care to share the bar with some baby-faced pre-teens, most of us just wanted to get out of the house. Rosalie was more interested in dancing than drinking and thought this would be a good opportunity to do that instead.

With the exception of Jess and Victor who opted for a quiet night at home instead, everyone got dressed up and made the long walk to the bar, glad to be out of the house. It was further than we expected and late by the time we arrived, almost 11:30 p.m. The doorman, who really didn't seem concerned with his job let alone a gaggle of latecomers, waved us in through the dark foyer without cover charge. We were taken aback by what we found inside.

Everywhere, the bar was littered with high schoolers, kids that looked anywhere between 14–17 years old. Barely anyone looked any older from what we could tell. On the dance floor, teenagers were grinding up against each other as remixes of popular pop/rap songs blared overhead, their dry humping clearly going unnoticed or ignored by everyone around them. Along the edge of the bar were several private booths where couples were aggressively making out or intensely groping each other, grasping at every part of their partners their hands could reach. It was a dry event, but these kids were drunk from cocktails of loud, lascivious music and intense hormones. Or they pre-drank beforehand, which I didn't doubt either. I had been to events aimed at young adults before, but had never seen anything like this.

Hazelton might have been a small, boring town, but compared to what I was seeing I might as well have come from an Amish community.

I was not alone in feeling old and out of place. Everyone from our group shared the same sense of awkwardness, but we had made the long walk there and Rosalie really wanted to dance, so the seven of us squeezed past the oblivious teens and found some space on the dance floor.

We tried our best to have a good time and dance, but the floor was simply too crowded. Any accidental bumping or jarring against another person yielded no apologies except from our end. After half an hour of the tightly knit dancing, the night began to wear thin quickly, and not just for us. A tall blond kid tapped Carlos on the shoulder with a bothered look on his face. Over the loud music, I could just make out what he was yelling at Carlos.

"Dude, don't touch my girlfriend's ass!" he yelled with a scowl. Carlos brushed him off, denying such a thing when we asked what happened. The two ignored each other and we continued dancing. A few minutes later, the same kid came back, lightly shoving Carlos now.

"Bro, I said don't touch my girlfriend!"

I stepped in between them, trying to be loud enough he could hear me but not so loud to seem confrontational. "Look, buddy, it's a crowded dance floor for everyone. If he did, it was an accident. We're just here to dance." Carlos had yet to say anything.

The blond punk walked away. Carlos waved him off, but Rosalie chided him to stop, worried he would make things worse. Wanting to avoid trouble, we migrated ourselves to another side of the floor and continued dancing. Luke was having none of it though. He crossed his arms and donned a scowl bigger than the blond jerk's, refusing to even sway to the music now. Probably one of the oldest people on the dance floor, he looked like a pouty adult, explaining he was still pissed off at Carlos' harasser. From across the floor, I spotted blondie again. He was whispering to what looked like his friends and was pointing directly at Carlos.

It was time to leave. I told everyone and we agreed to call it quits and head home. We got out of the house and burned off some steam, having done what we intended to do. Even Rosalie didn't feel like dancing anymore. Luke, Daniel, and I circled Carlos and the girls and walked towards the exit. Blondie hadn't seemed particularly threatening, but we didn't want to take a chance with him or his buddies in case they decided to jump or sucker punch our Katima-brother. I kept a vigilant eye for trouble as we emerged from the crowd, walked past the bouncer, and calmly left the bar. We made it outside with no further confrontations before I realized I had been holding my breath the entire time.

Everyone else exhaled breaths of relief as well. We slowed our pace and jovially walked back home through the lightly falling snow illuminated by streetlights overhead. Having avoided any potential trouble, Luke, Daniel, and my own male ego swelled with pride at our display of fraternal solidarity.

"We had your back, Carlos! We were ready to fight!"

"Yeah, we could have taken them if they pulled any stunts! Well, maybe not Daniel."

"Hey, I can scream a war-cry pretty damn loud! Did you see Luke? He looked like he was out for blood!"

Carlos appreciated the backup, but played the situation down. “Ehn, I’ve come across guys like that back home in Kingston. They’re all talk. They just want to seem tough.”

I wasn’t entirely convinced. Carlos didn’t exactly give off the vibe like he was street tough. Then again, I still didn’t know him that well. He and I may not have been very close, but that didn't mean I wasn't willing to defend him from an insecure asshole.

The conversation began to shift away from the threat now behind us. Luke and Daniel had walked ahead, now caught up in another enthusiastic discussion of video games with Erica occasionally chiming in. Carlos and Rosalie walked arm-in-arm behind them, leaving Bethany and I alone in the back. Normally I was a fast walker and would have chalked it up to the recent spike in adrenaline that night. That Carlos and Rosalie seemed to stay ahead of me and Bethany gave the impression the two of them were making a point to give us privacy to talk. I slowed my pace to match Bethany’s.

It dawned on me how little time she and I had actually spent together alone. One of the suggestions on my sheet from our workshop earlier that evening had been to learn more about others. This seemed like the ideal time to learn more about Bethany. Using my rudimentary French, I asked her about school, home, family, friends, any topic that popped into my head. The conversation we had wasn't particularly revealing given my limited vocabulary, but we were connecting. Bethany filled in my hesitating gaps of French while I filled in her English ones. Aside from the occasional word or phrase that eluded her, she had already shown great improvements in speaking English since when we first met. My French, much less so.

"I hope you keep practicing, Deyhve,” she giggled. “I like when you talk to me *en français*."

We continued walking and talking until we arrived at the house. Linda was asleep, but had agreed to make an exception in letting us stay out late that night, believing we wouldn’t get up to much trouble in attending a dry event for youth.

“Oh no! *Le pain*!”

Bethany was the next house manager, partnered with Victor. She realized she had forgotten to finish baking bread that night. She had started some dough that afternoon, hoping to get a head start to have fresh bread ready for us by breakfast the next morning. When we looked in the fridge, we found a billowing mound of dough mushrooming over the edge of a ceramic bowl. I offered to help Bethany finish baking it, hopeful that the dough hadn’t risen too long and that the final product could still be palatable. Luke and Daniel were still wide awake from that night's bar adventure and had a hankering for Taco Bell, so they left for the nearest one. The rest of the group, however, went to bed, leaving Bethany and I alone to knead dough and quietly continue speaking French in the kitchen.

She confided that she had been missing home. Bethany came from a small suburb outside of proper Montreal. She didn't really consider herself from the iconic city, unlike Luke who lived smack dab in the middle of it. Anytime someone asked where Bethany was from, it was easier for her to simply state the city. It was weird to think of your hometown not as its own place, but something that was constantly compared to somewhere else, always in the shadow of another town or city.

By the time Bethany finished putting the last batch of bread in the oven, my reservoir of French was tapped. I didn't know any words to start a new conversation and didn't want to risk repeating things already said. The two of us were finally feeling exhaustion set in from the day's events. Bethany assured me she could take out the last batch of bread herself when it was done. I wished her *bonne nuit* before quietly creeping upstairs, careful not to wake anyone. As my eyes grew heavy with sleep, I thought about Bethany and what we had talked about, as well as what we had *not* talked about that night. But when my head hit my pillow and I began to drift off, those thoughts began to dissipate. Instead of focusing on Bethany, they somehow drifted back to Ashley instead.

CHAPTER 11

December 2005. Sault Ste. Marie.

We had been so busy that I barely noticed how close Christmas was when there was finally a noticeable lull in our calendar. Any pre-Christmas volunteer engagements and events had been wrapped up and our work placements were letting us off work early. Most of them, anyway. Daniel and I were baffled when Demmy requested we still come into the museum, despite the fact that visitor numbers had taken a huge dive. Even Linda was convinced it was a waste of our time when we told her the two of us were just watching the front desk and were lucky if anyone, staff or visitor, came by. That in itself wasn't surprising. Christmas was less than a week away. People were spending this time with their family, friends, and relatives. They were bonding over holiday traditions, not checking out decommissioned bush planes.

As much as everyone in our group would have liked to have seen their own families for Christmas, it wasn't financially feasible for Katimavik to pay for participants to temporarily go home, especially at a time that it was already notoriously expensive and busy to do so. For most of us, this was going to be our first Christmas away from our families. I didn't mind. Had I been able to go back for the holidays, it wouldn't have been a full Christmas anyway. My oldest brother Derek was travelling in Brazil with his girlfriend. My other brother Kyle, however, was ecstatic to have the house more or less to himself whenever my parents stepped out and would have preferred to keep it that way. That didn't mean a Christmas away from home would be a bad one. It was just going to be a different one spent with new people.

There was a novelty to spending the holidays with strangers instead of family. With our new abundance of free time, we had the opportunity to create our own Christmas cheer, starting with a Christmas photo. We all stood in front of a giant snowwoman a few of us made on our front lawn, a feat which actually made the local news. The photo made for an excellent Christmas card. We may not have been with our families, but we were still receiving the love away from home with something in the mail every few days for someone. Anytime one of us received a package from home, it usually contained something that could be shared with the rest of the group or at least opened it in front of everyone with the intention of spreading the cheer that was sent along with it. The frozen cookies with cream cheese icing from Erica's parents were a group favourite.

We weren't completely alone for the holidays though. Carlos had invited a colourfully decorated man from Ecuador named Gael to the house as a guest and presenter one night. The two met through Carlos' work at the Red Cross after which he requested Gael come to the Katimavik house and present on Ecuadorian culture, art, and music. After a Latin-themed dinner the house managers were kind enough to put on, he showed us numerous bracelets he made and sold at the mall. Gael also played music he created with various drums which he let us all use in a living room jam-session. Carlos was excited to have a fellow South American educate us on a culture outside of Canada. He scowled venomously whenever he caught someone chatting or being inadvertently disruptive during Gael's talk. We enjoyed the taste of a new culture in the household. Even Daniel was open-minded and kept his snark to a minimum.

Everyone was relaxing in the post-presentation hours after Gael left. I was reading in the living room and listening to Erica strum her guitar in the girls' room. I was beginning to get lost in her soft-sung lyrics describing romance blossoming between a pair of lovers during an anarchist uprising against capitalist overlords when Luke emerged from the guys' room. He was about to sit down on the couch across from me when he noticed something on the tiny decorative plastic Christmas tree that sat on a wooden stand between the kitchen and the living room. We hadn't much in the way of decorations, but Linda did her best to make the house festive.

"What the… hey guys, check this out!"

We got up to investigate his find. Tucked between the plastic branches was a tiny toy crib with a folded note taped to the top of it. Luke grabbed the small ornament and opened it. Inside it read: *"Congratulations, it's a girl!"*

It took us a few seconds before we clued into what the message meant. We looked up at a beaming Linda who had heard us and was watching the scene unfold.

"Really? We're getting *another* girl?" I asked to be sure.

She nodded gleefully.

"The new participant is a francophone named Valérie," Linda said. "She's from Gatineau, near Ottawa, and she'll be arriving the same day as Tiffany."

Luke and I burst with joy, jumping and hugging like we learned we were going to be new parents. Erica ran about the house to share the news with everyone else. Linda smirked and walked back upstairs.

"Looks like you got your Christmas wish Devon," she said back to me. "You're getting a sister!"

Luke, Daniel, and I walked to Tim Hortons. We were craving hot chocolate and wanted to get out of the house. Once again, the topics of group relations and the potential of exclusive relationships came up. More specifically, we debated who we thought was likely to hook up within our own group. Luke and Daniel had been doing most of the talking. When they noticed how quiet I had been, they started badgering me, wanting to confirm if I was in the loop.

"You know all of this, right, Dev? Like, this isn't the first time you're hearing these things, is it?"

I tried to play dumb by admitting that I had heard some of the gossip they mentioned, though not all of it, which was true. I didn't want to make wrongful assumptions on hearsay. Luke and Daniel refused to let me take such a passive position and insisted they bring me up to speed as to what was *actually* going on in the group. It was apparently more than I realized.

It was like a plot ripped straight out of a romantic comedy film. Luke liked Rosalie initially, but she had mixed feelings herself. Now they talk, but don't really like each other. I took this explanation with a grain of salt as Luke was the one telling me this. Carlos and Bethany were supposedly dating, a reveal I found a bit shocking. Carlos also liked Rosalie, who, along with Bethany, wanted him to choose between the two of them. He decided neither but continued to flirt with them. Daniel was also having thoughts about leaving the group because his friend back home in Calgary had discovered she was pregnant, and he wanted to help her and her boyfriend out. Luke contemplated quitting the program himself because the girls were becoming increasingly bitchy and gossipy, an irony I tactfully decided not to point out. Erica didn't really like Daniel or Luke, but was fond of Victor. And Jess was a loner who considered herself closer to the guys, which was why she talked to us more than the girls.

I was floored. Just when I thought everyone was getting along so well, Luke and Daniel pulled back the curtain and revealed there was a lot more going on in our little group under the surface. I felt stupid and ashamed for having been unaware of these dramas, yet oddly relieved that I had also not played a role in any of them. According to Daniel, that was likely because I, along with Victor, were seen more or less as neutral parties, individuals who generally got along with everyone. Because we knew so little—whether by choice or simple ignorance—we weren't seen as a "threat," a word choice of Luke's I felt was utterly ridiculous. What exactly were we a threat to? Internal dating competition? People's comfort zones? My head swam around in deep silence as we walked home, trying to process everything I had just learned. We happened to cross paths with Rosalie who was on her way to the gym.

"Rosalie, you wouldn't believe what Devon doesn't know!" Luke told her.

You mean aside from everything? I thought.

"Does he know one of the girls liiiiiikes him?" she jested.

Well, we can add that *to the list.*

Rosalie had mocked me about Bethany before, so I assumed she was simply referring to her again. That she didn't say a name led me to wonder if it was indeed Bethany. I should have taken the high road and let it go, but given my precedence for ignorance, I thought it might be better to shift gears. I wanted to know who. Besides, I didn't want to give someone the wrong impression if I could avoid it in the future. I felt like I had already done that with Bethany. Maybe it was Jess, having developed feelings for me during our house managing? I hoped not. I doubted it was Erica. According to Luke and Daniel, she was enamoured with Victor and just seemed to put up with the rest of us.

"Alright, humour me, Em. Who likes me?" I asked, trying to downplay my curiosity.

"Nope, nuh uh. I'm not saying." Rosalie refused to spill any more beans and left with a giggling eye roll. Once again, I was left in the dark.

Between what Luke and Daniel had told me and now Rosalie's girlish mockery, I felt drained, frustrated, and confused, but mostly conflicted. Had my ignorance actually been through my own volition, or had I been left out of the loop? Was I supposed to feel foolish for having been blind to the dramas underneath my nose or frustrated because I wasn't a part of them? Just when it seemed like everyone was getting along, "norming" as it were, I learned we were barely more mature than the kids we had seen at the bar the other night. My group didn't want me to open up; they just wanted to drag me into these petty games. I couldn't very well unlearn what Luke, Daniel, and now Rosalie had told me though. Now I had to carry those little secrets with me. Katimavik houses were small, though, and as I found out, secrets didn't stay secret for long.

I found a small consolation in that I no longer had to be concerned by my supposed conflict between Ashley and Bethany. If what I heard was true and there was something going on between Bethany and Carlos, I could confidently drop any idea of a relationship with the tiny French girl and would avoid anything that could be misconstrued as flirting. Bethany had her own shit to deal with.

But once I started to pull at that string, everything else began to unravel. Had I been worrying about something that wasn't there to begin with? Was I doing that with Ashley? What if I was becoming fixated on something with her that was completely different than what I thought was going on? I'd have to eventually figure that out. It was a relief that Ashley didn't belong to our group. It would save us both a heap of trouble if this kind of drama was what was to be expected. Although it meant spending time together was that much more difficult, there were no inner group complications. It was me and her. No one else to get in the way, no one else to get hurt. But that didn't seem to be the way things were unfolding.

It was far from a quiet night in the Katimavik house. We were all stirring, much more than a mouse. No sugar plums were dancing in our heads.

"Who's up for a late-night drive?" Linda suggested.

"Where?" I asked.

"Don't know!" she said with a devious smile.

We all piled into the van, curious as to where Linda might take us. Spontaneous trips to nowhere were not a common occurrence, but Linda wanted us to burn off some of the pent-up excitement we had that Christmas Eve. Everyone had agreed to open gifts at midnight rather than in the early morning. We were going to take advantage of the chance to sleep in, whether it was Christmas or not, and no one wanted to go to bed early. So, Linda drove us around Sault Ste. Marie. We drove around the empty downtown mall parking lot, leaving fresh tire tracks in the wake of a fresh blanket of snow. From there, Linda parked in front of the Canadian shore of the St. Mary's River which separated us from the United States. Several of us pulled off our boots and dipped our toes in, drunk from the unbridled cheer Linda encouraged in us. She had read the situation perfectly—we did have a lot of energy to burn off.

By the time we returned home, it was just shy of midnight. We settled into the living room, huddling underneath blankets comfortably in our pajamas or sweatpants. One by one, we got up to give our gifts to our secret Santa recipients. The group had agreed on a Secret Santa style gift exchange with a reasonable $25.00 limit if gifts were bought. $21.00 a week didn't make it easy to save money. I didn't want to limit myself to making one person happy though. Everyone in my group was getting more than they expected.

After the last participant received their Secret Santa gift, I spoke up.

"Christmas isn't over quite yet, guys." I walked around and handed everyone a piece of paper. On each of them I had written a different location in the house: "Kitchen," "Downstairs Bathroom," "Guys' Room," etc. After I handed out the last one, I sat back down with a smug look and gave no further instructions.

Rosalie clued in quickly. "Can we go? Can we? Now!?" she asked with an eager grin, like a dog waiting for a ball to be thrown. I nodded permission and everyone sprinted away. Most found their hidden gifts quickly, some taking longer than others. It was surprisingly difficult to hide gifts in each room without anyone being the wiser, let alone having someone accidentally finding them. Somehow, I managed to find windows of time just long enough to do so. One by one, everyone returned to the living room, ecstatic at finding their presents.

Knowing well in advance that I would be spending Christmas with a bunch of strangers, I decided to make several gifts before I left for Katimavik. Twisting, knotting, and weaving hemp necklaces had been a hobby of mine, but more enjoyable was using my dad's electric Dremel to carve unique shapes out of bone for necklace centerpieces. I made just enough necklaces to give to each member in my group, including Linda. I kept them hidden in a small box tucked away in my duffel bag since we'd arrived so no one would see them and ask questions. With a selection of pre-made necklaces, each with unique centerpieces and different coloured hemp, I chose ones I felt fit each participant's personalities, personalities

I was still getting to know. I was happy with my choices for who received what, and so was everyone else. Well, almost.

"Why? Why did it have to be purple!?" moaned Carlos about his necklace which was weaved with purple and black hemp. I ignored his whining, but Rosalie punched him in the shoulder on my behalf. "I mean, thank you, Devon, it's a lovely colour," he muttered under his breath. "But why purple! Anyway, hey! Feliz Navidad everyone!"

CHAPTER 12

December 2005. Sault Ste. Marie.

We may not have spent Christmas with our families, but we did revel in the calming lull that tended to follow. Our group had fewer volunteer commitments after Christmas, but Linda refused to let us lounge around the house and be completely unproductive. She "encouraged" us to use our downtime to plan activities for after the holidays. We knew she was right. Her subtle guilt trip served to help us prepare for actual trips. After a few focused afternoons, we had put the finishing touches on some of our bigger excursions that required more extensive plans. Several days later, we were thrilled to receive confirmation that, aside from a few simple changes that needed to be made, several of our submitted plans had been approved by Head Office. As we watched a flurry of fresh snow through the living room window that evening, relieved to have such stressful things taken care of, we grew excited for our next upcoming excursion that had been recently approved: cross-country skiing.

I wasn't surprised to find it approved. After all, it had been one of the simpler excursion plans to write out:

"Excursion goals?"

"To cross-country ski."

"What activities will you be doing?"

"Cross-country skiing."

"What sort of reflection will you be doing post-excursion?"

"Talking about the cross-country skiing we did."

Even the big-wigs at Head Office could see that a simple cross-country skiing trip was a no-brainer. It was approved immediately.

When the day for our excursion arrived, Linda drove the loaded Katimavik van to the outskirts of Sault Ste. Marie where there seemed to be a lot more snow than in the city. It was a quiet ride to the small lodge where we picked up our rental skis and strapped in. Most of the group had never gone skiing before. I myself had only ever gone once. I knew cross-country skiing was different from its downhill variation though. I could appreciate the relaxing idea of slowly gliding through a wintery forest landscape muted by snow, with the silence broken only by the occasional bird chirping and the swishing of legs in snow pants. That, or the loud flailing of youth volunteers frantically trying to avoid falling down like a gaggle of drunken geese. It brought some comedic relief to counter the apprehension of first-time skiers. Even I was not immune to the clumsy tumble or two. Or three.

Once we got into the literal groove of cross-country skiing, everyone began to enjoy the outdoor adventure more. Some participants simply gave up when it came to climbing up short hills though. Rather than awkwardly attempting to waddle uphill with V-shaped steps, the less coordinated of us chose to remove our boots from their bindings and just walk up instead. The most exciting part was always on the other side of the hills when we got to go downhill. The acceleration in speed was short but enjoyable, and only made me miss snowboarding and flying down mountain sides at breakneck speeds more. When Linda informed us she had been looking into planning a snowboarding day trip later that winter, several of us voiced our excitement, me loudest of all. As much as I enjoyed the random antics our group seemed to get up to when cooped up inside, I enjoyed being outside on the nice winter days as well. I needed to move, to go fast. Being inactive inside for too long made me a little stir crazy.

Participants weren't the only ones that needed a break in Katimavik though. Just as participants could get 48 hours off, so did PLs. It only made sense that the individual responsible for a house filled with rambunctious youth would need some time away to recuperate. We thought we had been pretty good to Linda and were relatively well behaved, but we knew she needed some relaxation. It was time for Linda to leave her kiddies alone so she could spend her time off with her Japanese fiancé, Keiji.

The more she talked about him, the more eager we became to actually meet Linda's significant other. She made Keiji seem very interesting whenever she described him. In addition to being from another country, he was also a musician, an artist, a hacky sacker, and writer, just to name a few things Linda claimed he did. I thought of him as an Asian Renaissance man.

"There are very few skills or activities he can't pick up in the first five minutes of trying," Linda explained with thinly-veiled pride.

Shortly after Keiji's inaugural introduction to the group that evening, Linda's claims rang true. He was indeed a very articulate and interesting guest, easily finding some connection with everyone. I could certainly see how some of his pleasant sociability and polite demeanour might have rubbed off on Linda. He garnered even more of our favour when he left us his laptop to watch DVDs on while he and Linda were away. The two of them had planned a retreat out of the city at a bed and breakfast and wanted to simply relax in each other's company. We knew perfectly well what they'd be getting up to and it definitely didn't involve watching DVDs.

A DVD player may not have seemed like much, but our Katimavik house didn't have a TV. Most of them didn't. The volunteer program was old fashioned in that it discouraged TVs in Katimavik houses as they tended to encourage lethargy and laziness. If a house *did* happen to have a TV or DVD player, it was usually because the house came with one. On rare occasions, these would be used to watch educational videos, much like those days in school where a teacher would roll in a squeaky television stand into the classroom because their students were behaving well, the teacher had tests to mark, or there was a substitute teacher who didn't care to follow any sort of lesson plan.

But we didn't watch educational videos. We watched several seasons of *The Simpsons* that Keiji had also left us. None of us particularly missed television, but we knew a treat when we were handed one. Watching the antics of one of the most recognizable cartoon families ever to grace television gave me a novel sense of familiarity, if only because I was enjoying those laughs with new company in my midst. It was a renewed joy, one that had actually waned over the past few years.

I had grown loath to kill entire weekends in front of the television screen back home. Doing so left me bored, irritable, and depressed. This was only exacerbated when my parents had decided to purchase a satellite dish. I initially embraced the upgrade, having personally endured the excruciatingly limited four channels that many homes in the early 90's had, at least when the bunny ear antenna was bent just the right way. We soon had over one hundred additional channels to choose from. This also meant having over one hundred channels *to choose from*. Inundated with the sheer abundance of choice, I spent half my time channel surfing and would usually end up watching the same shows I grew up with, which included *The Simpsons*. The familiar characters, quotable quotes, quick adventures wrapped up in twenty minutes or so, plus the requisite couch gag; it was the entertainment version of comfort food in that you more or less knew what to expect. It was those kinds of familiar and simple jokes that filled the conversations between Bailey, Courtney, and myself whenever the three of us hung out back home. There were days I wanted to change the channel with my friends—figuratively and literally—but in the end, we always found ourselves watching and joking over the same old TV shows and films. At least in Katimavik, however, no one was complaining about our viewing options.

We couldn't remain completely glued to screens during Linda's absence though. Even without our trusty PL by our side, we still had activities to attend. With the pre-arranged help of our neighbouring Katimavik PLs acting as temporary drivers, we were driven to different places that were beyond a bus ride and a good walk. That weekend, it meant our snowshoeing excursion.

It took place outside an elderly woman's home, once again on the outskirts of the city. Underneath a large carport, a girl our age instructed us how to put on our snowshoes. We had previously met Astrid during an event we volunteered at on Christmas day. She was spending the remainder of her Christmas holiday at her grandmother's, who also happened to operate the snowshoe rental and own the property we would be walking around. Astrid became our unofficial tour guide for our afternoon stroll through a beautiful cedar forest and provided good company for the hotdogs and hot cider that followed afterwards.

Astrid's grandmother, coincidently, also led the quilt making workshop for the group back at the house the following day. It wasn't as well received as snowshoeing. The goal was to learn basic stitching techniques and sew together fabric cut-outs into a patch. We would combine our individual patches together to make a group quilt.

Somehow Daniel and Victor managed to skip most of the workshop, disappearing somewhere in the middle of it with Luke joining them later on. I found it to be incredibly rude, but Astrid's grandmother remained courteous and patient, understanding that sewing wasn't for everyone. No one had finished their patches by the time she began packing up her sewing kits. I tucked my fabric pieces into a plastic Ziploc bag, vowing to finish my patch later. I couldn't be bothered with it then. It was going to demand a lot of time and focus and there were too many other things to do. New Year's Eve was fast approaching, only days away.

Everything had been set. The venues were confirmed, meals planned and prepped, and Thessalon and Blind River's excursion plans were completed and consistent with our own plans. We even invited Keiji, who had graciously offered to DJ a small dance for us at the church hall. As with the arrival of any guests, we made sure the house was clean. For this, everyone pitched in, not just the house managers. Even though there weren't any participants from either Thessalon or Blind River actually staying at our house, we wanted to make a good impression.

The Thessalon group was the first to arrive. Their van pulled into our driveway in the afternoon on December 30th. Head Office couldn't very well give you a stamp of approval on an excursion plan just for a New Year's party, so Thessalon had to "leverage" their excursion itinerary to Sault Ste. Marie with other tours and activities, like a tour of the Bush Plane Museum.

Much to mine and Daniel's dismay, Demmy hadn't received the email from Linda requesting participants be excused from work for the last bit of the Christmas holiday. She still expected Daniel and me to come in, even after the failure in communication had been addressed. Both he and I, and now Linda, still couldn't fathom why Demmy needed us there. We begrudgingly acquiesced to Demmy's wishes though. Exactly as we expected, it was easily the most boring day of work. Not a single person came in. By that point, we had read most of the books from the gift shop. Even though it had been dull as hell, Daniel and I didn't mind since we got to play tour guide for the Thessalon group, knowing it would make their visit to the museum more enjoyable.

All the Thessalon participants were ecstatic to see Daniel and me when they poured out of their own white Katimavik van in the museum's parking lot. The feeling was mutual. Whenever you hung out with another Katimavik group, you were an outsider, albeit one who was welcomed more than shunned. You became privy to the hilarious stories, silly games, and other idiosyncrasies that other groups had. It was an exuberant, almost addictive energy, the kind that I fed off of. Even though I was fond of my group, the quiet fights and drama had slowly been tainting the program for me. As a guest to another group, however, you could keep your distance and not get bogged down by petty squabbles while joining in on the good times. And while doing so, they might vent to you about those things and vice versa, all while understandably sympathizing about the unique experience the others were going through. It was a support system that worked well. Daniel and I welcomed the Thessalon participants inside and began the tour.

I had only been volunteering at the museum for a month and a half, but had already amassed a favourite collection of interesting stories and tidbits about the exhibits and planes that filled the hangar: the progressive importance of Roberta Bondar, the first female Canadian astronaut; the evolution of fire suppression tactics via water bombers; and the adaptability and versatility of the de Havilland Canada DHC-2 Beaver float plane. The Thessalon group enjoyed our personalized tour so much, they invited us to join them in their subsequent tour of the Sault Ste. Marie Locks, engineered passageways that provided safe passage for ships between the Great Lakes. Daniel politely declined, but I was glad to continue on with them. It felt like I was being adopted by a loving family, one that wanted to spoil me and bring me along for the fun parts of Katimavik rather than dealing with the heavier stuff. At least, not in front of the new temporary member of the family.

When the Thessalon group dropped me off back at the house several hours later, I spotted a third Katimavik van in the driveway. The Blind River group had arrived, and that meant I would finally get to see Ashley. Inside, she and her group were already comfortably scattered about our small living room, socializing with my own group members. Ashley jumped up from the couch and threw her arms around me when I walked in.

"Oh my God, hi!" she squealed, squeezing me with a hug. I tucked my smile into her shoulder, not wanting to share the moment with anyone else in the room.

Our reunion was excitable, but short lived. The Blind River group was also on a strict itinerary which they had to adhere to. I was about to curse their damnable excursion plan under my breath before I realized it would take the Blind River group to the pool, which meant I could easily join them. My own group had no other plans that evening, so that was precisely what we did.

The pool quickly became a mad froth of waves and screams with two Katimavik groups filling the water. A few of us were doing cannonballs off the diving boards, others yelling Marco Polo, some relaxing in the hot tub. I was preoccupied with teaching Ashley how to swim.

"I'm not a very good swimmer," she said meekly. There weren't a lot of lakes where Ashley came from. Wheat fields weren't exactly the best places for prairie folk to learn to swim. For me, the closest pool available back home was in the next town over, so I learned to swim in the lakes and rivers that meandered between the valleys and basins across the region. Having mostly self-taught myself to swim, I was by no means a trained lifeguard, but thought I could teach Ashley the basic strokes that I knew.

"Yep, just push with your palms outward. Don't forget to kick with your legs," added Chris.

He was another member of Ashley's group. He also happened to be a lifeguard for several years and knew how to properly train someone of Ashley's skill level. I didn't want to risk giving her the wrong advice, so my voice quieted in place of Chris'. I knew she would benefit more from him than me, but that didn't change me secretly willing him to go away and train someone else.

When the gaggle of Katimavikers were pooled out, we walked back to our house. There wasn't enough space for two groups to stay the night, so Blind River and Thessalon were staying elsewhere in the city until New Year's Eve when everyone would be sprawled across the floor of the church hall. It almost seemed impossible with so many participants bobbing up and down the snow-covered sidewalks of Sault Ste. Marie, but Ashley and I managed to walk by ourselves and talk. I didn't know where Chris was and didn't care, so long as he wasn't walking with us.

Ashley proceeded to tell me how excited she was to hear from her family during Christmas, especially her little brother.

"And he's so smart. Ooh! And also, also, also… " Her bubbly refrains always made me smile. I let her do most of the talking. "My brother is really interested in Katimavik and thinks he might join when he finishes school."

I was confident his big sister would have lots of stories to share with him when she returned home.

New Year's Eve finally arrived. In true Katimavik style, everyone pitched in getting the church hall ready to ring in the New Year. Participants from all three groups moved chairs and tables, made an area for sleeping, and otherwise prepared for the party. Linda and Keiji had also returned that morning from their time away and were now joining in the madness. Keiji connected a pair of speakers to his laptop, making an adequate sound system. He had thousands of songs on his hard drive to keep us moving and grooving well into the night. We were thankful that he didn't need any complicated setup and could just play from the spare speakers he had. In Katimavik, simple was often better.

After everything was set up, we all took part in a massive dinner of delicious lasagna that Erica and I had prepared. The mountain of cheesy noodles everyone scarfed down didn't slow us down in the least. The three Katimavik groups were brimming with excitement for the coming end of the year. A few sips from concealed bottles of booze may have also had something to do with everyone's merriment.

We were hours away from ringing in New Year's Katimavik-style when I realized I had forgotten some important party supplies at the house. It was within walking distance and I wanted to ask Ashley to come with me, but I couldn't find her. I didn't want to miss anything and decided to leave immediately in order to make it back in time before the countdown. Rosalie saw me with a determined look on my face. When I told her where I was going, she offered to walk with me and grab the supplies.

Her company wasn't completely altruistic. She had immediately noticed how close I had been with Ashley since her group had arrived. Rosalie wanted the details.

"Are you going to kiss her? Oh my God, you should kiss her at the end of the countdown!"

I kicked a chunk of hard snow down the road, blushing.

"You better! It would be so romantic! Oh, I always wanted to be kissed on New Year's," she pouted.

It was hard not to think about that, especially given everything I knew about Ashley. From discrete conversations with others in her group, I had learned Ashley had not only never had a boyfriend, but she had also never even been kissed. I couldn't fathom how such an adorable and sweet girl had ever been denied such a deserving thing. I wanted to remedy that. I just didn't know how to make it happen.

"Aren't you going to do that with Carlos?" I asked. "Aren't you two a thing?"

"Ugh." Now Rosalie took her turn kicking the snow. "That's a mess. I don't even know."

She confided how she and Carlos found themselves making out the other night when Linda was away. Despite that—or perhaps because of it—the triangle between her, Carlos, and Bethany had not cleared up and the status of their relationship remained vague. If my previous conversation with Luke and Daniel had taught me anything, there was likely more to Rosalie's situation I was not aware of that she was probably not sharing. I thought about asking but didn't think she and I had enough time to dive deeper into a topic that surely demanded a lengthier chat. I was glad for her company, but I could offer no advice, only solace in the situation Rosalie was trying to deal with.

We made it back to the church hall with plenty of time to spare. It was exceptionally quiet from the outside, which I found odd. Katimavikers were almost never a quiet bunch. The reason was obvious when we walked through the door.

"Happy birthday!"

Ashley came out from behind a wall of Katimavikers singing happy birthday to me. She wrapped her arms around my shoulders, squeezing her cheek against the nook of my neck.

"I hope you have a really good birthday Devon," she muffled sweetly into my ear.

Someone brought out a large cardboard box wrapped in layers and layers of decorative wrapping and tape. Whoever had wrapped it had done an excellent job. It took me fifteen minutes to tear my way through boxes inside of boxes down to the gift buried deep inside: a signed scrapbook. On each page were pictures of my group, surrounded by random quips and quotes we had come to love and laugh at. Even the other group participants had signed it. I looked up at a winking Rosalie after flipping through the book.

You sneaky little minx, I thought, grinning a playful grin. It had been a good thing I had forgotten those things at the house. My group must have needed the chance to set the surprise up. Rosalie might have been tasked with distracting me anyway. I was glad their plans worked out, now if only mine would pan out just as well.

We still had an hour until midnight, but the party was well under way. DJ Keiji was getting everyone pumped with music, mostly consisting of top radio hits. I looked around hoping to see Ashley to ask her to dance, but I couldn't find her once again. I also didn't see Chris anywhere. I must have had a readable look on my face. Natalie, another girl from Ashley's group, came up to me. She could tell who I was looking for.

"Ashley's with Jim. He's been having some problems lately and they went on a walk to go chat," she said comfortingly. Knowing that put me at ease, reminding me of Ashley's sweet empathetic nature, which was one of the reasons I liked her in the first place.

I also happened to like Jim. He was a tall, lanky guy from Brockville, Ontario, who seemed born with his scraggly beard, but otherwise was a genuine guy. Ashley spoke fondly of him and painted him as a caring big brother. She had previously been concerned about Jim quitting Katimavik. During one of my phone calls to the Blind River house, Jim mentioned how he was feeling depressed and homesick. I couldn't help him get over his depression, but after a one-on-one phone chat between the two of us, I managed to convince Jim to stick around, at least until after the New Year's party that we had all planned. Even though he and I got along well, jealousy still scratched at the back of my mind, but I refused to give it the attention it demanded. Jim was probably lost in his own thoughts in the looming New Year and Ashley was probably doing what she did best in cheering him up. Before I could decide if it would be too intrusive to go looking for them and whether it was for the right reasons, I was unexpectedly dragged onto the dance floor by some of the Thessalon girls.

"Come dance, Devon!"

They weren't going to let me get away. I gave in. I didn't want to obsess over Ashley and reminded myself that the night should be spent having fun rather than being stressed, jealous, or paranoid. Once the music took over, I couldn't deny the girls some sweet break-dancing moves. Someone from Thessalon even taught a few brave Katimavikers a dance routine they had learned, involving impressive spins and careful flips between partners. It was around then that Ashley returned with Jim and I lost any interest in dancing.

I requested Jim take my place on the dance floor as I needed a break. Ashley and I found a corner of the crowded hall. More participants now returned inside the church hall as the temperature had dropped and it was too cold for them to smoke outside. It was still loud in the corner, but it was a bit quieter and more private away from the mass of people. We both sat down and watched the event unfold.

"Thank you so much for convincing Jim to stick around until the New Year," Ashley said, hugging her knees. "He's still dealing with a lot of family issues back home, but he's feeling much better about being here."

It wasn't just Jim's reluctance to stay. Several members of the Blind River group had been hit hard with homesickness, shared feelings that had started to bother Ashley. She had become particularly close to her group. Having been raised in a small southern Saskatchewan town, Ashley confided she hadn't had many friends growing up. It was one of the reasons she was excited for Katimavik, the chance to travel and meet new people. The risk of some of those people leaving, like Jim, left Ashley struggling to convince them to stay. Our group had lost Simone, and it still felt like there was a hole to be filled. I didn't want Ashley to deal with a worse version of that.

Our conversation was interrupted by people shouting for our attention. It was approaching midnight. Someone had found a TV tucked away in a closet which we kindly borrowed from the church. With a few engineer-minded Katimavikers, we finagled the TV's bunny ears well enough to display a Canadian channel hosting a New Years count-down. Everyone counted down in unison. The giant cluster of Katimavik youth volunteers who came from provinces across the country erupted into screams and hollers to chase away the ghosts of the past year and welcome the new one.

In the sudden confusion, there hadn't been any chance for a New Year's kiss. Once the countdown began, I lost Ashley again as she began hugging everyone in the throes of celebration. People were hugging, cheering, and giving hearty handshakes. As soon as the excitement settled, Keiji took the cue to keep the party going but at a slower pace than before and began playing songs to match the mood. Seeing everyone grab dance partners left me in a frantic worry, pathetically reminiscent of high school dances when the last song played, and people scrambled to find partners so they wouldn't be alone for it. I spotted Ashley across the room and walked over, refraining from bolting over and looking too eager. From the corner of my eye, it looked as though Chris was going to do the same thing, but I beat him to the punch.

"I believe you owe me a dance," I said to her. Ashley looked shyly down at the floor but happily obliged. We found our way to the centre of the hall amid a few others holding their dance partners. A popular country song played, with slow twangs for our hips to move to. I wrapped my arms around Ashley's waist and gently pulled her in closely, her head resting comfortably on my shoulder. She smelled faintly of a flowery perfume, a scent I somehow hadn't noticed at all that night. She mumbled something into the nook of my neck, but I couldn't hear her over the music.

"I said," she whispered just loud enough into my ear. "I just want to fall asleep right here."

I pulled her closer, slowly swaying her back and forth while slightly rotating on my heels. I didn't want to focus too much on dancing or moving without stumbling. I just wanted the song to keep playing, for the two of us to stay intertwined so that I could continue feeling her sweet, warm breath on my neck. I wanted that moment to last, but the insecurities in my head were already picking up pace, worrying about after.

So no New Year's kiss. What about this? What about now? What do I do next? The song is ending soon! How do I show this girl, this girl that I've been thinking about more and more, night after night, this girl with her arms wrapped around me right now that I—

The song suddenly stopped, taken over by a popular classic rock one that blared from the speakers.

"Ooh! I love this song!" said Ashley with a jolting perkiness as she joined a gaggle of girls who were already dancing.

And like that, the moment was gone.

CHAPTER 13

January 2006. Sault Ste. Marie.

We were always told that your world shrunk when you were in Katimavik, that it embodied the idea of six degrees of separation. I didn't realize how true that was until we had another guest for dinner. Her name was Jocelyn.

And we had met before.

Whenever our group introduced ourselves, it quickly became routine to go around and state our name and where we were from any time we met new people. Some participants were content to simply say the province they came from. Others however only needed to say their city, like Luke being from Montreal or Rosalie from Ottawa. I was obstinate enough to always include Hazelton whenever it was my turn to share how I was from British Columbia. It might have been just another small town in the middle of nowhere, but it was *my* small town in the middle of nowhere, damn it! Much to my chagrin, Hazelton had become the butt of a joke for the group. If someone had to describe something small or insignificant or otherwise unknown, Hazelton became the punch line.

"He thinks he's from a small town? Can't be anywhere near as small as Hazelton, right guys?"

"Oh, Devon? He hails from the great metropolis of Hazelton!"

"The amount of Spanish I know could fit inside of Hazelton!"

I could usually hear someone moan or see them roll their eyes when it became my turn to share where we were from. No one in my group ever expected anyone we would meet in Katimavik to have actually heard of Hazelton. That is, until Jocelyn arrived.

She was a PL from another part of Ontario, passing through town. I enjoyed having other PLs as guests. They felt like kooky aunts or uncles, telling us about cousins we never met with stories we could still appreciate. It turned out Jocelyn and I were closer than we expected.

"Oh, I know Hazelton very well! I was the PL for a group there a few years ago actually," Jocelyn said. Everyone around the dinner table stopped eating, a testament to the unbelievable thing our guest shared. I swear I heard someone drop a fork. Jocelyn looked around, unnerved by the sudden silence.

"Hold on," Luke spoke up, looking confused, almost frustrated. "You're telling me, you don't just know where Hazelton is, you actually *lived* there? And as a PL no less?" He laughed, throwing his hands up in the air. "Wow Devon. Maybe it's not as small as we all thought."

Jocelyn chuckled. "Oh no, it's still pretty small. What, like, two thousand people, Devon? The whole area, including Kispiox Valley?" I nodded. Jocelyn's face then lit up. "Wait, did you know the Sylvans?"

Now it was my turn to laugh. "Know 'em? My brother is dating one of them!" The Sylvans had been a billet family to Katimavikers for several years. The feedback from those who stayed with them was unanimously positive. Darcie Sylvan was a sweet spoken woman who worked at the hospital, always smiled, and was renowned for her delicious cookies. Her husband, Bill, used to teach at the high school and had been the wrestling coach for earlier grades before my time. The couple lived out in Kispiox Valley, a rural area about a twenty-minute drive out of town. They were one of the found members for the Kispiox Valley Music Festival, one of the biggest summer events back home. I didn't know their children that well, although I had graduated secondary school with one of their daughters. The family was a valuable pillar of the community and well liked.

Having mentioned the Sylvans, Jocelyn's eyes now widened with fond memories. "Hey wait, we had dinner there once. Yeah, I think you were there too!" she said, increasingly excited. "Graham and Sandra were there too."

Both of us were thrilled now. I *did* remember the dinner she spoke of. The Graham and Sandra she mentioned were the same volunteers I'd spent the summer landscaping the town with. The Katimavik stories they told during those hot afternoons spent working together outside helped stoke the fires for my eventual enrolment.

Jocelyn and I bubbled with cheer now, reminiscing about Hazelton. It had been more than a year since she'd been there, leaving me to bring her up to date.

"Did you know so-and-so's gone now?"

"Oh, and that place closed down."

"Was that building around when you were there?"

"What about this-or-that?"

The two of us inadvertently hijacked the conversation for the rest of dinner, but I didn't care. It was gratifying to talk about my hometown when the rest of my group seemed to have already grown bored with my stories. Small towns never seemed as exciting as the bustling city of Montreal or one with endless Canadian history like Ottawa. But home was home, and while I didn't mind the light mocking of it, it was nice to hear someone speak as fondly of Hazelton as I did.

Jocelyn was not our group's first guest. We played host to a surprising number of guests by that point: Kristie, our own Project Coordinator; Josie, another PL from Alfred, Ontario, on her way back to her group; and Marie-Eve, a Katimavik alumni whose PL had been Clara, the current PL for Thessalon. It was confusing trying to keep up with all of the connections, but it was always satisfying when we did.

Linda made it a point of asking us as a group if everyone was comfortable with having these Katimavik-related guests over for dinner, especially when they merely needed somewhere to stay for the night. We didn't exactly have any spare rooms, but the couch always sufficed for our guests and we loved new faces. Everyone agreed that if it wasn't a unanimous decision, we would politely decline overnight guests. Amazingly, we always found consensus.

Having guests did demand a bit more from house managers in order to accommodate an additional plate at the dinner table, but the extra effort was negligible. When you were already cooking for almost a dozen people, accommodating one more person wasn't a lot of trouble. Besides, our guests would always offer to help clean up afterwards, something those who were already scheduled to do so never complained about. I liked having guests for the same reason I liked hanging out with the other groups: different faces brought a new energy and new stories to the house. Our guests didn't see the rules or the pains of house managing or the pettiness between some participants. They would instead see and hear—usually over dinner—all the places we volunteered at, the weird but entertaining inside jokes, what activities we were planning as part of our committees, or maybe even just a funny story as we had already amassed quite a few. Guests kept Katimavik fresh and reminded us why we were doing the volunteer program in the first place.

We soon had new faces in the house. Not guests, but permanent additions. The day finally came when our Katimavik family got a little bigger with the arrival of Tiffany and Valérie. They were scheduled to arrive sometime while we were all away at work. As soon as I walked through the front door, I dropped my backpack and screamed in excitement.

"Whoo! New kids!" I rushed past the two strangers in the living room and proceeded to give Carlos a big hug. "Wow! You're shorter than I expected. But that's okay." I turned to the confused face next to me. "I promise I'll feed him and take him out for walks. But I *won't* clean up after him. That's Daniel's job."

Carlos slipped his arm around my head and put it into a headlock. "And this here is—*UMPH*—Devon, our very *special* participant. He's a little weird, but you get used to him." After some struggle, he finally released me. "Devon, meet Tiffany and Valérie."

With the ruse over with, I sat on the couch and properly introduced myself to the new girls. I started with the standard question of where they were from, and not just their province. Carlos had already warned them that they would experience that question a lot, among other things. He was one of the first members of our groups the girls met when they arrived, so I wondered what he'd told them about me. I'd have to make my own impressions. I started by asking them more about where they came from. Some people were content with a simple location to answer that question, but I wanted more details. Like Simone who had left, Tiffany also came from New Brunswick, but from a small town called Woodstock.

"Ah, so, bumfuck nowhere?" I asked after she described it. That phrase might have felt crude or derogatory, but it usually felt accurate. Tiffany agreed.

"Pretty much."

"Hey! Just like Devon!" Carlos laughed. "I'm sure you guys will get along great."

Despite Andre's jeering, Tiffany and I did in fact get along. She knew exactly what I was talking about when I lamented the struggle of getting to places when the next town was several kilometres away. Getting a car became a particularly important rite of passage as a small-town teenager. Having your own vehicle gave you mobility, which meant a new level of independence when you no longer had to rely on your parents to drive you everywhere. And in towns where everyone knew your parents, a reliable vehicle was helpful in getting away from watchful eyes, especially when the destination was a bush party. I was ecstatic that Tiffany knew exactly what I was talking about.

"So, it's a party… in the forest? The bush?" Carlos asked inquisitively, having listened to Tiffany and I talk.

"Or a baseball park," I explained. "But it's not really a party until some jackass builds a ten-foot fire with pallets."

"I know, right!" Tiffany had probably been to a few rougher parties herself. She was a stout girl and despite her stern face, smiled a lot. With wide shoulders and hips that didn't look like they would budge much if someone drunkenly bumped into her while standing around a fire pit, Tiffany had a tough-girl attitude only hinted at with her brusque but affable demeanour.

Valérie, on the other hand, was cut from a very different cloth than Tiffany. The thin blonde girl was from Gatineau across the river from Ottawa. I joked that she was practically neighbours with Rosalie who had since joined us on the couch to meet the new participants. She clearly did not like the comparison I had made.

"Trust me Dev, Gatineau is *very different* from Ottawa," she insisted, using hand gestures to drive her point home.

While Valérie agreed the two cities were not similar, she managed to find the humour in my comment. She had a slender, almost duckish face, but a very pretty one with deep blue eyes and puffy lips held slightly agape as we chatted. Valérie seemed timid at first, but when she did laugh, it revealed a goofy yet adorable grin of bright white teeth. I had no doubt she was going to make some of the girls jealous.

Later that evening, Daniel, Luke, and I took Tiffany and Valérie on a short walking tour to the nearby mall. While dodging piles of melting slush along the sidewalk, we told the girls more about the rest of the group.

"Rosalie loves to dance. Erica plays the guitar. Jess is into witchcraft."

"Wicca, remember?" Luke corrected Daniel. "She considers herself a Wiccan."

"So basically, everyone's a little bit weird. Gotcha," Tiffany summarized. "But what about Devon?" She jerked a thumb at me. "We've heard a lot about everyone, but no one's said anything bad about you. What are you hiding?" she scowled sarcastically before breaking into a giggle and playfully slapped my shoulder.

Luke answered on my behalf, which was relieving because I didn't know how to respond.

"Devon's kind of weird that way. We don't know much about him. He's not quiet, but he's not ... well, he doesn't share much."

I rolled my eyes. *Bullshit! I share plenty. It's just not enough, or not important enough to you guys.* I remained silent, however, having no answer to Tiffany's question. I didn't know how to go about describing my negative or weird qualities. It wasn't something someone openly shared, especially to new people you would be living with for the next seven months. Katimavik was supposed to be a fresh start, not another time to dwell on the past. We were having a casual conversation about personalities and quirks, not an interrogation. If I told them what I thought made me unique, I didn't want to feel compelled to live up to that reputation. I wanted to leave it to Tiffany, Valérie, and the rest of the group to find out on their own.

It had been a long day. The wet walk had left me with a chill. Most of the group was back in the living room once again, getting to know the new girls more. I had spent most of the day with them though, and wanted to escape people for a bit. Tucked cozily underneath a light blanket, I nestled myself away in the warm basement to make some phone calls. With my calling card handy and a list of contacts scrawled out on a piece of paper that I kept in my wallet, I called family and friends. The arrival of two new participants left me with exciting news I was eager to share.

I called home, but no one answered so I dialed another familiar number instead. The phone rang twice before Sydney picked up.

"Oh hey, bud! How are you?"

Sydney was my friend Jack's mom. She also happened to be my mom's best friend from high school. It was a neat coincidence that I naturally became friends with her son, even before I who his mom was. Sydney quickly became like a second mother, one who fed us, gave the occasional bit of life advice, and even taught my friends and I how to drive. She also loved to hear my stories from Katimavik.

Jack was originally supposed to have joined Katimavik after we graduated, but after getting into an accident that year that left him in a sticky legal situation, he decided to forgo the volunteer program until things had settled. He and I had a theory that because he declined acceptance into Katimavik, his spot went to the next person in the same area who had signed up—me. If this were true, then I was in the group Jack would have been in. Whenever I spoke to him about it, he was happy for me. With the way I described the group and what we did, Jack admitted he didn't think he would have gotten as much out of the volunteer program as I was.

So, Sydney and I caught up. I kept the conversation simple. Explaining to people what we were doing during Katimavik could sometimes be difficult. No one really knew what a PL was, why we volunteered at so many different places instead of just one, or exactly what our committees did. Sydney, however, had a good grasp on what the program strived to accomplish. After all, she was the one who had encouraged Jack to sign up in the first place. But as much as I enjoyed telling Sydney what I had been up to, thoughts about my mom crept their way to the front of my mind and eventually out my mouth. The last time I called home, my dad had mentioned how my mom had fallen ill.

"So, how's my mom doing? I heard she wasn't feeling well. The last time I called my dad, he said she had a pretty bad cold."

There was a pause on the other end of the receiver.

"Dev, your mom isn't sick. She had a heart attack."

CHAPTER 14

January 2006. Sault Ste. Marie.

Linda found me first.

The basement was growing small and hot and constrictive. I didn't know where to go. There was a rush of emotions I felt more and more on my face and in my body. They rushed me all at once, simultaneously filling me with adrenaline but also bogging me down with a queasy feeling that was draining me faster and faster and leaving me unable to think. I didn't want to walk upstairs past anyone who might see me struggle to explain why I looked the way I did. Outside it was open and cold, but I didn't even know where to go, couldn't think of where to go. I would have to walk through the kitchen, and then the living room in order to reach the foyer and put on my boots and coat, leaving me vulnerable to any curious eyes. No. I just needed to be somewhere else, anywhere else than where I was. Before I knew it, I found myself in the guys' room, my room, sitting atop my top bunk and tucked tightly into the corner with my back pushing against photos and letters I had sticky-tacked against the wall above my bed. The door to the room was open, but I didn't want to move. I wanted to hide, but I didn't want to close my eyes or get under a blanket. I couldn't tell if I was hot or cold, but I was definitely shuddering. Part of me wanted to be seen, for someone to walk to the top of the stairs and peer in to see me there, atop my bed cradling my knees, to see my eyes on the verge of overflowing with tears, to ask me what was wrong. It was Linda who looked in the open doorway and saw a vulnerable and scared child in the corner. I was glad it was her.

Linda had always been empathetic to her "kids." She had been quick at learning what her participants were like, understanding what made us tick, good and bad. I knew I couldn't lie when she saw me and calmly walked over to the bed before she asked me what was wrong. Between my ugly sniffles, Linda listened calmly as I told her about the phone conversation I had downstairs. Linda knew two things were on my mind: confirming my mom was okay and whether I was considering returning home. I didn’t know the latter at that point because I knew nothing about my mom’s situation. All I knew was what Sydney had told me an hour earlier. And I wasn’t likely to get any more information from her. In fact, Sydney hadn’t been happy to have inadvertently told me the news about my mom.

"Ooh, you little shit! I can't believe you made me... argh!" was Sydney’s frustrated response, but it wasn’t out of anger. She realized that by correcting what my dad had told me, she was actually the first to inform me of my mom’s hospitalization. Sydney had always been level-headed though, and quickly apologized for her outburst, downplaying my mom’s incident by explaining it had only been a small heart attack. Her exasperation at having been the one to break the news was not aimed at me and wouldn’t help the situation. I knew this and could tell with the way she backpedaled the conversation, but the damage was done. My mind had already begun to race by that point. Even though she had good intentions, I couldn't completely trust her explanation in that moment. I had my suspicions that my dad hadn’t been telling me everything, but I didn't mean to trick Sydney. Being a mother herself, she suspected my dad likely didn't tell me the whole truth because my parents didn't want me to quit Katimavik and rush home to make sure things were okay. I expected Sydney was right about their justification, but I still felt mad that both the truth and that choice had been taken away from me, leaving me feeling incredibly weak and powerless.

Linda calmly talked me through the emotions to reach that conclusion. She explained that if I wanted to, there was a process for requesting temporary leave from the program for exceptional circumstances such as extreme health issues or the death of a family member. Neither of us was sure if a near-death or medical emergency that wasn’t my own counted, but Linda said she would double check. But knowing full well how much I wanted to be where I was, she politely reminded me that a high percentage of participants who left, even for good reasons, didn't come back.

"Maybe call your mom at the hospital tomorrow and get updated on her condition before making any big decisions.” She reached up the bunk bed and patted my foot. “I know she'll be glad to hear your voice."

I was surprised when I called the hospital and was put directly through to my mom’s hospital room. I didn’t think it would be that simple, but I was glad it was.

"I’m sorry!” my mom apologized immediately when she answered the phone in her hospital room. “We didn't want you to freak out and fly home!"

"So instead, you had Dad lie to me? Sydney is pissed because she accidentally told me." I tried to speak calmly. I noticed my mom didn’t sound as quiet or tired as I was expecting, which seemed like a good sign, but I didn’t know how physically weak or sensitive she was after her heart attack. I didn’t want to stress her out anymore. It was hard to restrain myself as I voiced my frustration. I was so angry.

Apparently, I wasn't the only one my parents had avoided telling. My oldest brother Derek was in the middle of travelling through Peru. They didn't want him to cut his plans short either, opting to tell him when he came back to Canada. My other brother Kyle lived in Kitimat at the time, several hours drive away, but I wasn't sure whether they had told him yet either. I understood the rationale behind my parents' deceit, but it didn't make that pill any easier to swallow. Mom, wishing to alleviate my stress, gave me the details of her recent hospitalization.

She had been trying to quit smoking again. The combination of the stress from nicotine withdrawal and getting hit with a serious flu bug had left my mom particularly weak. While doing chores, she complained of her arm tingling and having chest pains out of the blue. Dad immediately recognized the symptoms and, ignoring Mom's protests, took her to the hospital. From what the doctor told her, it had indeed been a small heart attack. Dad's quick response in promptly getting her to the hospital minimized how dire the situation could have been. She was stable and currently under observation at our local hospital, but was going to be flown to Vancouver the next day for further testing. My mom promised to keep me and the rest of her sons in the loop from there on out. Continuing her lie would have been hard anyway. By that point, she had already been visited in the hospital by several friends and other family members. News travels fast in small towns and it was only a matter of time before Kyle and Derek knew.

"I promise, I'll tell them," my mom insisted. "Dev, I'm really sorry!"

As furious as I was, I knew it wasn't the time to make my mom feel any worse than she already did. I tried to soften my frustration by telling her how proud I was that she was trying to quit smoking. I had always rooted for her to quit the filthy habit, even when I was younger. It was an advocacy that began in the form of a worried son coming home crying after seeing a video in health class about the dangers of smoking and who would stubbornly hide her cigarettes, convinced he was helping. The thought that a heart attack might be the catalyst to get my mom to finally quit smoking was a small, comforting consolation over the next few days.

I brought up the family ordeal at the next house meeting when we provided our weekly highs and lows. I shared just enough information that it might satisfy everyone's expectations of me opening up, but it was also for cathartic purposes. Bottling up such a stressful event would eat at me from the inside. My fellow groupmates gave their requisite sympathy along with the expected offers to talk if I wanted. I didn't think I would take them up on that. Having them know that something deeply bothered the notorious energizer in the group made me feel vulnerable enough.

"Hey guys, come check this out!"

Most of us emailed family and friends with typical updates to our Katima-lives: exciting volunteer anecdotes, weird and hilarious happenings in the house, or whatever we thought might be interesting to share with those back home. To outsiders, these experiences were abstract and difficult to understand, but to anyone who had done the program, these were very much relatable. So much so that we began to scour the internet for Katimavik-related blogs, personal accounts from other participants' experience both past and present. One particular website we came across wasn't a blog or journal or anything of the kind. It was just an online list. With dancing hamsters.

It was a basic website consisting of a single, scrollable page, a beige background covered in writing. And hamsters. Each fuzzy rodent acted as a bullet point for a line of text underneath the header, "You know you're a Katima-victim when ..." Otherwise, it was essentially a list that went on and on. And nearly every single item on it was startlingly accurate.

"You've knocked over a house plant or two playing couch football." I did that the other day with a bad pass to Erica.

"Personal space becomes non-existent" In a group the size of ours, that was true enough.

"You have to ration cheese." Everyone loves it, but that shit is expensive. Linda warned us to go easy on it.

"You try to convince your PL that a group orgy would be "inclusive," not "exclusive." We made that exact joke the other day!

"There's at least one house meeting issue about 'flatulence'." It may have been brought up once or twice.

"Dishes will be the cause of World War III". True enough. Even with our accepted schedule of who did supper dishes, people still fought over who washed what and what was unnecessary dish usage.

Several of us crowded around the computer for the next half hour, nodding and laughing at how true so many of the statements we read were. If they hadn't been experienced already by our group, we understood how they could easily occur and likely would for us later. Eventually, everyone grew tired of standing and reading over my shoulders, but I continued to read, fascinated and entertained by the list. We were only two months into the program, but this collection of weird Katimavik-isms spoke wonders. It was eerily odd that despite the core essence of Katimavik being derived from the unique youth who came from different places across Canada and powered the massive volunteer engine, it yielded incredibly similar stories, experiences, anecdotes, and even lessons. Much like our emails to family and friends back home, anyone outside the program reading the list likely wouldn't understand.

But "Katima-victims" obviously did.

CHAPTER 15

January 2006. Sault Ste. Marie.

It was just me left.

Outgunned. Outnumbered. Outclassed. I was down to my last few rounds. But if I was going out, I was going out in a blaze of glory. I could hear the muffled screams of my fallen comrades elsewhere, but they soon faded. Even Ashley's.

I took a deep breath and slowly poked my head around the corner to see my surroundings. *Okay, they must be hiding over there. That means I should —*

Pa-THUNK. I dropped to the ground with a thud.

"Boom! Headshot!" I heard one of them cackle.

What did I expect? They were pros.

Our blended group of Katimavikers left the paintball arena still brimming with adrenaline and bits of sand wedged between every bodily crevice. We were the last group of people to play that night, but that unfortunately meant the overalls we rented were already covered in sweaty, broken paintballs, and dirty sand from everyone who had worn them earlier in the day. But we didn't care. We were just excited to shoot shit. I was also excited because Ashley was there.

It was Blind River's 48 hours off. Three members of their group decided to bus to Sault Ste. Marie to spend their free time. They liked the quiet ambience of their smaller community, but ours had more restaurants to dine at, activities to do, and of course similar-minded people to do those things with. Like protocol demanded for every other time we had guests, our group had to vote to see if everyone was comfortable with hosting Ashley, Natalie, and Xander. I would have been choked if my group declined. Fortunately, no one said no.

The trio from Blind River arrived later in the evening, which was convenient for us. Our group was out of the house attending yet another mandatory workshop, this one on teamwork. Linda planned for it to take place at a small park. I tried to be present as she briefed us on the goals of the workshop, but I couldn't focus knowing Ashley would be arriving later that day. Focusing didn't seem to be helping us much that afternoon anyway.

"The goal is simple," Linda explained for our first activity. "Working together, everyone will lift this broomstick handle off the ground using only your index fingers." We thought the task was simple enough.

It wasn't.

One of the rules was we couldn't curve or hook our fingers. They had to be stiff and pointed straight. The difficulty was compounded by the second rule, which was that everyone had to be touching the broomstick at all times. We assumed it would still be relatively easy. All we had to do was slide our fingers underneath the wooden dowel and lift it upwards gripped in V-shaped nooks, but even this proved much harder than it sounded. Some of us would lift too fast, others not fast enough, which meant the broomstick would quickly rise on one end while the other sank. The correction was easy to see, but with everyone yelling over each other the high end would soon sink and the lower end would suddenly jump up with some fingers still not touching it. We hadn't even raised the stick two feet off the ground yet before we started getting louder and more irate.

"That end is going up too fast!"

"You guys need to lift faster!"

"I'm not even touching it!"

"Then who's lifting, huh?"

"If we don't lift, it falls!"

"Aye aye aye aye aye!"

It was incredibly cumbersome and frustrating. We had been given a ridiculously simple task: lift a fucking stick. Yet ten young adults couldn't manage to get it higher than four feet.

"How about we move onto the next part?" Linda suggested.

Our second exercise involved crossing an imaginary lava pit with nothing more than a metal bucket that was immune. This was something where I expected to excel. I played similar games during my high school drama class. Creativity was highly encouraged for developing solutions in this game. One of the rules was that if someone slipped and touched the ground, we had two options: let them "die" and continue until the rest of us made it across, or start over and include everyone in our success. Ten minutes into the game, Erica was hopping awkwardly in the bucket across a packed section of snow when she slipped and fell to her pretend doom.

"Don't start over, just keep going," she insisted. "I don't really care if I survive anyway."

We fulfilled Erica's dying wish, but it wasn't long before Jess also fell into the imaginary lava in a frustrated huff. We debated whether it was worth starting over to have extra bodies to work with.

"Ugh, don't bother. I willingly sacrifice myself." She threw her hands up dismissively. By that point, we had finally developed a system of traversing people across the make-believe lava that seemed to work, provided no one else slipped. We finished with mixed enthusiasm. The moral of the activity was explained by Linda.

"Sometimes when you become so focused on the goal, it's easy to cast people aside."

There was unanimous agreement that the activity would have certainly been longer and more difficult if the goal wasn't as black and white as making it to the other side. Having such a simple goal, we didn't have to put a lot of thought into the consequences of sacrifices made in order to achieve it. Erica, who had admitted before she tended to be a pessimist, doubled down that she didn't mind that we carried on without her. Jess, however, felt shunned, disappointed that we hadn't debated as long as we had with Erica to keep her in the game.

"We were getting tired though, Jess, and we only haff so much time," Bethany pleaded.

Contextualizing the exercise was going to get us nowhere. We had passed the point where justifying our actions made anyone else feel better. Trying to rationalize every single decision each of us made was starting to tear us apart.

I could never tell if that was the point of some of those exercises. I read somewhere that when you join the military, the goal of boot camp training wasn't to merely endure the long marches or make it to the end the challenging obstacle courses, but to intentionally tear down new recruits. Intense hazing and drills beat the individualism out of recruits so drill sergeants could build them and their fellow soldiers back up together as a team, a unit. I had also read how an earlier version of Katimavik had military elements incorporated into it, intended to focus participants on geographical orientation and basic military skills. While the volunteer program might have moved away from its roughneck roots, those requirements for teamwork remained. Whatever the primary goal of that particular workshop was could be left to another day to ponder. Whatever the takeaways were, I was certain they would sink in over time, with the gears slowly moving in the back of our heads in our own ways.

In the short but intense workshop, I had briefly forgotten about Ashley and the other Blind River participants. They arrived at our house shortly after we returned. Once we got our guests settled in, Xander suggested we check out paintball after having learned there was an indoor arena in Sault Ste. Marie. His idea was exactly what our group needed to let off steam after our workshop. It seemed to have helped, but after removing our sandy, paint covered protective wear, my stress over Ashley quickly returned as we started walking back home.

New Year's had left me depressed. While the event itself had gone off well, nothing had come from it for me and Ashley. I was wishing for something to happen between the two of us, but nothing seemed to have budged. I hoped being out of the house would have helped me find a moment for just the two of us, but that didn't seem to be the case. On the walk down to paintball, Ashley talked to Daniel the entire time. I felt pangs of jealousy as I walked behind them. I tried to remind myself those feelings were petty and stupid, as I knew Daniel had no interest in Ashley. She was probably just caught up in the conversation. Daniel was an entertaining guy after all. Still, I couldn't completely suppress my frustrations. By the time we arrived at paintball, I was itching to shoot something. The walk back home was unfortunately no better. Ashley seemed to engage with everyone but me, painting what I could not avoid thinking was a pattern. But why? Wouldn't this have been an ideal time for us to walk together and talk at least? It wasn't as though we got a lot of those chances. I couldn't understand why Ashley didn't exhibit the same eagerness to talk to me now as she had over the phone many times before. Did I do something wrong? Was I overreacting? Underreacting? Was it foolish of me to invest this kind of energy into what was potentially a dead end? I couldn't understand it.

Despite the faint spark of optimism that still flickered and gave me hope that I might still squeak into an opportunity to connect with Ashley that night, it didn't seem meant to be. By the time we made it back to the house, everyone was exhausted. Ashley, Natalie, and Xander were quick to wish our group a good night, retiring to the basement where they had set up their sleeping bags. I ultimately decided to cut my losses. I didn't want to encroach on the little privacy they had and so let them be, but I was wracked by mental fatigue.

Maybe I *was* putting too much pressure on things. Maybe Ashley was just really shy. Maybe Luke was right, and I wasn't trying hard enough. But why was I the one having to deal with all the torture? When the small bunch of Blind River Katimavikers arrived at our house, I'd bounced everywhere in between waves of excitement, anxiety, and nervousness. Ashley, however, didn't seem to share any of the feelings I thought we had between us. Even her hug lacked her usual Ashley-esque bubbliness when she rose from the couch in our living room to greet me. She had apologized, claiming the bus ride into town had left her sleepy. It made me thankful she had enough energy to go out for paintball that night, but I started to question whether that was the real issue.

It seemed whatever we did during the remainder of Blind River's visit, Ashley intentionally distanced herself. It was like she had dropped any pretense of liking me: sitting next to others while bowling, playing chess back at the house when we all wound down, reading a book even when she was alone. Had I misread everything that had happened between us or was it all in my head? I didn't want to pry her away from her group like a needy child demanding attention. I also didn't want to make a move if she wasn't going to be receptive. I didn't even know what making a move meant! Wasn't that what I had been doing? Wasn't putting ourselves in situations of privacy or semi-privacy a key first step in order to build some sort of momentum? A build up? A spark?

The intense marathon of overanalyzing that night left me emotionally drained and restless in bed. As I grumpily urged myself to fall asleep, I begrudgingly tried to accept that nothing was going to take place between me and Ashley.

Before they boarded their bus back to Blind River, Ashley, Natalie, and Xander wanted to go out for dinner downtown. They had grown tired of the limited restaurant options they had to dine out in their host community, which consisted mostly of Chinese/Canadian joints. They invited us to join them, but most of our group was tired from the busy weekend and politely declined. Only Luke and I took them up on this offer.

I was glad he came. Luke had been supportive of me doing whatever it was that needed to be done to connect with Ashley. His advice was also much more helpful than Daniel's, which more or less consisted of inserting body part A into orifice B. With fewer members of my own group present, I statistically had a greater chance of finally getting Ashley alone. And then… well, I would have to figure that part out. A few scenarios ran through my mind, but I knew how well those had worked in the past.

At the semi-authentic Mexican restaurant, I barely paid attention to the conversations that took place over the course of dinner. Once the bills were paid, it was time for our friends to return to Blind River and a steady routine of volunteer life.

The five of us walked to the bus station, not far from the mall. Despite previous circumstances, Ashley and I somehow managed to be alone, walking together far behind everyone in front of us. I swear I caught Luke looking back at the two of us, opting to believe that he had performed some quality wing-man duty keeping Xander and Natalie occupied. Even with the rare, coveted private moment between me and Ashley finally taking place, it *still* seemed like nothing had changed. Our conversation was strained and slow to pick up to levels I had grown accustomed to and looked forward to. If there couldn't be anything new between us, then maybe I could hold onto what we had at least. She was still the sweet and innocent prairie girl I'd catch looking down at her feet anytime she said the slightest embarrassing thing about herself. Eventually, she began to laugh and smile in the same way she always did. It was uncanny how seeing and hearing her like that made me forget everything that had happened in the past two days, or had *not* happened. I just wanted to keep on walking with her, past the bus stop, away from the members of our group, away from house managers and PLs, away from Katimavik and its rules.

But of course, we couldn't do that. The Greyhound bus arrived at the station shortly after we walked through the gate, our timing impeccable. Natalie and Xander were tired from the walk and immediately boarded the bus. Even though it wasn't leaving for another half hour, they wanted to sit. Even Luke had disappeared onto the bus with them, still eager to chat until the last minute. Or perhaps giving me that opportunity I pined for.

Ashley and I stood there, two silhouettes hidden away in the cement tunnel while snow drifted outside in the light of the nearby lamp post. The bus station was surprisingly empty of any other transit-goers. After two very long days, Ashley and I were finally alone. No one was within eyesight or earshot. And in that moment, there seemed to be nothing but silence, etched away by the soft patter of snowflakes falling from the night sky above.

Say something, you fool. She's probably just as nervous as you are. Now, now! You won't get another chance.

The seconds ticked away, each one urging me on.

This is it. You wanted the opportunity, this is it! It's now or never.

I turned to Ashley.

Just do it. Kiss her!

I could see her face buried underneath the fur-lined hood of her winter jacket. She looked up, allowing the lamp posts to light up her face. I had barely uttered her name when I heard shouts erupt from behind us.

It was the rest of the Sault Ste. Marie group, my group.

No! Guys, no! NO!

They all jogged over, yelling excitedly. Xander, Natalie, and Luke stepped off the bus, rushing to hug the unexpected farewell crew. After declining to have dinner with us, the rest of the Sault Ste. Marie group had decided they still wanted to properly say goodbye and see Blind River off. Their timing, while perfect for them, couldn't have been any worse for me. Despite the sudden injection of people into the bus compound, no one seemed to pay me or Ashley any attention. We managed to look at each other for what seemed like the first time again. But Ashley had caught the silly energy emanating from the laughing crowd next to us, tossing aside any hint of intimacy.

"Hug!" she said, turning back to me. It sounded more like a request. We embraced stiffly.

The moment was gone. Again.

Ashley broke away, and for a brief second we found ourselves looking at each other again. Her blue eyes sparkled against the light of the street lamp in a way they hadn't before.

Wait ...

"Ah! Oh no, the bus!" she turned her head. "I think it's leaving. I have to go! Bye Devon! I had so much fun this weekend!" Ashley grabbed her bag, now covered in a light dusting of snow, and skipped away to board the bus. She didn't look back.

It was like someone dropped my internal organs right on top of my heart. I couldn't believe it. Did Ashley really think the bus would leave, with her standing just feet away from it? Even someone as dumb as me recognized there had been a second chance there and I wasn't going to get it back.

I didn't bother glance back to see if Ashley was looking out the bus window. I slunk away and joined the rest of my group who was waiting for me inside of the bus depot.

Everyone chatted vibrantly in the Katimavik van as Linda drove us all back home. I just looked out the window silently.

"Hey, you okay Dev?" Rosalie asked. I barely heard her.

"Yeah, I'm just… tired." I really was tired, but it was definitely more than that and Rosalie knew it.

The sting from that night failed to subside. I remained quiet and sullen for the next few days, playing the bus station scene over and over in my head. Each time I heard Ashley's cute little gasp or saw her walk towards the bus, I became more frustrated, disheartened, and even bitter. What if it wasn't my fault that nothing seemed to be developing? Maybe she wasn't trying hard enough. She knew we had an opportunity at the bus depot, didn't she? I gradually began to resent the whole situation and resolved myself not to speak to Ashley, at least not for a few days. I needed to let muddy waters settle. I simply didn't want to think about it anymore than I already had, hoping the whole ordeal would fade away.

Our Katimavik winter holidays came to an end and we all resumed our regular schedules. As dissatisfying as it had become, work at the Bush Plane Museum helped distract me. Most of the staff were away in Detroit for a plane exhibition. Daniel and I had helped the week before they left in disassembling a de Havilland Otter bush plane. This mostly involved ratcheting bolts along the wings and, with the help of other bush plane volunteers and aficionados, carefully loading them into the back of a long cargo truck. They were lighter than I expected for being part of a functioning and technically airworthy plane, but still heavy to lift. I didn't believe it when we were first told we were going to put a plane into the back of a truck, but I was proven wrong. With most staff out of town showcasing the plane and one of the more exciting things we had done now completed, Daniel and I were tasked with a new and exciting job: window washing!

The upper half of the entire southern wall of the hangar consisted of two rows of glass panels. Each rectangular panel contained a 7x4 pattern of square panes of glass, stretching all the way from the corner of the work bench area to the staff room. This accounted for a lot of windows to wash, or according to Daniel, "a metric shit ton."

"I want you two to wash them," asked Eli, one of the exhibit curators. "I'm not going to lie, it's going to probably take you a few days."

We believed him. Every pane was filthy, with the dirtiest ones near the top. We assumed this was because they were hard to reach and had accumulated more grime. Eli supplied us with buckets of hot soapy water, a pile of assorted rags, and a large clunky rolling safety ladder to reach the upper windows. Surprisingly, sunlight still managed to shine through even the grossest ones, but there was no doubt they were dirty. It took no time at all before our buckets became a dark soup of greasy grey gunk. Daniel and I hoped that the bucket of shit water meant we were making progress on a necessary task and that the windows would be sparkling clean by the time we were done.

They were not.

After spending the entire morning on just the first few panels, Daniel and I stepped back to view the progress of our work.

"Wait, we cleaned those ones, didn't we?" I asked, pointing to the left where we started. We tried to use as much elbow grease as possible without breaking the fragile windows. We had even experimented between using more soap and letting the dirtier windows soak in foaming bubbles. Whatever our effort, it didn't matter. The results were noticeably negligible. Despite how many times we had replaced our buckets of water, the remaining dirty windows to our right looked more or less the same as the clean ones on the left. We couldn't fathom how that was possible. Eli and one of the chairs of the museum board, Marv, came to inspect our work. They agreed.

"And you guys are sure those windows are clean? There's not much of a difference," said Marv.

"They are. We spent all morning on them." I was worried they wouldn't believe us, find us incompetent, or would ask us to clean them again. I didn't know what was worse.

Marv looked at the mobile stairs we had been using.

"Are you two using harnesses when you're up there?"

"Harnesses?" It was the first time anyone had mentioned them. I thought it was just a ladder. Even though Daniel and I were perfectly comfortable with the heights we were at and didn't need to put ourselves into any sort of dangerous or precarious positions, Marv started to voice concerns over safety and liability. These worries became moot that afternoon when the sun came out. We looked up at the windows and could see the sunlight shone through the remaining dirty windowpanes just as well as the ones we insisted we had cleaned. It baffled us all. With the futility of our work now confirmed, Marv relieved Daniel and I of window washing duty and instructed us to assemble some large metal shelves in a back room instead.

"Take your time and do a *real good job*," Marv told us. Daniel and I deciphered his emphasis as code for, "Stay in there so we aren't bothered to keep you two busy again." Even though we took our sweet time—which was easy working with Daniel—we eventually finished assembling the shelf, flawlessly put together and with every bolt tightened. The two of us were silent in our unanimous agreement that the remainder of the day would be a much lazier one. Seeking to stay out of the limelight lest we be rewarded with more work, I decided to spend my break in the object theatre.

The object theatre was a dark room decorated with the front half a bush plane set up among a forest and lake backdrop. Across from the set were benches for visitors to sit on while they watched a short film about a pilot named Ron and his Jack Russell Terrier co-pilot, Charlie. Together the pair described the magic of flying and the history of using bush planes to travel, transport goods, and even fight fires, all while flying their own vintage Beaver model bush plane. As they explained the different kinds of cargo that could be flown in a bush plane, the same props were lit up on a fake dock via spotlight. Rather than simply playing a video on screen, however, the film was projected onto the door of the plane, giving the illusion of a pilot leaning out of the window of the cockpit and telling the story in person to the audience. It even depicted what it was like flying through a thunderstorm. The setup was very clever.

It was one of the more intriguing and unique exhibits in the museum. Prior to hitting the start button for the show, the warm, dark theatre had the ambient noise of nature playing on the speakers on a loop. The sound of crickets, frogs, and other small forest creatures gave the impression of sitting on the shore of an isolated lake tucked away in the Canadian wilderness. It made for a great spot to take my break and even sneak in a nap or two on other occasions. I was surprised I got away with it for as long as I did before Marv caught me one day while he was giving some corporate big-wigs a tour. Even though he had a good laugh at how relaxing the room was, I stopped napping in there after that. Daniel and I seemed to be bumping heads with Marv more and more often while Demmy was in Detroit. I started to think napping wasn't the best idea anyway. That's when I always found myself thinking about Ashley.

The house phone rang. "Does anyone want to talk to the Blind River group?" Erica yelled from downstairs. I bit my tongue and hesitated for a moment before I grabbed the phone from her. I'd wondered what their group had been up to recently, but I didn't feel up to speaking to Ashley. We had continued communicating through online messages and email, but our conversations had become staggered. They felt clunky and mechanical, and noticeably lacking in something we had before. It was like her personality had been removed from her emails. And in between our digital conversations, neither of us brought up the moment I thought we had at the bus station.

Thankfully it wasn't Ashley who answered the phone. It was Natalie.

"Oh, hey Nat," I said. "How's the gang?"

The Winnipeg girl and I made small chat, informing each other who was house manager that week, what activities were coming up for our groups, and what general anxieties were on our mind before we moved to our next communities. There was growing talk around "Rotation Camp," several days of out-of-town workshops intended to help ease Katimavikers transition over to their next community. I didn't feel like giving it much thought though. Despite my best efforts, I always ended up thinking of Ashley. And even though Natalie and I had skirted around her name as we talked, I secretly hoped she would bring Ashley up. Whether it was a courtesy or merely a coincidence, Natalie didn't. Finally, in an unexpected moment of controlled panic, I broke down.

"Nat… do you know what happened at the bus station the other week? With Ashley, I mean?" I asked her calmly. Girls talk. They always talk. Hopefully Natalie knew something. And to my surprise, she did.

"We were watching you two from the windows actually," she said. Natalie knew exactly what I was referring to and wasted no time in informing me what apparently had gone down that night. "You probably know by now that Ashley is a shy girl. She *wanted* something to happen, Devon! Ashley's never done any of this before. This is new to her. But she felt terrible that night and told me all about it on the bus ride."

There it was. Confirmation—I was right! There *was* something there. I wasn't crazy. I should have trusted my instinct and done something!

"But it seemed like you were mad at her. She didn't really know what to think."

"Well, I was," I stuttered. "Kind of. Not when you guys showed up. It's just that … I didn't know ..." I tried to explain how I wasn't mad, more confused. This news shattered my world like a rock thrown through a dirty hangar window. As quickly as I had been elevated upon hearing Ashley did in fact have feelings for me, I fell back down into a frustrating pool of self-loathing.

I had fucked up. I'd really fucked up. I couldn't think of how to process the glitter bomb of feelings and emotions that went off in my brain. Somehow banging my head against the wall seemed like a good idea.

How could I have been so stupid? I was mad and frustrated at Ashley for her mixed signals, but it turned out I was the one giving them, and for nothing. Being mad at someone was pointless if they didn't know you were mad at them. She probably felt just as confused as I did. Shit!

Natalie interrupted, still on the phone. "Hellooooo?"

"Nat, can you put Ashley on the phone?" Fuck everything that had happened before. Fuck my anger, fuck Ashley's shyness. There was no better time for a Hail Mary play. I was tired of letting those opportunities slip by. Not anymore.

A familiar voice picked up. "Hello?"

"Ashley, I'm going to just put all the cards on the table here…" And I told her everything. How I felt about her, how I had been confused and frustrated at her on account of my hesitation, but also her mixed messages. And finally, what happened at the bus depot.

"I wanted to kiss you, Ashley. But… well, you practically ran away!"

"Oh geez! I'm so sorry Devon. I thought the bus was leaving!" she explained with a hint of disgusted shame. Ashley really *did* think the bus was going to leave. She even thought she heard the bus driver start the engine. "I'm so so so so so sorry, I didn't want you to think that I … you know ... I actually wanted to kiss you too." Both ends of the phone line went quiet.

Ashley and I felt horrible that the weekend had not gone the way we wanted it to. Romantically, anyway. She continued to describe how jealous the rest of the Blind River group was after hearing everything she, Natalie, and Xander had done during their two-day visit. As much as they enjoyed themselves, Ashley regretted that she missed the opportunity to have made it more memorable. While it was a huge weight off my shoulders to finally know where Ashley and I were at, I still felt like an ass for how I had treated her in the past few days. Isn't that what they say about 'assuming?' There were always two sides to a story and I had been so caught up in mine. Even though I was by no means an expert, I did have more experience with relationships than Ashley. I wasn't good at this, but this was *completely* new to her. Maybe I needed to take the reins, to take Ashley's hand and help her through this. I didn't know exactly how or what to do, but next time I wouldn't hesitate to show my affection. I vowed that in future circumstances, I would confirm how the other person felt and avoid the traumatic hell I had put myself through for the past week. Honesty wasn't easy, it was better in the long run, awkwardness be damned.

When I finally hung up the phone, Luke and Rosalie found me dancing in the kitchen afterwards. I ignored their jeers and mockery. I didn't care.

I liked a girl, and she liked me.

CHAPTER 16

January 2006. Sault Ste. Marie.

Before Katimavik, I had never even heard of the term "billet." It wasn't long after the holidays that we were discussing this integral part of the program every day.

Billet families were people who were willing to take a Katimavik participant into their home for two weeks. They didn't have to necessarily be a nuclear family with a spare bed like I initially presumed. Sometimes they were single adults who wanted a young person to hang out with, and other times they were elderly couples who'd grown bored of their empty nest and wished to fill it once more, even temporarily. Regardless of which billet family we were assigned, all of them were vetted by Linda beforehand. She had to ensure billets had a stable living arrangement and weren't just going to use us for free labour, a situation we heard *had* happened in the past. While it was normal for participants to be expected to help around their new "home," the billeting period was intended to offer participants a unique experience from the perspective of a community family. If that family played their cards right, they could potentially score a free babysitter so long as they fed said babysitter and occasionally brought them along on family trips. Everyone heard stories of participants who were utterly spoiled by the families they stayed with, but obviously this wasn't a typical experience. You wouldn't really know what would happen during billeting until you were sent off with your family.

The group had the expected anxieties for the upcoming change, but the excitement was bolstered by our trust in Linda. Even prior to our arrival in Sault Ste. Marie, she had begun putting out feelers out for potential billets. She insisted that participants didn't have to do much with the process of recruiting billets aside from acting as stellar volunteers. It didn't stop us from telling our coworkers or anyone else interested in Katimavik, directing them to contact Linda if they wanted to know more about billeting us. We felt like foster children trying to look cute and convince strangers that it would be worth it to adopt us for a short while. The combination of Linda's networking efforts and our public charm must have worked. Once she had enough potential billets, she coordinated a night for us all to meet. Our house was jam-packed with an assortment of Sault Ste. Marie residents.

It was Linda's idea to host the night as an open house style event for the billet families. The selection process was similar to how we did our workplace interviews. With billets stationed at different parts of the house, each participant would rotate between them and tell the other about themselves. This was much easier in the large United Way office space, but even as cramped and loud as our tiny duplex became, we made it work. Participants told billets where we were from, where we worked, what our hobbies were, etc., while they told us what their lifestyles were like, where we'd be sleeping, and otherwise what we could expect from living with them for two weeks. These informal conversations helped gauge if we would be compatible with our billets and avoid potential friction. Some of the older married couples preferred someone who was quiet and would occasionally help out around the house, whereas the young adults in their late twenties and early thirties proudly described their active social lives and how they'd like to include us in them. Most of us resonated with these families, excited by their promises to take us skiing or snowboarding and bring us to dinner parties and family gatherings, showing us off like a shiny new toy. Some of the billets in the room had hosted Katimavikers before and were familiar with the expectations, but the others were new to the concept and were understandably unsure of what they were getting into.

Linda assured us there was nothing wrong with having our own billet wish list. Some of us, like Erica and Victor, wanted a quieter billet family, potentially one that lived outside the city and didn't do much aside from read and relax. Carlos and Rosalie wanted an outgoing billet family who would take them on trips and maybe share an illegal beer or two with their underage billets although this was obviously not condoned by Katimavik. I wanted something akin to the latter, a billet family who would show me a side of the city we hadn't had the chance to explore yet on our own. There was still so much I wanted to do and see in Sault Ste. Marie and there seemed to be a few candidates who could help me with that. Regardless of what people wanted, everyone agreed Linda had secured an excellent mix of billets.

At the end of the night, Linda spoke up loud enough for everyone in the crowded house to hear. "I want to thank everyone for coming. From what I saw, the *interviews* went really well. I'll do my best to match the participants up and I'll be in touch soon to finalize everything. Drive safe!"

Before the billet candidates left, Linda handed them a form to take home and fill out. She then gave us the same form, instructing us to write down our preferences for which billet we wanted to stay with.

"I'll collect them once you're all done," Linda told us as we thought about the people we'd just met and what living with them might be like. "And once I get those same forms back from the billets, I'll make a decision on where everyone will be placed."

It would be another week before we found out who we were to billet with.

In the meantime, our volunteer lives continued, occasionally broken up by committee activities and workshops. With the biggest, more strenuous workshops out of the way, the ones we started doing were more diverse and simply more enjoyable as we learned new knowledge or practised a new skill. I don't know how we managed to incorporate a massage workshop in our calendar, but I was sure we were able to justify it loosely somewhere under the category of healthy lifestyles. It was no surprise that everyone looked forward to it more than any other workshop.

From the comfort of our kitchen table, our facilitator showed us which points of the body were prone to stress and then how to massage and relieve it. As a final exam to the brief lessons we were taught, the group formed a circle and massaged the shoulders of the person in front of them. Valérie was particularly enjoying the work of my hands.

"Mmmm, Meester Fleen," she said, her Québécoise accent seeping through her moans of satisfaction, "You do such a good job back d'ere."

Valérie, or Val as her friends called her, was no stranger to being touched. She had unusually soft and smooth skin, despite claiming to use no skin products. Several investigative pokes from the rest of us confirmed she was indeed a squishy individual. She did request that we avoid pinching her soft skin as she bruised easily.

Appearance was important to Valérie. She often talked about her dream of becoming an actress, to be in film, or possibly a performer on stage. Though my experience in acting was limited to a few years of high school drama class and volunteering with a local theatre group back home, a fondness for acting was something Valérie and I shared in common. Long after others in the group lost interest in the topic, she and I would talk about the past roles we played, funny moments that happened on stage, or what we thought of famous actors. Valérie was intrigued when I brought up my experience with historical acting. She wasn't sure whether she would like dressing up in musty pioneer clothing for summer tourists, preferring dramatic scenes in front of a camera instead.

Valérie might have dreamed of becoming a famous actress, but I couldn't see myself ever achieving Hollywood celebrity status. I hated the idea of being watched like a hawk by paparazzi, having to stay ever vigilant and careful in what I did or said lest something be taken out of context and used against me. On the contrary, Valérie loved the idea and thought she might be able to help people by publicly inspiring them to achieve their own dream. Even though we shared the same passion, we enjoyed it in very different ways.

"I'm just saying, the next ones can only get bigger and better."

We were talking about my birthday that had recently passed. I had long since expressed my compliments to the surprises, gifts and company present for the celebration, perhaps too much. Some of the group suggested it had set the bar for how future birthdays should be celebrated. This left some people disappointed upon realizing that their birthday was outside of the nine-month program and would unfortunately go uncelebrated. This included Luke, who jested that we celebrate his conception day instead, rather than his "escape from his mother's vagina." We came to the consensus that even though the slush fund was initially intended for birthdays, we should find ways of celebrating individuals with their own celebrations.

Bethany was jealous of the idea of celebrating Luke's non-birthday and wanted in on the fun.

"Aww come on guys! Why Luke get a birt'day?" she said sadly before suddenly perking up. "Hey, I have h'idea! Why don't we celebrate 'Bethany Day'!" she suggested with a childish grin.

No one denied her this. We agreed we would celebrate yet another unique Katima-holiday in the future. We didn't set a specific date for Bethany Day, but Luke decided to surprise her the very next day.

"It's perfect!" he explained. "Beth won't expect it to take place so soon after she suggested it!"

The timing wasn't just to maintain the element of surprise. Luke wanted to do it before we left for billeting, convinced we would likely forget about the idea and lose enthusiasm for it over the two weeks we'd be living elsewhere. Everyone agreed. With our support, Luke went out and bought a pile of foam swords from the nearest dollar store while Carlos went for a walk with Bethany so we could set up the surprise. When the two returned, she was bombarded with cheers and given a celebratory plastic ninja vest before we promptly attacked her with the rubbery weapons. This turned into an all-out brawl around the house that left everyone sweaty and giggling. Bethany Day was satisfactorily concluded with puffed wheat snacks I baked on a whim.

Seeing how well Bethany Day was received, Jess politely requested for some attention to be focused on her. She had previously mentioned how she wanted to share a pagan full-moon ritual with us. It just so happened that there was a full moon the same night after we finished a djembe drum workshop and had nothing planned afterwards. No one seemed particularly eager to go, but we felt Jess deserved the chance to educate us on her religion that none of us really understood, no matter how many times she tried to describe it. If we could celebrate a pretend day just because a wee French girl demanded it, surely we could accommodate Jess in something a little closer to her heart. She had attended other pagan events in town on her own time and would often invite us, with no success in gaining our presence. But our curiosity and Katimaviky open-mindedness had caught up with us and compelled us to see what the whole Wiccan thing was about.

"Who knows, maybe we'll accidentally summon a demon or something," Luke whispered.

In the middle of the same small park we held our teamwork workshop in, isolated and darkened by a surrounding crop of trees, Jess laid out different items on a blanket: candles, a cup of juice for us to drink from, and a plate of diced apples to eat. She said a prayer aloud to the gods of the North, South, West, and East.

"Now, we spin and welcome the moonlight into our bodies!" she declared with a smile. We hesitantly did as we were told. I opened my arms, raised them high to the bright moon in the sky and ...

Nothing.

No raspy voices from an ethereal realm. No heavenly light show. Not even a faint howl of the wind. It was just as I expected. Granted, I was skeptical well before my lackluster and vague introduction to Wicca.

I didn't really get religion. I never did. The concept seemed to me like it was similar to hypnosis in that you had to already be susceptible and suggestive to it to really believe it. To be fair, I hadn't been exposed to many religions aside from Christianity at a young age. Most of my religious experience consisted of social gatherings motivated by games and food.

At first, it was an evening group called "Kid's Club." It was hosted by some members of the church near my house that welcomed young kids in the neighbourhood. After an hour of playing ball and tag games, there was a light Bible reading where correct answers to questions were rewarded with candy. Once I hit high school, this weekly activity was upgraded to a more mature version in the form of a youth group. The games were a little more complex and held outdoors, candy was traded in for snacks, dinners and potlucks, and there were budding female teenagers attending whose company and attention I desired. Even with those things at hand, the religious aspects of the group still managed to land on occasion.

One teenager a few years older than me gave a talk one day, sharing how he decided to become a Christian. He had been going through the typical trials of being a teenager—hating his parents, difficulties at school, and of course, endless questions about life. One day, someone introduced him to Christianity and the teachings of Jesus. He'd become intrigued. The more he learned, the more the particular religion seemed to answer the questions he had about life. I was happy to hear how he came to have a profound religious experience and found comfort and guidance in it. I had asked myself many of the same questions he did, in addition to different ones. After deep reflection, I considered whether Christianity answered those questions for me, or at least most of them. The resounding answer that came to my mind was simply: no. I could get behind the wholesome ideals and virtues the commandments represented, but I didn't like the idea of having to devote yourself to an imaginary being in order to live by those same virtues. They always seemed to boil down to the golden rule: be a good person. Even that seemed overly simplistic. There were too many factors to consider. Was it as simple as following a good deed checklist? Or did you have to embrace an authentic and unshakeable feeling that you were on a righteous path, even if others disagreed?

Religion hadn't answered those questions for me and neither had Jess' attempt at introducing Paganism. The same questions still haunted me. Maybe I wasn't asking the right ones. But then again, maybe I hadn't found the right religion.

"Now I want everyone to go around and say a small prayer. This can be something you want the strength to endure or to let go," our facilitator said. He was an Ojibway man who spoke with an understanding, yet powerful calm. "You don't have to share if you don't want. This is a safe, supportive space."

We hadn't learned much about local First Nations culture, even though Ontario was home to numerous bands. Our latest workshop had Linda drive us to Garden River, an hour and a half outside of the city. The town's wellness centre boasted the Dan Pine Healing Lodge, a spacious octagonal building. Inside, long benches sat between thick wooden columns that held up a tall roof. In the centre of it was a large hole that let smoke out and light in from the winter sky, illuminating the dark space inside. The building wasn't quite enclosed nor was it completely exposed to the elements. On the centre of the gravel-covered ground was a smouldering fire pit that our facilitator stoked into a healthy flame, warming those that sat around it. He gave us a brief introduction to his people, traditions, and their land.

"This facility has provided programming for First Nations, especially Ojibway, that have faced rampant alcoholism and drug abuse," he explained. "But everyone needs help, not just those groups. Sometimes people just need help letting go or to cleanse themselves." Using a cindering stick pulled from the fire, he created a smudge from a small pile of leaves resting atop an abalone shell which everyone passed to the person beside them. We each waved the smoke curling upward from the shell towards our bodies to bathe ourselves in the cleansing curls while our facilitator chanted a quiet prayer.

I was always nervous around any sort of prayer or confessional. My problems never seemed as important as others, especially those of First Nations. I was a young, healthy, white male who had never experienced abuse or neglect, alcoholism or drugs, or a systematic destruction of my own culture. I could appreciate their efforts to do so as individuals and together as a community, but my struggles were nowhere near the hardships these and many other First Nations had endured and were trying to recover from.

I quietly passed the smudge along when it came to me. Rather than speaking my own thoughts I focused on respectfully listening to everyone else share something personal about themselves. Valérie teared up when she admitted how worried she was for her mother whom she hoped would quit smoking. I could relate, given how recent my own mom's heart attack had been. I noticed family was a common theme. Everyone voiced some desire to protect or pray for those they loved. But these prayers, these confessions of hope, were just words to me, a delay, a distraction on the way towards changing or improving one's life or even letting go. Recognizing one's pain might have been part of the process, but I didn't want to waste time praying to some invisible deity to help me or my friends or family. I wanted to know what the next step was, what it was I needed to do. Talking was one thing, but action was another.

"You guys are going to bake a cake," our facilitator instructed us.

Lou was a staff member of the United Way, one of Rosalie's coworkers. He was thrilled to provide us with some team building exercises in yet another workshop. I thought we were already done with team building, but Linda insisted another workshop would be helpful. I didn't blame her. The last exercise felt more like a team breaker than a team builder. Besides, this one seemed much more enjoyable given how there was cake involved.

Everyone murmured at how easy the task seemed. Rightfully cautious, a few of us remembered how that sort of thinking bit us in the ass last time. We waited in anticipation of what the catch was.

"The catch is, you have ten minutes to do it. The cake must be *in* the oven by the ten-minute mark," Lou elaborated. "Does everyone understand?" We all nodded. The intensity in the air tripled. "Go!"

People scrambled, yelling out tasks we knew needed to be done. Nothing had been planned beforehand.

"I'll get the eggs!"

"I know where the cake pan is!"

"Someone start the oven. It's got to warm up!"

Our kitchen was small though. Within minutes, most of us found ourselves getting in the way. Practically, only one person could blend the cake batter at a time, the role which Erica was already performing with gusto. I briefly believed I might be able to do the task marginally faster, but I let the fleeting thought go. Time was of the essence. As eager as we all were to help, there was nothing else left to do except pour the mixed batter into a cake pan.

"Hm. I guess this is kind of what they mean when they say too many cooks spoil the broth," I mused to Lou as the prepared cake pan was placed into the oven to bake. No matter how much we wanted to help, there were some situations where we were better off just staying out of the way. It seemed like a disappointing lesson to me. I was normally a firm believer of the more the merrier, that many hands made light work, but here was a stark example of how that was not the case. There were limitations; at a certain point, we had to be content with our contributions and take a seat, regardless of how eager we were to do more. We couldn't argue with the results though. For how quickly it had been prepared, we baked a pretty damn good cake.

It was once again my turn to take on the role of house manager, this time partnered with Bethany. The two of us both had new recipes we were itching to try.

It was after our healthy meals workshop that we realized how lacking our dishes had been in protein, a key component to a nutritional meal. Linda had suggested we incorporate textured vegetable protein—TVP—into more of our meals. Commonly found in the bulk section at the grocery store, the small rocky granules looked similar to bacon bits, which I found ironic. I was still unfamiliar with how to use the ingredient or how I might incorporate it into my latest kitchen concoction, a veggie casserole à la Devon, which could have benefited from some TVP. Despite its lack of flavour, it was still one of the better meals I had cooked that week. Bethany's tuna and rice casserole on the other hand already had more flavour than we anticipated, but also less… shape.

"It's more like tuna and rice *soup*," Rosalie said at the dinner table. Her bemused face showed a quizzical expression as she ladled herself a bowl.

Bethany went on the defensive. "Hey, at leest we tried someting new!"

She and I didn't worry about the comments that much. It had been a busy week of workshops and we were only house managers for one more day.

We were relieved when Linda offered to give us a reprieve on our first night and make supper. She claimed she found it relaxing. We joked that she hadn't mothered us for quite some time and was probably missing the role she took on when we first arrived. Luke kicked my foot from under the table, quietly reminding me to tread carefully lest Linda retract future offers to cook. Convincing house managers to let you take over a meal was never a hard sell though. They were always glad for any break they could get.

Bethany and I got along very well, much better than Jess and I did when we were house managers. Since the two of us had been house managers at least once now, we knew what to expect, even if our most recent meal was a flop. We spoke French to each other half of the time in an effort to improve both of our second languages while still maintaining a modicum of understanding. Bethany's language skills had vastly improved, whereas mine seemed to have peaked. I knew the basic verbs to get by, but I needed more vocabulary, a translation for everyday nouns and objects. Rudimentary high school French only took me so far. I hoped to improve more by the time we arrived in Quebec.

I was worried that there might be some tension with Bethany given everything that had previously happened—or at least, what had been said—but that didn't seem to be the case. I was still smitten with Ashley and thought about her constantly. Bethany joked sparingly about her, but I tried to avoid bringing her name up in conversation. I didn't know how Bethany felt about Ashley and me. For all I knew, she was jealous or upset that I had chosen Ashley and simply remained polite for the sake of working together. Wherever Bethany stood, I felt more comfortable when I avoided discussing Ashley. Bethany and I were in a good place. There was no need to shake that up.

Even though we had worked together relatively well as house managers, I was looking forward to wrapping it up and experiencing another integral part of Katimavik which was just around the corner—billeting.

CHAPTER 17

January 2006. Sault Ste. Marie.

Neither of us said anything on the drive home. It was one of those silent moments where the radio hits a quiet, hypnotic lull and you briefly forget the world for a moment. I stared at the passing lights along the road somewhere in the northeast of the city, faintly noting the growing silence in the vehicle. In the absence of conversation, I said the first thing that came to my mind.

"Really, really, ridiculously good-looking," I mumbled, quoting Ben Stiller's memorable line from the *Zoolander* movie. We had watched it earlier that night at a birthday party for one of Andrea's friends. The thing was, she happened to quote it at exactly the same time I did. We both looked at each other and burst out laughing at the incredible timing and coincidence.

My billet was awesome.

When the day came for everyone in the Katimavik house to leave for billeting, we all waited in the living room with our bags packed, eagerly waiting to be picked up by our new temporary families. I was no doubt the most excited, evident by the snow pants I was already wearing as instructed by my new billet. I tried to tone down my smile when Andrea pulled into the driveway so as not to make everyone jealous. When the two of us drove away, we didn't even drop off my personal bags at her house. Instead, she drove the two of us straight to Searchmont Ski Hill to go snowboarding. Though the smaller Ontario hill made me dearly miss the larger mountains I was accustomed to back home, it was refreshing to simply get into a vehicle and go. No drawn-out details, no excursion plans, just two people who wanted to do a fun winter activity and made it happen.

Andrea made it clear that what she wanted to do for the next two weeks was show me a good time. In turn, I made it equally as clear that I would be a willing participant to whatever she had in mind. It was likely why we were each other's top billet/billeter choice. From the second I hopped into her truck, we immediately hit it off, bonding over commentary of the Top 40 radio hits that played during the drive to Searchmont, our choice in gas station snacks that we grabbed on the way there, and the gnarly wipeouts on the hill we both shared. Andrea was living her best life and I was coming along for the ride.

She was a single woman in her late twenties and had a circle of friends who were as high energy and active as she was. They all dabbled in snowboarding, cross-country skiing, even underwater hockey at the YMCA pool. I only joined her in the latter once. I was a decent swimmer who was capable of aquatic frolicking, but not the thrashing and three-dimensional swimming necessary to move and control the weighted puck, all while holding your breath. After nearly drowning the first time I tried, I was content with being a spectator.

Andrea took me almost everywhere, including her friend's birthday party that night. She and her friends were fun and a joy to be around. Most of them didn't have children and were keen to take advantage of the consequent excess of time and disposable income that choice gave them. Those couples who did have children, however, seemed to really enjoy their night away from their kids. They were as happy playing board games during a party as they were watching the latest Ben Stiller comedy on DVD after demolishing a diabetes-inducing chocolate birthday cake. The biggest go-getters would work off their hangovers the next morning with a winter hike. Life was a fleeting bundle of opportunities they didn't want to squander. I was treated more as a younger peer in their midst rather than a ward who needed to be cared for. Most days, I forgot about the structure of Katimavik that I had grown accustomed to, a break from which I didn't mind.

Billeting had come at a good time. Our normal day-to-day routine felt stale. Even with our periodic excursions to break up the monotony, winter had kept our group cooped up in the house more often than we wanted. Everyone was getting antsy and seemed constantly on edge. We were only two months into the program, but there was a collective itching for some change. It seemed an opportune time for everyone to get away from each other for a little while. The need for some extra space might have also been prompted by a recent incident.

I had come back from the gym to find the Katimavik house stark empty. That was itself a rare phenomenon. Living with so many people, there was always someone present, tucked away somewhere. I went upstairs and was about to toss my gym bag onto my mattress except I couldn't—there was no mattress to toss it onto.

It was gone. All the mattresses, in fact, had disappeared from the guys' room, with just the empty black metal bunk bed frames standing there like skeletal furniture. I stood in the doorway silently, speechless at what I was seeing. Or not seeing. I approached the empty bed frames and carefully reached out my hands, but touched nothing but thin air, disproving my brief theory that the mattresses and bed sheets might have somehow turned invisible.

I heard the front door open.

"Saluuuuuuut?" It was Valérie. She had been at the gym with me earlier, but stayed behind to finish her workout.

"Val, come here!" I yelled at her from upstairs. "I need you to confirm if I'm crazy or not."

"C'est quoi de fuck?"

She had the same reaction I did. When she wondered if the same thing had happened to the girls' mattresses, we quickly bolted downstairs to investigate and discovered that the girls were victim of the same mystery: no mattresses. They weren't thrown outside or jammed into any of the closets. After a thorough search of the house, Valérie and I eventually found all the mattresses tucked away in a far corner of the basement hidden beneath a sheet. It shouldn't have taken us as long as it did to realize we should check the room with the most abundant space in the house in order to hide something, but the shock and ridiculousness of the prank stripped us of rational thinking. It wasn't long before everyone else returned to the house and we eventually learned what had happened.

The culprits had been Luke, Daniel, and Tiffany, who hid the mattresses as a practical joke. Linda's mattress was the only one that remained untouched. No one would dare mess with Linda's stuff for risking the wrath of our Katima-mom, even if we believed she would have found the humour in it. After all, it was just a little prank. I found it funny when all was said and done. Others did not. The next day, a house meeting was called.

"This is about respect and personal space," Carlos said. I tried to argue that it was a harmless prank, even though I had nothing to do with it. Everyone had their mattresses returned immediately, but that wasn't enough for Carlos. "Fine, let me move your things around and see if you like it!" I pointed out that my mattress had in fact been moved, but nothing could deter the angry Colombian. Some members of the group had clearly reacted more seriously than Luke, Daniel, and Tiffany anticipated.

I didn't want something so harmless to be a turning point for group relations. Thankfully, billeting took place shortly after. I hoped the two weeks living away would give everyone a chance to forget about trivial things and that by the time we all got back, bygones would be bygones.

As much as we needed a break from each other, everyone in the group kept in contact via email and online messages during billeting. We would update one another as to how our respective billet experiences were going, what we had done with our hosts, and what they were like. This was obviously easier for me and Daniel because we worked together. He and I would share what we heard, getting a more complete picture of how everyone was doing and what they had been up to. After the first few days of billeting, we confirmed that Bethany and Jess had unfortunately become sick the day we left for billeting, Valérie got drunk with her billets, and Erica did very little with her older billet family but was content to catch up on a lot of television and reading. We hadn't heard much from the rest of the group.

As much as I knew billeting was a good way for us to take a break from each other, I was beginning to miss my group. Even Carlos.

It wasn't as though we wouldn't or couldn't see members of our group for the next two weeks. We simply weren't living together. Even during billeting, we were required to uphold our wide range of volunteer commitments. We had previously committed several evenings to help at the Bon Soo Festival, an annual event in Sault Ste. Marie, which was facing its own challenges that year. One day the temperature was too warm, melting the "Fantasy Kingdom" snow castles; the next, there was a blizzard that cancelled the sleigh ride. Organizers were scrambling to ensure that different activities for the event continued as best they could, despite the conditions that seemed to change at the drop of a hat. All we could do was wait for instructions from the appropriate people in charge and help as best we could when possible.

For one evening, that meant donning a heavy mascot costume. Everyone thought I was best suited to be "Buckles," the anthropomorphic life-vest mascot for one of the Red Cross programs. Even Hoopie the Owl was present that evening, although it turned out to be someone other than Daniel that time. I got a taste of the joy that came with bringing massive smiles to children just by waving a cartoonish hand. It hardly felt like work at all.

In between the various volunteering gigs, whatever activity Andrea was inviting me to join her in, and the occasional visits to participants' respective billet homes, I made a point to carve some alone time for myself. I needed to catch up on some personal paperwork.

I was in the process of applying for another program called Canada World Youth. It was another volunteer program similar to Katimavik, but designed on a more international scale. Participants in CWY lived three months in a Canadian community and three months in another country. Some of the potential countries included Brazil, Africa, even China. Partnering with different organizations in both countries, participants focused on building knowledge and leadership skills to develop and assist with projects in the respective communities they would live in. From what I had read and heard from the information package I was sent, these projects were usually focused on sustainable community development.

The similarities between Katimavik and Canada World Youth were not coincidence either. Both volunteer programs were actually developed by the same person: Jacques Hébert.

The renowned Canadian senator was a close friend of Canadian Prime Minister Pierre Trudeau. The two had travelled together to China in the late '60's to learn more about our Asian neighbors and meet influential leaders at a time when the communist country was a very closed society. The two friends shared a passion for travel and the lessons that could be learned when abroad and observed how visiting other countries helped foster cultural understanding, curb xenophobic attitudes, and solidify geopolitical relationships both at home and abroad. Trudeau himself was a fan of hitchhiking, having hitchhiked around Europe and the Middle East as a young man before going on to become Prime Minister. He encouraged others to do the same, advising youth to drive and hitchhike across Canada and see their own amazing country. With their respective travel experiences having shaped their political views, Pierre Trudeau and Jacques Hébert would go on to shift the future of Canadians in their own unique ways. Trudeau became the 15th Prime Minister of Canada. With the political and moral support of his friend, Hébert founded Canada World Youth in 1971. He saw it not just as a way of connecting foreign countries through their youth, but as a way of developing their communities and promoting world peace. With the help of former Minister of National Defence, Honourable Barney Danson, Hébert would then go on to found Katimavik in 1977.

Canada World Youth was intended to expand the role of youth in developing their communities and offer international education while Katimavik encouraged cultural discovery and civic engagement within one's own country. They were two volunteer programs with admirable and praiseworthy goals. Oddly enough, they didn't always have the support one would expect for them.

In 1986, the federal government threatened to shut down Katimavik. Jacques defended the volunteer program, the oldest and largest the country had seen, and completed a 21-day hunger strike in protest. His valiant efforts paid off and Katimavik returned. Jacques was willing to go to great lengths to defend something he felt so passionate about.

It didn't seem like many individuals would do that these days. I respected that others opted for more civil routes of enacting change, such as writing strongly worded letters to government representatives or marching in a protest with succinct signs in hand. A hunger strike, however, was different. Fighting a basic human need—to feed and sustain yourself—indicated you were willing to put yourself at risk of harm for a cause you believed in. I admired the senator and his level of commitment.

I hadn't travelled much when I was younger, but programs like Katimavik seemed like a wonderful opportunity for young people to get out of their own Hazeltons and see a bit more of the world. Though I wasn't even halfway through Katimavik, I started to wonder about Canada World Youth. The countries Jacques Hébert must have seen were no doubt different from the ones waiting for me out there. If CWY was anything like Katimavik, it was a great way to see them and bound to be an amazing adventure.

CHAPTER 18

February 2006. Sault Ste. Marie.

Our first rotation was coming to a close, faster than most of us expected. But true to the essence of Katimavik, we couldn't simply pack our bags and be on our way without a planned moment for deep reflection.

Every group was required to give a final presentation at the end of their rotation, a summary of the past three months spent volunteering. Precisely what a final presentation looked like was left to interpretation, but Linda gave us a good run down of one.

"Typically, groups gather community members and give them an overview of your accomplishments over the past three months," Linda explained. "This typically entails what the group had learned, both as a team and personally, while sprinkling in some pictures and entertaining anecdotes throughout."

Rather than remaking the wheel, that's exactly what we decided to do. Execution, however, was the issue. With each passing day, the preparation that needed to be done for our final presentation began to feel more like homework. We had to pick away at it whenever we had the chance, but we would eventually need to produce something worthwhile at the end. It was a group project of the ultimate caliber and the scathing memories we all had of those in school were still fresh. And like begrudging students, we dragged our feet until the last week before the event, humming and hawing whenever Linda asked us about the progress of our presentation. She always looked worried whenever we told her. Our lack of work was only highlighted when she reminded us of who was going to be attending.

Linda had invited all our co-workers, managers, and supervisors from our work placements, anyone who was involved with any of our workshops or excursions, and of course our billet families—practically anyone our Katimavik group had become affiliated with. Just as I was beginning to wonder if the invitation list was becoming a bit excessive, Linda prematurely answered, elaborating on the purpose of the event.

"I know some of you might think of it as just another form of reflection, but your final presentation is also a way of advertising the positive impacts of Katimavik," she told us. "I need you to make a good impression with everyone involved so that I can recruit and maintain community support for the next group."

We read what our Katima-mom was putting down. She needed us to get shit done, and get it done soon. With a mutual desire to avoid disappointing Linda and an invigorated level of focus driven by guilt kicking our asses into high gear, everyone started to really sit down and flesh out what the hell we were going to do. We split into sub-groups to talk and joke about billeting, group living, and workplaces. This eventually turned into a framework for who would speak, in what order, and on what topics. Digital photos were gathered and organized into a PowerPoint presentation, something almost no one had any experience doing. And finally, speeches that were to be delivered by pairs of participants were written and rewritten. The next time Linda asked us how our presentation was coming, we felt a lot more secure in our answer.

"Don't worry, Linda. We're going to do you proud," I told her confidently.

"I want to thank everyone for coming out for this Katimavik group's final presentation," Linda said, addressing those sitting across from us in a small conference room on the Sault Ste. Marie College campus. It had everything we needed, including a screen to project our PowerPoint onto, chairs, and a half dozen round tables which were crowded with people listening attentively to Linda. Several tables behind them remained empty. There were fewer guests present than I expected at what was effectively our goodbye party.

"I know Thursday evening in the middle of winter isn't convenient for a lot of people, especially with the fresh snow covering the roads," Linda continued. "But what my wonderful participants may not know is how I have spent the last week on the phone inviting people like yourselves to tonight's presentation, people the amazing young people behind me have met, volunteered for, worked with, learned from, and otherwise befriended in the past three months. While our audience may be small, I want to assure both you and my participants that everyone, and I mean everyone who I reached out to, wanted to be here tonight."

The welcome and introduction was Linda's only part in our final presentation, and she delivered it in spades. Everyone waited patiently, eagerly waiting to hear about the Katimavik experience from the participants our PL had praised so much. The rest was up to us.

My part in the final presentation eventually came. While everyone was given the opportunity to speak specifically about their own work placement experiences, I was tasked with speaking on the broad value of work placements in general. I bit my tongue when I was first given the role, especially given recent events. The absence of my former Bush Plane Museum boss at our presentation, whether intentional or not, made my speech easier. I actually preferred that she wasn't there. Demmy and I had not left on good terms.

In December when I was still planning the New Year's party, the pastor who would eventually agree to let us use his church as a venue for the event had emailed me. He wanted to discuss the arrangement, but was only available in the day, during my work hours. I was desperate to secure confirmation on a venue, so I left the museum immediately at the start of my lunch break to meet him in time. I had to catch the city bus and I missed both the one that would take me there and the returning bus by mere minutes. As a result, I was an hour late when I returned to the museum. As calm and cool as ever, Daniel was sitting at the front desk with his feet kicked up when I returned. He didn't even look up from his book when I walked through the front doors.

"Demmy wants to see you in her office."

Just as I expected, it was about my absence. I apologized profusely and explained the struggles of planning the event and how, despite my brisk walking, I managed to miss both buses which made me late. Even though it was a one-time situation, I promised it wouldn't happen again. Demmy accepted my apology.

"Just let me know when you're leaving so I know what's going on," she requested nicely. In hindsight, it was something I should have done anyway, but I didn't want to waste time looking for my boss who wasn't always in her office, delaying myself further. Escaping any punitive action, the situation was resolved. Or so I thought.

At the end of each three-month rotation, participants received two reference letters: one from each PL and one from each work placement. We may not have been official, paid employees, but these letters were intended to give us a glowing review and help us gain employment once we returned home at the end of the program, touting our volunteerism and work ethic. After our work placements had officially ended, Daniel and I bused down to the museum to pick up our reference letters from Demmy, but also to say our goodbyes to the staff. We had an amiable working relationship with most of the employees and the other volunteers at the museum. Demmy was away at the time, attending another exhibition in Detroit. Before she left, she wrote up our reference letters and left them in envelopes at the front desk. Upon finding them, Daniel and I opened them up and gave them a read before we made our way back home. We were both surprised by what we read.

"Devon found his daily tasks challenging and required supervision and direction," I read aloud slowly. *"Initially he didn't understand the importance of adhering to our dress code and punctuality policy."* I stared at the letter with a blank look of confusion.

"Wait, what?" Daniel said, snatching the letter from my hand.

I knew what she was referring to.

About a month into our work placement, Demmy gave Daniel and I Bush Plane Museum t-shirts, emblazoned with the museum's logo on the front. We mistakenly thought they were a gift, not a uniform as Demmy explained to us weeks later when she noticed we hadn't worn them each time we came to work. After reminding us the one time, we had no problem wearing them every day, though Daniel refused to wash his in childish—and eventually smelly—defiance. The issue of our uniforms was never brought up again. Yet here we were, reading it in a reference letter from our supervisor as though it had been a reoccurring issue. Demmy had actually taken other several small issues with our work and felt the need to mention them in our letters.

I was flabbergasted and didn't know how to react. The issues she pointed out were exaggerated and lacked context. Had they been as problematic as she claimed, they could have easily been addressed. Counter to my reaction, Daniel was delighted in the disdain Demmy had shown him in his letter. He refused to show me though. Perhaps it was a courtesy in that he saw how much Demmy's comments had bothered me and thought whatever she had written about him would upset me further.

"You know what—screw her, Devon," he said. "In fact, let's show everyone what Demmy thinks of us." Despite my better judgement, Daniel and I sought out the museum volunteers we had been closest to. Not just to say our goodbyes now, but to show them our reference letters and perhaps see if Demmy was as off base as we thought.

"You guys should have just come to me for a letter, I'd 'a written you up something better than dis garbage," said Ed, one of the oldest mechanics working in the back of the hangar. "I know you didn't always have much to do, but youse two were alright." His thick East Coast accent was coming through in his confusion. He read the letter over a second time, brushing his scrubby white beard. "Why they put two of youse here, I don't know." I shrugged, having asked myself the same thing.

Before Daniel and I left the museum for the last time, we photocopied our reference letters and left copies on the desks of employees so they could read and express their own reaction to it.

"'*Handles constructive criticism immaturely,*' she says? Oh, we'll show her mature," Daniel said while the photocopier finished spitting out the last copy.

The act seemed petty, but with Demmy out of town, we knew we'd never get the chance to confront her. Worst case scenario? The other staff members read them, confused as to why the letters landed on their desk, and tossed them away. Best case scenario? They'd lambaste Demmy for her unfair judgement of the two unpaid volunteers who jumped at her beck and call. It seemed like a small form of justice.

When we arrived back at the house, I showed the letter to Linda. I wanted to know her thoughts. She was good at sifting out the positive from such situations. As she read my letter, I explained my side of the issues Demmy mentioned, hoping Linda might be able to provide me with some perspective. I omitted the part about us leaving copies of the letters for other staff to find. Upon reading the last bit of my reference letter, Linda let out a disappointed sigh.

"You simply can't use this reference letter, Devon," she told me. She gave me a hug in a comforting mom fashion and told me not to worry about it. I could only imagine what comments Linda knew Daniel's letter contained.

Few people in the group liked Daniel. While he certainly had his annoying moments, I considered him my foil: Daniel was clever, but lazy, whereas I was simple, but dedicated. He could shrug people's comments off easily and laugh at them—both the comment and the people—but I took those concerns to heart. I cared what people thought because I believed that reflected something about me. If someone was proud of my work, it was because I put effort into it; if a member of my group voiced that I was not being open, it meant I was disconnected. And now, Demmy's letter left me feeling disappointed and vulnerable. Just as I couldn't use Demmy's unflattering letter of reference, I couldn't very well put "successfully caught over seven mice" on my resume, no matter how good I thought I was at it. If I was going to make something out of this program, I was going to have to make the effort. My first volunteer work placement may not have been difficult, but it left much to be desired. I hoped to gain more from the next three months in Quebec than just sitting around and being used when convenient. I wanted my time in Katimavik to mean something. If I was going to glean—and share—any sort of lessons from our first rotation, our final presentation was the time to figure out what those were.

I made sure not to let any lingering bitterness poison my speech on work placements. It wasn't the time nor the place for it. Hearing snippets of wonderful things my group had to say about their own work placements in their own speeches gave me hope for the remainder of Katimavik. I may not have had as rewarding a work placement experience as everyone else, but the mood of the night inspired me to look for the positive. Rather than giving a bad impression of the Bush Plane Museum, I described it to the audience as an interesting place and how I wished I had the chance to do more during my time there. This was the point of our final presentation after all—to inspire the residents of Sault Ste. Marie. We wanted to remind them of the range of organizations in their community they might never have otherwise known about, but also give glowing reviews of them, looking past the rare instances where that wasn't quite the case.

Almost like a reference letter.

Our speeches were followed by a slide show that Carlos and Rosalie had put together with the inclusion of everyone's digital photos. Most of the ones they used had been taken by me. I had become the de facto photographer for the group simply because I remembered more often than others to bring my camera any time we left the house. Though I occasionally pissed people off by whipping out the camera, I knew everyone would want pictures of the many places we helped out at, explored, or visited. Sometimes we needed reminders of just how much we saw, other times we simply did crazy shit and needed proof for a good laugh.

Though we omitted the stories and pictures that would have gotten us in trouble, those we did share with the small crowd of guests that night left them impressed. To wrap up the presentation, each of us returned to the small stage to give our final comments about our time in Sault Ste. Marie. Our closing comments were met with heartfelt applause from the audience. I was certain that we wouldn't have had the same reaction had we presented to complete strangers. We worked with, volunteered for, learned from, and lived with these people. They understood our Katimavik jargon and shenanigans because they had put up with it. If the same presentation was given to friends and family back home, we would have been left with blank stares and strained laughter.

The group was elated when the presentation was said and done, not only because of how it had turned out better than we expected, but because it was our last mandatory activity before rotation. I had mixed feelings about it. Being a required activity made it more like a formal school assignment than an impassioned public speaking event. Despite the success, I wanted more festivity behind it, for it to be more of a celebration rather than a larger-than-normal period for reflection. If this was to be our going away party, I guess I was expecting more party than presentation. I said nothing to ruin the mood, though, especially for Linda's sake. She was the most excited for us.

"Oh my goodness, you guys!" She hugged all of us in a congratulatory group hug. "You did such an amazing job! You know, I wouldn't normally say this," she said in a hushed tone, even though most of our guests had left by that point. "But your presentation blew my previous group's presentation out of the water!" We didn't know much about the group she had before us as Linda rarely mentioned them, but at least we knew we were better than them!

Having wrapped up our last official activity of our rotation meant our time in Sault Ste. Marie was one step closer to ending, which made the impending move to Quebec that much more real. With that on our minds, we felt celebrations were in order while we could, celebrations of a less formal variety. And with our final presentation freshly behind us, this night was as good as any other.

Lyndsey, the same Katimavik alumni we had spent time with previously, knew what an accomplishment it was to survive a Katimavik rotation and invited us over to her house. Linda knew what this meant and agreed to turn a blind eye to any illegal consumption that might take place, so long as we promised to be safe.

Thankfully Lyndsey didn't live far from us. After a quick freshening up back at the house, we made our way to her address. It took no time before video games were set up, drinks were flowing, and the "Katimavikers-are-leaving" party got going. Being sober allowed me to sufficiently kick some ass at Mario Kart. Luke took his loss admirably. Drunkenly, but admirably.

"Devon, you should *totally* have a drink with us in Quebec. Like, for real!" he said, wrapping his meaty arm around my shoulder, squeezing me in a brotherly fashion. "I totally respect your decision to not drink, but it would be fun! And it wouldn't even be illegal because the drinking age there is eighteen!"

As drunk as Luke was, I had considered the idea. At a party, being sober often felt like being forced into the role of babysitter to everyone else who was letting loose. Even though I was one of the younger members of my group, I would be ashamed of myself if someone was to get hurt when I was capable of preventing it. But I also hated the idea of missing out on something that everyone seemed to enjoy. Even Jess appeared to have cast off her usual nanny role. A few drinks in and she was noticeably friendlier, giving out extra hugs. She had previously complained about feeling like a mother at times, something people openly told her was unnecessary and unwanted. Jess wasn't our PL, something she tended to forget. I was glad to see her letting go of those supposed responsibilities she felt she needed to burden herself with, even if she was the one placing them on her shoulders in the first place. Maybe I could do the same?

Katimavik encouraged new experiences, and while underage drinking definitely wasn't one of them, could it reasonably be something outside my comfort zone worth trying? I wanted to make the most of the opportunities presented to me, even if that included safely sipping a few beers with fellow volunteers that I lived with. After three months, I trusted these people.

I decided to be content with remaining sober that night, even if we were celebrating a final presentation well done. I would wait for the right time to get drunk with my group, even if that meant waiting until Quebec when it would lose that rebellious taste of deviant behaviour.

Our walk back home from Lyndsey's took a lot longer than it took to get there. Luke stumbled and struggled to hold both Erica and Rosalie up, Daniel and Tory were joking about Bethany puking in the snowbank, and Tiffany and Valérie were venting about men to me.

"Why, why eet so hard to find a good man? Can you tell me dat, Devon?" Valérie drunkenly pointed her finger at me while staggering on her feet. "I want—*hiccup*—a nerdy boy! A sweet, smart boy with glasses. And not blond!"

I smirked, knowing someone well who fit her description.

"Someone who likes me, not just wants sex. But likes bungee jumping, biking, being adventurous. And he 'as to be funny!" She threw her arms up in the air. "He 'as to be able to make me laugh and smile. Like you do, Devon!" She poked me in the chest and smiled a drunken smile. I rolled my eyes when she turned away. If only other girls were as forthright in explaining the type of man they wanted, especially when that man was walking right beside her.

We stumbled into the house in no way quietly or discreetly. It was only midnight, but everyone except for me was quite drunk. Linda surveyed the scene from atop the stairs with the quiet calm of a mother who was only slightly disappointed before remembering she was the one who allowed her children the autonomy that night to make their own decisions. She and I shared a look of mutual understanding as everyone shuffled around the house to sort themselves out. Several of the girls invaded the bathrooms, Daniel demanded food, and Bethany accidentally ripped the stair handrail out from the wall. In her defence, we had previously noticed the screws and their hold were beginning to strip in the wall.

After Linda and I managed to put the handrail back up as best we could, the household finally seemed to quiet down. Everyone was quickly settling into their own rooms and beds. Valérie and I were the last ones awake, waiting for the two bathrooms to be free from whoever was in them. We waited on the couch, slowly fighting against falling asleep ourselves.

She leaned her head tiredly onto my shoulder. "Mmmm, I'm so drunk Meester Fleen. You were so nice to me on the walk, listening to me."

“Mhmm,” I hummed in minimal agreement. I didn’t want the inebriated girl passing out on me and thought of how I might shift her off to bed to avoid any potential awkward situation.

She lifted her head and gave me a hug. "No, you don't understand. Most guys would take advantage of dat. But not ‘chu. You are a nice guy. A funny, nice guy with glasses." Her wide drunken smile settled for a second before her glazed eyes closed. Valérie leaned forward and kissed me.

It caught me off guard more than I expected. I backed away, but she draped her arms over my shoulders.

"Val, no, you're drunk."

"No, you're right. See? You're *such* a nice guy. Okay, okay." She pulled her arms away from my shoulder but then slid them along the front of my shirt, pulling me towards her. "Just one *d’oh*? Kiss me once," she pleaded. I calmly placed my palms over her fisted hands. When they relaxed their grip, I leaned forward and kissed her gently on the forehead.

A toilet upstairs flushed, and the bathroom door clicked open, allowing me to take my turn. I made my way to the stairs.

“Good night, Val.”

CHAPTER 19

February 2006. Poverty Lane.

Linda broke the long silence in the van.

“Okay, so here’s the deal..."

Everyone shook themselves awake from their groggy reverie of the morning. Given that we didn’t have work, volunteer, or even learning commitments, the last few days at our house were not as restful as we’d expected. They had been gruelingly spent not only packing our own belongings, but cleaning and readying the house for the arrival of the next Katimavik group, just as another was doing for us. While doing so, we took it upon ourselves to include a welcome letter and hide emergency condoms around the house.

"They'll be like, 'Why is there a condom on the ceiling fan?’ or 'What's this doing underneath the silverware drawer?'” Luke explained between fits of giggles. It seemed people had forgotten the drama created by the mattress prank which had only been a few weeks prior. This was different though. Aside from the fact that no one’s personal belongings were being moved, we also didn’t know the people who would be moving into our house. Everyone in our group enjoyed the humourous idea of condoms popping up in random places. It helped break the tension for the oncoming change.

There was a unique sense of excitement and nervousness for the rotation. We weren’t exactly moving, as we were only bringing our personal belongings, but it also wasn’t as simple as merely relocating. Everyone was starting to get used to each other by this point, understanding (or at least learning to put up with) the foibles, habits, and attitudes that would follow us through to Quebec. Linda, however, would not be joining us. Project Leaders stayed in the community they were assigned; just the groups of participants moved. We could tell Linda had been holding back the tears of letting her kiddos go. She had been very quiet about her feelings on the whole transition. Rotation was no doubt a different experience for

PLs, which is what made us curious as to what she had to say in the van that morning.

"You guys aren't coming back to the house. This is the last time I'll be seeing you." She choked back something. Tears, a smile, a chuckle. I wasn't sure. "You don't *have* to if you don't want to, but now is the time you can tell me *everything* you did at the house that I didn't know about, and I promise you won't get in trouble. Unless it's a level three violation, I won't care." Level three violations meant immediate expulsion from Katimavik. These were big no-nos, like hitchhiking, leaving the country, and illegal drugs. "You don't want to get in trouble, and I don't want to do paperwork. Oh, and you can ask me questions if you want to."

A few of us looked at each other with hesitation. There was *always* something a group or participant did that they weren't supposed to. This became evident very quickly whenever we spoke with other participants, past or present. These deviant behaviours weren't always deliberate either. They just sort of… happened. When you put a bunch of youth together under the same roof with a lot of "don't" rules, trouble was bound to happen. But Linda was like that favourite teacher in school that everyone in class liked. They seemed cool, but you knew they also had their limits. You wanted to test those limits, but no one wanted to be the one responsible for pushing them too far and ruining an otherwise great relationship. Linda had been wonderfully kind and understanding throughout the past three months as our PL. None of us wanted to ruin her pristine image of her amazing group that would never—

"You *totally* looked in the boiler room for booze, didn't you?!" Tiffany blurted out from the middle seat, cackling.

"I may have looked once or twice," she laughed.

Ha! I knew it!

There wasn't much more anyone had to confess. I contemplated sharing the time I hitchhiked once, but bit my tongue. I had become terribly lost along a long stretch of road after a solo trip to Walmart. It was snowing hard, and I lost all sense of direction. I was worried I was walking out of town. Not knowing what else to do, I got my thumb out and hoped someone might take pity on the poor fool on the road in the middle of winter. Eventually, someone did stop. Despite the driver's kind offer to drop me off directly at the Katimavik house, I had to insist they drop me off away from the house so I could avoid being questioned. I explained the reason behind my odd request, but I already felt terrible for stupidly becoming lost, risking an act that could get me kicked out, and then having to keep it a secret.

I was certain that given the circumstances, Linda would have understood my course of action. Regardless, I decided it was best to keep my mouth shut. Thinking about my own secret, I realized I may not have been privy to what troublesome acts everyone else may have gotten into. If I wasn't sharing, there was a good chance the others in the van weren't either. As far as I knew, no one in my group did hard drugs, no one had travelled across the border, and no one had killed anyone. I was about to crack a joke about how if we had to make bets on the latter, I would put my money on the quietest one in the group. Then I realized that was probably me…

As transparent as Linda was letting us be, the conversation naturally diminished. We continued the long drive, quietly watching the last bit of Sault Ste. Marie go by as suburbs and gas stations were replaced with farms and fields in the distance. Our first rotation was coming to an end. The group had survived the first three months of Katimavik, but we were now several participants shorter.

Daniel and Victor had left.

They had both informed us of their decision shortly after our final presentation. Victor explained that he simply didn't care for the rules and didn't feel like he was gaining much from the program. He respected the regimented structure of personal learning goals and volunteering that Katimavik offered, but preferred a freer form of expression and learning instead. He was an artistic individual and had occasionally shown us pictures of some of his past projects—ceramics, painting, pottery. I couldn't blame him. Katimavik might put you in a workshop here or have you visit a museum or gallery there, but hands on artistry wasn't something one could pursue in-depth during the program. Victor had a calling to his passion he needed to follow, so waiting another six months to do so was a waste of time.

Daniel was the other side of that coin. He understood the rules, if only so he could break them. He was a jerk, but he was also a smart guy. He had proven this on a few occasions. On a particularly slow day at the museum, we were stationed at the front desk. Daniel found himself reading a volunteer manual tucked underneath the cash register. Not only was the building a museum, it was also located next to the waters of the St. Marys River, and served as a functional dock for float planes. Every so often we would be reminded that bush planes and float planes were still flown, that they were functional and practical vehicles, not just dusty exhibits in a hangar. Sometimes they were flown as a hobby, but being a bush plane pilot was still a very real job that existed. As such, planes were sometimes docked outside the museum. Their pilots were charged a large fee for this service. Daniel was pleased with himself in finding a loophole to paying this fee: if the pilot of said plane paid the daily admission fee of $3.00, then the regular docking fee would be waived. Eager to call him on his bullshit, I looked at the manual myself. After reading the section several times over, the wording appeared to prove Daniel right. We both suspected Demmy would have argued against this loophole had we brought it to her attention. I wouldn't have been surprised to find Daniel arrogant and combative enough to share his gem of a policy with her if only to piss her off. Daniel never grew fond of Demmy, but at the end of our work placement, neither had I.

"We're here!" Linda announced.

We arrived at our destination: two cabins down a quiet road called Poverty Lane. We all had a good immature chuckle at the street name. Our group had been the last to arrive, but not by too long by the looks of it. Participants loitered in front of the cabins that would house us all for the next few days, a blend of Sault Ste. Marie, Thessalon, and Blind River. I eagerly looked for Ashley in the crowd of participants as we disembarked from our white van, never to be driven by Linda again. I found Ashley, but could only squeeze in a quick hug. We had to unpack our bags from the van, bags which were brimming with more contents than what we arrived with in Sault Ste. Marie on account of things purchased or sent to us from home. It would be a relief to send winter clothes home prior to our last rotation.

When the last bag was pulled out of the back of the van, we said goodbye to Linda. Before she left, Erica pulled out something from behind her back. Linda started to well up as soon as she saw it—a poster board filled with a photo collage of us doing workshops, hanging out, events we had volunteered at, and an assortment of adventures we had been part of over the past three months.

"Oh, you guys," she said between tears. "Bring it in one last time." I had mixed feelings about making our former PL cry, but it was for the right reasons. We gathered for one last group hug and photo with Linda before she forced herself to leave, hopping back into the driver's seat and driving away.

She didn't get far. Linda got the van stuck.

We ran over to her, trying to keep ourselves from falling over laughing. Luke and I immediately began pushing the rear of the van forward as a few boys from the Blind River and Thessalon groups came over to help. Several of the girls were talking to Linda to make sure she was okay. She had driven through a deceptively deep snow drift which pulled the van into the ditch, but she wasn't hurt at all and in fact shared in the fits of glee and laughter. Meanwhile, Carlos yelled at those of us pushing.

"Come on you poo-sees! Push!"

Luke and I both swore at him under our breath.

A familiar voice joined the peanut gallery. "Consider this a final teamwork exercise!" It was Kristie, our Project Coordinator.

With a final shove, Linda and the van were soon free and driving away, honking wildly. Her kiddies were now left alone.

We gathered around with the Blind River and Thessalon participants. Someone pointed out that it didn't seem accurate to refer to us as the Sault Ste. Marie, Blind River, or Thessalon groups. We didn't live in those places anymore. Soon we would be the Saint-Élie group, but not for a few more days. What were we to call ourselves during our period of transition then? I brought this question to everyone's attention, but no one had an answer.

"Welcome to Rotation Camp," Kristie declared to the large group to gather our attention, putting a sudden pause on my quandary. She spoke loudly, ensuring she was heard over the participants chattering in the back. Our PLs were gone, so Kristie had her work cut out for her. There was only one Project Coordinator, but there were more than thirty participants now under her direction. Since this was new to all of us, Kristie explained what we could expect.

Rotation Camp was intended to not only be a period of transition between our communities, but a time of reflection and preparation. The camps were often held at actual campgrounds or other isolated places. The intention was to remove Katimavikers from urban distractions like malls, theatres, and stores. Even so, talk amongst other participants suggested it was still a kind of respite.

"Pft! We're in the middle of nowhere in the middle of winter. We couldn't go anywhere even if we wanted to!" said Rosalie. I snickered once she started to quietly mutter worries about bears. The city girl was unaware they were hibernating.

Kristie continued. "I'll be running several workshops and activities. These will involve not only debriefing the past three months, but also preparing you for what you can expect in the next three."

The second rotation was going to be our "French" rotation. Each group would be living in a French community somewhere in Quebec, although sometimes the French-speaking communities were in other provinces. We were warned that communication would likely be challenging between participants, but also at our work placements and during billeting. Kristie elaborated that the language barrier and shock from the immersion into French culture usually exacerbated the "storming" phase of a group. This was a period where people pushed against established boundaries and conflict tended to arise. I had a bad feeling that this would likely happen, but I accepted that my group would cross that bridge when we came to it.

It was hard not to dwell on what to expect in Quebec, but my attention was focused on Ashley who was standing at my side. The gears were already grinding away in my head as to what the next few days would look like for the two of us. I needed to do something with Ashley: make a move, kiss her, something. Anything. This really was the last chance.

For reasons unknown to us, our cluster was not staying together. Thessalon participants were going to Val D'or and Blind River participants to Ville-Marie, more than 800 km away from Saint-Élie-de-Caxton. We would have two new groups as part of our cluster, groups who were in their own Rotation Camps at the time and would soon be going to the Quebec communities of Shawinigan and Trois-Rivières. New groups, new participants.

Ashley and I discussed the idea of visiting each other, potentially using our 48 hours in Quebec to meet each other somewhere in the middle. Even with our hearts set on seeing each other again, I had a sinking feeling that the two of us meeting up again during Katimavik wasn't likely to happen. Even after our rotation in Quebec, her group would then move westward to Alberta, mine eastward to Newfoundland. Time was ticking and a hug goodbye wasn't going to cut it. I didn't know what I needed to do, but I had to do something. Words weren't going to cut it this time. I had to show Ashley how I felt.

"But first, let's get you guys settled in!" Kristie finished.

We piled into the two cabins rented for us on Poverty Lane. We were so accustomed to everything Katimavik-related being in threes. Now having to accommodate three Katimavik groups into two cabins, even temporarily, felt… off. More practically, the cabins were not large to begin with. The bedrooms were small, there were limited beds, and every room immediately became crowded. Participants were forced to share beds, couches, floors, even requiring sleeping in the open living room and kitchen. Only a few complained, but their bouts of whining were quickly replaced with shouts of glee. Something else caught our attention when we stormed the cabins with our backpacks and duffle bags.

"Dude! We have satellite!" someone yelled. It wasn't long before the boob tube was turned on and captured several participants' attention. Though there was TV and ample channel selection, there was no internet, which left some people uneasy and more homesick than ever. I didn't care for any technology at that point. I couldn't have any distractions. Seeing how small the two cabins were made me realize how difficult it would be to get Ashley alone, a problem I was already familiar with. Privacy was usually limited in Katimavik houses, but during Rotation Camp it was nigh impossible except for venturing into the cold outdoors.

The lack of privacy wasn't the only thing that bothered me. Ashley didn't seem nearly as intent on spending time with me as I was with her. Every workshop we had, she sat far away; if she was part of the massive dinner-making sessions we had been assigned by Kristie, she was too busy; if she was washing dishes after dinner, there was always someone else helping her. The look I got from Ashley's groupmates was filled with empathetic pity. Some of them gave me supportive thumbs ups, encouraging me with "go for it" well-wishes. As I watched Ashley deep in conversation with her dishwashing partner that night, I didn't care for the looks of pity anymore. Enough was enough.

I should have asked to wash dishes with her, I realized. *Stupid! It would have been a great time to talk to her. Well, no more! No more waiting!* I walked up to her as she was handing over a series of semi-dry plates to someone from Thessalon and politely interrupted their conversation. My heart was full of bravado, but my body was a quivering pile of nerves.

"Hey Ashley, when you're done, d-do you want to go for a walk with me?"

Her face lit up, just like it always did. Even when I thought about Ashley, I pictured her face lighting up with that same cheery smile.

"Oh sure," she answered casually, like I'd asked if she wanted a piece of candy. I left her alone to finish up the dishes. I thought about offering to help, but I didn't want to pressure her or make it seem like I was rushing her. I wanted her to think about what I'd asked her, to get excited to be alone with me. While I waited, I pretended to watch TV with some of the other participants in an effort not to seem like the panicky mess I was. Participants on the couch were watching *The Simpsons* for the umpteenth time, which kept everyone's attention except mine. I couldn't help nervously glancing at the clock every minute as discreetly as possible.

Finally, Ashley walked over.

"You ready?"

I wanted to tell her that I had been ready for a long time.

We exited the warm cabins into the wintery night. It had grown much colder. I worried Ashley was going to say something about the temperature and wish to go back in, but I was relieved when she didn't. Our bulky winter jackets made the walk a noisy endeavour, but the isolation and silence of Poverty Lane made it ideal for me. I took Ashley's left hand with my thick glove. I suddenly realized it was the first physical romantic gesture we had ever shown each other. Her hand felt small, but I was sure it was soft and warm. Seeing how she forgot her own, I offered her my left glove to wear.

"That's okay," she declined.

God damn it. Why can't anything just go smoothly?

Neither of us said anything at first, but eventually we opened up and started talking more about our anxieties about rotation. I listened to Ashley talk about Ville-Marie, what she had heard about her new community, her new PL, and potential workplaces she and the rest of her group could be assigned. I tried focusing on her words, but I could only think about what was going on right then, like where we were walking to, if her exposed hand was warm enough, what I should say next.

"I really liked the gift you got me," Ashley said. Her head was tucked so deep into the collar of her jacket, I almost didn't hear what she said, but I had.

It was February 14th that day. Valentine's Day. I wasn't about to let that slide by. We might have been away from any sort of stores, but I came prepared. Earlier that afternoon, before I was rushed to help prepare supper alongside two other participants, I managed to pull Ashley aside and give her a present—a rubber football to replace the one she had lost when we first met. On the side of it in large bold letters were the words, "*DO NOT THROW NEAR WATER*" written in permanent marker. Knowing Ashley liked it gave me a glimmer of hope, but only for a fleeting moment. I didn't think I could have given her a better gift, but beyond her conciliatory thanks, it didn't seem to make a difference for us.

The conversation unfortunately dipped as cold as the temperature, although I hoped it was actually because of it. Neither of us said anything else as we continued walking. Eventually, we walked past a graveyard on our left. All the gravestones were covered in a deep blanket of snow, making the graveyard barely discernible in the darkness except for the decorative gate.

"I didn't know we were close to a graveyard. Do you want to go in?" I asked.

Ashley giggled nervously. "No, not really."

Of course not, stupid! Why would she want to go into a graveyard? Don't turn this into a B-rated horror film for the poor girl!

We continued walking. Silence took us over again except for the maddening screams of embarrassment in my head over what I had just asked. *Shouldn't have said that. Should not have said that ...*

"Do you want to head back?" she asked quietly. "I'm getting cold…"

Fuck. No, I don't. I really don't, Ashley.

We turned around and continued walking. I squeezed her hand tighter, hoping she would notice. We didn't say another word until Ashley stopped just out of sight of anyone standing outside the cabins. The few streetlamps ahead of us and the light spilling out of the curtained windows of the cabins were the only illumination in the dark of Poverty Lane. Suddenly, Ashley turned and hugged me. I said nothing and only squeezed her back.

Seconds passed.

Then minutes.

We continued to hold each other, fighting against the cold, until finally I spoke.

"If … if I don't do it now, I'll never forgive myself."

"... I know, it's just … I've never been kissed before."

"I know."

We slowly lifted our heads, looked each other in the eyes for a moment. And our lips met.

CHAPTER 20

February 2006. Saint-Élie-de-Caxton.

When Ashley and I returned to the crowded cabins, it was like nothing romantic had even taken place. She quickly sat with some of her group on one of the couches and joined them in mindlessly watching television. No one was invested in what was on the screen by that point. We were all running out the clock until our chartered bus arrived to take us to the airport. Rotation camp was almost over.

I didn't know what to do. Nothing was registering in my mind except for a hazy list of questions marred with confusion. I wanted to hold Ashley, to be close to her. So why wasn't I? What happened? What was I doing wrong? We had kissed. I had finally shown my feelings, not just talked about them, actually *showed* them. Before, it was all talk and no action, but now something had happened, something had clicked between me and Ashley. So why did I feel worse than ever?

Whatever progress I thought I had made was ripped away, torn up, and laid at my feet. And there I was, regressed back to my former paranoid, overanalytical self. I had just kissed a girl and now she was sitting several feet away from me while I stewed. Hollywood had spoiled me with its climatic scenes of romance. That, or I never saw the particular movie that turned out this way, a nice romantic comedy that would show me what to do after leaving audience members in suspense, starring a protagonist without a fucking clue on what to do or say.

The early morning hours agonizingly ticked by until our bus finally arrived at Poverty Lane at 3 a.m. Some participants had attempted to stay up until then, opting to nap on the bus or at the airport once we were checked in. Others succumbed to the whims of sleep and napped until it was time to leave. My confusing and sour mood had exhausted me. I hoped a few hours of sleep would help ease the heartache, but it only moved it to my neck instead. Sleeping on the cabin floor underneath the kitchen table didn't help either.

"Bus is here," someone shouted. Everyone groggily grabbed their bags, put on their winter boots, and trudged out the door. As we boarded the bus, it didn't seem like sitting next to Ashley was going to make a difference in her demeanour either.

"Oh my goodness, I'm so sleepy," she said before pulling up the hood of her sweater and resting her head against the window. It was a reasonable reaction given what time it was. I was tired too, but wouldn't that have been a good chance for us to be together in our final moments? What I wouldn't give to rest my head on her shoulders or have hers against mine. I wanted to hold her hand again, but I noticed she hid them in her pockets. When she did finally pull them out, it was to clap along with the others in thanking the bus driver when we arrived at the airport hours later. Ashley seemed almost determined to find excuses to avoid any sort of connection with me. I didn't just feel cheated, I felt like a coward. What was the point of even trying anymore?

Our flight to the Montréal-Pierre Elliott Trudeau International Airport was uneventful, but we were left with a long wait for our connecting flights that would take us one step closer to our communities. My group's flight was the last to leave, meaning we had the most time to wait. I didn't want to be around people though, and instead wandered around the airport until I found a nook in a restaurant booth to hide in until it was time to board. A few members of my group managed to find me. They knew exactly what was wrong.

"Woman problems, eh?" Luke tried to console me, but I was simply too tired to care. We all were at this point, given the travel and poor sleeping conditions. Pouting felt right, a rebellious emotion, an unhelpful but nonetheless soothing antithesis to the emotional investment into something that had proven to go nowhere.

Over the intercom, I heard the call for Blind River's flight. They would be boarding soon, the first group to leave out of all of us. Despite my deep frustration with how things had gone with Ashley, I wanted to at least say goodbye to them. It was the right thing to do.

The girls in the booth had grown tired of my sulking but were oddly enthused at the idea of me saying goodbye, especially Rosalie who loved the cheesy and romantic idea of an airport farewell. I was running on a severe lack of sleep, but I somehow found enough gumption to push myself up from the dining table and leave the restaurant. Unfortunately, in my drowsiness, I lost my bearings in the Montreal Airport. Soon I was running across the airport, down corridors, and up and down different flights of stairs and escalators. I was about to pass through a gate when a security guard stopped me.

"Do you '*ave* a flight *t'rue* '*ere*?" he asked with an arrogant Québécois accent, missing almost every '*h*' in the sentence he spoke. Without the conviction nor energy to lie, I sheepishly admitted I did not, for which he immediately refused to let me through. I tried explaining as best as I could how I simply wanted to say a final goodbye to a girl I loved without sounding like it was a lame line from a John

Hughes movie, but the security guard remained obstinate. Whether it was my poor stuttering explanation in English or he was just an unromantic prick, the *tabernacer* wasn't having it. Just as I started wondering how fast I would have to be to bolt past him, how much it would hurt to be tackled by the large man, and whether Katimavik had a protocol for releasing participants detained by airport security, someone yelled my name.

"Devon!"

It was Ashley and the rest of her group. They hadn't walked through the gate yet. I hadn't missed them! There they were, all the members of the former Blind River group. They had already said their goodbyes to the other participants except me. Under the scrutinizing eye of the security guard, I had to say my strained goodbyes to them all, but especially Ashley. It was hard with everyone standing there.

She stepped forward though and we found ourselves once again in a tight embrace. I held her tight, hoping to somehow commit to memory the smell of her hair or the soft give of her body against mine, even under her plush winter jacket. I closed my eyes and for a moment let go of the reality that a security guard who took his job too seriously and Ashley's wishful groupmates were watching us. For a few seconds, the world disappeared, and it was just me and Ashley. I leaned my head gently to her ear.

"One last time?" I whispered carefully, hoping to kiss her, to kiss her with gusto. To hell with everyone watching! Awkwardness be damned!

She whispered into my shoulder nervously. "No… not in front of everyone."

My heart shattered.

The Blind River participants walked away and so did Ashley.

A heavy sigh dropped my shoulders with the weight of a thousand black holes. Somewhere behind me the security guard was ushering me away, but I wasn't listening.

Welcome to Quebec, I guess.

CHAPTER 21

February 2006. Saint-Élie-de-Caxton.

I tried calling it Mass-O 2.0, but the name didn't seem to catch on.

We were crowded around a classroom somewhere in a Shawinigan high school. It was our second time meeting the Shawinigan and Trois-Rivières participants. The first was when we all landed at the Montreal Airport. It was easy to pick Katimavikers out of a crowd. All you had to do was look for the large mass of sleep-deprived youth waiting for or already carrying their overstuffed duffle bags, backpacks, and suitcases. These could easily be any other group of young travelers, but the key was to look for the diehards, those amongst them who wore the green and orange Katimavik logo on their shirts, hats, or bags. Katimavikers were not a subtle bunch. After passing several other groups of Katimavikers in the airport that day, groups who wouldn't be part of our new cluster, I started to wonder if every group rotated on the exact same day.

Once everyone had their bags, the Saint-Élie, Shawinigan, and Trois-Rivières groups boarded a chartered bus to drive us to our new communities. With the hustle and bustle of the airport behind us, everyone relaxed and began to get to know each other. I wanted to capitalize on the spike of excitement that came with meeting new faces and hoped it would help distract me from the bitter funk that had plagued me over the previous few hours. Just like when we first met other groups, I started talking to everyone. These were faces that we would be seeing often, and I committed names to memory early. I was a social butterfly that chattered away, but in the back of my head was a ghost with a lingering, haunting presence. As long as I kept talking, I couldn't give it the attention it demanded.

I might have had girl problems, but no one else felt particularly jolly either when we arrived in Saint-Élie-de-Caxton, mostly on account of the long day of travel. Once again, our group was the last to be dropped off. Thankfully our bus was able to pull up right to the front of a large two-story brick house, our new home for the next three months. Atop the front porch stood our new PL, Anne, waiting for our arrival.

"Où est la douche?" were the first words out of my mouth. Asking where the shower was may not have been the warm welcome Anne expected from us, but I couldn't help it. It had been an exhausting trip, both physically and mentally. I was also very sweaty. Hoping to escape stringent weight restrictions for luggage as well as make extra space in their bags, some participants wore their thickest and heaviest winter clothes, myself included. Despite taking my jacket off, the bus was very warm. Our bus driver may not have understood our English requests to turn the heat down. Saving an excessive weight fee at the airport came at the price of being irate, tired, and sweatier than I anticipated being when we arrived at our new home.

It was the following day when Anne drove us to a Shawinigan high school where we met the Shawinigan and Trois-Rivières participants once again. We were still acclimating to our new communities and the surrounding Québécois culture. The suddenness of it all had led me to misunderstand how our cluster gathering was in fact not a second Mass Orientation, but rather a behaviour standards workshop. If Anne had told us otherwise, my mind had obviously been elsewhere.

The workshop was more or less a lecture, a reminder not to be exceptionally stupid or reckless in our Katimavik houses and the potential consequences of doing so. By that point, everyone wasn't just aware of what not to do, we were also better at not getting caught. I was more focused on continuing to get to know people than paying attention to flip charts and the PLs talk.

I tried to recall participants who had introduced themselves on the long bus ride. It had been difficult to introduce yourself to everyone without yelling to the front or back of the chartered bus, especially when some of us were sleeping. There was the same bubbly fervour when meeting a new group, even if we were now asking the same questions we had grown accustomed to by people who had never heard of Katimavik. We could, however, dig a little deeper though and ask about things in progress: What was their last placement like? How well was their group functioning? Who could speak French and who was expecting to struggle?

Rather than looking for secrets or hidden agendas, I talked away, full of jokes, energy, and enthusiasm. I took to my new friends quickly. There was even a girl from Saskatchewan who seemed funny and easy to talk to. I was excited to get to know these people. It seemed worth doing so, as we would remain a cluster for this rotation as well as our third and final rotation. This meant we would actually be spending *more* time together with the Shawinigan and Trois-Rivières participants than with those from Thessalon and Blind River. It was never explained why our original cluster wasn't sticking together, it was just the way things worked out. Mixed emotions followed that realization.

I was the only one who seemed to have any enthusiasm about becoming acquainted with the Shawinigan and Trois-Rivières participants. I noticed the rest of my group was noticeably distant and reluctant to socialize not only with the new participants in our midst, but even amongst the Thessalon and Blind River participants during Rotation Camp. It wasn't long ago we were crammed into those two cabins on Poverty Lane, only a few days. During that time, everyone in my group had tucked themselves away in one of the tiny rooms which somehow managed to fit Luke, Carlos, Bethany, Erica, Rosalie, Tiffany, Valérie, and Jess. I had been preoccupied with Ashley, but I hadn't been actively antisocial like they were starting to act now. If they wanted to continue being reclusive, that was fine, but I wanted to mingle. I wanted to embrace the new, whether it was getting to know the participants in that room during our behavioural standards workshop or the French-Canadian culture we were steeped in. Even novel things, like seeing "*Arrêt*" on the octagonal red signs rather than the traditional "Stop" drove home the reality that I was in a very different place than where I had been before. Despite a lingering exhaustion from travelling and nights of poor sleep, I was willing to let myself be overwhelmed with these unfamiliar settings and new friends, scattering my attention to the winds. I didn't want to reject those things simply because I was tired. Deep down, I knew that by enjoying everything that was now different, I was avoiding confronting the reality that I was beginning to miss the other groups, that they were gone, and so was Ashley.

Even a week after our arrival to Saint-Élie, we all still felt drained. Whatever "norming" looked like, it didn't seem to be happening for us. Whether it was an invisible, undisclosed stage of the Katimavik group process or just the close-quartered travelling and living, most of us felt like crap those days. The cold weather kept us inside most of the time where sickness flourished. When one participant got sick, it was almost inevitable that the rest would follow. Homesickness, combined with the regular kind, weakened our immune systems and group relations. It took much coaxing, cajoling, and the occasionally thinly-veiled threat to convince everyone to go outside and explore our new community, even what was just in our backyard.

Saint-Élie-de-Caxton was a small town, mostly inhabited by employees of Mauricie Park and their families, or *Parc Mauricie* as they called it. More than half of our group had grown up in large urban cities. Jess and Carlos fought me hard that Kingston and Kitchener were not big cities no matter how much I argued about relativity. This difference between us seemed more evident as Saint-Élie was the first time the city dwellers had actually *lived* in a small community. There were no office buildings or towers, no Tim Hortons or Starbucks, and much to Rosalie's dismay, no shopping malls or even thrift stores. There were, however, two small convenience stores, a small school and youth centre, and not one, but *two* bars.

Our new Katima-home itself was a prominent building in the community. We lived on the top floor of an old parish home located beside a Catholic church, complete with stone exterior, tall arched windows, and a white steeple over the front entrance. Behind the church was a large cemetery. All the graves were covered in snow except for the taller headstones. There was enough of the white stuff that we could simply step over the spiked iron fence that was intended to keep the dead in and nosy volunteer kids out. Behind our house, a road ran past the cemetery and turned into a narrow path that wound up a hill decorated with small statuettes along the way. Atop the pimple of a hill was a large cross which Anne told us lit up at night and could be seen throughout the town. Beneath the giant ode to Christ was a small cement mausoleum. Upon our first visit to the site, we managed to squeeze in the already-ajar door buried underneath snow. Inside we found it contained a frighteningly real statue of Jesus laying in a glass case next to three Wise Men watching over him, a scene real enough to give the few of us brave enough to look inside a scare. I had no doubt we weren't supposed to be in there, but the door was unlocked, and we were only curious, wishing to respectfully examine the aged statues with their peeling veneer and paint.

The religious side of Quebec was still foreign to most of us. No one in our group was particularly pious. Carlos claimed he was Catholic but never discussed his faith much. I suspected it was more a familial upbringing than true devotion. We had never seen him go to church or even pray. The closest any of us were to being religious was Jess who practised her Wicca quietly. We all retained a modicum of respect for the various elements of religion we found in our new community and across the province.

As far as I knew, Katimavik had no official stance on religion, merely policy that encouraged respect and understanding for those that practised. Linda had once told us a story of a participant who had billeted with an extremely religious family. He thought it would be funny to turn all the crosses in the house upside down one day while the family members were out. Upon returning, they did not find it amusing, a far worse crime than messing with someone's mattress. The billet family considered the act incredibly offensive and disrespectful, enough that the participant was kicked out of the program. It sounded a lot like something Daniel would have done. I kept the anecdote in mind, but I wasn't worried. Aside from the religious elements and the French culture, I found Saint-Élie quite similar to Hazelton. While some of my group may have felt a bit agoraphobic and apprehensive about the lack of amenities they were accustomed to in larger cities, I felt more or less at home.

Churches and the like weren't the only places of devotion in Saint-Élie we checked out. By the end of our first week, Luke had visited one of the local bars on his own. He pleaded with us to come out and join him the next time. With Victor gone, Luke was now the oldest of us. He admitted to being self-conscious about sitting in a bar by himself, but with the drinking age being eighteen in Quebec, we would all be legally allowed inside the boozy establishment.

Our inaugural visit to the bar just so happened to coincide with karaoke night. After a pitcher split between Luke and a few of the girls, we soon found ourselves singing Aerosmith's "Don't Want to Miss a Thing." It wasn't long before Valérie was dancing with a drunken patron, another regular was air-guitaring a solo on the dance floor, and the whole bar learned of our invented dart game, one of the more stupidly immature yet fun diversions we played.

The dart game consisted of making direct eye contact with someone and pretending to blow a "poison dart" at them. If they weren't fast enough to look away in time, they had to drop where they were, "paralyzed" for three seconds. Silly but fun, especially in certain situations that raised eyebrows from those who weren't aware of what the hell was happening.

After we felt like the bar had provided sufficient fun and decided to head back to the house, a large burly man, easily mistaken for a lumberjack, put his sausage fingers on Luke's shoulders and turned him around to say something. I could barely understand his *authentique* rural French over the blaring bar music. The fact that he was drunk did not help.

"What did he say?" I asked after he let Luke go.

"He said we shouldn't leave, because we brought the bar to life. They hadn't had that much fun for a while," Luke explained as we walked home. He assured the French bear of a man that we'd be back.

It was when we all got ready for bed that night that I realized we weren't the only ones who had left an impression. My clothes stank something fierce of cigarette smoke and cheap alcohol spilled on me while dancing. Quebec was currently in the middle of banning smoking from bars like the rest of Canada, but the provincial law wouldn't take effect until later that spring. Despite the friends we made that night, the acrid stench left me very reluctant to return to the bar.

Not all the residents of *la petite ville* were whiskey-soaked boozehounds. Every so often we would visit the local youth centre, the *maison de jeune,* where precocious teens loitered. I was never entirely sure what we were doing there. We weren't tasked with a specific goal of volunteering, no event to plan or facilitate, no fence to paint, no heavy equipment to move. We just hung out with the teenagers there. They seemed to enjoy the company of people just a few years older than them, especially that of the anglophones. They loved to ask me questions in broken English.

"What do you for … ehhhh," one scrawny teen would ask, trying to think of the English word he was looking for. "... fun? *Oui, oui.* 'Fun!'" They were usually ecstatic when they made the accurate translation. The feeling was mutual, even though they did most of the talking. The majority of my socializing wasn't contingent on conversation. Inside the compact youth centre was a bright and open room filled with games and a small kitchen. Every wall was covered in colourful posters with model teenagers standing in model positions to indicate they were sharing model sound bites of positive or helpful advice. They were the same kind of posters that covered the wall of any typical secondary school, albeit *en français.*

"Stay in school."

"Wear a condom."

"Don't smoke."

The last one I thought particularly helpful. Half the kids seemed to smoke cigarettes casually outside. Despite the onset of future lung disease, it impeded them in no way, shape, or form when it came to competing against Luke or me in their console version of Dance Dance Revolution while the rest of the group—mostly francophones Bethany, Rosalie, and Val—would tell them about Katimavik. It frustrated me that I couldn't tell them the number of entertaining stories that I already had under my belt. I couldn't offer worldly advice about life after graduating high school or share my volunteer experience or really say much at all, unlike the francophones in our group. All I could do on our visits to the youth centre was dance, play games, and entertain them with some weird Anglophone mannerism which the teenagers often found oddly hilarious, even if I didn't. As enthusiastic as they were when we showed up, our visits to the youth centre usually left me feeling somewhat hollow. I was only there because my group was there.

"Best two out of three?" I asked. But Erica was having none of it.

"Just go do it Devon, so we can leave!"

I grumbled away as I put on my boots and brushed the foot of snow off the van. Mornings were hard. We were still adjusting to our new living arrangements and the Quebec winter in general, especially the snow. Anne politely but firmly put the task of clearing the van of snow onto the participants.

Saint-Élie was actually Anne's hometown. This was her sixth year as a Katimavik PL and we were getting the impression that she was ready to move on to something else. There were no buses or public transit in Saint-Élie, which left Anne to drive us everywhere we couldn't walk, which turned out to be a lot. Our workplaces, most workshops, and practically all our excursions took place outside of Saint-Élie. If they weren't held in Shawinigan, they were in Trois Rivière. Anne had grown tired of the constant driving. This also included venturing out into the cold early in the morning to start the van, and brushing off any snow that might have covered it the night before. Anne wanted participants to take a more proactive role in the travel arrangements and was even looking into the prospect of having Erica granted special permission to drive the van as she was one of the few of us with her full licence. That morning, she and I played Rock Paper Scissors, with the loser having to deal with the many inches of fresh snow that covered the van. I was the sore loser.

"Today is going to be very busy, you guys," Anne told us as we drove to the park. Not only was it our first visit to Mauricie Park, we were also doing a first-aid course in the morning followed by job interviews in the afternoon, just like in Sault Ste. Marie. Our first-aid course facilitator was very patient with our antics, which seemed to be at an all-time high as we were really getting into the dart game. Carlos was pissy when I refused to fall down, despite my reminder that we were right in the middle of training.

"Fucking cheater," he whined quietly, kicking my shin under the table. It was getting harder to let Carlos' attitude slide those days. He was usually the mature one between the two of us, but his reaction left me thinking otherwise. Being silly in our own domain was fine, but pulling that shit in the middle of a course seemed incredibly rude to the facilitator who was standing right at the front of the small meeting room we were in.

For our job interviews, we met a tour guide at the main park complex. Viv was an attractive park employee in her early thirties. Anne drove us around to other sections of the park while Viv sat in the front seat of the van sharing the history of Mauricie and the role employees played in maintaining park. At least that's what I think she was describing. Once we started driving around, she spoke mostly in French. Luke occasionally translated for me, but stopped after a while, struggling to listen himself. I politely asked twice for our guide to speak slowly. She would briefly, but eventually ended up returning to her normal pace of speech, still far too fast for my comprehension. I gave up attempting to understand and just looked at the passing sights out the window which I assumed she was describing. It looked like a lovely park, but most of it was covered in snow.

"Does anyone have any questions so far?" she asked.

Oh sure, that she says in English.

She looked at me expectantly. I had many questions, but to ask them would be as much struggle for me to ask as it would be for her to answer. I said nothing, pursing my lips and shaking my head instead.

Our drive took us to five different stations around the park. At each one we met a different supervisor, only two of whom spoke to us in English. They discussed their job and the potential work we would be doing. There were four main jobs, each of which required two participants who would be partners. After our meeting with the last supervisor, we were given printed sheets to write on and describe ourselves, select where we hoped to work, and why. I took a crack at writing mine in French, something I was more adept at than speaking. Someone in charge would look at our answers, discuss it with Anne, and get back to us in a day or two with decisions on where we would be placed. Anne must have already started reading our papers, because later that night at the start of our first house meeting, she let loose a loud chuckle.

"Devon, how good is your written French?"

Her question left me puzzled. "Better than my other French skills." I hoped. "Why?"

"Do you know what you put on your application?" she asked. Everyone sitting on the couches that circled the living room listened intently, eager to know what was so funny. "'*Je t'aime l'exterior?*'"

I recalled writing that down. "Yeah. *I like the outdoors.* I want the job that will have me working outside. I thought they'd like to hear that."

"That's not what that means. You said, 'I love you outside.' They thought it was hilarious. All the supervisors had a good laugh in the office when we saw that," Anne explained in between giggles.

Thank you, high school French class. I wanted to impress the people at the park, but I had instead confirmed for them that I couldn't speak French worth shit. I said nothing else in response to Anne.

At least I made them laugh.

That was the fun part of the house meeting. The rest went downhill after that. Everyone was already fed up with the existing house relations: participants were purposefully avoiding others, some were spending too much time with each other, and some were simply excluding themselves from the group overall. Erica and Bethany felt a lot of the comments were aimed at them. Whereas I thought they had simply grown closer as friends, Luke explained to me after the meeting they were supposedly "dating." This had not been explicit in people's comments during the meeting as I couldn't help but notice everyone had avoided saying the d-word, at least in front of Anne. Despite the concerns, everyone remained relatively civil in explaining how we all felt left out in our own regards. There seemed to be no resolution, however, when the house meeting finally came to a late close, and perhaps there should have been. Relations in the group only got worse.

I myself was very withdrawn those days. At first, I thought it was only during Rotation Camp. While I had been preoccupied with Ashley, my group had stayed in the tiny bedroom for most of those three days, rarely socializing with the others. But now, Ashley was gone. Our group might have been back living in a house instead of a cramped cabin, eating at a dinner table, and sharing couches during weekly house meetings, but it felt like I was sitting on the sidelines. This, compounded with my *très* shitty French skills, made me feel even more alone.

As it was our French rotation, we were expected to speak and practise French in the house and during house meetings. I tried my best to follow the discussions, but it wasn't long before I became lost, tired, and often frustrated. Jess and I couldn't comprehend spoken French. It wasn't Carlos' second language like it was ours, but his third. He seemed to manage alright, or maybe he hadn't let on whether he was as confused as me and Jess. Meeting agendas were given to me and Jess in brief, rushed translations, like what activities or excursions were planned, but usually only the important details. My poor second language skills also meant I could do very little to help in the planning of these, which furthered my frustration.

Planning excursions entailed hours of visiting and reading through websites and making phone calls. Most of these websites were strictly in French and required me to translate in order to understand anything or to constantly request help from someone else who was around. The few times I called the contacts from the websites were utter failures. Only once did I speak to someone who was bilingual, which I knew was luck and not something I could rely on happening often. Every other time, my requests for information ended in strained conversations, stalemates where the Québécois person on the other end of the phone didn't know how to answer my questions in English, nor did I know how to ask them in my pathetic French. They would kindly ask if I had someone nearby who could translate, but by that point, I was basically getting other people from the group to do my work for me, which they obviously didn't wish to do. Even writing out the itineraries was a pointless exercise. As part of our French rotation, they had to be written in both languages in order to be approved by Head Office. Considering they were documents that required specific information regarding pricing, travel, scheduling, availability, and descriptions of activities, even the English draft couldn't be trusted for accuracy.

Just when I thought I was getting the swing of the planning elements of Katimavik, I was now set back drastically. It was like getting a handle on calculus and then having to go back to counting to ten on my fingers, although numbers would have been easier to understand than some of the francophone receptionists I spoke with. I could write French acceptably well, read it only marginally better, but my oral comprehension was the worst of all. Nowhere did this seem more evident than during French class.

The anglophone participants were required to participate in French language lessons. Our teacher was actually Anne's mother. The older Québecoise woman certainly bared resemblance her daughter, but also remarkably like a poised Anjelica Houston. While she had a thick provincial accent, her English was surprisingly easy to comprehend. I suppose that's what made her ideal for the task ahead of her.

Just like a normal class, we had assignments and occasionally homework, often simple tasks, like translating a list of words or creating a basic dialogue with newly learned vocabulary. I insisted to our teacher that my problem wasn't my grammar, but comprehension, and to a lesser degree, my limited general vocabulary. If I couldn't understand a Québécer's thick accent when they spoke a phrase I already knew, how could I understand them if they spoke a phrase I *didn't* know? She was patient with me and my struggles. We both agreed that practice was key: to speak, to be spoken to, and to repeat until understood.

The theory was sound, but practice less so. I found very few people had the patience for such a strained conversation with someone who had to constantly repeat themselves. No matter how often I asked them to *parlez lentement,* whether it was a stranger on the street or another participant sitting across from me on the living room couch, they would inevitably revert to speaking at their regular pace and cadence, leaving me in the conversational dust. The more I tried, the more frustrated I got which led to neglect in my practising.

I was physically comfortable with where I was in Katimavik. The rural setting didn't bother me like it did others in my group. But emotionally and linguistically, I was constrained. I had taken a huge step back from what I had accomplished in my first three months of Katimavik.

My lack of practise and effort in French started to become problematic even outside of lessons. As weeks went by, I was failing to keep up in house meetings. Relying on translations from the French speakers for both meetings and my committee work quickly wore thin on them. Some of them passive-aggressively suggested I start "catching up" with my French skills. But no one was about to slow house meetings down just for my sake. I couldn't blame anyone since those meetings tended to drag on to begin with.

As a result, I started to mentally check out. Rather than intently listening to French spoken, I tuned it out instead, unless someone said my name. If something was discussed that I forgot about, I blamed it on having been said in French and not translated for me. How could I be expected to remember something if I didn't understand what was being said? As weeks went by, this excuse became less accepted by the others who began to insist that no, the discussion had in fact been in English. This was hard for me to accept. I was certain that if English was ever spoken, my ears would have perked up and clued into the familiar native language I had grown up with. I didn't know whether my groupmates were telling the truth or were becoming spiteful of me and my lackluster efforts to practise my second language. Whatever it was, the gap between me and my group grew wider every day.

So, I couldn't understand what our group had planned, it was rare and difficult for me to get involved, and nothing seemed to work. Electronics helped bridge the gap that language had left. I dove into my Game Boy SP to entertain myself. At least in the fantasy worlds of my video games, I could understand the characters' dialogue or the story. I could be involved in driving the plot forward in the action adventure or roleplaying game. My video games may not have been a solution to the problems I faced, but they provided a good escape. And thankfully, it wasn't the only one.

The phone was starting to become a coveted item around the house. Thankfully our home phone this time was cordless, which allowed homesick Katimavikers an important and more private link to the outside world. Despite its size, the layout of our house still meant privacy was rare as you never knew when someone could come around the corner of the long hallway. Everyone's rooms were located around the edges of the massive living room: Luke, Carlos and me in one; Tiffany and Bethany in another; Erica and Valérie; Rosalie and Jess; and Anne of course in her own private room. A conversation in any one of those rooms would easily be overheard though. Instead, a popular nook to hide out with the phone was inside a large walk-in storage closet around the corner from the stairs that led up from the kitchen, the furthest distance away from people's rooms short of going downstairs. Inside were two shelves filled with board games, outdoor toys, sports equipment, random knick-knacks, and boxes of assorted Christmas decorations. It might have been cramped, but it was the best spot for privacy.

Everyone was missing home, despising someone in the group for some reason, eagerly looking forward to our final rotation, or just pissed off about something. A lot of us seemed to have triggers, so it was probably for the best that talking about something someone did that irked you was best done in private where there wouldn't be backlash. Even if our confidants on the other end of the phone line didn't understand the complicated web of volunteering, communicating in secondary languages, and otherwise living in a group that seemed to be glued together more those days with strife and stress than the desire to get along, phone calls were an outlet during a period which couldn't be anything other than us "storming."

I was feeling particularly mopey one day and had managed to snag the phone. Inside the closet, I propped up an extra mattress that had been placed in there and proceeded to get comfy. I burned through many well-spent minutes from my calling cards to contact family, friends, and eventually, after things had settled somewhat and she emailed me her phone number, Ashley.

As painful as the moment at the airport with Ashley had been, I didn't feel resentful or spiteful. I wasn't happy about it, but I didn't want that to ruin a friendship that made me feel less alone despite constantly being surrounded by people. Rather, the event highlighted my growing struggle with communication. I felt that if I couldn't make much progress with French and communicating with my group, then I would do so with Ashley. In English, of course. Doing so through the safety of a distant phone call as opposed to face-to-face felt pathetic, but I needed to start somewhere. If I couldn't express my thoughts and feelings to a trusting friend far away, in English no less, how could I ever expect to do the same with the people I lived with?

It took a few phone calls between the two of us for me to work my way into broaching the subject, but I eventually confronted Ashley how the event at the airport had made me feel. All of it: the embarrassment, the disappointment, and the struggle I faced since the bus drove away from. She confessed that she had felt horrible. Ashley, like most of us I suspected, was coming to terms with who she was. Being away from home, meeting new people, and living in strange places were scary experiences for a lot of us. Ashley confided that she had been making progress in breaking away from a shy and timid nature that she resented herself for, but in the last few days of Rotation Camp, she had fallen back into those old habits. The time at Rotation Camp was very embarrassing and she felt a lot of pressure from watching eyes.

"I wasn't embarrassed by you, but more by how indecisive I had been," she told me. "I… I hate that part of me. I've hated it for a long time."

We both went quiet. Before I had begun dialing the long string of numbers for the calling card toll-free line, my card pin number, and her Ville-Marie phone number, I went through a spectrum of negative emotions. I had been angry, disappointed, and miserable. Now I just felt horrible. It had never occurred to me that the other person in a weirdly distant and complex relationship might be struggling to come to terms with her own personal insecurities. We both admitted to our own guilt but continued talking. Eventually those negative emotions over what happened faded and just became part of the past.

When we finally hung up, I felt much better. At least the giant acidic knot in my stomach had subsided. I had made a big step with Ashley. I had told someone I cared about how I felt. It seemed stupid that something like that should be so hard, but it was.

I had been able to finally communicate with Ashley and come to what seemed like an amicable understanding of things between us. Could I do the same with my group?

CHAPTER 22

February 2006. Saint-Élie-de-Caxton.

Who knew a scavenger hunt could be so disastrous?

It was supposed to be a simple French activity. The items on our lists were disguised as questions written in French and intended to guide us around Saint-Élie. We were split into teams with Tiffany, Bethany, and me put together. The teams were shuffled at the last minute when someone pointed out that the activity might be extra challenging for a team composed of all anglophones. The well-intentioned thought seemed pointless once we learned there were words on the list that even our token francophone Bethany didn't know.

I asked Tiffany what the questions on our list were. She yelled back venomously that I had already asked three times already, even though she hadn't answered me and had resolved to mutter to herself. With Tiffany reading the list and Bethany translating over her shoulder, this left me to lead us around town. I tried to inject enough levity into the activity to strike a balance of fun and progress in our task, but the girls were having none of it. Even with a crudely drawn map provided for the scavenger hunt, I still managed to get us lost, which further dampened our already sour moods. Hours later, all the teams returned to the house, more bitter than when we started.

Everyone was in a bad mood those days. It made me surprisingly glad to be house manager with Luke that week. House managing with Luke was a welcomed change. Not only would we be the first all-male house managing pair, he was the only other guy in the house I could tolerate. It was like Carlos had a personal mission to piss me off every day, a mission at which he often succeeded. A silver lining to house management was its hefty requirement of spending much of my time in the kitchen, which helped put some distance between the two of us. While normally a chaotic part of a Katimavik house, our kitchen in Saint-Élie was different.

At our house in Sault Ste. Marie, everyone bottlenecked in front of the tiny boot closet right in front of the entrance before they had to walk through the living room and then the kitchen in order to go either up or downstairs to access either the first or second floor bathrooms or bedrooms. Entering our Saint-Élie house immediately brought you into a spacious, tall-ceiling kitchen with ample space to spread out our snow-covered winter clothes and boots. While our only entrance still took us through the kitchen, it wasn't nearly as disruptive. The kitchen was the furthest room from the living area upstairs where we usually gathered. You had to go up the stairs, around three corners of a hallway, past the small statue of Jesus on the wall (that genuinely scared us half the time we came around the corners in the dark), and into the wide open living room before you could get to your own room. If we weren't on our way out or in from the entrance or sitting at the dinner table during mealtimes, the kitchen made for a surprisingly quiet place, great for removing oneself from the group, especially when the phone nook was already occupied. When meals were ready, house managers in the kitchen could usually hear the rest of the group stampede down the hallway and bump into each other as hungry participants bombarded down the slick wooden stairways. Many bums were bruised from accidentally slipping on them. It was hard not to laugh when people took spills down the stairs in such cartoonish ways.

I also liked being house manager with Luke because he was on board with me in shaking things up on the menu. The group's culinary skills had taken somewhat of a dive since we had arrived in Saint-Élie. Everyone was excited to hear Anne admit we didn't *technically* have to bake bread like we thought we had to.

"It's more of a suggestion," she explained. "I'm okay with you guys buying bread. I don't care, really."

Whether this news was actually true or not, we didn't bother to argue. Anne had been a PL for an impressive six years. We knew she had likely eaten her fair share of burned or undercooked bread made by participants and was probably sick of it. I didn't want to lose my bread-making skills though, and would occasionally sneak off to the kitchen and attempt to make some late at night when I wanted to be alone. Although I was far from an expert baker, I still enjoyed making it. Everyone was content to buy bread, but no one minded having a few extra slices on hand.

Anne's lax stance on bread let us get away with a few things in cooking in general, especially when it came to accommodating Jess. With Linda and Victor absent, she was the sole vegetarian in our group. It seemed like we forgot most of our lessons from our past cooking workshops and had trouble cooking wholesome vegetarian meals, but so did Jess. While we were loath to admit boiled vegetables weren't exactly a proper substitute for a main dish that contained meat, we all agreed that Jess' constant snacking on junk food wasn't helping her stomach aches or bad moods either. If she wasn't willing to make an effort to follow her own voluntary diet, then neither were we.

Even so, Luke and I agreed we needed to try something new as house managers, anything to bring some excitement into the meals plans. We wanted to spice things up, minus the spices. He and I weren't sure if everyone was ready to try a completely new recipe, so one night we tested the waters by adding food colouring to Thai chicken dish. It was a meal I'd previously made and had been well received, but even with rainbow coloring of noodles being the only difference, reactions were not positive.

"These are dees-gusting," Carlos sighed petulantly. "Why, why, why would you do this?" According to Carlos, "something new" automatically translated into Spanish as a colourful attempt at poison.

"It's literally just food colouring! You can't even taste it," I protested. Nobody believed me. Rosalie insisted she could taste a difference, but couldn't explain precisely how or what it was when I asked her what that difference was.

There were lots of leftovers.

Blue, red, and green noodles weren't the only surprise for dinner that day. While Luke and I were busy preparing the last of the dishes, someone snuck cards underneath everyone's plates. When we sat down and noticed them, we pulled them out and read what was written.

They were wedding invitations.

Earlier that week, a random conversation during dinner had brought up the topic of middle names. With pressing curiosity, everyone shared what their middle names were. Once it was revealed that my middle name was William and Erica's was Elizabeth, girly-girl Rosalie lost her mind.

"Oooooh, it's like royalty!" Rosalie gasped loudly. "Oh my god! We should have a wedding! It would be so cute!" The rest of the girls chimed in.

"Yeah, a Katima-wedding! We can have a cake and invitations! I can be a ring bearer and we can have flower girls!"

Erica looked about as enthusiastic as I was. We both rolled our eyes at the ridiculous idea, but we knew it would be a losing battle. She and I gave in to the persistent squeals and let everyone have their fun.

Days after Rosalie's suggestion, there remained whispers of a wedding here and there. I started to get nervous when I spotted Bethany jotting down wedding notes. I had almost completely forgotten about the asinine idea until we pulled out the handwritten wedding invitations from under our plates that evening at dinner.

"Are you guys still on this?" I pleaded. There was no dissuading Rosalie though, who was obviously the wedding planner/mastermind/instigator of the whole thing.

"Yes, Devon, and you're going to dress up and be handsome. And Erica's going to dress up and be beautiful. And it's all going to be *lovely*!" There was a hint of intensity in Rosalie's tone that I thought best to leave alone. Things were already rocky in the house. I decided to let it go and let everyone have their fun.

A few days later, I was married.

Having soon forgotten about the silly idea after the wedding invitations went out (there had not been a specific date set) I walked into the living room one day and was momentarily confused to find the couches had been moved and chairs set up facing the other end of the wall. It didn't take long before I realized it was a wedding aisle. Sitting in some of the chairs were stuffed animals facing forward. One part of me wondered who they belonged to, as I hadn't seen any of them around the house or knew the girls to own any. The other part of me wondered whose side of the family they belonged to.

The girls came out from their rooms dressed up. They even had makeup on. Bethany had volunteered to be the priest and borrowed a black dress shirt from Carlos. Around her neck was a strip of white paper, a makeshift priest collar. In her hand was a Bible, further adding scary authenticity to the event. I couldn't believe the elaborate effort the girls had gone through for the joke, but it was enough that I couldn't deny them a groom. The ridiculousness of it made for a good laugh, one that we all needed. I also knew they would never forgive me if I ditched my own wedding. I dressed in a tuxedo t-shirt, a gift I had received for my high school graduation and arguably the most suitable shirt for the occasion. I decided to bring it to Katimavik, thinking there might be situations to wear it during the program but so far had only worn it once. I couldn't think of a situation any more perfect that demanded this exact combination of sarcasm and formality.

Despite my shirt's appropriateness, I felt woefully underdressed when my bride-to-be came out from the bedroom. Erica had a sheer white bed sheet pinned behind her in a yoga style that somehow accentuated her girlish figure, something she tended to hide with looser, more drab attire in comparison to the other girls. Valérie had curled Erica's already naturally curly hair into perfect ringlets that bobbed in front of her face as she walked down the aisle. I suddenly felt lucky that a running joke had placed me into a mock wedding with this lovely girl in front of me.

As this was our French rotation, everyone was adamant that my and Erica's vows be spoken in French. Erica was more or less bilingual and was capable of saying her own vows. Bethany, aware of my language handicap, offered to say mine on my behalf. I was scared into agreeing, "*Je fais*" to whatever the faux French priest had stated on my behalf, waiting for me to confirm. I felt slightly more comfortable knowing Erica thought the ordeal was just as silly and awkward as I did. We gave each other a quick—and much to Rosalie's dissatisfaction, "lame"—smooch when the time came to kiss. Our fake ceremony was followed by a fake reception that consisted of cutting a real peanut butter cake that someone had baked for the occasion, as well as juice spiked with real booze that Tiffany had smuggled away somewhere. Anne was away for the day, leaving us to celebrate the reception party and briefly forget the stresses that had been plaguing the group those days.

"They just need some extra hands to help move things and organize stuff. I'll drop everyone off and pick you up in a few hours," Anne told us.

It was a sudden volunteer request. We didn't even know what we were agreeing to except that it was going to take place at a homestead. It was a historical site where people would dress in old pioneer clothing and describe how people lived in the past. Anne hadn't been able to tell us much about the homestead or the work they needed done when we asked. I couldn't tell if it was me missing details we'd been given earlier or if we were all left a little bit in the dark.

We were getting used to Anne's disappearances, but still felt disappointed by them. We had been reminded at Rotation Camp that PLs were people too. They had responsibilities and needed to be there for their participants when necessary, but they also had their own lives outside of Katimavik, their own schedules to follow, and their own things to do. We saw this in Anne who tended to keep to herself and would only tell us where she was going if it was pertinent to our travel plans. Her mysterious nature was the topic of debate while we painted baskets and cut out various cardboard and paper shapes at the homestead, a task given to us by our volunteer contact.

"Who wants to bet she's banging Isaac," said Tiffany who was gluing cardboard pieces together with confident fervour. Isaac was the PL for the Trois Rivière group. The last time we saw them, they had shared similar theories that there was a thing between our two Project Leaders. Luke disagreed.

"Has anyone else noticed the severe lack of crime in Saint-Élie? Anne's clearly being called away to punch loud-mouth drunks in the face *because she's a superhero!*" I applauded Luke's creativity and straight face in delivering his explanation. "But you know, maybe less like Batman, more like Captain Planet!" We all took turns trying to remember the names of the culturally diverse cast of the teenage Planeteers and what power their magic rings had bestowed upon them.

Our jump to childhood cartoons reminded me of other programs I watched when I was younger. "You know who my superhero was when I was younger? Mr. Dressup! That guy was the shit!" I was also fond of the Canadian icon because he looked a lot like my grandpa.

"I loved him! He was usually on after that weird *Beetlejuice* cartoon, I think. Did anyone watch that when they were younger?" Jess asked. Most of us had, even some of the francophones. Bethany asked if we had heard of Babar or Tintin. She was delighted to hear that we had indeed known of those shows that had French origins. But then she mentioned the name of an obscure television show that none of us had ever heard of.

"It's because it's Frey-nch, isn't eet?" she pouted sarcastically. Claiming we didn't understand something because it was French was Bethany's go-to comment to both lighten moods and express her disappointment. "What about de…umm…what was the name of dat polar bear on da CBC?"

"Basil!" we all chimed in at the same time, fondly remembering him and other characters from *Sesame Park*, the Canadian version of *Sesame Street*, as well as other Saturday morning programs that we all grew up with.

The woman in charge of the homestead walked into the room and commended us on the quality and efficiency of our job. I thought we had actually been rather distracted. She cheerfully gave us more cardboard to cut as well as baskets to paint, leaving us alone to our task once again. Our conversation carried on right where it left off. Even though we were sitting in a house built over fifty years before any of us were even born, surrounded by memorabilia that stood as a testament to French pioneer culture, we were more interested in cartoons, movies, books, video games and other bits of pop culture from our youth, our own form of nostalgia that apparently transcended the provincial borders across Canada.

It had been a busy week. Most of us relished the break from volunteering and our work at the park and were looking forward to a more casual day trip to Trois-Rivières. We were able to further justify the day excursion by joining the Shawinigan group on a joint tour of a prison/museum, led by a guide who had apparently been a previous prisoner there. Whether this was true or not, I couldn't verify. The tour was given in French. Rather than getting frustrated and disrupting the tour for others by requesting translations, I ventured off on my own to learn more about the prison. I was able to glean more information from the descriptions and signs than by listening to the guide, even if they were written in French.

Vastly different from the prison section which focused more on history, the museum section of the building was incredibly interesting. It was filled with plenty of unrelated exhibits describing the historical significance and engineering of bicycles, the evolution of firefighting techniques, explaining human kinetics using wooden stick figures, and how different apparatuses were used by Foley artists in making different sound effects. For some reason, an exhibit focused on nature included a captivating story about a forest troll. I never did learn exactly what the lore was because the description beneath an artistic depiction of the troll was, much to my repeated frustration, solely in French. I filled in the blanks of what I was unable to translate with my own version of events.

One final exhibit was much more interactive than the others. It was an entire room filled with mirrors and explorable tubes and tunnels you could get lost in. Some of the tunnels brought you face-to-face with hidden cameras that were connected to monitors in another room that your friends could spy on you with. As fascinating and well-designed as the exhibits were, I still couldn't determine how they were all related. If it was science, why was a fictional story about a troll included? If it was fantasy, why were engineering and physics explained in depth? Whatever theme brought the exhibits under one roof, I was thoroughly impressed by it all and would have gladly taken it over the Bush Plane Museum, but I doubted they were taking volunteers. Even if they were, it would have gone to a lucky participant from the Trois-Rivières group, not mine.

As fascinating as its prison and museum were, Trois-Rivières' shopping malls were just as enthralling to members of our group. Malls weren't just something

Saint-Élie severely lacked; they were a beacon of familiarity of those of us from larger cities. While the stores might have been ubiquitous across large malls throughout the country, they still provided enough change in scenery, something we were all craving those days and in more ways than one.

With an afternoon at the mall at our disposal, Erica and Tiffany took the opportunity to get their lip and eyebrow pierced. I was content with my piercing in my left ear, but I was still among those looking to shake things up. My hair had grown out and the blue colouring had faded into a greasy, dull shadow of its previous hue. It might not have helped that I was letting the girls recolour it with whatever permanent markers they could find during some of the more boring evenings. I knew markers would not actually dye my hair and probably weren't good for it, but I didn't care that much about the condition of my hair and enjoyed the physical attention. Still, I thought it was about time to dye my hair again. I promised Erica and Bethany they could choose the colour as long as they helped dye it for me, saving me from performing the messy job myself. The chocolate brown they chose was met with a great response when I stepped out of the bathroom later that evening with the finished result. Erica curled her finger around her hair, proud of her work, while an enamoured Bethany swooned.

"It looks so good!"

"*Oui, très beau*!"

It was a nice end to our week before returning to our regularly scheduled jobs at the park. For me and Luke, this meant painting.

It seemed there was always something that needed to be painted at *Parc Mauricie*. Our supervisor was a short, white haired Québécois man in painter overalls named Étienne. Though he spoke English well, he rarely did. Since our first introduction, he immediately knew I was not fluent in my second language. He would give directions to Luke who would relay them to me, even if I was standing right next to him at the time.

Winter was apparently the best time to paint the park offices as they were mostly empty during the off-season. Luke and I painted walls, doors, shelves, whatever needed a fresh coat of paint or two, sometimes three if it really needed that true *authentique* sense of paintiness. Or if we missed a spot, which seemed inevitable no matter how hard we tried. After every project Luke and I painted, Étienne would calmly walk over to quietly inspect our work which would go one of two ways: it was satisfactory, which Étienne would indicate with a bored "*bon*"; or it was unsatisfactory, in which case he would look at whatever we had painted with even more scrutiny and find spots we had missed. Even when we were adding second coats, Étienne always seemed to find these spots regardless of how much paint Luke and I seemed to throw at the surface. Half the time, I couldn't fathom how he could even tell, but to his credit the old timer had been with the park for over thirty years. If he said I missed a spot on the wall, who was I to argue? Painting had become my job and I wanted to do it well. It wasn't as though there was much else to do. It was too cold, wet, snowy or any combination of the three to do any sort of painting outside. Noticing just how many buckets of paint we were going through, I began to wonder how much of the park's budget was put aside for paint, brushes, trays, and turpentine alone. As different as it was from working at the Bush Plane Museum, painting at the park quickly became monotonous.

Working with Luke made things easier though. Everyone agreed Carlos and I would have killed each other, and the girls were easily aggravated those days. Even though there were rare moments when I got along with others, there was a creeping feeling that I was slowly drifting apart from the group. I found it hard to connect with anyone on an individual basis. The one exception of course was Luke, with whom I had the best relationship out of anyone else in the group. During those long bouts of painting, we told as many bad jokes as we could think of, sang the chorus of horrible pop songs over and over, forgetting or butchering the rest of the lyrics. I was convinced he and I were experiencing some form of synchronized insanity as a result of paint fumes, but it all helped make the hours we spent together fly by. When we weren't cracking jokes or singing off key, the two of us talked about everything, from battle tactics from our favourite RPG video games, to who would win a battle between Iron Man and Batman. And as everyone was wont to do at some point or another, we talked about the group: Carlos, Anne, the girls, and just women in general.

The topic of home also came up often. It seemed so long ago I had left Hazelton, but for Luke, home was just a few hours drive away. He had made plans for his dad to pick him up in Saint-Élie and drive them home to Montreal for our group's 48 hours off. Everyone agreed to have ours next to St. Patrick's Day, making it a 72-hour holiday for us. Luke was insistent that I join him in Montreal.

"You'll love Montreal, Devon! I'm telling you, we have the most beautiful women in the world!" he assured me. Luke was also excited because I had agreed to have a drink with him on our time off. Not just a sip or a single beer, but a whole night of drinking. Luke knew of my apprehension and explained we were just going to have a good time with no specific goals.

Erica and Valérie had also expressed an interest in tagging along. Neither Luke nor I had any qualms about the female company. We got along with the two girls well enough. I wanted to make the best of our time off. Having some other members of our group in our midst aside from Luke might give me the chance I had been looking for to reconnect with people. It was already beginning to feel like there were fleeting opportunities to do so. We were half-way through our nine-month program and things seemed to be picking up speed. I didn't want to wait until the very end to do something big. I loathed the idea of missing opportunities and wanted to do something special with these people while I had the chance, something outside of the basic routine and confines of living and volunteering together. Partying in Montreal seemed like it would fit the bill. Luke was gleeful at the prospect of witnessing my proper inaugural inebriation, but I was concerned I might overdo it. The last thing I wanted to do was become an annoying, sloshing, stuttering slob like I had witnessed happen to my friends in high school, scenes which had turned me off from drinking to begin with. Luke's casual expectations helped relieve some of the self-imposed pressure. Rather than worrying about things prematurely, I would commit to going with the flow instead; whatever happened, happened.

It wasn't just going to be us sitting in a living room knocking back drinks either. Luke's older brother, Greg, had agreed to take us out for a night on the town. I had only a vague idea of what this entailed, but I was excited to see what the city of Montreal had to offer. I was not the only one. We later learned that most of the group was also planning on going to Montreal, albeit with their own agendas: Bethany was going to visit her family, Tiffany and Rosalie were doing their own thing, and Carlos was meeting up with his friends from Columbia who were visiting Montreal as well. None of us knew what Jess' plans were, but no one seemed to care.

Jess had been growing noticeably snippy. While touring an iron forge museum in Shawinigan one day, our tour guide gave us a small task that required partners. Jess was looking at a display and when we called her over to join, she refused to participate and instead grumpily walked out of the lobby. We tried to chalk Jess' attitude to having a bad day, but her behaviour only seemed to grow worse.

When we first arrived in Saint-Élie, Rosalie had bit the bullet and agreed to share a bedroom with Jess when no one else would. The two had gotten along well enough at the beginning of our second rotation, but even Rosalie had had enough and begun voicing her frustrations about the living arrangement. We did our best to again be inclusive to Jess but despite our best efforts, nothing improved. It was mildly reassuring to hear that everyone's relationship with her had grown thin and strained and not just mine. This became evident at a conflict resolution workshop hosted in Shawinigan for all three Katimavik groups.

"Think of a conflict you've had in the group. It can be something small or something big. We're going to have everyone talk about it using the skills you just learned today and resolve it," our facilitator instructed. We all felt pathetic when the only thing our group could sheepishly agree upon was that we didn't have a major problem to resolve; our supposed conflict was that *we didn't have a conflict.*

It was a blatant lie. No one wanted to mention the elephant in the room: a mutual frustration with Jess. It wouldn't be fair to have everyone turn against her in a crowded setting, no matter how true it was or how constructively we approached it. Our problem with Jess wasn't even specific. She was just getting on everyone's nerves, but no one knew how to tackle such a vague issue. Whatever the root of her annoying behaviour was, the problem would have to run its course in the future and not during a workshop surrounded by peers.

We stuffed down our post-workshop guilt with homemade pizza made for an indoor "beach party" event the Shawinigan group hosted at their house afterwards.

It was the change in tone we drastically needed. Despite the exasperations earlier that afternoon, all the participants present were having a good time. Even some of my own group members managed to crack some smiles as we mingled with participants from the other groups. Some of us munched happily away on our third slice of pizza, others played an impromptu game of Twister in the living room, and in another room people were dancing to obscure French songs. The Shawinigan house was a-rockin'.

My ears perked when I recognized one of the songs that played from the iPod dock in the kitchen. I had heard it on the radio plenty of times in our own Katimavik van. French pop music, French country music, even French rock music sounded different than their English counterparts. It wasn't merely listening to lyrics sung in another language. They just sounded more… French. Maybe I was picking up on the subtlety of Quebec solidarity and distinctiveness of francophone culture, a foundation for francophone music in the same vein of how rap and hip-hop was derived by the angst of those coming from the street or how the blues was a musical narrative of the struggle of African Americans in the Deep South. I enjoyed the music I heard in Quebec, but it continued to bother me that I never knew the damn lyrics.

There was one particular pop song I enjoyed until one day I noticed I could suddenly understand what was being sung. I thought I was losing my mind, like someone had comically hit me over the head with a frying pan without me realizing it, but giving me super translational powers to understand French lyrics with ease. That is until Erica assured me that the song in question just so happened to have a single verse in English and that the singer was simply switching between French and English. My excitement disappeared as fast as the English lyrics in the song did.

As Shawinigan's indoor beach party continued, I observed the differences between their Katimavik house and ours in Saint-Élie. I became engrossed in their monthly calendars which looked very similar to our own hand-drawn grids on coloured poster board. The only difference was theirs was much fuller. Each day had something rousing penned on them: an intriguing tour, fun-themed dinner, interesting guest speaker, full-day outing, etc. Samantha explained some of their activities.

"We're going to the pool and then downhill sledding that day, visiting the museum that Matthieu works at the day after, and checking out an indoor garden sometime after our 48 hours off," she said, pointing at the upcoming week before backpedaling a little. "To be honest, it's been pretty hectic."

I was jealous, especially since I hadn't been able to help much with any sort of committee work that might contribute to our own planned activities. Bethany had been kind enough to switch spots with me from the French committee to the community committee. At least on the community committee, I could potentially plan activities on my own. I was tired of feeling like a meek and helpless English-speaking kitten, dead weight to everyone else around me. The more incapable I felt in Quebec, the more equally excited I became for our final rotation in Newfoundland where I could plan excursions and activities. I could feel my resolve solidify, much like it did the year prior.

As I neared graduating from secondary school in Hazelton, I had resolved to go out with a bang, not a whimper, a line from T.S. Eliot's famous poem "The Hollow Men" that I found great inspiration in. I later learned not only did I have the line backwards, but the author was believed to have been referring to post-World War I disillusionment and despair and most certainly not the fear of a teenager missing out on a good time. Regardless, I took from my English Literature class what I did. Only having one high school graduation in my life, I intended to make it as awesome as possible and thus became involved with every single fundraising activity in my final year with the intention of making our dry grad party more successful than any past or future graduating classes. With that same attitude, I knew that the closer my Katimavik experience came to its end, the more compelled I would be to make the most of it. For our rotation in Quebec, however, I was constrained, limited to what I could contribute to either my group or the community I lived in. I would bide my time until I could unleash my potential.

Until then, all I could do was endure.

CHAPTER 23

March 2006. Shawinigan.

"Well it's not my end! I'm pulling!"

"Who's slacking then?"

"For the third time, I am!"

"I'm telling you guys, if we just designate people as the corners, it will work."

Little success was coming from everyone shouting over each other. Everyone had something to say and little of it was helpful.

"Hmm, no. Not quite. One end is pinched," Isabelle, our Quebec Project Coordinator told us.

Reminiscent of similar workshop activities, the instructions had been simple: In this case, to make a square. Each of us was given a section of a long white rope to hold in our hands and make the shape with. As expected, I knew it couldn't be that easy and patiently waited for the hammer to drop.

"You can talk as much as you want, but the catch is, you can't see!" Isabelle added. She proceeded to give us blindfolds to put on ourselves.

The problem wasn't just the visual handicap though. We all had different ideas as to what the solution was. Those who were confident in their ideas spoke the loudest, at least until those who had previously remained silent had to now shout in order to be heard. Like most of the workshops we had taken part in during our second rotation, we finished feeling more embittered than when we started, and only slightly more enlightened.

The exercise wasn't part of just any workshop. It was part of our mid-rotation reflection that Isabelle was facilitating. It was effectively the halfway point to our entire nine months of Katimavik, a detail that hadn't escaped most of us. In addition to the exercise that gauged our communication skills (spoiler: they were bad) it was also an opportunity for us to review Anne as a PL.

Our consensus of her was one of the few things we could agree on those days. Everyone more or less liked Anne. She reasonably fulfilled her role as a PL, but we wanted her to be more involved with us in our group activities. Many times, she would simply drop us off and pick us up afterwards rather than joining us. Some of us theorized that Anne's behaviour was actually typical for a PL, that Linda had in fact coddled us and left us with beyond average expectations for future PLs. For all we knew, maybe distancing was part of some behind-the-scenes Katimavik training, a more conservative approach that was intended to teach us to be responsible and mature adults capable of solving our own problems or, alternatively, leave us to implode or kill each other in the process.

We never did discover exactly what the inner machinations of our PLs were. We did what we were asked for the sake of the workshop activity, answered the few questions Isabelle asked of us, and were left to examine our emotional foundations on our own after having them thoroughly shaken up.

The aftermath of the workshop did, however, reinvigorate my desire to reconnect with my group and practise effective communication. Doing so in my native language was still a struggle, but doing so in my second language remained a stuttering disaster. The recent changes Anne's mom made to our French classes helped a little. Rather than talking to Carlos, Erica, Jess and me as a group and asking each of us a question one at a time, she decided that teaching us one-on-one would be more effective. Rather than answering a question for the sake of moving on, we would actually converse, slowly, addressing each of our French needs personally. She also provided me with worksheets to help expand my vocabulary. I felt somewhat more inspired to learn French and make the effort to speak it. Only a little, but it was a start.

Our workshop that day also netted us a reward in the form of a trip to Trois-Rivières to attend an improv show. Anne woefully informed me it was in French, but tried to lessen the blow by insisting the group had been known to do the occasional sketch in English. It was a marginal consolation, but I didn't let that get me down.

I loved the zany antics on the popular improv show *Whose Line Is It Anyway?* and hoped the entertainment that night would be similar. I knew that much of improv was physical anyway, comedy delivered via expressions and gestures. I wondered if perhaps the improv actors could have turned our communication workshop earlier that day into something funnier and more lighthearted than what it had been. It had the perfect makings for an entertaining sketch—props, misunderstanding, escalated frustration. These guys needed to run our next communication workshop.

Thankfully I was right and managed to enjoy the silly scenes that were performed. It was a huge relief to find that humour managed to transcend language, as I was able to grasp most of what was happening on stage. Even Luke's translation of the scenes or key lines surprisingly managed to retain the efficacy of the punch lines or gags. To top it all off, the last scene was performed in English depicting a hyperbolic mockery of the expensive costs of stereotypical American lifestyles. The exaggerated impersonations were hilarious to listen to, especially with the hint of thick Québécois accents underneath them.

The genuine hilarity of the show wasn't a big surprise. Quebec drew many comedians from across the country who would eventually find success on the *Just For Laughs* stage in Montreal. It seemed only natural that the communities of entertainers surrounding Montreal would breed funny with such a famous comedy venue nearby. Watching the wild and unscripted antics take place on stage reminded me of my high school drama class and acting with Bailey and Courtney. Behind my laughter was a pang of homesickness.

We were back at a Shawinigan Elementary school, our second time volunteering there. The first was assisting in a winter fun day for the students. Outside across the school yard, different winter sports and activities were taking place. Though it wasn't an official activity of the day, I found myself watching a group of young children making a snow fort. The weather had been cold and dry lately, creating a hard, crunchy top layer of snow. The kids had stacked broken chunks of this rigid snow to make walls high enough that they towered over the adorable engineers. I was impressed by their winter architectural skills and even helped lift the smaller children up to place chunks on the higher parts of the walls, watching for any precarious leaning, in case the icy structure fell on top of them.

Minding that particular group of kids hadn't been a part of our volunteering duties for the day, but I enjoyed doing so. I didn't even need to speak French with them. Once the mixed group of children learned I could barely speak their language, they quickly became entranced by the out-of-place adult anglophone amongst them. Some of the brighter children started pointing at random objects or miming actions to help us swap translations. The unexpected language lessons were cute, and although it was encouraging to know that I was helping teach a second language, it was embarrassing that my learning had to be done with children as my teachers.

For our second visit to the Shawinigan elementary school, however, my groupmates and I were inside, helping out for a kind of "food awareness" day. Not as many volunteers were needed that time around, so only Tiffany, Erica, Bethany, Valérie and I went. The coordinator of the event was a grizzle-bearded teacher who looked like he should have retired from teaching ten years ago. He showed us different table stations set up around the perimeter of the school gymnasium. There was a breadmaking station with bowls containing dough of varying levels of gluten, a snack table filled with assorted vegetables and a homemade yogurt dip, and even a trivia table with a spinning roulette wheel that determined what questions the children would get asked. There was a plethora of activities for the students to learn about healthy foods.

Erica babysat the kids with their sticky hands in the bread bowls, Bethany and Valérie covered the quiz game, and Tiffany helped out with snacks. Because I couldn't speak French very well, it was thought best that I did not man a station alone. Rather than bother the irate coordinator of the event any further, I opted to float between the tables and help the girls however I could. They all had a good handle on their stations though, and insisted they didn't require any additional assistance. I didn't want to annoy them by getting in the way, so I went elsewhere. At another station was a volunteer juicing vegetables and fruits to provide the kids with healthy drinks. She didn't look like a teacher and made me wonder if she was one of the student's mothers who volunteered for the event. She understood enough of my French to figure out I was simply another volunteer, one who currently had nothing to do. As slow as her station appeared to be, she allowed me to help her peel carrots. Finally, I was being helpful.

The coordinator from the morning noticed me helping the woman and came over. He asked me something in speedy French, but the look of sheer confusion I gave him clearly indicated that I did not have the answer he was looking for. I hadn't understood a single word and didn't know where to begin in responding. The woman I had been helping heard whatever he had said, but did not translate. After a curt exchange between the two, the coordinator said no more and just walked away.

When all the carrots were peeled, I thanked the woman for letting me help and walked over to Bethany's station. She was standing at the table alone, informing me that Valérie went to the bathroom. I asked Bethany if the coordinator seemed to mind that I was simply floating and helping out where I could.

"No, he don't mind. He just tink you don't get along wit us. Dat you have like ... social problems? Or some ting like dat." Apparently not understanding French was on par with lacking basic social skills. His observation didn't seem entirely off base.

The food awareness event was a success. It was well-attended by plenty of excited kids who had behaved exemplarily from what I saw. With the exception of peeling carrots with a complete stranger, my feelings of uselessness were at an all-time high and no one around me seemed to care. It was another quiet van ride home when Anne picked us up. I stared out the window and let the girls describe to Anne how the event went in French, incomprehensible gibberish to my tired little brain.

The feelings of loneliness and isolation that had been haunting me were more prevalent than ever, and not just because of the solo volunteer situation that day. I wasn't *performing* with my group. I was simply there, an extra body in the room wherever we volunteered, and even that felt hollow. It was like they were all participating in the program beside me, not *with* me.

The combination of missing Ashley, missing home, and longing for a more active role in the group left me feeling tired and irritable often. Even though I caught myself most of the time before my anger became noticeable, I didn't seem able to recharge or bounce back to normal. I was barely present at house meetings and more often zoned out, waiting for them to be over. Agenda items discussed were either completely spoken in French or I had just stopped paying attention at all. I never knew what was said anyway. I was so exhausted from trying to understand French that it felt like my brain was being pulverized underneath a dirty boot whenever someone spoke to me in a language that stubbornly refused to stick. How Carlos and Jess seemed to be coping left me in the dark just as well. As our 72 hours approached, I felt more and more hopeful that a good break from things might shake me out of my funk and that when it did, I might have the energy to somehow connect with my group afterwards.

There was a frantic rush when everyone returned from work on the eve of our 72 hours off. Participants were running in and out of the bathrooms and bedrooms to pack. Luke's dad arrived at the house to pick up me, Luke, Erica, and Valérie. We had driven half an hour down the road and were about to connect to the highway when Valérie realized she'd forgotten her wallet at the house. No wallet and no ID meant no bar. I bit my tongue at the delay, even though I specifically asked if everyone had everything before we left. The constant routine of coming-and-going with so many people had hammered into me a habit of always double-checking whether people had what they needed, because someone would always forget something. We called the house phone and thankfully Carlos was still there. He was willing to bring it to Montreal and would connect with Valérie later to pick it up. With that situation resolved, we continued on. An hour later, we were in the heart of Montreal in a neighbourhood called *LaSalle*.

Luke was eager to walk us through his old stomping grounds. We passed by a video store to see a friend of his, a park where music festivals were held in the summer, and the restaurant where Luke had his first job. Even away from the core of the city, the streets of Montreal were busy and lively, not slowing down as evening came: pizza shops, bakeries, laundromats, grocery stores with boxes of fruit and vegetables laid out beneath awnings, historical churches on street corners right across from buzzing vendors—Montreal was alive wherever we walked. Even the simple diner Luke took us to had a story.

"Trust me Devon, you can't leave Montreal without trying *au jus* smoked meat," he told me, assuring me the diner we were in had some of the best in the city. It was my first time trying the signature sandwich and was indeed satisfying and filling, a hearty meal in preparation for another first that would take place that night. On the way back to Greg's apartment where we were staying, we stopped at an SAQ liquor store to buy alcohol. I skimmed the shelves and coolers containing a vast array of bottles and cans of beer, liquors, wines, and spirits. There were too many choices and I couldn't decide what I wanted. Gin. Vodka. Beer. Brandy. Whiskey. I'd just have to grab something and see whether I liked it or not. Wanting to avoid jumping into any drinks exceptionally strong and potentially dangerous, I grabbed a six-pack of something called Rev. The light blue liquid inside the clear plastic bottles seemed as good a choice as any for my first legally bought alcohol.

Back at Greg's apartment, we began to play a competitive game of Quarters. Even though I had never played the classic drinking game, I still knew the rules having watched it unfold at parties. Erica and Valérie didn't seem to mind losing against my and Luke's admirable coin-bouncing skills. We finished our *Au Coq* rotisserie chicken take-out dinner (the au jus sandwich hadn't been enough) and waited for Greg to return from his work. He was our tour guide for the night and had offered to take us to the strippers.

"I'm telling you, Devon, Montreal has some of the most beautiful women in the world!" Luke assured me once again, forgetting the previous times he had already told me. He was very proud of his city, something I could appreciate what with all he had shown us. Montreal by day was incredible, but now I was going to see it at night. Valérie and Erica were even willing to join us on our dirty journey.

"But only if we're drunk," Erica said. "If I'm going to watch you two get dirty stripper tits shoved in your face, I need to be liquored up." It was a prerequisite that didn't take long to fulfill. The four of us took one last shot of Erica's whiskey before we left on my first drunken adventure.

CHAPTER 24

April 2006. Saint-Élie-de-Caxton.

Our 72 hours off had indeed been fun. While we had not seen or done everything Luke had set out for him, myself, Erica and Valérie in that short timeframe in Montreal, we had definitely enjoyed ourselves. Thoroughly. Drunken times were had, many stories of which (but not all) we shared with the rest of the group once we got back to the house. The brief vacation had indeed helped release some tension, but after three weeks of more regular, almost boring Katimavik programming afterwards, there was still a lot of "storming," and the usual stresses of confined living quarters reared their ugly heads again. Our allotted Katimavik vacation days for that rotation might have been used up, but we all needed another bout of respite.

Thankfully, that opportunity had come again. It was time for the lightning round. The mid-season twist. It was that kink in our routine that we desperately needed not only to shake things up, but as a way of giving everyone a break from, well, everyone.

It was billeting time.

Our bags were packed, but unlike in Sault Ste. Marie where our billets picked us up, Anne was going to drop each of us off, but not before pumping us all full of sugar first, like a doting aunt sending her nieces and nephews back to their parents.

Sugar shacks—*cabanes à sucre*—were an iconic Quebec activity. All the Québécois in the group had been to a sugar shack before and wouldn't stop telling the rest of us how amazing they were. Their comments left me eager to visit one.

"Just imagine maple-flavoured *everything,* Devon," Luke explained. He wasn't kidding.

Our tour guide met us in a forested area just a short drive outside of Saint-Élie. The woman also just so happened to be Luke's soon-to-be billet mom. She led us to a small wooden shack amongst a grove of maple trees. The trunks of most of them were already tapped, the beginning stages of syrup production. The plastic buckets at the base of the trees already had about an inch of liquid at their bottoms. It would be two or three days before the buckets were swapped out for empty ones. The full ones would be brought into the shack. The interior of the small building was sweltering, but the dozen bodies of young volunteers crammed inside didn't help. If it wasn't for the chimney-looking extension sticking out from the roof with tin slats to allow for ventilation, it would have been hotter than a sauna. Our tour guide explained what the different large metal apparatuses around the shack were and how they were used to boil, evaporate, and otherwise create a thicker, more refined finished product.

Ushering us back outside, we saw a display had been set up, filled with a variety of foods for us to sample. They were all soaked, sautéed, spiced, or somehow flavoured with maple syrup. Ham, eggs, hot dogs, pancakes, pudding cake—everything had the sweet taste of maple, overpowering or subtle. All the food was delicious, a testament to the craft of the chef that whipped them up, but in my opinion, some of it could have gone without the maple flavouring. My favourite, however, was a classic maple staple of the *cabane à sucre* that I had somehow gone my entire life without knowing about. Maple syrup was poured into small impressions made in fresh snow. Using a Popsicle stick, you rolled the cooled and congealing syrup up into a lickable treat called *tire d'érable*. Our guide assured us she had taken her time finding the purest and freshest snow. Spring was beginning to arrive, so it was difficult to find snow that didn't have dirt or debris in it. Her effort was appreciated, but not surprising. Québécoise take syrup very seriously. Bethany reamed me out one day when I (foolishly) commented how real maple syrup tasted similar to generic brands.

"Dat stuff eez shit! It is *not* da same!" she argued defensively.

After a few meals of pancakes with the real stuff, I later agreed. I learned a lot of syrups in grocery stores are not maple syrups, but in fact maple "flavoured." Even after an authentic tasting, however, I still wouldn't put the classic Canadian condiment on my eggs.

Once our tour of the sugar shack concluded, we crammed back into the Katimavik van. We weren't going home though. One by one, every participant was booted out onto the doorsteps of their respective billet homes. There were no drawn-out goodbyes.

I was dropped off in front of a two-story home in a suburb that looked to be part of a new housing development. There were only six houses I could see spread far apart along the road. I lost my bearings as Anne drove us through new parts of Saint-Élie/Mauricie, beyond the parts of town that we had walked or explored. I was unfamiliar with the area and had no idea where I was.

"He's expecting you," Anne said as I stood awkwardly in the car bay of the unsuspecting home. Armed with that little bit of information and little else, I grabbed my bags and knocked on the front door.

"Come in!" I heard someone yell, surprisingly in English. "You must be Devon," a bald man said when I poked my head around the corner wall of the foyer. He walked over to shake my hand. "Come, leave your bags, join us."

I had arrived at Louis' home in the middle of the English class which was taking place in his kitchen. It was the last class with his students, a small group of energetic Québécoise women in their thirties and forties. The gaggle of women were excited to practise their English conversational skills with the new young boy who would be living under Louis' roof for the next two weeks. They spoke English quite well, with only a few of the older women struggling to find the translations for words or phrases they wanted, a testament to the success of Louis' informal but effective lessons. I didn't have much to say to the ladies, aside from the well-versed regurgitation of where I was from, what Katimavik was, and what I was doing while I volunteered at the park. I remained mostly quiet while they cackled and crooned, boisterous behaviour encouraged by the drinks in their hands.

" Louis, donnez le garçon un verre du vin ou de la bière!"

"Ahh ahh! En anglais!"

"Boy! You drink wit us, yes!"

I politely declined. I had a few family members that I was used to seeing knock back a few and get a little rowdy, but this was new territory. I had literally just met Louis and wanted to make a good impression. Although I swear I could still taste the alcohol from my 72 hours in Montreal, those three days had left me confident I could control myself from drinking too much, as well as my behaviour while under the influence. Regardless, I suspected these were the kind of women that weren't shy about filling a cup with more than you wanted.

Louis and his wife Charlotte had two young daughters, eleven-year-old Noémie and seven-year-old Gabrielle. They were as adorable as little girls come. I was grateful they spoke English exceptionally well which allowed us to talk about cartoons or their time in school. Kids were easier to relate to compared to drunken Québécoise cougars.

Once I felt like I had satisfied my due diligence of introductory pleasantries, I excused myself to my room. I decided to take a nap before we went out for supper that evening. When it came time to wake me up, Noémie and Gabrielle thought it funny to stand at the end of my bed and quietly whisper my name louder and louder until I finally rose from my dead sleep. It was rather cute, especially when I feigned anger as I whipped off my blankets and chased them down the hallway and downstairs, both girls playfully screaming all the way.

After a dinner of pizza that night, we attended a hockey game. I was unaware that Louis had so much planned for us that evening. Unlike most Canadians, I wasn't a big hockey fan, but kept my mouth shut so as not to impose on the abundant hospitality he had shown in such a short time. I was surprised to find Rosalie present in the spectator stands as well. Apparently Louis was friends with her billet family and the two of them had planned the night out for us all.

As the players warmed up, Rosalie and I swapped stories from our first day of billeting. It was hard to ignore my pesky billet sisters making kissy noises behind us. I turned around and gave them empty threats in my paltry French. It was hard to be intimidating in your second language.

"Arrête! Maintenant … S'il vous plait ..." The sternness in my voice was lost as I cracked a smile at their innocent playfulness, but they relented and let us be.

The hockey game ended with fewer bouts between players than I hoped. I may not have cared much for hockey, but I loved a good fight. It was the weekend, so Noémie and Gabrielle were dropped off at one of their friend's houses for a sleepover. I thought we were returning home ourselves, but was mistaken when Louis pulled the vehicle into a parking lot and brought us into a bar.

"What kind of beer do you want, Devon?" he asked me once we sat down at a table. Again, I politely declined the offer from my billet. I simply didn't feel like drinking. He awkwardly offered me tonic water instead. It tasted like carbonated bitterness, but I said nothing so as not to insult his offer. More of Louis' friends arrived and sat with us, commencing the same predictable question and answer routine I'd done a hundred times already.

"Hazelton, British Columbia."

"Between Terrace and Prince George."

"Saint-Élie."

"At the park."

"Painting. Lots of painting."

I could tell I wasn't being the most social individual. I didn't mean to be rude, but I couldn't seem to find the enthusiasm to elaborate on my answers. The jump into billeting had happened so suddenly that I wasn't appropriately receptive to the kindness of the family who had taken me in. My mind began to wander, and even though everyone in my group had been more than ready for billeting, I was already starting to miss them.

No one asked any more questions of the quiet kid at the bar table and continued chatting like good friends. And even though they spoke in English, I rarely joined in.

Maybe I should have had that beer.

It wasn't a movie I cared to see, but the girls were excited for it. All the movies at the Cineplex were playing in French, so even if there was one I'd been itching to see, everything would have been lost in translation.

Noémie, Gabrielle, and I watched *Eight Below*, a movie about lost sled dogs in Antarctica and their owner's desperate struggle to reunite with them. The more I thought about it, the more appropriate the movie seemed for me. It was mostly about dogs and dogs didn't speak French, or at all for that matter. I heard part of the movie had been filmed in Smithers on Hudson Bay Mountain, the next town over from Hazelton. I watched the aerial shots of the opening scene closely hoping to catch a glimpse of a recognizable part of a highway I'd been on over hundreds of times. I didn't spot anything familiar, but watching the film made me homesick anyway.

My billet sisters may have also been excited for a movie about sled dogs for more personal reasons. Their father owned eighteen sled dogs himself and ran a small tour business in the winter. My interaction with the pets was unfortunately minimal. Louis was very particular about feeding and socializing with his dogs. He recruited my assistance only a handful of times over the course of billeting to help fill the aluminum food bowls for the hungry, but lethargic, dogs. The running season was over for them. The snow was melting with the warm weather and most opportunities to try dogsledding were long gone which left me disappointed. I had never gone dogsledding before and it was something I would have loved to have tried. Still, billeting allowed me other new experiences.

I enjoyed spending time with my billet sisters. Having grown up as the baby in my family with two older brothers, I never knew what it was like to be the mature one. It was a new experience to socialize and care for someone younger than you, even though the sisters were quite mature for their given ages. It also meant I had to be careful with my actions and words, lest the two girls were more impressionable than I expected, but that wasn't a problem. It was surprisingly easy to relate to Noémie and little Gabrielle: we watched cartoons together, played card games, and usually did whatever the girls felt like doing. I was a temporary guest, so I might as well be a fun one, or at least a helpful one.

I was reading in the living room when they came to me for help one day. They smiled brightly and asked me sweetly to help them get a kite down that they had tangled in a power line outside the house. I felt like an older brother and obliged. Having an extra person to play with or help out was probably something different for them as well. The family lived in a rural area with neighbours far and few in between. If the girls wanted to have a sleepover, they needed one of their parents to drive them to their friends' homes far away. Noémie and Gabrielle were busy given their age, often needing to be dropped off or picked up at soccer practice, dance, or something school related. This did leave me a few occasions of being alone if Louis and Charlotte were out for a date night or visiting friends. Having the house to myself allowed me the chance to work on planning something exciting for not just our group, but Shawinigan and Trois-Rivières as well.

Billeting might have changed our living arrangements, but the status quo at work remained, with one exception: Erica had been given permission to drive the Katimavik van so that she could pick up those of us who lived relatively close and drop us off at our respective workstations at the park. The others were dropped off in the morning by their billet families, some of whom also worked at the park.

A freak snowstorm one night left me and Luke plenty of white stuff to shovel from doorways and sidewalks the next day as instructed by Étienne. The physical labour we were often tasked with was simple but satisfying, but our work was still staggered and sporadic. When we thought we would be giving a wooden box a second coat of Varathane that we had painted the previous day, Étienne would instruct us to paint a metal railing instead. While that dried, we had to move lumber. One day, electrical breakers were inexplicably blowing and leaving us in a blackout, so we were instructed to take an extra-long break because Luke and I couldn't paint in the dark. Étienne rarely explained why we were moved from project to project when we asked.

"*Parce que*," he would reply bluntly before going back to his chewing noise. We finally noticed one day that Franc never actually chewed gum. It was just an odd quirk of his you couldn't help notice, one of many.

Luke and I would usually take our break in a computer room where Étienne could easily find us when there was work to be done. When there was ample downtime, we got creative and found ways of entertaining ourselves.

"We're clear." Luke came back from peering around the hallway. "They're taking their lunch now."

We were in the mechanic's shop. Various pieces of industrial equipment lined the walls. Some of the equipment flattened things, some cut things, and others drilled things. We didn't know what half of the tools did, but we had used the paint mixer several times as part of our job. The first time we used it, Luke joked about using the machine to shake up a can of pop. We had both seen *The Simpsons* episode where Bart shakes Homer's beer with a paint mixer, a prank that ended with disastrous results. Given the opportunity, we had to try. We had low expectations that it would work that way in reality, but we were curious nonetheless. More to the point, we were bored.

I purchased a can of Coke from a nearby vending machine that, despite its dust-covered surface, was stocked regularly. I brought the pop over to the paint mixer. The machine had faded from its factory green finish after years of use. Luke carefully turned a lever to raise a platform normally reserved for larger cans of paint. It took a lot of turns before the small can was finally secured tightly, sandwiched between the platform beneath and a plate up top. We donned safety goggles like the brave pseudo-scientists we were and turned on the machine. We ran the mixer for a minute before shutting it off, wanting to ensure the bubbly contents had been thoroughly shaken up. Luke lowered the platform while I removed the can with intense care, like I was transporting an unstable container of dangerous chemicals. With both of us in deep anticipation, we took the can outside the bay doors to open it to avoid any spills or carbonated explosions. I held the can away from my body, my face flinching in preparation as I slowly pulled the tab.

KACHEWsssss ...

There was a quick fizzle and then… nothing.

Not exactly nothing, but the experiment was definitely a flop. Shaking the can of pop by hand would have yielded a more explosive reaction. Luke and I were very disappointed. We weren't expecting anything comparable to what a cartoon might have depicted, but surely something slightly more exciting. At least we had given it a try and could provide a dramatic telling—or outright lie—when everyone returned from billeting.

I was excited when Louis told me they would be bringing me along for a family trip to Quebec. "The city, not the province," I explained in my emails to friends and family back home, but I suppose that went without saying when you lived here. Sometimes geography denoted those little nuances. Back home in BC, if you told someone you were going to the island, it could be Haida Gwaii or Vancouver Island, depending on who you were speaking with and where at the time. The same could be said about explaining you were from "up North." Telling that to someone from Burnaby would get you a different reaction than someone from Fort Nelson. I wondered if Americans had the same problem regarding Washington state and Washington DC. In any case, I was thrilled to be part of the family trip to the namesake city which pulsed with history.

We drove through the quieter suburbs and past the occasional church or random building that looked more noticeably aged than those around it. Most of the older architecture looked like it held some grand historical value which could be talked about at length if you found the right francophone to spill the wealth of knowledge he held. As rich a history as there was to learn, we wouldn't be seeing much more of the province's capital. It was Louis' father's birthday, and as I eventually inferred, this was more or less a family visit.

I connected surprisingly quickly with the ageing senior when I was introduced as the newest and temporary member of my billet family. Not only was Louis' father familiar with Katimavik, he had actually *met* Jacques Hébert, having the pleasure of introducing him at a fundraiser in Shawinigan more than twenty years ago. He showed great admiration for the founder of Katimavik which led to an enjoyable discussion between the two of us on the value of hands-on volunteerism. I might have even been more social and talkative with Louis' father than Louis himself, though if only because of the passion we shared. I was grateful to bond and connect with someone through my billet family, although it certainly helped that he and his wife spoke English. Their age and life experiences must have taught the two geriatrics to speak slowly and concisely, conversational attributes I had grown to miss dearly after so many failed attempts to strike up a conversation with devout francophones.

That evening, we met up with Rosalie's billet family once again. They were also visiting Quebec City. Rosalie later informed me the two families were related, that the fathers were not jovial friends, but in fact brothers. I was embarrassed and felt guilty that I still seemed to be missing key details in plain sight. With that relationship explained, it made much more sense that everyone was staying at Louis' brother's home that night. The parents went out for dinner and drinks while

Rosalie, the kids, and I were allowed to order pizza. It might have also been an enticing bribe for the two of us to babysit the children, including Rosalie's own billet brother, Marcel.

Shortly after the parents left, Noémie and Gabrielle asked to go swimming in the apartment's outdoor pool. Rosalie and I sat comfortably in lounge chairs and watched the two girls jump and splash around, but twelve-year-old Marcel had no interest in aquatics whatsoever and remained in his room playing video games.

"He plays in the morning, he plays during the day, he plays at night," Rosalie complained. "He barely talks and isn't very sociable. Hey, he's like you and Luke!" she chuckled. I knew she was joking, but I rebuked her comment nonetheless. I explained that while Luke and I enjoyed our games, we still interacted with our group. Gaming was a hobby that we were passionate about, but we weren't absent or ignorant to what was going on around us. Intermittent escapism was one thing, but extreme detachment was another. Luke and I had both heard stories of people who were guilty of this and knew that level of addiction was an unhealthy form of gaming. Rosalie apologized, but her sincerity was questionable when I caught her rolling her eyes.

The parents were still out after Noémie and Gabrielle were done swimming, so Rosalie and I ushered them to get ready for bed. They were surprisingly agreeable and went about their routine. Marcel, meanwhile, still looked heavily invested into his online computer game and hadn't moved an inch since we left him. He wasn't part of my billet family, so I left Rosalie to deal with him. Being a bit older than the pair of girls, I assumed Marcel had a later bedtime. Either way, I knew he had plenty of time anyway. The last week and half had proven Noémie and Gabrielle were not the quickest at getting ready for bed.

I could hear the sisters begin to bicker behind the locked door of the cramped apartment bathroom over who needed to brush their teeth first when I heard the front door of the apartment open.

"We're home!"

The parents returned. Louis and his brother stumbled through the doorway a bit, embarrassing their wives at having drunk a bit more than expected over dinner. Charlotte didn't seem particularly upset, stabilizing her husband with a loving hand on his chest. It must not have been the first time he and his brother had done this.

"Thank you both for taking care of the children," she said to me and Rosalie, insisting they had been no trouble. "Maybe you two can go for a walk if you'd like and get out of the apartment for a bit, hmm?"

We took her up on the offer and left. Along some unfamiliar but well-lit streets, Rosalie and I continued talking, catching up on topics that we hadn't discussed much with the kids around. I was surprised to find ourselves touching on things that neither of us had shared much of with the group: homesickness, our own personal excitement for Corner Brook, the odd relationship between her and Carlos, and of course, the one between me and Ashley.

As I explained to Rosalie, it had been two weeks since I heard anything from her, phone call or email, leaving me ricocheting through a spectrum of feelings. We had gotten over the hump of emotions and both expressed a desire to stay in touch, but Ashley's lack of communication usually left me feeling disappointed and hesitant to call her first. Back at the Katimavik house, I was constantly calling people—family, friends, and on occasion the Shawinigan or Trois-Rivières group. It would have been nice for someone to reach out to me for once. I *wanted* to be wanted, and more so, I wanted Ashley to want me to some degree, to carry on what we had, even if we were… whatever it was we were. Friends, I guessed.

But distance be damned, the least she could do is make an effort.

Upon Rosalie's and my return to the apartment, the adults hadn't slowed down one bit. An open bottle of wine was sitting out on the kitchen table and boisterous laughter filled the apartment. Rosalie and I were both offered a drink, but respectfully declined. Our walk had been longer than expected and tired us out.

"Okey dokey," Louis said with a noticeable slur to his speech. I wished them all *bonne nuit* and took advantage of the empty bathroom before Rosalie could hog it, as I knew she was apt to do after having lived with her for almost half a year.

My sleeping quarters were in the spare room where a cot had been set up next to the family computer. It was the same computer Marcel had been gaming on.

"He must have finally been told to go the fuck to bed," I thought. I couldn't blame the kid. I might have done the same thing.

As a result of living outside in the outskirts of Saint-Élie, my billet's internet was spotty. It took several minutes before I saw anything load on a web page and was slow enough that I eventually gave up on checking emails. Instead, I checked my email on my work breaks at the park where the bandwidth was much faster and I wouldn't waste much time waiting. I still anticipated emails or updates from Ashley in my inbox, but they never came. Whenever I did finally receive an email from her, my short half hour lunch breaks never afforded me enough time to properly craft a response that sufficiently explained how my French rotation was going or how I was still missing her.

Charlotte had mentioned earlier that I could use the computer if I wanted to. Now that Marcel was off, I figured I might as well while I could. Zipping through my emails, I saw the name attached to one that I craved so much to see. I opened Ashley's email, but as I scrolled down the wall of text, I saw it was longer than her typical emails which were normally short but scattered with thoughts and ideas in a flux of coming and going. She did the same thing when she spoke, one of the little idiosyncrasies I realized I missed about her.

I abruptly closed the web page before my own doubt and habit of second-guessing could spiral out of control. I didn't want to revere her email like a love-sick puppy, but I did want to read it when I had more time. A lengthy email from Ashley filled with her adorable, if scattered musings, might provide some comfort and make her feel like she wasn't so far away.

I was dropped off at the home of Luke's billet family rather than returning to my own after work one day. The two of us were to give a presentation about Katimavik to a Scout troop that his young billet brother was a member of. It was one of the promotional activities required as per our public relations committee. We expected it to be easy. By now, Luke and I knew the ins-and-outs of what Katimavik was about and what these activities demanded: go in, hype up the program, encourage kids to look into it when older, high fives all around—boom, done by dinner.

Scouts are known for embodying many virtuous qualities: helpful, friendly, courteous, obedient. But these kids were fucking *psychotic.*

Luke and I stood in a community hall and watched as twenty or so Scouts kicked, screamed, punched, grabbed, wrestled, bit, and committed other acts of violence against each other.

The zoo of prepubescent French wildlife also included Luke's billet sister, Gabrielle. Only a few years older than most of the boys who were somewhere between eight and twelve, she was holding her own and wrestling several of them at once. I didn't know what kind of relationship Gabrielle had with her younger brother, but he and his friends appeared to be both afraid of this tween girl, yet bravely eager to piss her off. This madness seemed to be the norm as few of the Scout leaders showed any signs of concern. Eventually, the kids were brought to order as Luke and I began our presentation. While Luke spoke his part, I could see Gabrielle quietly threatening some boys who weren't paying attention. Luke had mentioned a suspicion that his host sister had a schoolgirl crush on him. I didn't know if she played the bully card as a way of garnering Luke's affection, but I couldn't deny her effectiveness in bringing about a semblance of strained order to the room.

At the conclusion of our question period, things quickly descended back into chaos. Once we were done talking, the kids no longer needed to listen. They pounced on each other like animals that had been at heel but were now overwhelmed by vicious instinct. The Katimavik pamphlets we had handed out were littered across the floor and tables, destined to be torn apart by the untethered Scouts. I was about to consider the event a wash until I saw one young boy pick up a pamphlet and flip through it. Even some of the Scout leaders themselves expressed some interest in Katimavik, being closer to the age where they would have to begin thinking of a plan after finishing school. Surely their vast experience in wrangling chaotic groups would serve them well in their applications.

After the Scout's hall was tidied, everyone received some authentic maple toffee. I didn't think the kids warranted any sort of treat for their appalling behaviour, but I was fully aware from Katimavik dinners that full mouths were usually quiet ones. I didn't have much of a sweet tooth at that time and politely declined a second treat. This almost seemed to upset the Scout leader handing them out. He couldn't fathom why I wasn't ecstatic for more toffee. I made a mental note, reminding myself once again that Québécois really, *really* loved their maple!

When I returned to Louis' later that night, Noémie and Gabrielle were asleep. Louis and Charlotte were out for the night, so I thought it was a good time to check the email I had received from Ashley the other day. The internet connection was excruciatingly slow, but I had all night. Fifteen minutes later, the email was there in its entirety. I read through, savouring each sentence as Ashley explained what had transpired in the past two weeks during her own time billeting.

She had been in the same boat as me in that her billet family didn't even have a computer, but she still felt bad that she hadn't spoken to me. Further to that, Ashley was mad at herself. I continued on, reading how she blamed herself for what happened—or didn't happen—between us.

"*It's not the first time I've confused people by what I've said or even how I said it,*" she wrote. She described how her indecisiveness had a habit of leaving her depressed, sometimes to the extreme in feeling that she didn't deserve anyone to love and if she did, she would eventually hurt them.

"*I feel like I'm psycho sometimes, do you know what I mean?*" she wrote.

I did. Sometimes the biggest frustrations weren't in what you were feeling, but the inability to express that confusion in a relatable manner to others. But Ashley admitted she had been struggling to break out of her shy shell, and our kiss was a small step in doing so. As disappointed as I had been with how things had turned out, hearing her version of the story made me feel oddly honoured and proud to help someone grow into a better person. I quickly shushed the comedian in the back of my head suggesting that if that were the case, I should kiss more people.

If someone could benefit from a situation that had otherwise caused me so much stress and anxiety, maybe it was worth enduring.

CHAPTER 25

April 2006. Saint-Élie-de-Caxton.

There were no tears when I left my Québécois billet's house. I actually had to coax Noémie away from a sewing project she was working on just to get a hug goodbye. Considering I hadn't been the first Katimavik participant to billet with the family, she might have gotten used to the experience of strangers living with them and then leaving, but I hadn't. I accepted the temporary arrangement for what it was though. Billeting was over, and as necessary as it was for the group, I was excited to return to our Katimavik house back in Saint-Élie. By evening, everyone from the group had returned and we'd found ourselves back in the living room sharing the highs and lows from our two weeks away. The transition period was brief and it wasn't long before we were back into the full swing of things, including new volunteer opportunities outside of our regular work at the park.

Our first post-billeting volunteer gig was a long 12-hour day at an ice rink in Shawinigan. Everything involved setting up for a large show that was going to showcase lots of performances—figure skating, belly dancers, even a boxing match between the provincial champion and a rising contender. I never did find out exactly what the event itself was that involved such a diverse arrangement of entertainment. Answers varied depending on who I asked, but after a while I quit inquiring, falling back into the habit of merely doing what I was told. For the day, that entailed hanging curtains, stapling drapes from a stage, and setting up long strands of lights.

I had hoped that billeting would have refreshed group relations, but that didn't seem to be the case. We were quickly back to our usual routine and attitudes, myself included. Quicker than expected, I found myself easily frustrated: Rosalie and Erica spoke French, leaving me unable to participate in their conversation; Tiffany snapped at me when I asked her to hand me a nearby hammer; and Carlos huffed and puffed at any little thing I said. I didn't know if I was the common denominator, but I found myself leaning towards working alone whenever I could. If someone asked if I was mad, I no longer pacified them with ambiguous answers, but instead answered succinctly and honestly, the result of which was their avoiding me. Rather than tearing down walls, I was right back to putting them up. There seemed to be nothing I could do about it short of lying about how confusingly frustrated I felt, which seemed to be for no good reason a lot of the time. I hoped billeting might have provided me some clarity or improved my mood enough to be approachable and repair relations, but it hadn't. I didn't know what to do except try to put up with people, but I knew the reality was they were putting up with me.

The long day of volunteering hadn't been enough for Anne though. She must have spent the two weeks away from us setting up different all-day volunteer gigs, a mission to keep us busy and occupied. Sometimes this meant pulling us away from our regular workplaces at the park in order to help out elsewhere. I didn't know what arrangements she had with the park regarding our volunteer placements, but it made for a very irregular schedule.

Even so, we didn't mind volunteering for things when it got us out of town, even if it was for all-day commitments. The following week, she set us up for a volunteer gig in Montreal. Not only did it net us a full day away from working at the park, but gave us another chance to return to the beautiful city that so many of us had fallen in love with during our 72 hours off. As we drove past the last few houses of Saint-Élie and made our way to Montreal, I quietly joked with Luke in the back of the van.

"Luke, do you miss painting at all?"

He stifled a laugh. "Hmm, let me think about that." He exaggerated a ponderous expression. "Hmm, nope, I think I'm good. Guess painting will have to wait!"

That particular trip to Montreal served a double purpose. In addition to volunteering, we were also going to tour the Katimavik Head Office.

"So this is like, *the* Head Office?" I asked to confirm, lest it turned out to be some satellite office or something other than what I envisioned in my head. "Katimavik Headquarters? Where the big kahunas who sign off on our excursions work?"

"Yes, Devon," Anne said with a slight chuckle. "The same place."

Most of us were surprised when we arrived in front of the unsuspecting cement building across the St. Lawrence River. Outside, there were no colourful, boisterous signs that suggested inside was anything other than a boring, bland, multi-office workspace and not the epicenter of Katimavik, filled with the people responsible for putting us where we were right then. The first indication we were in the right place (aside from Anne's annoyed reassurances) was when we walked past a hall with a large glass sign on the wall: "Katimavik. Bureau du Quebec/Quebec Office." The green and orange colours on the sign alone invoked the same spirited energy of the thousands of Katimavikers whose applications were processed just beyond the frosted glass doors of the entrance, beckoning us inside to learn more.

It was exactly what I pictured.

Katimavik Headquarters was not a soulless office filled with stuffy cubicles and miserable paper pushers hunched over desks. Easily visible beyond the front reception desk, the bulk of the Katimavik office space was spread out across an open floor with high ceilings. Instead of square cubicles, employees sat at wavy desks arranged in flowing patterns, their tops all decorated with colourful toys, knick-knacks, photos, and personal items that showed the employees had interesting lives. Every wall was adorned with some sort of artifact from past Katimavik groups: large-print posters of smiling participants, a quilt woven in the shape and colours of the Katimavik logo, collages and murals depicting tokens of appreciation from a host community. The employees themselves appeared as vibrant and enthusiastic as participants themselves. No one within eyeshot was wearing bland office attire, but had instead adopted a more casual dress code which seemed to have the desired effect: everyone was keenly typing away at an email or talking on the phone with soon-to-be participants, PLs and PCs, billet families, work partners, and program funders. Whatever task they were doing at that time, I suspected they were proud of the work it was contributing to.

I heard it was common for Katimavik employees to be former participants themselves, which didn't surprise me. Diverse, passionate people, united in a goal and willing to work together to achieve it? Throw a couple years of work experience in there, and you've got yourself the ideal staff. There might have been different departments, but everyone there was an important cog in keeping the massive machine that was a national volunteer program alive and moving. This was an office as unconventional as the program it ran, an alternative option for youth pressured to figure out what they wanted to do at one of their first major crossroads in life.

We were introduced to Madelyn and Carter, a pair of smiling co-workers in their late twenties. I recognized their names as the two Katimavik employees I had communicated with as part of the interview and pre-departure stages before leaving Hazelton. When we introduced ourselves and where we were from, I was ecstatic to hear Madelyn had remembered me from our conversation on the phone despite likely having spoken to hundreds of participants since then. There weren't a lot of participants from Hazelton, a detail that seemed to have distinguished me. I found it to be a pleasant, if peculiar joy to match a face to a person you had spoken to six months prior, even if that interaction was brief.

Much to our disappointment, however, Madelyn informed us that there was no single employee tasked with putting a Katimavik group together. It wasn't in any one person's job description to play the role akin to the Harry Potter Sorting Hat, selectively choosing unique individuals from across the provinces of Canada in an attempt to reflect our country's demographic distribution. The placement of participants with each other was the result of a computer program, the decision process more or less random except for a few key pieces of information factored into the mix. We had no one to thank—or blame, depending on who you asked—for the assembly of our group.

After our visit to the mysterious entity that had been Head Office, we drove directly to our designated volunteer gig for the day. In true Anne fashion, we remained out of the loop as to exactly what it was we were doing until we were already there. Rather than concerning myself with what to expect (or because I simply might not have been paying attention earlier), I decided to roll with whatever was to come. I was also pleasantly distracted by the colourful façade of the building we entered once we found a parking spot in the busy downtown core of the city. The Montreal Convention Center was decorated with a rainbow mosaic of glass panels that adorned the western side entrance where we came in. A bright April sun illuminated the grey cement stairway we walked up to reach the upper floors, filling it with bright colours and warmth.

"Ah, you must be the Katimavik group." We were quickly met by a youthful coordinator once we walked into an open lobby area. "Here, let me show you what we're doing today."

Between two sets of narrow staircases leading up to the next floor were several large tables. On tables sat piles of black backpacks, another pile of various printed information pamphlets that needed folding, and on the last were stacks of small magazines with a title I didn't recognize. Our job was to form an assembly line that would fill the donated backpacks with information packages, pens, pencils and other knick-knacks. The backpacks were to be distributed to high school students at another event the following day by other volunteers, an event which we wouldn't be part of. Some of those same volunteers who would, however, joined us that afternoon. They were surprisingly not a Katimavik group, but student volunteers. I had to briefly remind myself that Katimavikers didn't have a patent on volunteerism.

Once friendly introductions were out of the way, all those present spent the next few hours assembling the backpacks. Me and several of the students walked around the tables grabbing one of each item and stuffing them into the empty backpacks which were then deposited onto a cart to be rolled away to be stored elsewhere. Though it was a bit monotonous, everyone was jovial and in good spirits. The promised reward of pizza also helped. I wondered if Henry Ford could have increased productivity levels if he had embraced the power of pizza for his workers.

Once the pizza boxes and tables were both empty, Anne gave us a free hour to explore downtown Montreal before we drove back to Saint-Élie.

The spring weather had been surprisingly warm and very welcome those days. The bright sun highlighted a lot of the vibrant graffiti painted on the sides of large brick walls, between alleyways, and sometimes even on the streets themselves. Everything seemed like a canvas in Montreal, an exciting city where there was always some display of artistic creativity: stained glass windows around Place Des Arts, a mural of an evil-looking chicken off of René Lévesque Boulevard I deemed "Ze Devil Coq", even the panoramic view from the top of central Mont-Royal looked like it came straight out of a painting. The city was filled with beautiful combinations of art and culture in a variety of forms. If it wasn't an installation of art that demanded a long second glance, it was something else that was grabbing your attention: there were jazz festival, comedy, buskers, musicians, parades, religious celebrations, business sales, protests, marches. There seemed to always be something going on in the city, something that would stir the emotions of a wandering passerby, be they tourist or resident. Montreal was a place where everyone had an interesting story to tell, whatever their medium.

Easter arrived at Saint-Élie. Jess celebrated by making us a pancake breakfast. As we sopped up the puddles of *vrai sirop d'érable* on our plates, she cleared her throat.

"There's an Easter service at the church next door," Jess said sweetly. "I kind of want to check it out. Would anyone be interested in joining me?"

"I would," Erica said, kindly gathering the empty dishes from the table.

I was surprised. Jess' Wiccan might have been a Pagan religion, one that believed in many gods, but Erica didn't strike me as religious whatsoever. I expected her to sooner scoff and wax atheistic pragmatism rather than indulge Jess of all people. Whether it was the breakfast sugar high or a shared curiosity, we all agreed to attend with the two of them out of support and solidarity. I went primarily because of curiosity as to what those wafers that represented the body of Jesus really tasted like. Dry and bland I found out. Carlos insisted that if I wasn't Catholic that I shouldn't be eating the communion bread. Despite my protest that I wasn't there to offend, he was decidedly pissy for the remainder of the morning when I tried it anyway. The pageantry of the service was beautiful, scripture beautifully spoken in the French language, but I was left bored and spiritually unenlightened at the end of it all.

With the last bit of energy at the tail-end of the day, Luke, Rosalie, and I went for a walk. Notwithstanding the relatively drama-free church experience that morning, we three acknowledged that group relations still remained rocky, and not just on account of me. Hearing this helped relieve a bit of my anxieties.

"You and Carlos still don't like each other, huh?" Rosalie confirmed. "Why? Why is that?"

I did not have an answer. The reason for that remained a mystery. In fact, the friction seemed to have grown between the two of us. Any time we found ourselves having to speak to each other, it wasn't long before things escalated. Our verbal fights had grown increasingly prone to turning into sweaty wrestling matches. By the end of them, we were both too tired to sling insults at the other.

According to the unabashed gossip from Rosalie, Erica and Bethany were also still an item. They would hide themselves away at any opportunity for privacy and always sat together during group activities. If one was ever called out or picked on at a house meeting for whatever reason, the other would be quick to jump in and defend.

And Jess was ... well, Jess.

Tiffany had been the most vocal with her annoyance. While Tiffany's baseline mood seemed to be mild anger at everyone those days, it was tolerable, but Jess got the brunt of it. Tiffany vowed that if Jess pissed her off enough, she was going to speak her mind or punch her in the face. Knowing the feisty New Brunswick girl already had little filter to begin with, this made us worry that Tiffany would likely follow through if she and Jess ever had to work together unsupervised.

Luke grew noticeably jittery when we brought up the Jess problem. He lacked subtlety in his facial expressions and clearly had something to say. His moans of frustration gave that much away, something Rosalie and I both noticed. Normally I steered away from drama, but I was already an unwilling participant in the conversation. Given the topics that had already been discussed, my hands were dirty; if I was already getting wet, I figured I might as well jump into messy waters.

Refusing to let Luke keep whatever little secret he was holding onto, Rosalie and I prodded him to spill his beans. He finally caved with an exasperated sigh.

"Jess… cuts herself."

Luke told us her confession with great unease. We knew Jess could be depressed. It was something she occasionally voiced during house meetings, but we brushed it off. We were all a little homesick and depressed, so her words weren't shocking. Hearing the details of what Luke knew though, we immediately expressed a concern that Jess might be suicidal. None of us had the training to confront that kind of situation.

A sullen dullness grew over the three of us as we began to walk back toward the house. We suddenly felt powerless to change anything with the new information. Our response of simply "putting up" with someone, including Jess, now seemed like a terribly poor way of handling things. We had all tried in some capacity to get along with Jess and all of us had failed. But she was still part of the group and we now felt some responsibility to do *something*. There was a truly roiling pot of mixed emotions, leaving a bitter taste in our mouths that made us feel like shit for the next few days.

After spending the better part of a morning and afternoon helping Luke's former billet family clean up after their final maple syrup harvest one day, Anne called us into the living room for a surprise house meeting. Once everyone had settled onto the couches, Jess stood up.

"I'm going home," she informed us, looking around the room. Jess didn't seem filled with confidence per se, but she certainly wasn't shying away from news that was clearly difficult to deliver. "I've got some family problems at home that need to be sorted out. And although I've learned a lot from living with you guys for the past six months," she started to tear up, "I just can't stay here."

A few of us looked around the room to see the others' reactions. We didn't know whether Jess really had problems back home or if she was lying, but whatever the true reason was, we went along with it. There was a restrained sense of elation, but we all bit our tongues and offered kind words.

"You'll get to see your family!"

"You can make money! More than three bucks a day!"

"No more excursion plans Jess! You can just *do* the things you want to!"

The recent issue of a member of the group harming herself seemed to have resolved itself. I only hoped genuinely so.

Even though no one had bonded with her as much as others in the group, we didn't wish any negativity on Jess and gave her the appropriate pleasantries. I couldn't tell if our well-wishes were fake or sincere, but I think we all agreed that Jess deserved clarity, good friends, and happiness. The unfortunate reality was she wasn't getting those things from us. It created a bitter feeling in my gut that suggested that maybe she wasn't the problem, but *everyone* else was.

Whatever emotions I knew I'd have to navigate, there was no denying that Jess' decision to quit Katimavik appeared to lift a lot of weight off everyone's shoulders, including her own. She was extra huggy in her last few days with us, but we let it slide. Jess didn't seem so uptight anymore and neither were the rest of us, leading to the last few days with her more enjoyable than they'd had been before. Whether the shift was intentional or situational, attitudes were refreshingly and noticeably better.

Even so, there were goodbyes on the day Anne drove our former groupmate to the airport, but no tears. The only exception was Jess'.

Spring was quickly making its way to Quebec. Everyone inside the Katimavik house was ready to break free of the winter doldrums that had dragged us down. We were ready to see Saint-Élie-de-Caxton emerge from beneath its snowy cover. It was hard to tell whether it was Jess' departure that brought about a much-needed change or the progression of seasons. Had she been a magnet for our shared frustrations and her new absence dusted off stale group dynamics? Or was it the vitamin D from the bouts of sunshine that gave us a childish glee in seeing grass emerge from the melting snow on the ground? Whatever it was, I had a welcomed vigour, a pleased gladness for the improved relations between the group that seemed more affable and slightly less explosive those days. I felt like I'd reclaimed much of something that had been lost. I didn't know if anyone else felt quite the same, but I didn't want to keep it to myself. I wanted to spread those feelings and share the good vibes I was having those days. And I had just the thing:

The Katima-lympics!

I liked the way it rolled off the tongue when it first came to me. Out of all the other words and phrases we had thrown the flexible Katima-prefix onto, that one sounded the best. The idea had been brewing for a while, but it was during billeting that I really started putting pen to paper. I planned out the games and events that teams could compete in, how scoring would be done, time and material costs, and even the possibility of having it count towards a committee activity. If it qualified, we could use some of our budget towards it.

Part of my passion for my new idea was because I finally had something to contribute to house meetings. I didn't need to speak French with people at visitor centres, reception desks, or businesses. This was something I was capable of doing, and I took great pride in it. I was easier to get along with when I talked about my plans because I was exhibiting a passion and enthusiasm that had been buried. I felt more like my optimistic and energetic self, like a deflated balloon filling back up to its original shape again, slowly but steadily. And most of all, it was another excuse to bring the Katimavik cluster together, this time to little ol' Saint-Élie. Many of our one-off volunteer gigs took place in the larger cities of Shawinigan or Trois-Rivières. As much as we enjoyed our trips to our neighboring communities, we wanted to share Saint-Élie with those groups for once. Being the smaller of the three, however, we had less to offer. Anne was in support of having them come to us. Not only had she voiced a concern about overspending on our fuel budget, she was also getting tired of the long drives. Considering how much planning I had invested into the event, it was comforting to hear the consensus of support for the Katima-lympics amongst my group. I wanted it to be a great success.

When the big day arrived, everyone was brimming with excitement. The Shawinigan and Trois-Rivières groups screamed with rousing enthusiasm when they exited their vans in our muddy driveway. They were in awe at the beauty of our little town and the size of our house when they poured in through the kitchen entrance. The mood was electric with impatience to see what crazy events I had in store for everyone. I couldn't keep everything a secret though. I had to divulge some information about the event and games. In order to turn the Katima-lympics into an approved excursion for Shawinigan and Trois-Rivières, they required certain information. Thankfully it was an easy enough excursion plan for them to write as none of the events were dangerous or risky. They also weren't contingent on the weather.

I planned for most of the Katima-lympic games to take place outside regardless of inclement weather. Everyone still hoped for a break from the days of rain we'd been having in time for the event, but in true Katimavik fashion, that wasn't the case. For brief moments that morning, it rained harder than some of us had ever seen! The weather showed no signs of letting up, but that wasn't going to stop us. My optimism must have worked as everyone remained committed to participating in the events with full gusto. I did, however, rearrange some of the events so we could begin with the indoor ones just in case the rain subsided later in the afternoon.

The first event was the burping contest. Chosen "athletes" had to chug a can of pop and let loose their best belch. It was odd to have people drinking carbonated beverages so early in the day, but the rush of sugar and caffeine and the infectious laughter at the deafening burps woke everyone up even more.

Next, teams swapped out their pop-chuggers for new athletes in the blender food competition. Every group brought a food item to contribute to the communal container that would be blended and consumed: peanut butter, mustard, marshmallows, corn starch, stale bread, soggy lasagna noodles, and as a *pièce de résistance*, fried pork tongues. It was only for this game that I set a flat set of points to be awarded to participants and their team who swallowed a complete spoonful of the awful concoction. This prevented those with an iron stomach from abusing the system and racking up unlimited points. It didn't stop Ryan from Trois-Rivières from chugging the nasty blend, successfully grossing many of us out.

Even after lunch, when we continued the remainder of the games outside, the rain still refused to let up. The next event involved standing on a bucket and avoiding water balloons being thrown by opposing team members. Even though everyone seemed to enjoy it, the appeal soon waned. Getting hit by water balloons while standing in the rain just didn't have the same impact as having it happen on a hot summer day. Furthermore, few balloons were popping. The wet rubber slid off the wet bodies of those Katimavikers being pelted. The balloons were still fun to throw, but it lacked the same satisfaction as soaking a dry target.

The remainder of the games were received just as well. Plenty of rain, but with equally as plenty laughs. This continued into the afternoon as we made our way into the closing ceremonies. As a way for us to celebrate the end of the Katima-lympics, I requested each team to bring a cake. The snack allowed me time to tally up the points to declare a winning team. As much planning as I'd put into the games, I had neglected to consider how difficult it was to judge. I considered electing the three Project Leaders as judges, but I wasn't sure they would understand the games and their criteria for victory. It also left the door open to bias and the likelihood of them judging in favour of their own participants. Considering I was the one who had planned the Katima-lympics and had the best grasp of the games and how they were played, everyone agreed that I would be the most neutral party to act as judge. Despite my insistence that I would be as neutral and fair as possible, I quickly found out how difficult this was. Every event had someone contest my decisions.

"His burp was longer, but ours was louder!"

"We should get points because we had fewer people!"

"He dropped the ball for longer than two seconds!"

I reluctantly wavered in some of my decisions, but in the end, I decided to firmly put my foot down and decided it was a three-way tie between all the teams. Few accepted this decision but I insisted it was true. The points really had been that close, although I downplayed the discrepancy between different scoring methods I had devised. The calculations hadn't been as straightforward as I would have liked, which meant there was likely a margin of error, the grounds for which many challenged my decisions. Some participants understood why I had come to the decision I did, accepting the necessity of the "everyone-is-a-winner" approach.

Thankfully, the burning desire to determine the true winning team was soon extinguished with the sugar crash from the cakes and the need for teams to return home and finally dry off.

The three groups had vastly enjoyed the event, which was what I was most concerned about. Content with the success, I would remember to be more bold and resolute in future decision making. I was sure there would still be plenty more times in my life where I'd have to make tough choices and would need to stick to my guns.

CHAPTER 26

April, 2006. Lake Rosée.

Saint-Élie rained itself out shortly after the Katima-lympics. The change in seasons couldn't have been more evident or welcomed. The storms helped wash away much of the snow piles which continued to shrink with the warmer temperatures and the sunny days that took their place. Saint-Élie wasn't the only thing changing scenery though. Once again, our bags were packed and loaded into the van. Our group was leaving the Katimavik house for the next three days.

We were going to camp! The regular kind, not rotation.

Staff at the camp on Lake Rosée needed help preparing for the upcoming spring season of campers. We were filled with chatter on the drive there and shared some of our fond childhood camp experiences, but Anne felt the need to put on her PL hat.

"I know you're all excited, but keep in mind that you're not there to have fun. You're supposed to be helping."

She wasn't wrong, but considering the details we were told beforehand, I disagreed. Camps were fun places! We could enjoy the fresh outdoor air but without the struggles of traditional camping. We weren't sleeping in tents, but indoor bunk houses (that we likely had to clean, but still). Rather than cooking as house managers or even outdoors over an open fire, our meals were going to be cooked for us by the staff we were assisting. Our needs were met. Even if it was another volunteer gig, most of us expected it to feel less like work and more like a vacation.

Once we arrived and settled into the bunkhouses we would be staying in for the next few days, we were quickly introduced to the skeleton crew responsible for getting the camp ready. Bobbie was the camp cook. While we were busy lifting and moving various things, the jolly young man was busy in the kitchen, stocking the freezers and fridges, but also making our meals during our stay. Cute, rosy-cheeked, and bespectacled Savannah was coordinating paperwork and performing inventory. Christoph, the caretaker, had been there the longest, probably longer than the other two adults had been alive. He had seen hundreds, maybe thousands of kids enjoy the camp he worked at. He spoke very little English, but was patient and understanding in the midst of the clueless Anglophones. I managed to pick up on his occasional joke, something I had often failed to do with monotone Étienne. We were to help Bobbie, Savannah, and Christoph in whatever they needed. Bobbie and Savannah needed to dive into their own work before they could figure out where best to put us, but Christoph already knew exactly what needed to be done on his end. We gathered around the seasoned man who began delegating tasks in broken English.

"Need *deux*," he said, holding up two fingers. He then flexed his arms in an exaggerated muscle-man pose. "*Deux* tough, strong people. Move heavy tings."

"Devon and Erica," everyone else said at once.

We both looked at our group, incredulously.

"What the hell? Really, guys?" Erica protested, sharing my attitude.

We didn't drag out the debate and delay work any further. Erica and I were used to being offered up for such tasks. Luke was a big guy, but didn't exactly have a fit physique and Carlos was a bit shorter than me. I was far from muscular, but I was no stranger to physical labour. As for the girls, Erica was certainly the more rugged out of timid Bethany, feminine Rosalie, or squishy Valérie. Tiffany would have been helpful, but she was the loudest among the people who volun-told us. *BC Boy* and *Alberta Girl* would once again do most of the heavy lifting.

And lifting is what we did for the most part. Christoph instructed Erica and me to move several boxes out from a large garage in order to access canoes that had been stored at the far end. The long, cumbersome watercrafts hadn't been hung from the rafters or stored on any sort of shelves over the winter season. They were simply piled lengthways atop each other. Once Erica and I carefully pulled each one out onto the grassy lawn, we loaded them into the back of Christoph's pickup truck, which he drove a short distance down to the lake shore where we unloaded them into the water. Christoph thought it would be faster and more efficient if we moved the canoes across the water rather than moving them directly to the dock with his truck. The access road from the garage to the docks on the other side of the lake was pitted with holes and craggy rocks exposed from the recent rains. Floating the canoes across the lake circumvented the need to tie the canoes down with rope to prevent them from falling out of the truck from the bouncy drive, rope Christoph couldn't find anyway. His pickup truck was also the only one at the camp which would be needed to transport large, heavy things elsewhere. Erica and I were content with the tactics at hand. It also meant a relief from additional heavy lifting.

Once all the canoes were out of the garage and bobbing in the water next to each other, we tied each end of them together with rope, creating a train of canoes that we paddled to the dock on the other side of the lake. While Erica and I paddled the lead canoe across the water, dragging a line of connected canoes in tow like obedient children holding hands, we couldn't help gloat as the rest of our group watched us from the lake shore, jealous of the "work" they had a role in giving us. If we were going to work hard, we were going to play hard, suckers!

No one else had the chance to gleefully paddle watercrafts like me and Erica, but eventually we all got our own chance to play hard. The campground was well stocked with fun things to do. There was an archery range, rock climbing tower, mud pit, obstacle course, trampoline, and even a picturesque bridge across a small inlet of the lake that extended into the forest that surrounded the northern half of the camp. When we were done with our work for the day, we were given permission to use the facilities so long as we were careful and left them in a clean condition. But we were helping to open the camp the next week. Equipment needs to be tested, *mais non?*

The three days we spent helping at the camp never seemed like work. For every bit of jealousy we felt for how much fun kids would soon be having there, we were equally glad to know that our help was necessary to get things ready so they could have those memorable times. It reminded me of the camp our elementary school would go to every second summer. It was nowhere near as equipped as this one, but I still had fond memories nonetheless. Our camp leaders usually consisted of parents volunteering as chaperones, my own mom included. The fun ones would let the students in their groups stay up late, sneak in junk food, and have conversations late into the night in the cabins with your friends after a day spent swimming in the lake, playing games in the fields and the forests, and singing feet-stomping chants in the covered mess hall. I wanted the kids attending this camp to make those kinds of memories as well.

I must have shown exemplary work ethic as Christoph trusted me enough to let me drive the camp quad for some of our other tasks. It also probably helped that I was also the only one who had ever driven one. For most of the morning on our last day, everyone raked leaves and loaded them into the small trailer hitched behind the quad. When the trailer was full, I would drive it out to dump into a shallow pit in the forest away from the camp. Every time I did, I brought someone along for the ride and would secretly let them drive back just before we came into eyeshot of everyone so it seemed like I did all the driving. The girls were ecstatic with the rebellious opportunity, especially Rosalie who was very nervous. I repeatedly reminded her to go slow and use the brake in case she suddenly forgot where they were when the time came to use them. There were no incidents.

The sunny weather and satisfaction over a job well done had left us all quite amped up. Everyone wanted to do something crazy and fun before Anne came to pick us up from camp later that afternoon. We decided to do a polar dip in the lake. Lake Rosée was freshly thawed, the last remnant of floating ice having literally finished melting that morning. No one expected the temperature to be anything but freezing, but the brave polar dip was our own way of celebrating that spring had indeed arrived. I was amazed at how committed everyone was to jumping in when it was first suggested—everyone except for Carlos. Knowing how stubborn he could be, we didn't bother trying to convince him to join us and jumped into the cold lake with the expected high-pitched squeals. As we lumbered out of the frigid water like stiffened zombies, Carlos stood on the shore edge, calling us all "poo-sies" sharpened by his Colombian accent, berating us for not staying in the water longer. He ran away when we threatened to throw him in the water fully clothed. Choosing not to join us was fine, but mocking us while he sat on the sidelines pissed us off more than we expected.

Our group was saddened to leave when Anne arrived. Most of us had expressed how it had been our most positive experience in our Quebec rotation thus far. The courteous staff, the excellent food, the enjoyable work—all of it felt like something we needed those days. I wasn't sure whether we needed time to let those good vibes sink in or if our upcoming excursion to Quebec City would keep them going. It would be one of the bigger trips that rotation. I would just have to go along with the plan and see.

Even while walking through downtown Quebec City, we couldn't escape the presence of Katimavik. As Anne parked the van outside the Museum of Civilization, we noticed a bunch of kids our age screaming and waving at us. The surprise wasn't that they were another Katimavik group, but one from Ontario! French rotations in Katimavik didn't necessarily have to be in Quebec though. Sometimes they took place in French communities in anglophone provinces. The notion that Canadian French communities existed outside of Quebec was novel to me, but people assured me it was true. The group from Ontario took this one step further. As part of their excursion, they had driven a very long way to the epicenter of French-Canadian culture.

Quebec must have had a stronger attraction to Katimavikers than I expected. While we were perusing a quaint candy shop, two random girls approached a few of us and asked if we were in the program. They had noticed our group earlier when we were watching a street mime. His body and clothes were completely covered in gold paint, and his rhythmic dance and juggling entranced the captivated audience. And not a minute later, we ran into the Trois-Rivières group! We hadn't spoken to them since the Katima-lympics. By sheer coincidence, they were also on an excursion to Quebec City, something they must have neglected to mention in passing conversation. One of the Trois-Rivières participants explained everything on their itinerary they were expecting to do and see, including several museums, a visit to a celebrity hall of fame, and a tour of a chocolate factory! It all sounded more thrilling than what we had planned.

I had appreciated the work Carlos and Rosalie had done in planning our excursion to Quebec and all the sights to be seen and places to visit, but we always seemed to be in a rush, running late to be somewhere. It was a struggle to find parking, which meant meandering was minimized. If I found myself enjoying an exhibit or viewpoint, it was inevitably cut short. While I was still stunned by the beauty of one of the oldest cities in Canada, it wasn't enough to deter the mood from turning increasingly sour over the course of our trip. I intrinsically knew my attitude was selfish, but I felt like a tourist. Less than a tourist even, as I had no control. We went where Anne drove us, got out where planned, and were given a negligible amount of time to look or see or observe or learn. As much as I tried to enjoy our excursion, I was just along for the ride.

Our final activity for the night was bowling. It had nothing to do with Quebec or French culture, but was merely a fun activity tagged onto our excursion plan. I wasn't finding it fun though. I couldn't seem to hit any pins, which was unrelated to my dour mood, but served to make it worse. By the end of our first round of ten-pin, I was gutterballing almost every time and just wanted my turn to be over. There was no rhyme or reason to my attitude. I was pouting like a silly child. I knew this, which upset me more. Not knowing exactly why I was grumpy meant I didn't know how to respond to the few people who noticed. I didn't want to ruin what was clearly a fun activity, or the entire excursion itself, and bit my tongue into a frustrated silence so I could suffer alone. For all intents and purposes, the collective attitude was better than before: things weren't perfect, but our group functioned, jokes were still cracked, and we accomplished our tasks during volunteering gigs. Hell, we were currently enjoying one of the biggest excursions planned during our French rotation, except for me. Katimavik was happening right before me, whether I liked it or not. I observed these things, but it didn't feel like I was part of them, merely present. Why couldn't I get on board and feel the way I knew I was supposed to? Why did I feel bitter and miserable instead? I thought I was making progress.

What I did know for damn sure was that I didn't want to feel the way I did. I wanted to get better but didn't know how.

Luke was house manager again, this time partnered with Tiffany. That meant I was painting alone. Painting had grown tiresome by then, even before I had to do it solo. I felt like I had learned as much as I could—or cared to—about proper brush stroke techniques, how much paint was too much for a roller to spread onto a wall without dripping, and the short-term effect paint thinner fumes had on Katimavik volunteers. Within the first hour that morning, the small wooden brush felt like lead in my hand. I wanted out.

"Étienne, I need a change of pace from painting, *s'il vous plait*," I asked, hoping my pitiful addition of French might soften the little paint elf up. His mood had always been difficult to tell, even as he chewed his invisible piece of gum, slowly pondering my request. I held my tongue waiting for his answer.

"... Ok," he finally responded. "I talk to someone. *Attend ici*."

I waited per his instructions. Étienne returned quickly.

"You go with Gilles. *Vide merde de chauve-souris*."

We met Gilles in the lobby. He was a rotund man with a large moustache. I had only seen him a few times around the park, occasionally taking a break with Étienne. The two of them spoke without a word of English passing between them. They spoke in their thick Québécois accents quickly and casually, their words weaving into each other far too fast for me to catch anything. I didn't care. Wherever I went, I wouldn't be painting.

When all was said and done, Gilles began to walk away. Étienne waved his hand, ushering me to follow my new co-worker. I followed, getting into the passenger seat of a park truck outside that Gilles started up, driving us down a dirt road for half an hour. Mud was beginning to seep through the softening snow making an ugly mess of the roads. Gilles and I said nothing. I wondered what we might be doing so far away from the main park building I had grown accustomed to working at. I tried to remember what Étienne had said, if there was anything in his conversation with Gilles that I might have understood now that I had time to think back on it.

Wait, did Étienne say "merde?" *Didn't that mean…*

I spoke up.

"Gilles, Étienne didn't tell me what we were doing," I said, hoping to coax the man into telling me details of our work, any details. He said nothing though. The large man simply turned to me and chuckled to himself, smirking behind his bushy moustache.

"*Parle pas anglais*," he said quickly. I heard that phrase enough times to know exactly what he said, even if it was in French.

"Well shit. This is going to be fun." I glanced over at him, driving the road without a care in the world, enjoying each bump along the way. Both his face and his large belly pressed against the steering wheel, making him look as though he were driving to the candy store. "So, you have no idea what I'm saying right now, do you?" He looked over and smirked his bushy smirk again.

"*Comprend pas*," he shrugged.

I know. I know you don't understand.

We arrived at yet another cabin in the middle of the park. I noticed how there appeared to be the same style of cabins spread everywhere about the park. I never knew who they belonged to. I suspected they were used by rangers or maybe reserved as seasonal homes for park employees and their families, sites of refuge against the nastiest of Quebec winter storms. I scanned the inside of the empty cabin through the front door when Gilles grabbed my attention. He raised his hands and began to gesture something in what I assumed was an attempt to mime our work plan.

"Charades? This might work." I was pretty good at charades.

Gilles made a loud humming noise which I correctly guessed to be vacuuming. And the squeaking hand flailing was ...

"Not bird… no… hand? Bat? Yes! Bat!" I said ecstatically at how fast I guessed the answer. "We're vacuuming bat shit out of the cabin!" He nodded and smiled at my enthusiasm of having guessed correctly. I suddenly realized what I was saying. "Wait, we're vacuuming bat shit?"

Gilles laughed at my reaction. At least it wasn't painting.

We started by putting on painter's overalls and masks. Once those were donned, Gilles and I helped each other duct-tape our ankles and sleeves shut to protect against the fiberglass insulation we would be working around and possibly the fumes given off by the bat shit. It felt excessive at first, but I reminded myself that I was neither a bat expert nor a park expert. I had no grounds to question the need for the precautionary equipment no matter how hot it got in the rafters below the cabin roof. Upon fully sealing ourselves, we carefully climbed up a ladder on the side of the cabin and through a small hole in the outside wall, leading us into the attic. Stepping carefully over wooden beams with blankets of pink insulation sticking between them, the two of us worked diligently vacuuming up guano from the rafters, careful to avoid shingle nails sticking through the roof just inches above us. It was hot and dangerous work, but I would not give Étienne the satisfaction of hearing how I wanted to go back to painting.

Finally, it was lunch. We ate downstairs in our overalls, sitting on empty buckets flipped over to use as seats. There had been minimal talk all morning and I was itching to try to start a conversation. If Gilles and I were going to attempt to talk, the onus was on me. Though definitely weak, my French skills were noticeably better than Gilles' English. I told him as long as he *parle lentement* to me, we might understand each other. And somehow, we did.

I managed to tell my new co-worker that my oldest brother Derek had come to Quebec once for firefighting, but I couldn't recall specifically where he had been stationed. Currently, he was training to become a conservation officer and could very well end up working in a park like the one I was at. I also told Gilles about the recent Katima-lympics and the other participants from my group, some of whom he recognized when I mentioned their names.

He also attempted to share tidbits of his life as best he could. He mostly spoke about his family, his daughters, and how old they were. When I tried to explain which province I hailed from, Gilles couldn't quite follow, confused as to where Vancouver, Vancouver Island, and the provinces of BC and Alberta were in relation to each other. Had this fellow been so entrenched in Quebec provincialism that he hadn't learned something that most elementary students were expected to know? I meant no insult to Gilles' knowledge of Canadian geography, but was more surprised than anything. I was obliged to sketch him a quick map of the West coast and better answer his question.

By the end of lunch, Gilles and I managed to have a poorly-grammared, but enjoyable conversation, slightly more complex than what I would have mustered in some of my high school French classes. He would occasionally translate necessary words into French for me, and vice versa for him. That I managed to hold a conversation with a complete stranger in another language felt incredibly rewarding, regardless of the trivial topics covered. I was not a completely helpless anglophone. As long as the other person was patient and we spoke slowly, I could manage to communicate. There was hope for me yet.

Instead of our weekly French lesson, Anne had us begin work on our final presentation. There'd been plenty of chatter amongst our group on what we hoped our last rotation in Newfoundland would be like, but little talk about our transition out of our current rotation in Quebec. We started to discuss whether everyone wanted to do something similar to our first final presentation. Carlos was particularly opinionated.

"Why, why, why don't we just do the same theeng?" he cried. "It worked! Show pictures, share some stories." It didn't matter what we suggested as an alternative, Carlos refused to even hear anyone out. His constant argumentativeness had grown thin for all of us. Tired of being quiet, I spoke up.

"We're not against the idea of doing the same format as our first final presentation," I said. Hearing myself say the phrase "first final presentation" made me aware of the oxymoron, but I focused back on Carlos. "We're just spitballing ideas for something new and frankly, you're being an ass about it." I knew that would get him going, but I didn't care anymore. Telling him that to his face would mean more coming from me, the silent one in the group, than from any of the others. Carlos' response was exactly what I anticipated.

"H'okay *puta*, let's go." He threw down his pencil. The girls quickly grabbed the notebooks they'd been writing on from the floor before he and I clashed on top of them. The couches squealed against the floor as we slammed against them. Carlos grabbed my waist and tried to twist me to the floor, but I had a good grip against the aged wooden panelling in my bare feet and stood my ground. His shoulder pushed hard into my gut, so I reached down and locked my wrists into a fingered clasp under his stomach. I heaved, flipping him backwards onto the floor with a loud thud.

"Whoa!" I heard Tiffany shout. I wasn't paying attention to whether people were still watching. Usually they rolled their eyes the minute mine and Carlos' metaphorical gloves came off and walked away, leaving us to fight. But not this time.

Rosalie spoke up. "You two are always wrestling. We want to wrestle!" Even with Carlos and me in the middle of our bout, her comment left me confused. He and I didn't wrestle because it was fun; we were wrestling because we were sick of the other's shit. It hadn't solved any problems so far, but the act usually tuckered us out enough to the point that we no longer cared about whatever it was we were fighting about. Why would everyone else want to join in? Carlos and I didn't need an audience for us to sort our beef out, but everyone's sudden interest in wrestling was bizarre. The girls ignored us and began to do their own thing while he and I continued to throw each other around.

"Hey, it's raining outside. Let's go wrestle outside!"

"Yeah, mud wrestling!"

The snow on the front lawn was completely melted except for a few remaining dirty piles of it in the shadow of the fences just out of reach from the sun. The sparsely grassed lawn was covered in puddles from the constant rain that Saint-Élie had over the past few days which had turned most of it to soft mud. The next thing Carlos and I knew, there was a three-way wrestling match between Tiffany, Valérie, and Rosalie in the front yard which Carlos and I found ourselves stopping to watch. Luke walked up behind us and joined.

"Umm… what's going on?"

"The girls wanted to mud wrestle," Carlos answered with a shrug. "It was their idea actually."

"Oh."

The three of us continued to watch with an unspoken bemusement at the unexpected scene. The girls were immediately soaked as they rolled around in the mud, laughing as they playfully pushed each other over.

"Hey, do you know what would be great right about now?"

"…popcorn?" I suggested.

"Popcorn."

The three of us nodded, suddenly forgetting the stresses and precipitating event that brought us to that entertaining moment playing out on the front lawn.

Saint-Élie-de-Caxton wasn't just a tiny town that housed *Parc Mauricie* employees and their families. It was also the home of Phil Frédérique. He was a renowned celebrity in Quebec, but I had never heard of him. Valérie and Bethany definitely knew who he was, and Luke and Rosalie had heard his name a few times growing up. The hometown hero seemed less exciting for the two teenagers who grew up in urban Montreal and Ottawa where more celebrities came from. To the rest of us, Phil Frédérique was an obscure and random name, which was soon to change.

Phil Frédérique was a well-credited writer, singer, and performer. His stories were apparently a blend of fantasy and magic either about or inspired by the history of Saint-Élie where he was born. He had won multiple awards, given praise-worthy spoken performances, was a published author, and was even rumoured to be working on a film. Phil sounded incredibly successful, having made it his life's goal to let the world know about the quiet *village de Saint-Élie*. Anne had apparently been trying to get him to come over to our house for dinner for some time, but he had always been working or travelling and otherwise busy with one of his many projects. She was excited to let us know Phil was finally free from his commitments for a brief period and agreed to a visit so that we could finally meet this enigmatic man.

I did not like him.

Phil had an air of subtle smugness. Maybe it was his round glasses or how he pursed his lips when he smiled that seemed fake to me. He wasn't necessarily cocky in telling us about his various accolades, but he did request that no one take any pictures of him, his wife, or his recently born daughter. I couldn't imagine why we would. I'd never heard of this man before arriving in Quebec and no one back home would even know who he was. Most of our visit with this pseudo-celebrity was spent listening to him speak with the francophones of the group while I listened for the occasional word in English. I was more preoccupied with trying to decipher why I had an irrational dislike for the Where's-Waldo look-alike. Aside from common courtesy, I had no reason to like this man who could easily be a stand-in for an adult Harry Potter. Maybe it was the way Anne had so fondly described him to us, a performer who was revered for sharing stories about his hometown filled with mischievous elves, fairies, and trolls that pranced through people's backyards. It was easy to tell that everyone in town loved Phil. We were often asked by our coworkers if we met Phil yet as he didn't live too far from our house, just down the street really. I could now tell them, with a mild shrug in my shoulders, that I had, omitting the part where I didn't care about having done so.

Except that I did. It took me aback when I realized my dislike of Phil was actually a mask for jealousy. He had become, and continued to be, famous for sharing stories about a small town that otherwise never would have been recognized on a map for anything special. I wanted—and actually, had been striving—to do just that. Even across the country in rural Quebec, I still made it a point to tell people I was from Hazelton whenever I was asked, a habit which no longer annoyed my group but one I remained committed to. I wanted people to know. I didn't want to be another Joe Schmo from the middle of nowhere, I wanted to be *someone* from *somewhere*. Phil had achieved exactly that through a combination of historical and fantastical storytelling, but all I was doing was volunteering: moving things, changing mouse traps, babysitting kids, filing papers, boxing knick-knacks, and endlessly painting. I wanted to be proud of my hometown, but did that involve coming from a place that already had a reputation? Or did someone need to put it on the map somehow?

Phil and his family left later that night, leaving every participant a signed copy of his book. Even though my ability to read in French was better than my ability to speak the language, I doubted I would be able to make much sense of the book. I was glad to recognize that Phil did not deserve to be the target of my misplaced anger, but also confused as to where the strong desire to do good by my hometown had come from. I couldn't fall asleep that night and stared at the dark ceiling from my top bunk, dreaming awake of fictitious people wishing to visit Hazelton, the birthplace of Devon Flynn, a man famous for doing something ...

"Luke, Devon, get up! You guys are late for work!"

So much for that dream.

Our last few weeks in Quebec quickly became as busy as they had in Sault Ste. Marie. It had been a steady pace of getting driven to work, mindlessly painting, getting picked up, all sprinkled with the rush of preparing for an excursion somewhere. On our last few excursions I had managed to keep my mood mostly likeable, but the consistently rushed pace continued to bother me—rush, see, break, drive, visit, picture, snack, drive some more, attend, and then drive home. I liked that we were seeing so many things, reminding myself Katimavik wasn't about being tourists. That wasn't the point of the volunteer program. I shut the hell up and tried to just enjoy wherever we went and whatever we saw. I knew it was foolish to think making it to Corner Brook would fix everything, that a fresh start would magically change my mood. Putting the pressure on the change in scenery might even be more disappointing if my attitude didn't change, but I was confident that more time in Quebec wasn't going to fix anything either. I was ready to leave. Everyone was coping with the mounting stress of finishing excursion reports that needed to be sent to Head Office. These were a mandatory part of the excursion process, summaries of our trips that described how well we had followed our original plans and explained any deviations. In addition to these reports, we were also putting last-minute touches on our upcoming final presentation and finishing off our last days of work in various ways.

It wasn't just a rotation we were getting ready for, but a drastic change of seasons. Spring was most certainly welcomed, but we had to prepare for summer as well. Now that winter was over, there was no point in bringing our thick heavy winter jackets and boots with us to Newfoundland. The eastern province wasn't exactly tropical Hawaii, but we definitely wouldn't need snow pants, at least not for the time we were there anyway. Everyone had at least one box worth of seasonal belongings they no longer needed. Anne had found a scale for us to weigh our taped-up packages before making a van run to the post office to ship our belongings home. The girls—every single one of them, I noticed—weighed themselves on the scale.

"I put on five pounds!"

"Oh my God! *Sept* pounds!"

"Ugh, just… ugh!"

I stepped onto the scale out of curiosity. "Huh ... Would you look at that. I lost weight." I stifled my laughter. "And I'm even using one less notch on my belt. Never noticed that." The girls did not appreciate my objective observation. I jokingly referred to them all as fatties, even Valérie, the thinnest of all of us. It might have been uncalled for, but the tone of my insult was soaked with sarcasm, intended to point out the ridiculousness of how they all sounded. The obvious insincerity of my words held no ground no matter how much I pointed out I was clearly being sarcastic. None of the girls spoke to me for the rest of the afternoon.

We visited the *maison des jeune* kids to say *au revoir* one last time. There wasn't a lot of time for a visit or long goodbyes unfortunately. After some hugs and exchange of French farewells, Luke stayed behind afterwards to speak with the young teens a bit longer. As the only male in the group who could fluently speak French, he had a stronger connection with some of them. They either looked up to him as a role model or he was a figure of adolescent attraction for the younger girls.

When he caught up to us walking back to the house, he informed me how one of the younger girls cried because she was going to miss me.

"Me?"

"Yeah, dude. She called you her "*drôle anglophone*," Luke said with a bemused grin.

It was touching. Just when you think you didn't really bond with a group of people, they end up saying something like that to you. Maybe Saint-Élie *was* going to miss our group. Maybe it was unfortunate timing that our group arrived during the dead of winter and in the heat of our "storming" phase instead of a time when we could see the town and its residents for the pleasantness they had rather than the ugliness inside ourselves.

"Come. We go," Étienne said.

"*Où?*" I asked.

Étienne said nothing more when he pulled me and Luke away from our final paint job. It was our last day at our work placements in the park. There hadn't been any sort of celebration or acknowledgement, at least for Luke and me specifically. There was to be a small luncheon in a few days but that was for the whole group and was expected to be low key, according to Anne. "It's not a big thing though," she said, lowering our expectations. "It's too complicated to get all the staff you guys have worked with together. This was the best they could do." For that day, however, it remained business as usual, which meant more painting for me and Luke, until Étienne interrupted the work we'd been doing on an office wall. He ignored my question and gestured for the two of us to put our paintbrushes down. We did as instructed and followed Étienne outside where we got into one of the small park trucks and drove away down one of the many park roads.

We had no idea where Étienne was taking us. When Luke asked, this time in French, Étienne gave another vague answer.

Luke turned to me and gave me a shrug. We gave up on asking.

I doubted Étienne was whisking us away to some surprise going away party, although I'd never know with how straight-faced he always was. I don't think I'd seen him even crack a smile the entire time we worked under him at the park. I didn't mind if we didn't have a specific destination though. A drive, especially those days, was always a nice reprieve from the park work Luke and I had grown accustomed to doing. No office walls or furniture to paint, no bat shit to vacuum or shops to clean. Our supervisor was anything but lazy, but it didn't seem like we were driving to work elsewhere. Étienne didn't seem concerned with where we were going, but he also wasn't particularly talkative. The three of us drove mostly in silence. I found myself focusing more on my growing awe of the scenes of nature passing by the window.

Étienne had worked at the park most of his life. He'd seen all four seasons there, many times over. He and Gilles and others we'd worked with knew what was coming to the park and what it would look like—the arrival of something beautiful. They hadn't just seen the majesty of the park and the nature it consisted of, but they had also helped shape it, lived it, breathed it in at work and at their homes. Something had drawn them to work at the park and stay in the area and made them appreciate what was around them. As I looked out the window, it felt like I was just starting to see a little bit of what they saw. Like the rest of Quebec, *Parc Mauricie* was casting off winter's harsh hold quickly. Lakes sparkled with lively reflections on their watery surfaces. Any ice still present drifted towards revived streams that connected the lakes. Everywhere in between, trees were budding, each at their own pace, but all making clear progress that brought a smile to my face.

Others in the group had expressed similar lamentations that we'd be missing the park in its most lush and vibrant state. Our coworkers unintentionally made us feel worse when they said the same thing, voicing their disappointment that we wouldn't see the park in its peak splendor during the late spring and summer. We wouldn't see the park the same way Étienne or any of the other park staff did, and probably never would. It was an unfortunate and unavoidable park of Katimavik. In three-month rotations, participants only ever witnessed snippets of a community, never the whole. And as excited as we were for it, Newfoundland would no doubt present the same problem. Even if we could choose the season to be a part of the communities we volunteered in, there would always be something we'd miss. All we could do was share those moments, good and bad, with those around us and appreciate the beauty of it all.

CHAPTER 27

May 2006. La Pointe-du-Hameau.

"They're going to claim this is another 'team building exercise,' aren't they?"

Raking leaves was not something we expected to do during our second Rotation Camp, but no one from the three groups seemed to mind. Even though the Quebec skies were dark grey, the rain held off while we raked the wet leaves on the ground that had been revealed underneath the spring snowmelt.

The camp that hosted us for our second Rotation Camp wasn't as isolated as Poverty Lane had been. In fact, La Pointe-du-Hameau was a small *village* just across the river from Trois-Rivières and hardly seemed like a camp at all. With not just a group, but a cluster's worth of Katimavik volunteers on hand, the leaves in the field were raked quickly, leaving the participants from the three groups plenty of time to wander the area and explore.

Our debriefing workshops were much shorter than our first Rotation Camp, mostly consisting of providing feedback on our work partners and PLs from Quebec. More importantly, they prepared us for our final rotation. We were given suggestions on how to make the most of it, how to use what we had learned from the program thus far and apply it to our last three months of Katimavik. We were encouraged to continue "performing" if we were at that stage of group dynamics, or to continue working towards it. It wasn't an end goal, we were reminded, just progress.

My thoughts were more focused on the workshops during this Rotation Camp than at Poverty Lane. Ashley wasn't there to preoccupy them this time around. There were also fewer workshops than at our previous Rotation Camp, so it wasn't nearly as draining to pay attention. Most of the workshops focused on being present and listening, rather than planning or discussing. For one activity, we passed flames from candle to candle. The premise was to share something we appreciated about the rotation, passing on our personal flames so that everyone might feel enlightened and illuminated. It felt hokey, but I knew it was probably best to transition to our last rotation with some optimism. We were reminded several times that feedback was important for the growth of both the participants and the program. No matter how challenging that rotation had been for us all, it still seemed better to leave with a smile than a frown.

When it was my turn to share what I appreciated, the first thing that came to mind was the group's improvements—or at least the efforts that had been made—in regards to communicating, and not just in French. There had indeed been lots of fights and arguments amongst the group, but conflict meant we were at least facing those problems. We still had a long way to go though, and I knew a lot of it involved me figuring myself out. While I hadn't resolved most of my problems, whatever they were, I felt I would be in a better position to do so come Corner Brook. I figured it was better to deal with those struggles sooner rather than waiting until the end. With those plans in my head, I tried not to get so caught up with the future that it removed me from the present and the shared excitement the three groups were brimming with. In a few days, we would be in our new, and last, Katimavik homes.

Once workshops were over, we mostly goofed off. Knowing Newfoundland was looming just a day away, everyone had an abundance of pent-up energy. Most participants stayed up through the night playing a loud circle game of Mafia or mindlessly watching movies on a TV someone had found tucked away in one of the sleeping quarters. Others chose to sleep, taking advantage of our free time to be well-rested for our 4 a.m. shuttle bus. Or perhaps they were sick from the purple potato shepherd's pie and burnt spaghetti that had been the main course of our supper that night. I was amazed anyone could get shuteye considering how loud and heated some of the circle games had gotten. When the bus finally arrived, over thirty sleepy youth boarded quietly and settled in for the long ride to the Montreal-Pierre Elliott Trudeau International Airport. The towns we drove through were blanketed in darkness with only passing cone-shaped snapshots of them available for us to watch, fleeting illuminated scenes provided by the streetlamps overhead. Several hours later, the soft light of dusk took over and brought the world around us back into view.

Considering how little traffic there was in the early mornings, I wasn't the only one miffed with how little time we had to catch our shared flight. Our rush through gates and down hallways left little chance for even the remote possibility of running into Ashley. I had forgotten to email her and ask about her travel itinerary. I assumed that since she was also flying out of Quebec, there would be a good chance she would be going through the Montreal Airport, the largest in the province. I kept expectations low, but the thought that she might be looking for me as well put both a spring in my step as well as a reason to slow down as the three groups raced for our plane.

When we landed at the small Deer Lake Airport we were welcomed by our new Project Coordinator, Keith, and a woman from Head Office. The two of them assured us that despite the rainy weather that welcomed us to "The Rock," Newfoundland would be an amazing finale to our nine-month program. I believed them.

The Trois-Rivières group—now dubbed the Deer Lake group—were picked up directly from the airport by their new Project Leader, Sandy. She was a tiny thing with a high-pitched voice, a curly mop of light brown hair, and an adorable smile. The Shawinigan-turned-Stephenville group would be dropped off last, our group before them. From Deer Lake our chartered bus drove south, eventually passing through a valley flanked by steep cutbanks alongside the Humber River. The highway brought us upwards again until we were looking down at a busy, bowl-shaped city that overlooked where the same river we'd followed now flowed out into the Bay of Islands. We were on the West Coast of the most eastern Canadian province, in the city of Corner Brook.

The chartered bus drove us through the city's downtown core at the bottom and then back up a short hill. It turned slowly and precariously between a pair of rectangular buildings and down a narrow alleyway and into a small dirt parking lot. The driver backed up and inched forward, and then again once more.

"Sorry kids, I can't make it down that steep road there. You'll have to walk." The bus driver opened the front doors of the bus. "Don't worry, it's just down that hill and around the corner."

We bid the Stephenville participants on the bus goodbye, grabbed our bags, and heaved them the short distance to our boxy two-story house on Laites Lane. Keith and the Head Office lady had driven ahead and were standing there, waiting for us. And with them was a dimple-faced redhead named Julie, our third and last PL. She waved excitedly and gave us all hugs, reciting our names.

"It's so good to meet you all!" she said, beaming. "Just drop your bags off in your rooms before we do the whole getting-to-know-you-guys thing." Everyone rushed into the house to get out of the light rain falling on us.

"Guys have the first room on the left, girls the other two rooms," Julie yelled up to us as we stampeded upstairs. The room assigned to me, Luke, and Carlos was painted a brilliant blue with a lime green ceiling. Posters and art left by previous participants covered the walls. None of us felt any need to take them down and enjoyed the bright and happy decor they brought to the already colourful room. There were two sets of bunks on one side of the room and a single bed on the other. I grabbed one of the top bunks, while Luke took the bottom of the other bed. This left Carlos with the single. He looked across the room, watching as Luke and I began to unpack our bags, using the empty mattresses beside us as shelves.

"How is that fair for you two to have extra storage?" Carlos was quick to complain. Luke and I looked at each other in agreed disbelief.

"Because you get a bed to yourself," we said together.

"Yeah, and Luke snores!" I added.

"Wait, what? No I don't!" He did. Carlos would still hear it, but he wouldn't feel the reverberations of Luke's sleep apnea on his side of the room. It was one of the reasons I took the top bunk, to distance myself from the snores as best I could.

Julie walked by to see how everyone was settling in.

"Hey, when everyone's done, does anyone want to join me outside for some hacky sack? It's stopped raining and the sun's coming out."

We joined Julie in kicking the small bean bag toy around, learning more about her. For starters, she was quite active.

"I sometimes go for runs in the morning out at Massey Drive which you're welcome to join me on."

She wasn't just vegetarian, but *vegan*.

"You guys can still totally buy eggs and milk and meat, just be mindful about the dishes you use to avoid cross contamination. But you'll have to give my walnut burgers a try. I swear, you'll think they're better than normal burgers."

She was quite bubbly and enthusiastic.

"Sometimes I get so excited for things I forget stuff, but I'm getting better. I'm just stoked to have you guys here for the summer though! Newfoundland is so nice then!"

Julie reminded me of a younger, more concentrated version of Linda, only lacking a discernible enthusiasm for Japanese culture. No one agreed with my comparison between the two. When everyone went for a walk around town later to explore, it didn't take long for the question to come out.

"Sooooooo… what does everyone think of Julie?"

Some of the girls were hesitant to answer. Bethany was ambivalent and thought she was okay. Rosalie was a bit unsure. I thought it was jealousy, but knew to say that aloud was to dig a grave I had been trying very hard to escape. Being the youngest PL we'd had at twenty-four years old, Julie's age was a game changer. She, Sandy, and Alice, Stephenville's PL, were all just five or six years older than the participants they oversaw. The small age gap felt like it could be a hindrance or an asset in teaching and leading a group of youth. Those few extra years gave them life experience and a maturity that was helpful in fulfilling PL duties while still allowing them to relate to us without coming off as standoffish authority figures. This grey area worried Luke, the oldest participant in our group.

"She's only three years older than me Devon!" he whined with marginal seriousness in his voice. "What if she hits on me?"

"Then you win 'the game,' duh!"

This game—one of many we had taught each other and continued to play—had arisen midway through our Quebec rotation. I couldn't recall how it came about, but the repressed hormones of youth cooped up together in a house likely contributed to its creation. Hooking up with someone within your group was a Katimavik trope, almost expected even, but to do so with someone outside the group became a challenge, a mark of pride even. The idea became a game, a joke really. One of the punch lines being that if you slept with the PL, you automatically won the silly competition. It was a stupid rule which no one took seriously because the situation was ridiculous and unlikely. The girls felt it was unfair because all our PLs had been women, leaning towards a fictitious victory for me, Luke, or Carlos. Only now, that silly idea seemed plausible. Julie was the youngest PL we'd had and was attractive to boot. Her fondness for hacky sacking, light hippy-isms, and positive attitude admittedly had me a bit smitten. These characteristics made me think of her as a mature embodiment of my friends back home.

"Pft, the girls have a better chance of sleeping with Julie than you would Luke," Tiffany shot him down. I liked to think that anything was possible in Katimavik.

Before heading to bed, I checked my email and updated family and friends with my initial thoughts of Newfoundland. A personal email from Ashley contained the same thing on her end regarding her group's arrival to Elk Island National Park in Alberta. I was glad to hear from her. There had only been wafting thoughts of Ashley with all the travelling and settling in that had been going on that day. Having been reminded of the stupid game dug up buried feelings and thoughts about things that could be, as well as those that could have been. I skimmed over Ashley's email that described her group's own Rotation Camp and flight to their third and final community.

According to her email, Ashley did in fact have to fly out of the Montreal Airport. She had also hoped that we might cross paths there. I noted the time her flight left the airport and then pulled out my old flight itinerary from the garbage. I looked at them and compared the two. Our flight left the airport at 8:55 a.m. Hers had left at 9:00 a.m.

Fuck...

CHAPTER 28

May 2006. Corner Brook.

All of us were getting two jobs.

I didn't care where I worked, so long as I didn't have to paint. I hoped to be placed at the Roger's television station or the YMCA, but those both went to Valérie. My next preference was for Cycle Logic, a bike shop which put on several bike-related events around the city. That went to Carlos, whom everyone threatened to hurt if he got it. Somehow Carlos always seemed to get both his top work placement and billet choices, something he also noticed and began gloating about. I was the last on Julie's list as she read aloud.

"And Devon, you're going to go with Corner Brook Stream Development, but for your first few weeks, you're going to help out at Junior Achievement."

We didn't tour our workplaces like we had in Sault Ste. Marie. When we gave her our preferences, all we had to go off of was Julie's description of them, which didn't always paint the fullest picture. I had never heard of Junior Achievement before. After a quick search online, I learned the non-profit organization helped inspire youth business ventures, educating kids about entrepreneurship and financial literacy through different programs. Students developed confidence and skills, helping them become the next generation of business and community leaders. The organization provided a great opportunity to kids, which was one of the main reasons I wanted to work at the YMCA. Junior Achievement sounded like it would alternatively be a good fit for me, even if it was only for a few weeks.

As for Corner Brook Stream Development, it was kind of what it sounded like. It was a landscaping company with work taking place almost completely outdoors. I'd be digging up trails, laying sod, watering flowers, etc. I cringed when I realized there might indeed be some painting, but at least there would also be some substantial variety. I wouldn't be stuck inside dusty offices with everything covered by plastic tarps and a lack of ventilation for the paint fumes.

"Oh, and you'll be working with Erica," Julie added. BC Boy and Alberta Girl were once again given the tough job. No one was surprised. Rosalie would have had conniptions if she had to perform heavy lifting and Valérie would be a distraction. I wasn't sure if it would have been up Bethany's alley, but Tiffany would have fit in well, a young woman in a safety vest cracking wise with her coworkers. Luke and Carlos weren't dainty, but both seemed pleased with their work placements where they would avoid getting their hands dirty.

"One of these days, you two are going to have to do some physical labour, even more than painting, Luke," I said. "And Erica and I are going to be gone or busy house managing and you'll *finally* have to pick up a freakin' shovel and won't have a damn clue how to use it." They laughed at my empty threat.

"Oh, the trail guys don't meet here," the receptionist explained.

Julie accompanied me to the Stream Development office for my first day. It looked, well, like an office—desk, water cooler, printer, computer, the works. The receptionist at least knew who we were and why we were there. She understood why we might think the office was the place for me to go for my first day.

"No, the work crew meets at a giant green shipping container near one of the trail heads. That's where they store their tools and equipment." Looking at some notes on her desk, the receptionist described the trail the crew was working on that day and where we might find the people I would be working with. The trail network in Corner Brook was impressively lengthy, however. They could have been anywhere along it, doing any sort of project put forth by their boss, my supervisor, Bret.

"But if you're going to be working on the trails, you'll need a pair of steel-toed boots," the receptionist insisted.

Protective footwear was mandatory for both employees and volunteers of the organization, something Julie had not been made aware of beforehand. Knowing I'd need them before I could work, we spent the rest of that morning shopping at thrift stores to find a pair of steel-toed boots for me. Considering I was only going to be in Corner Brook for three months, I wasn't about to drop some hard-earned Katimavik cash on a brand-new pair of expensive boots. We only found one pair that fit. They were a bit snug, but they would have to do.

The next morning, I arrived early, easily finding the shipping container at the trailhead where the receptionist had said it would be. I wanted to make a good impression and avoid missing anyone for my first real day of work. It was 8:40 a.m. when Terry and Shawn arrived. Terry was a chubby man in his thirties with a goatee, curly hair, acne scars, and thick-rimmed glasses. He struck me as a guy who still lived in his parents' basement spending his free time playing World of Warcraft. Shawn, on the other hand, looked a bit older. I joked with him how he looked eerily like a thinner version of my dad, moustache and all.

"Oh, I dunno there, buddy-guy. For all I know, I could be your daddy!" he said with a notable uptick in his Newfie accent.

"If that's true, you have a lot of child support to pay back and my mom will fight you tooth and nail for it," I retorted. If I was to work with these guys, I knew I'd have to give out as much ribbing as I took. I wasn't some soft-handed kid who didn't know his way around a few tools. I was here to get shit done.

Shawn unlocked the sea can shipping container so we could grab what we would need for the day. Inside the large metal box was an assortment of tools and landscaping equipment lined up against the walls: lawn mowers, weed whackers, saws, watering cans, goggles, overalls. I had used a few of the larger pieces of mechanical equipment before, but some were foreign to me, leaving me clueless as to what they did. Maybe I would find out.

Our job was exactly the kind of grunt work I expected to be doing: cutting trees, moving rocks, shoveling this, raking that. Terry had work to do further along the trail, leaving me and Shawn to work by ourselves. Shawn cut down overgrown branches that hung over the trails while I picked up garbage that had accumulated over winter. It wasn't long before he was distracted by someone walking by. I assumed it was someone he knew, a friend or maybe another employee on their day off. By the time I filled up five bags of garbage, Shawn was still talking to the man. I tried to be aloof to the fact that I was almost done with my task whereas he had barely even started his, so I carried on with the other work I knew had to be done. I would soon learn that this was to be the norm.

My first day at my outdoor job hadn't been particularly taxing. It consisted mainly of trimming of shrubs and small trees with an extra-long lunch break in between, strongly encouraged by Shawn. Nonetheless, the work took its toll on me faster than I expected, particularly on my feet. My thrift store steel-toed boots were tighter than I first thought. When I pulled them off at home that evening, my big right toe was bleeding, rubbed raw from the tight inside edge. Julie was a sweetheart, but not as sympathetic as I expected when I told her.

"Sorry Devon. Katimavik doesn't exactly have a budget for shoes. If you can't wear them or find a pair that fit, I guess you'll have to work full-time at Junior Achievement then." I told her I'd give it some time before I figured out a solution. I liked the experiences my two volunteer positions gave me, especially considering how different Junior Achievement was from landscaping. I didn't want to give up on it within my first week.

"Just like the name says, we want you to 'dream big'!"

In addition to facilitating financial education programs through Junior Achievement, my supervisor, Valerie, also ran the "Dream Big" program. She explained it in further detail during her introduction to a workshop which brought both Deer Lake and Stephenville groups into the small Junior Achievement office that week. Dream Big was normally aimed at high school youth where facilitators helped aspiring entrepreneurs set life goals and teach them to develop and execute action plans to achieve those goals. Valerie had adapted the program to Katimavik's mandate and encouraged us to explore our own personal goals—dreams, if you will—and plan the steps and objectives necessary to achieve them. One of the exercises included writing a bucket list.

"How many of those items on your bucket list are you capable of doing tomorrow? In a week? A month? A year, even?" Valerie asked everyone with a slow, drawn-out inquisitiveness. The room broke into chatter over ideas, goals, and dreams. Valerie eventually quieted us down to reflect in silence and eventually translate these aspirations from thought to paper. When we were done, some of us shared our lists. Many of our goals involved travelling, having lofty careers, advancing our education, or even finding romance. At least three girls joked how they wanted to marry a rich man. A few of us almost strained our necks we rolled our eyes so hard, but Valerie wasn't bothered by their romantic aspirations. In fact, she humoured them, asking if they insisted that was truly their goal, what specific and measurable steps could they take in going about finding Mr. Right?

I was familiar with the idea of bucket lists but had never made one before. Hearing everyone's dreams made mine seem weird in comparison when I looked down at what I had written.

"Grow a garden."

"Finish Katimavik." *Well, give me a few months.*

"Write a book."

"Adopt a child."

"Marry someone I love."

My bucket list seemed almost comical, like stereotypes pulled from a movie or fairy tale. Suddenly, snagging a wealthy hubby didn't seem as silly. I bit my tongue at having been so critical. No one should mock someone else's dreams, least of all when they make an effort to make them happen. Maybe mine weren't as lofty as I first thought. What I did like was that my goals had range. They were challenging, yet achievable. I hadn't grown a garden before, but it couldn't be that hard; a book seemed like a cool project, even if it would take a while to write; and I wanted to impact someone's life, be they a child of my own or my spouse. With a few exceptions, I noticed my goals were contingent primarily on me. Was I willing to make the sacrifice to achieve them? I looked at the diverse group of people around the room. With what I knew about them from the short period of time we'd known each other, I wondered who was just writing things down for the sake of the activity and who would go on to achieve their goals and make their dreams come true. I expected the majority of what was written on the sheets of paper in front of us would never come to fruition. "Dream Big" wasn't about achieving dreams, I thought, so much as it was about planning, taking a step back and truly contemplating what it took to make something happen, whether that was through sheer determination, will power, or just dumb luck. Whatever the case, writing them down on paper was a good start. It made them tangible, visible. I had read somewhere that if you write down your goals, you are more likely to achieve them. The logic seemed valid—the more you come across that list, the more you'd be reminded of what you wanted to achieve, a kind of self-nagging reminder, I guess. Whether writing a draft to an essay, a to-do list, or a personal letter, the slow and methodical process of handwriting your hopes and thoughts was an effective start. Writing words down gave them power, certainly more than the ones in our head.

I wrote down a second bucket list, one specific to Katimavik. On that piece of paper, I scribbled down the goals that I wanted to achieve before the program finished. I thought it was a good habit for me to get into anyway. I didn't have a good memory to start with, and it seemed to have been worse those days. Re-reading some of my past journal entries during Quebec seemed to demonstrate that. I had too many fleeting thoughts—dreams, questions, worries, aspirations, desires, anxieties, fears. People would occasionally ask me why I wrote in my journal whenever they saw me writing in it on the couch or while laying on my bed. I never had a good response except for a vague answer of hoping to have an account of what I did in my past. Doing so didn't help me sort things out as much as I hoped, but it gave me some recollection of what was going on at the time and what was on my mind. Maybe journals were a link to the past, whereas bucket lists could be stepping stones to the future, a helpful reminder for present-you what past-you wanted. Knowing our last rotation would go by faster than the first, my new bucket/to-do list would help me keep track of what I wanted to accomplish before the end of Katimavik. It didn't take much time before my list grew long. By the time I was done, it reminded me how I was still working on improving relations with everyone in my group. Even if I accomplished what was on my list, it would mean little to me unless I could enjoy those things with the people around me.

Before the Stephenville and Deer Lake groups drove back to their communities after the Dream Big workshop, we urged them to join us at Cyber Zone, one of our new favourite places in Corner Brook. The owner welcomed us with open arms when he saw the extra bodies we brought with us.

"Hey guys, how's it going? Ho, geez? Are you guys multiplying? I swear there were fewer of you last time you came in here."

Jordan was in his mid-thirties but looked to be a bit older. The true blue Newfie had a bit of a gut and a hairline that was beginning to recede, but a youthful smile. He and his wife Molly ran Cyber Zone, the laser tag maze/arcade in Corner Brook, one of the first places Julie insisted we check out when we first arrived. Jordan and Molly were very supportive of Katimavik and loved having large groups of enthusiastic young people in his midst. He considered himself a child at heart, which was one of the reasons he ran the business that he did. Jordan was the nicest guy in Corner Brook and not just because he would occasionally comp us a free game of laser tag. Sometimes we would pop into Cyber Zone just to chat with him when we were bored and wandering around that part of town. We were glad to spend our hard earned Katimavik allowance at his establishment. Every $5 round was well worth it.

Amusement arcades like Jordan's might have catered to children, but he made it fun for everyone. Despite there being a "no running" rule in his laser tag maze, it was amazing the workout you could get from walking so briskly. Everyone was always incredibly sweaty from the adrenaline-filled games. The no-running rule was also in place because the laser guns were made of a hard plastic which seriously hurt if you ran into someone unexpectedly coming around the corner. We had some close calls, even at walking speeds, and could attest the rule was a good one to have. Our group was ecstatic to share this gem of Corner Brook any chance we got, especially with our Stephenville and Deer Lake friends.

"Since I gots a bunch of youse here, what's to say I throw on the cape and we do a round of vampire?" Jordan asked. "On the house!" We accepted his offer with great enthusiasm.

"Vampire" was a version of laser tag in which Jordan would quietly stalk people around the maze and shoot them. Once you were shot twice, you "turned" into a fellow vampire and had to help the main vampire hunt the remaining players. Jordan wore a black cloak which he claimed could conceal him in some of the darker corners of the maze. Several of us saw this in action through the window of a waiting area near the maze entrance where visitors could safely watch players walk by in the middle of the game. Sure enough, Jordan would hide in a dark corner just before a laser tagger would walk right by him, none the wiser until he would turn and shoot them, leaving them clueless as to how they'd missed the villain, now cackling before disappearing around the corner to prey on his next victim. The Deer Lake and Stephenville participants voiced how jealous they were that our group had such a fun place to go to.

It had been an exhausting day, mentally and physically. I was glad for it to have been in that order and not the other way around, or else people would have been falling asleep in the Junior Achievement office chairs earlier. With most of our group getting ready for bed or already there, I slumped down in front of the house computer to check my email shortly before doing the same. I was surprised to find I had received an email from Anne of all people. As far as I knew, participants didn't tend to keep much contact with their former PLs. Our parting with Anne at rotation camp had been abrupt, but otherwise typical.

I wondered what her email was about and read it with timid curiosity. Reading all the way to the end, my heart took a dive. I scrolled back up to the top of her message and read it again, then once more. I could feel the panic in my stomach grow worse every minute. All I could think of was how I had fucked up. I had fucked up real bad.

I was going to be kicked out of Katimavik.

CHAPTER 29

June 2006. Corner Brook.

I couldn't sleep.

Luke and Carlos were already snoozing by the time I came into the shared bedroom. The entire Katimavik house was sound asleep while I lay in bed, staring at the ceiling. I hoped for anything to distract me from the worry and paranoia that wracked my brain, like someone getting up to go to the bathroom or late-night chatter on the other side of walls, but there were only muffled snores and the occasional sound of someone shuffling in bed, nothing like what I needed. My anxiety finally exhausted me enough that I eventually fell asleep. I woke up with a gut-wrenching pit in my stomach though. There was no rationalizing the situation I was in, no justification. I had simply fucked up, which made me feel worse.

When Katimavik groups rotated to a new community, other groups would take their place. Unlike those in a cluster who would occasionally work together and eventually rotate together, we would never meet the groups of participants that Linda and Anne would end up with. That wasn't to say there couldn't be interaction with them. Before leaving Sault Ste. Marie for our first Rotation Camp, I wrote a letter for the next group to arrive after us. I thought the idea would be fun and maybe even helpful to have a perspective from a fellow participant, someone who'd slept in the same house, worked in the same places they were likely to work at, and had the same PL they'd now be living with for the next three months.

I did the same thing before we left Saint-Élie. In that letter, I wrote about the large Katimavik house, filled with its own unique history. I mentioned places in the town to visit, interesting people they might meet, brief information about billet families that I had gleaned from other's experiences, and of course what living with Anne was like. My intention was to prepare the participants who would replace us so they could avoid the pitfalls and challenges that we had endured during our time in Saint-Élie. Corner Brook had already made a wonderful impression on me, but I still would have been thrilled to come across a letter of my own and would have welcomed any advice on how to make the most of our final community, a plan that was very much in place even before we'd even arrived.

The new group in Saint-Élie found the letter. I had left it on my old bed where it couldn't be missed. They read it aloud at their next house meeting, but according to Anne's email, their reactions upon reading it were not what I'd hoped for. The participants did not find the contents of the letter amusing, but instead made them uncomfortable about their PL sitting in front of them. Anne was embarrassed and humiliated after having heard my description of her, describing her as lazy, a recluse we never got to know as much as we'd have liked. The matter of the fact was, she did more than we knew. The constant driving between different work placements spread out in the park left Anne exhausted, something she had already struggled with. There were also certain restrictions she faced while driving, details of which she refused to expand on in her email. My description of some billet families, particularly Luke's younger billet siblings, had also come off harsher than I expected, the result of which screwed Anne out of two families in a town where she already struggled to get billets. In my letter, I had encouraged the participants to sneak into the second basement of the house, an act Anne explicitly explained would immediately net any participant who did so a warning as that area was not part of the rental arrangement Anne had with the property.

From Anne's perspective, I had not taken advantage of the available opportunities to discuss these frustrations with her. As a result of writing that letter, I made her already difficult job that much harder. In the end, I had made unsound judgments which were not mine to share. Not only that, I had deprived that group of participants the chance for a positive start for their final rotation. My letter had achieved the exact opposite of what I intended.

Every minute that went by made me feel increasingly more stupid for having written the letter in the first place. How could I be so fucking selfish? Anne was right. Who the hell was I to make those kinds of judgments and pass on my own frustrations to complete strangers? That letter had been a horrible, horrible mistake. Anne's email wasn't filled with malice, but she hinted that repercussions might be worse than guilt:

"I don't know what Head Office will do about the matter, but I felt the need to express myself. We all face consequences from our actions."

This wasn't something I wanted to sit on. I had to apologize immediately. The silver lining to my restlessness the night before was having plenty of time to rehearse my apology. I knew most of what I wanted to say when I woke up. Even if I ended up in serious trouble, I wanted Anne to at least know I was sorry. I rushed to the computer first thing that morning. It wasn't normally in use at that time as people were busy getting ready for the day. I sent Anne an email, profusely apologizing and explaining my actions. I wouldn't be content with that though. I had to speak to her over the phone so that she could hear the sincerity in my apology. That kind of private conversation couldn't be rushed, though, and wasn't going to happen that morning. I didn't want to talk to Anne while participants, on her end and mine, were noisily stomping through the house getting changed, grabbing breakfast, and getting ready for work, something I had to do soon myself. It had to wait until I got home from work. My day spent watering plants and freshly planted sod along trails gave me no reprieve from the plague of guilt, but plenty of time to refine what I was going to say. As practiced as my apology was going to be, it was going to have to wait.

"No, sorry man, Anne is on her 24 hours off," said the participant who picked up. I called the Saint-Élie house as soon as I got home from work.

Julie was coincidentally taking her 24 hours off at that time as well, leaving our group alone and unsupervised that night. I had to endure another day of sickly impending doom in my gut that left me hot and short of breath. I flagellated myself with barbs of blame, scolded by a punishing voice in my head. *You only want to apologize so you stop feeling bad. You're not sorry, you're just a selfish prick.* I told myself that wasn't true, that it was the right thing to do even if it did make me feel better. Hopefully. I couldn't take back the things I said, but I had to say something. As dreadful as the thought of going home was, I would accept that punishment if it came to it, but I couldn't bear the idea of Anne holding a completely warranted burning hatred for me. I deserved it. I deserved to feel like this, to feel like shit, like I was going to vomit at any moment.

It didn't take long before my group started to notice. With the way I felt, my expressions couldn't have been subtle. One by one I eventually told everyone in the group why I had been acting exceptionally sullen and withdrawn.

"Oof, that sucks man," Luke sympathized.

"Hey, we all felt that way, so don't feel bad," Tiffany chimed in.

Even Carlos was supportive. "Yeah, even if you didn't mean for it to go that way, I think you're overreacting. Just chill, hombre."

Everyone was convinced that I wouldn't get in trouble or at least not be sent home.

I tried to embrace their words, if not for my own sense of comfort, then for everyone else's sake. My pity party wasn't about to put a damper on things while Julie was gone for her 24 hours. Someone pulled out a mickey of vodka and everyone began to have casual drinks. Understandably, I declined. While I was still interested in having drinks with the rest of the group, I wasn't in the right state of mind that night. Not only would combining alcohol with my mood have been dangerous, I also didn't want to risk any other activities that would get me into more trouble. I was in enough hot water and the stress was already unbearable. I did manage to eke out a brief but wry smile at the irony at play that night—everyone was doing something they could be kicked out for, which was the exact thing I was worrying about. I didn't point it out though. I didn't want to ruin the small freedom that was being taken advantage of. While everyone was rambunctious and jovial, I sat quietly among them, still haunted by Anne's final words from her email:

"*We are responsible for our actions.*"

Erica playfully nudged me, making me lose the staring contest I had with the floor.

"Hey, I know you're stressed, but there's nothing you can do for now. Just try to relax."

The group might have been taking predictable advantage of Julie's absence, but I couldn't wait until she came back. I needed to talk to her, as a PL, to get advice on how to respond to my situation. I needed to know what was likely going to happen and what to be prepared for when I finally got a hold of Anne. For the rest of that night, I worried about how disappointed Mom and Dad and my friends back home would be if I got kicked out of Katimavik, and how my group would fare without me.

It was later in the evening the next day when Julie returned. She arrived shortly before our planned hike to Cook's Monument. The monument was part of a historical site dedicated to the captain who charted numerous Newfoundland coastlines in the 18th century. It also gave visitors a pleasant viewpoint overlooking Corner Brook, one we had all been encouraged to check out. I didn't want any more excuses though. I wasn't going to wait for things to get better, not this time.

"Hey Julie, I know you just got back," I said, speaking firmly. "But I have something really important I need to talk to you about."

Julie was bubbly, not ditzy. I wasn't coy in my request. She could clearly see that whatever was on my mind had me upset. "Sure. What about on the way back down from the monument? Will that work?"

I agreed.

It was a steep walk up Crow Hill to the lookout. The bronze sculpture of Captain Cook joined us as we gathered around to listen to Julie.

"I've been learning a lot these last few days," she explained. "I know it's only been about a week since you guys arrived, but I've been hearing a lot of different things about appreciation, things we wouldn't normally expect from people and tend to take for granted…"

It was a casual speech. Julie's words weren't part of a workshop or anything formal. She had simply been experiencing some personal epiphanies, some newfound wisdoms that she wished to share with her group. Her timing with the unexpected yet eerily relevant topic was uncanny. It felt like someone was twisting a knife already painfully lodged in my chest.

As soon as we started our way back down the steep hill, I caught up with Julie. We walked behind the rest of the group as I explained what had transpired over the past few days.

"You're not going to get kicked out," Julie assured me after giving me a well-needed hug. She explained that while I might get a CTI, a final warning was unlikely. Julie knew my talking about the issue was difficult and was proud that I was taking responsibility for my mistakes and showing initiative to apologize. I felt only marginally comforted after our talk, which made sense. I hadn't atoned yet.

The steep walk drained a lot of us, prompting several participants to crash on their beds when we returned to the house. I tried calling Anne again, hoping to take advantage of the privacy.

"Oh. Hi Devon! How's it going?"

I was surprised to not only get a hold of her, but have Anne be the one to answer the phone. Normally it was participants who picked up. Anne even sounded the tiniest bit excited to hear that it was me on the other end. Wanting to avoid the pitfall of small chat, I immediately launched into my apology, trying my best not to speak too fast or break down.

Anne was surprisingly calm when I finished. She acknowledged I was likely not in the right mind space when I wrote that letter. I realized it was true, even if I didn't know it at the time. I'd been so focused on Corner Brook that I hadn't been able to focus on the good things that happened in Quebec. I admitted how she was right, that the storm our group had endured should not have been another group's to bear. Anne also admitted that she could have done more to engage with us and that perhaps she might have unknowingly been in the process of closing her own chapter in Katimavik. She'd been a PL for several years by that point and was beginning to tire of the job.

"You know, it might be time for me to start looking for something else," she said.

Once the emotional baggage had started to lift, the conversation between Anne and I turned casual and friendly. I caught her up with how everyone in the group was doing, making it a point to focus only on positive things. Likewise, she shared with me how her group was adjusting to Saint-Élie and what changes were taking place at the park since we'd left.

I was relieved that things had been resolved between the two of us, but the tension during the phone call wasn't only about Anne. I hadn't just made a simple mistake. I had unfairly shared with the world my own pain which I had not dealt with first. It was humbling, reminding me that I still had a lot of learning to do. I might not have managed my experiences in Quebec very well, but I was not going to make that same mistake in the last few months of Katimavik.

Julie had a renewed passion in her after her return from her short vacation. She was excited to show us the different hikes and trails and scenic spots of Corner Brook that she'd learned of in her six months of living on The Rock. Winter might not have been the most pleasant or safe time to attempt them, but now Julie was able to enjoy these recreational opportunities, and with people who were equally as excited to do the same. Her last group may not have been keen on the outdoors, but she reciprocated our enthusiasm to get out and explore what the area had to offer.

One place Julie wanted to show us was the top of Steady Brook Falls alongside Marble Mountain just outside of town. We immediately agreed. It was a steep but fortunately short hike. Before long, our group had made the climb, wading in the pools atop the falls. And that was *all* we were allowed to do.

"No dunking your heads under water. As soon as you go under, you're more or less *swimming*, which means this becomes an official excursion. Which it is not. If it was, there would have to be lifeguards. Which there aren't…" She looked at me. "So we can wade, but no swimming. This means you, Devon."

I said nothing. I wasn't about to ruin the opportunity Julie had given us by opening my mouth.

The weather had been exceptionally hot and humid, or "muggy" as the Newfies called it, and none of us wanted to go swimming outside more than me. Most of the city-raised participants didn't know the satisfaction of swimming in a classic water hole, having grown accustomed to chlorinated indoor pools and crowded public beaches. Erica and I were the most excited out of the group, but that may have been because we worked outside, performing physical labour in the hot sun. Since I learned that the creek that ran through Margaret Bowater Park was dammed in the summer, allowing people to swim in it, I'd been badgering my group to go there as well. It was no secret I wanted to jump off every cliff, climb every mountain, and swim in every bit of water deeper than my waist. Julie knew this, but she couldn't put us in a position that would get her in trouble.

It had been almost a week since my phone call with Anne. I hadn't heard from Head Office regarding any form of punishment, punitive action, or anything for that matter. I felt like I was out of the woods. They might have followed up with Anne, but I assumed she shrugged the matter off and explained that I had apologized. I was finally calming down from the nervous wreck I had been. Even so, I didn't want to tempt fate by getting into any more trouble. I knew I wasn't going to be a saint, but I remained cautious of my actions. I considered Julie's position and the necessity of her drawing a line in the sand. The temptation was real. I mean, if we were already that close to doing something we technically weren't supposed to, what was the harm in going that last little bit? Just a quick dunk in the water, some light swimming, nothing dangerous. I knew it wouldn't end there though. That kind of thinking was a slippery slope, which wasn't something you wanted next to a waterfall. Julie wasn't averse to bending the rules, but they were most certainly broken if someone was to get seriously hurt. Comprehending these risks, I pouted in silence, wading around the cool flowing water in an odd mixture of glee and disappointment.

Carlos' boss from Cycle Solutions, Ethan, had informed us that below the top pool of Steady Brook Falls was a second pool, just before the creek turned into the sixty metre falls it was named after. Two massive boulders split the creek, causing the water to go left, right, and through the centre butt crack of the rocks into a surprisingly calm pool. The rumour was that it was supposedly deep enough to dive into. Ethan told us that along the flat edges of the bowl-shaped pool, people had tossed long logs and tree branches into it in an attempt to touch the bottom. They never did, Ethan told us, giving the relatively safe impression that the second pool was deep enough to jump into. We mentioned this to Julie, who was already nervous about the inherent danger of the off-the-books trip and threatened us all with immediate CTIs if we did such a thing. It was definitely not worth arguing with her and none of us tried. When it came to Katimavik, you took what you got when it came to PLs turning a blind eye and didn't push your luck.

We didn't let the restrictions spoil things. Everyone calmly floated about or lay on some rock with their body half submerged, relaxing or idly chatting. It reminded me of swimming in the river during the Kispiox Valley Music Festival back home. Up the road from the festival grounds there was a bridge you could jump off, as well as a small nearby cliff for the less brave. The sudden jump into the river helped you acclimatize to the cold waters faster, but it was worth it. Floating down the calm river, you were surrounded by the smells and sounds of nature with friends splashing not far away. Unfortunately, I was going to miss the festival by two weeks by the time Katimavik ended.

In the meantime, our shallow wade atop a waterfall sufficed in satisfying the merman in me.

"You'll laugh! You'll cry! You'll swoon!"

That's what it said on the cover. And it was an apt description.

Practically every participant by that point had heard of it—a book written about Katimavik. It casually came up during a house meeting one day and by sheer coincidence, Julie just so happened to have a copy. She was hesitant in lending it out, not because she was particular about loaning out her books, but because she didn't want it to affect anyone's experience. The book was older than I expected, published in 1998. *I Was a Teenage Katima-victim* was author Will Ferguson's personal account of his Katimavik experience in the early '80s. It was an acclaimed book that was purported to have accurately described Katimavik through the eyes of a participant. That was precisely why Head Office hated it.

The quality of Ferguson's writing was applauded, leaving his book with mostly positive reviews. The controversy came from Katimavik itself. Ferguson described participants as eager, naive youth, full of hormones and a penchant for getting into trouble. PLs ranged from motherly hippy types to bearded lumberjacks, adults who were thrown into leading the program in much the same way as the teenagers participating in it. The narrative painted Katimavik like a getaway camp for free-loading youth using the program as an escape from conformity and getting into trouble in a different province than their own, albeit while making some fun memories and learning a few mild lessons along the way. It was not the image the current Katimavik program wanted for itself, even if it was eerily accurate. Katimavik already faced enough critics who considered the volunteer program a socialism-soaked version of babysitting for youth who could be contributing members of society in better, more productive ways. Those same people, however, tended to be as critical of the program's efficacy and cost as it was a Liberal Prime Minister and senator who started it. Having Ferguson validate those concerns was enough for Katimavik higher-ups to develop a disdain for his book.

The book continued to be both lauded and loathed. His narrative may not have been flattering, but damn was it accurate. Some Katimavikers were eager to read another person's account of the program, myself included, while others refused to do so as not to sully their views of the program they were currently involved in. It was like being given a chance to see your own future—spooky for some, enticing for others.

I knew the program had evolved since Ferguson's time as a participant and was curious to see how much Katimavik had changed since then. I read whenever I had the chance. Whether it was after house managing chores were done, when riding in the back of the van to wherever destination we had that week, or sitting down for my lunch break after working on the town's trails, I took whatever free time I had and dove into Ferguson's Katimavik experience of volunteering in Kelowna, BC; St. Thomas, Ontario; and Saint-Canut, Quebec. And I was floored.

Even though Ferguson's nine-month adventure took place more than twenty years earlier than mine, it seemed like Katimavik had barely changed at all. The similarities between our experiences were staggering and left me impatient to turn the page: hippy-ish PLs, emotional exclusive relationships, unexpected life lessons, unrelenting sexual tension, bitter rivalries between participants. Ferguson's group had even planned their very own Katima-lympics! I was disappointed to learn my idea hadn't been original, but in hindsight it was foolish to think that in twenty years no one else had thought of the Katima-lympics. I hoped to see a satisfying conclusion to Will and Francois's bitter rivalry for each other, thinking it might provide some sort of answer for the problems between me and Carlos, but I was left hanging in that regard. *I Was a Teenage Katima-victim*, however, performed the same wonders that most enthralling non-fictional books did, leaving me yearning for more to quell the uneasy emptiness that filled my soul after the final sentences were read.

But it was only a story. Even if it was about something real, something I was currently experiencing myself, it was still someone else's story. It was not mine. My story had its own characters, its own protagonist, with his own conflicts. And it was up to him to conclude the story, however it unraveled.

"Devon, don't tell us the whole freakin' story, just take the shot!" Luke yelled at me. He'd bugged me to go for a walk, finding he had a hankering for some delicious donairs that evening. Luke was no stranger to street meat, what with the succulent options available to him in the bustling *rues* of Montreal. I was also craving some juicy protein. Having overheard us, Erica and Tiffany joined us for the late-night stroll. What I didn't realize was that our quest for a savoury snack had an ulterior purpose.

Luke wanted to get screeched.

It was during our walk to the other side of downtown Corner Brook that I brought up the Katimavik-focused book that I'd finished reading. I was passionately beginning to describe how the program had—and hadn't—changed since Ferguson was a participant when Luke thrust the bottle of Screech at me. Inside it was real Jamaican rum.

"Bit harder than the stuff we had the first time, huh?"

We had joined the Deer Lake group weeks earlier to take part in a time-honoured Newfie tradition. Our "screeching" that day wasn't technically an authentic ceremony, unfortunately. With the strict Katimavik rule restricting alcohol, even as part of a cultural event, our certified master screecher had to improvise. In lieu of the customary rum people normally slammed back when getting screeched in, he had us take shots of a sugary, alcohol-free cocktail syrup. Once we'd taken our stand-in shots, our emcee, donned in an accoutrement of weathered olive-green rain slicker and yellow bucket-style rain hat, had us collectively recite an age-old Newfoundland creed:

"From the waters of the Avalon, to the shores of Labrador,
We've always stuck together, with a rant and a roar.
To those who've never been, soon they'll understand,
From coast to coast, we raise a toast, we love thee Newfoundland!"
Once we drank our screech-substitutes, our emcee roared again.
"Alright, now who's ready to *kiss the cod*?"

A large Atlantic fish was pulled out of a freezer. Given the fact that we weren't even using real Screech, our emcee was lax on the usual requirement of kissing the Newfoundland food staple. The fact that several lips had already been on it by the time it got to him did not stop Deer Lake's Ryan from kissing the cold cod with gusto.

It had been a fun evening. We appreciated our PLs coordinating the event, but the participants quietly agreed it didn't feel authentic. We wanted the real deal. And that meant real Screech.

While we might have lacked a proper master screecher and only had a few of us in company, we made do. Luke admitted he was getting impatient waiting for the right time. Julie was away for the night, leaving us to fend for ourselves, so that seemed as good an opportunity as any.

I grabbed the small mickey of rum from Luke and downed a glug without hesitation. It took a second before a smooth, alcoholic burn began to slide down my throat.

"Wow, you didn't even flinch. Good job!" said Erica, taking the bottle. I was on the cusp of giving a vigorous hoot in reaction, but restrained myself so as to hold onto the essence of Erica's compliment and also to avoid drawing attention to ourselves. A quick scan around revealed it wouldn't have mattered. No one else was on the street outside the small burger shop where we collected our greasy meat wraps. As much as the donair hit the spot, I would have welcomed any excuse to get out of the house.

Carlos had been getting on my nerves and I found myself at a boiling point earlier that evening. I had simply grown sick of his out-of-the-blue shit talking and told him as such. It had launched us into yet another wrestling match. And it was a doozy. I held his head firmly locked under my armpit, but he bucked like a raging bronco and pulled out. He dove for my legs, but I sprawled away from him in time, causing me to fall on top of him. Wrapping my arms around his torso, I leaned back with all my weight, flipping him onto his back. His landing pinched my shoulder, but I didn't care. Nothing else mattered—my straining arms, Rosalie yelling at us to stop. If Julie hadn't been gone that evening and witnessed us fighting, she likely would have written us up on account of the ferocity we fought with. Play wrestling was fine, but obviously fighting was a no-no. And that's what it was. Carlos and I weren't having fun. I wanted to hurt him. Those were the words I huffed to him as I caught my breath in between our tussles, locked in whatever awkward wrestling hold we had on the other. I wanted him to feel the repercussions of his insulting words. I wanted to hear him say, "No more." If we were going to keep fighting, I wanted one of us to walk away in physical pain. Maybe if one of us won one of our stupid wrestling matches, we would finally be able to get past whatever it was that caused us to inexplicably hate each other. Maybe with a victory or a loss, there could be some sort of catharsis, some progress or change that meant things weren't going to stay the same. I hoped so, because I was sick of draws.

The hard liquor and greasy donair helped numb the last bit of frustration I had with Carlos. I passed the bottle back to Luke, who was already tipsy. Before we left on our late-night adventure, he, Carlos, Erica, and Bethany had shared a few drinks with the neighbours across the road from us.

They were a group of young men who loved to party and play music. We had only met the trio in person a handful of times, normally hearing them more often than seeing them. They played in a garage band, calling themselves *The Embarrassments.* The aspiring musicians were mostly nocturnal, but occasionally came to life in the afternoon, using that time to rehearse in their living room. We didn't mind for the most part, but on the few occasions when we were having house meetings, Julie would ask for them to keep it down. She had befriended them before and didn't mind speaking with them curtly when the situation called for it. They had invited us over to their living room to play a small concert earlier that night. The amateur band even dedicated a song to our group. The gesture was more pleasant than their music was, but it was kind, nonetheless.

The unexpected mini-concert, delicious donairs, and secret screeching helped relieve the stress that Carlos had been causing me, like hocking loose an acid-laced loogie that had been lodged in my throat. We took our sweet time walking back to the house and enjoyed the lulling serenity of the muggy Newfoundland night.

CHAPTER 30

June 2006. Corner Brook.

No one was surprised, not even me. It couldn't have been any other way.

Carlos and I were billeting together.

"Geez, it's going to be like marriage counselling for the two of you," Erica joked. It felt oddly accurate. Carlos and I had recently been paired as house managers and somehow survived each other, but not for lack of effort. Crossing paths with a partnering house manager was unavoidable, but it was made easier by doing most of our chores alone, muttering thinly veiled insults whenever we had the chance.

"I'm going to go clean the bathroom, asshole."

"I'll sweep the stairs, douchebag."

I wasn't proud of our system of pettiness, but it seemed to work. The group was fed, the house was clean, and I was productive. Once it became clear that Carlos flat out refused to be social or even make any semblance of small chat, I decided to direct my energies into actual causes rather than lost ones. I buried my head into planning upcoming excursions. I was doing my best to make a river rafting trip happen. The proposal looked good but lacked a budget and a chosen date. These had to wait until we had details confirmed for other future excursions that were already in the works. I would show my worth and make sure the last rotation was a blast for everyone in the group, even if a certain individual was committed to being a shithead.

Just when we thought we had escaped each other's company, Carlos and I were informed at the next house meeting that we would be billeting together. It wasn't due to some twisted form of karma though. Both of us had expressed a preference for outgoing, active billets, people who might take us somewhere to show us a side of Newfoundland we hadn't seen yet. We also both wanted to billet with a participant who would give us a different experience from living with a family alone. It wasn't uncommon for a billet family to take on two participants if they were able and willing.

Larry and Ruby were the only family who were willing to do just that, and they fit the other criteria Carlos and I sought. They might have been an older married couple, but Julie assured us that despite their age, they were wonderful billets who were surprisingly mobile and loved sharing their home with Katimavikers.

"In fact, their daughter Anna was very involved with our first two groups. She was one of my best friends here before she moved to Sault Ste. Marie just before you guys arrived," Julie told us. "She loved to travel and had so many great stories. You guys would have loved her!" It was too bad we didn't get the chance to meet Anna. The way Julie described her, she would have been a great person to meet, but her parents sounded like they would make good company in her stead.

Although the group was looking forward to the change of pace that billeting brought, many of us expressed a desire to spend time together. We were quickly approaching the halfway point of our third rotation. That left about six weeks until the end of Katimavik, and everyone knew they would fly by. Time was ticking away, and we wanted to make the most of it, even during billeting.

"Before we wrap up the house meeting, we need to talk about ... exclusive relationships," Julie announced. "They don't have to necessarily be between two people," she added. "The problem with exclusive relationships is that they're *exclusive*, to the point where you're shutting yourself off from the group. This kind of extreme isolation can even happen with electronics. Things like music players or portable game systems can be problematic if they get in the way of other relationships."

My eyebrows went up. Considering how Luke and I were the only two with Game Boys, that comment must have been aimed at one of us. I had been playing mine more often those days, but mostly because I was trying to finish a game I had borrowed from Luke and wanted to give it back to him before Katimavik ended. I immediately spoke up, insisting that if people thought my gaming was problematic, I'd quit, cold turkey. If there was going to be a conflict between me and the group, it sure as hell wasn't going to be because of video games. No one said anything.

As Julie wrapped up her vague concerns, I realized that perhaps the conversation likely wasn't aimed at the gamers of the group. Erica and Bethany seemed to have cooled down in their relationship, or at least moved things behind closed doors. Luke had also been getting pretty close with Krissy, a participant from the Deer Lake group. And as far as I knew, Rosalie and Carlos had not recuperated from their own falling out. Exclusive relationships were a tricky maze to navigate and we were all finding our own way of doing so without them becoming a noticeable problem.

Billeting was different the third time. Whereas we had embraced billeting in Sault Ste. Marie and Saint-Élie as a relief from the mounting stress that naturally came with group living, that wasn't the case this time around. Billeting brought with it certain freedoms, something participants normally wanted to enjoy with the families that had taken them in and made those possible. After all, those families had signed up for an experience as well—they were billets, not babysitters. We knew the intrinsic value of spending time with these residents of Corner Brook and didn't want to deny either party those joys. However, no one seemed eager to say sayonara to the rest of the group for those two weeks. Our unstructured hang outs usually took place when our families were busy or working during the day and we weren't, a healthy balance of how our time was spent, careful to avoid neglecting our billet families.

There was a shared, quiet reluctance to be alone for too long, resulting in everyone being keen to hang out together. Doing so felt different during billeting, refreshing almost, now that we had fewer responsibilities looming over us. Maybe it was an indicator we made progress through the storming phase that plagued so many Katimavik groups. People don't tend to want to surround themselves with those they fight with and would surely prefer the company of people they got along well with. Perhaps that was indicant of the performing phase all PLs aspired their participants to reach. Or maybe it was because the end of Katimavik was nigh and those opportunities were fleeting. After living with the same people for the past seven months, there was something to be said about getting used to that kind of company.

Carlos was the only snag. I couldn't stand to be alone with him, whether it was house managing or billeting with Larry and Ruby for the next two weeks. Whenever it was just the two of us around, he remained a dickhead on a mission to be a pest, but when we were surrounded by the rest of the group or socializing with our billet family, he behaved. If he refused to change his behaviour on my account, then he would have to do it for others.

And so, with a Newfoundland summer out in full force, we wanted to enjoy it with as many people as possible: a joint BBQ at Rosalie and Bethany's billet, laser tag with Rosalie's billet brother who had never been, showing Antoine and Joe from the Stephenville group around town when they bused into Corner Brook, going swimming with Julie's visiting boyfriend, even spelunking with Ethan, Carlos' boss from Cyclic Solutions.

We were especially excited for some cave exploration. It was an exceptionally dangerous activity which would in no way be approved by Head Office as an excursion. But since we were billeting, the rules were a little more lax, even if we weren't doing it *with* one of our billets. What Julie didn't know wouldn't hurt her, though I was sure Ethan would inevitably tell her over some beers after the program ended and we were long gone.

Everyone walked behind our host as he led us through a forested trail on the edge of town. As our Katimavik house was right in the lower bowl of the city, we didn't spend a lot of time near the upper rim of Corner Brook, although we occasionally made the walk up to the McDonald's next to the Walmart to redeem some of the free ice cream coupons that covered the wall of Erica and Tiffany's room when we arrived. I don't know how the previous group scored over a hundred individual coupons, but we made sure to keep some in the Katimavik van in case we ever went in that general direction.

After a few minutes of hiking, the trees grew thicker. A canopy of leaves shaded us from the sun's hot rays, even in the late morning. Each of us sported a coloured helmet with an attached light on the front. Luke and I bonked our helmets together, giving them a good durability test. Rosalie scoffed at our antics, but soon everyone was doing it, gentle enough that we didn't risk damaging the equipment Ethan had graciously lent us. Rosalie continued rolling her eyes but ran away when I chased after her with my rhino impression.

"Sheesh, it's hot today, even underneath the trees!" Luke panted as we continued walking towards our destination.

"Don't worry. Within five minutes, we'll be deep enough underground that it will be cooler. It doesn't really change temperature after a certain depth," Ethan informed us. "Ah, there it is."

After a brief safety talk, Ethan had us enter one by one into the cave hidden deep in the forest. He was right about the temperature. We had barely walked into the damp hole in the ground before we noticed how much cooler it was, even close enough to the cave entrance for us to see sunlight. Carrying on, we travelled deeper into the earth, walking, climbing, and crawling past chambers filled with stalagmites and stalactites and even wading through pools of water deeper than our heads. It was a truly unique feeling to be swimming deep underground. If we all turned off our lights, we would be enveloped by complete darkness, a suggestion that no one was willing to try. After an hour or so, a new tunnel of light appeared in front of us, indicating our exit.

We ate a brief lunch sitting just outside the cave entrance. Everyone was munching away happily on the sandwiches that Ethan had been kind enough to pack us. When I leaned against the rock wall at my back, I noticed something lodged in a small nook beside me. I pulled out what looked like a small Tupperware container. Thinking it was one of Ethan's containers he'd used to pack the sandwiches, I passed it to him.

"That's not mine. Wait, where did you find that?" he asked. I showed him where it came from. "Oh, that's a geocache! I heard there was one out here."

"Geocache?"

Ethan explained. Geocaching was an outdoor treasure hunting game played with GPS devices. Boxes or containers much like the one I was holding were hidden around the world, filled with logbooks and little knick-knacks that people could trade. Looking inside, I found a small notebook and pencil, along with a bracelet, some stickers, a set of dice, a coloured rock, and what looked like a small toy you might find in a Kinder Surprise Egg.

"You can take something, but you got to leave something behind. Or you can just sign the logbook," he explained further. I passed the container around to let everyone else have a look. "Sometimes people find them by chance, so we'll have to make sure we put it back."

The concept was still mind-boggling to me. "Are you telling me, there are boxes like this hidden everywhere around the world? And I just happened to find one right now by chance?" I asked.

"Yup."

I was flabbergasted. It was like real-life treasure hunting! Sure, the "prizes" seemed small and meagre, but Geocaching sounded like the coolest thing ever to me. I loved treasure hunts, scavenger hunts, and the like. How had I never heard of it before?

Once we returned to our respective billet homes after our spelunking adventure, I looked up Geocaching online to learn more. Just as Ethan had said, there were Geocaches around the world. Millions of them! There were over twenty in Corner Brook alone. Looking closer at the online map, I found there were five hidden around Glynmill Pond, a popular scenic area in the centre of town where several trails converged. It dawned on me that I had likely walked by these little treasure troves over a dozen times and never even realized it.

Geocaching seemed like an excellent way to explore a familiar area even more. I didn't have a GPS like the game suggested, but I was confident I could find these Geocaches without one. Most of them had detailed descriptions about where they were hidden, some including a hint. I began drawing crude maps on paper, marking out the Geocaches' general locations. I couldn't wait for the next time when I'd be working on the trails. I planned on using my lunch break to hopefully—and this time, legitimately—find my next geocache.

Breaks were well needed at work. The weather had been sweltering all week. Not only had the sun been blazing relentlessly almost every day, the stream and trail work crew had spent most of their time shoveling rock and moving sod. After Terry and Shawn had laid the square brown and green lumps, Erica and I were usually tasked with watering them until the grass could take root and survive on its own. Sometimes that meant watering the same piece of sod several times throughout the day. This wasn't as difficult along sections of trail that followed a creek; Erica and I could simply dip our water cans in to fill them instead of walking long distances to find a spigot, ponds, or other water sources. We didn't mind the occasional cooling splash from carrying the heavy watering cans, but there were some days where it was tempting to jump right into the source. It was a miracle Erica and I had enough strength to lift our arms and play laser tag at the end of work.

Even over the course of billeting, we still made the occasional visit to Jordan at Cyber Zone. Luke didn't have to though. He was billeting with Jordan and thrilled to be staying with a cheery friend to the group. Luke had gleefully and remorselessly told us all the extra games he had been privy to play. Jordan would occasionally throw Luke into random groups who were playing if they were small or to balance out unfair teams. In addition to free laser tag practice, Jordan had also given him lots of tactical advice accumulated from years of running the business and playing the game, giving Luke a distinct advantage over the rest of us. He called it "an edge." We called it cheating. By turning sideways and strafing down the corridors of the maze, you minimized the exposure of your lit vest targets which the infrared laser had to strike to render you "hit." Luke, however, kept holding his gun up to his chest, physically blocking his targets and making him practically impossible to hit. Everyone caught on to what he was doing and soon our entire group was using the same tactic. The usual screams of glee and excitement were soon marred with cursing and grunts of frustration. Mine were especially loud. Laser tag had changed and now wasn't quite as fun.

This was especially true when Carlos and I were on opposite teams. We still actively despised each other. Our first week of having billeted together hadn't changed that. Even in the normally fun laser tag arena where we could put our differences aside for a short period of time, he continued to be a dick. While we played, he stalked me throughout the maze, rarely going after anyone else. Whenever a player was shot, their vest would power down for five seconds, giving them a chance to escape from the player who shot them. Carlos would deliberately follow me until I powered back up and then shoot me again.

"Dude, fuck off!" I bleated as he wandered after me again with a bored expression. "You can't just follow someone the entire game." As per Jordan's rules, we weren't allowed to run in the arena, so I couldn't escape Carlos if I wanted to.

"It's not a rule," he reminded me, free of any anger or even joy in his voice for that matter. Technically he was right, but it was an incredibly cheap way to play. Carlos wasn't subtle or sneaky in his commitment to annoy me, and would idly wait to shoot me, even risking getting shot himself by everyone else playing. He only cared that it bothered me, going well out of his way to piss me off. I tried not to let it, but it did. Even the others were annoyed at his immature tenacity. If he was going to make me suffer, at least there was collateral damage which would bite him in the ass later.

Our additional volunteer commitments continued during billeting. Julie had done well to set these up in advance prior to us leaving the house for those two weeks. They were light affairs, events that didn't demand too much time away from our billets.

One of them was a bike race that Cycle Solutions was hosting. Ethan was running the event and asked Julie if she could spare some extra volunteers. Given his generosity in taking us spelunking, we were glad to help him out.

Upon arriving at the event, Ethan quickly sent us to different areas of need. Some of us were tasked with setting up equipment and others with taking registrations, but when Ethan asked who among us was a good photographer, my name was quickly offered up. As the de facto photographer for the group, I was deemed qualified enough to take candid photos of mountain cyclists along the route. I assured Ethan I wouldn't settle for some boring static photos of cyclists at the gate, but would get him some sick action shots, which were exactly what he was looking for. Just before he was pulled away to give an interview for Rogers Television, he handed me his digital camera and quickly showed me how to use it, ensuring I was familiar with the basic zoom, settings, and view photo functions. When Ethan pushed the button to review the photos currently saved on his camera, he winced.

"You know what, *don't* review the photos. Just… take pictures and bring the camera right back to me, okay?" His reaction left me perplexed. Before he could say anything else, an announcement came on, letting everyone know the race was going to start soon. Ethan excused himself to give his interview. I also hustled, readying myself to go to work.

Looking at the map of the race route Ethan gave me, I walked to a section I thought would be a good spot to capture oncoming mountain cyclists and give me time to fiddle and adjust the camera settings. I decided to climb a tree that I thought would give me a photographic advantage and keep me out of everyone's path. After I was comfortably nestled on a sturdy branch, I waited. It was going to be a while before any of the racers came by on their first lap though. Double-checking to confirm no one was nearby, I turned on the camera and reviewed the photos on the memory card. Had Ethan not said anything I wouldn't have bothered looking, but curiosity got the best of me. I already had an idea of what I might find. As it turned out, I was right. After quickly panning through the photos—twice—I shut off the view screen. I could spot cyclists coming off in the distance and readied myself to capture some candid action shots.

I changed locations twice more to snap photos. I felt confident I got something Ethan could use. When the last circuit of racers passed by me for their final lap, I walked back to the registration tent. Volunteers were already busy packing things away. Ethan was nowhere to be seen, but I recognized his girlfriend. She was busy taking banners and posters down.

"Hey, I took pictures for Ethan, but can't seem to find him. Can you give this back to him?" I handed her the camera. The woman grabbed it from me, then hesitated.

"You didn't look at the photos already on here, did you?"

"No," I lied, somehow with a straight face. She smirked slyly at me.

"Suuuuuuuure you didn't."

Maybe I wasn't as convincing a liar as I thought.

The next day, we had another volunteer gig, this one in the evening. Julie had organized us to help at a Nature Stewardship BBQ at Margaret Bowater Park. Upon our early arrival, we sought someone who looked like they were in charge.

"Oh hey, you must be Julie's volunteers," said one of the organizers. "Sorry guys. We had more people offer to help than expected. It looks like we have most things covered, but you're more than welcome to stick around in case we find something for you to do."

A few of us managed to squeeze in to flip burgers on some BBQ's and set up a Frisbee golf course, but with the abundance of volunteers, the rest of us were left to stand around. Volunteering had kind of become our main purpose, something I like to think we'd gotten good at, so it was a peculiar disappointment to find our presence wasn't necessary, especially considering we were asked to be there in the first place. I started to wonder if Julie was just finding a way to keep us out of trouble while we were away billeting. Preoccupied Katimavikers tended to stay out of trouble, right? We were conflicted when all the volunteers were instructed to join the lineup for burgers, us included. It was intended as a small token of appreciation for our "help." We felt more comfortable doing so only after all the other volunteers had gone through the line first. It only seemed fair; they helped more than we did.

Once we each had a plate of food in our hands, our group found a spot on the grass, away from all the other volunteers. No one was particularly eager to meet or socialize with the new people we were with. There were lots of volunteers at the BBQ besides ourselves, including a bevy of cute girls who caught my eye. I chatted with the organizers of the event, played Frisbee golf with some strangers, and eventually talked to some of the girls. While casually tossing a Frisbee around, I told them about Katimavik and how I ended up there. If we weren't going to actually do much while volunteering, the least I could do was some promotional work.

Once the BBQ ended, Carlos, Luke, Erica, and I began putting chairs and tables away. Our idle chatter turned onto the topic of the silly games the group played.

"Oh yeah, we never did declare a winner between the guys, did we?" I said without thinking.

Erica raised an eyebrow. "What game?"

Both Carlos and Luke shot me angry glances. "Shhh!"

But I had already said too much. The obvious secret had piqued Erica's interest, and she pressed us for details. We caved.

It was probably the stupidest out of all the silly games we played. The goal was simple: who among the guys could masturbate the most. It was based purely on the honour system as no one had any way—or was willing—to verify. We had only started it a month ago, but billeting had distracted us. We had completely forgotten about it and who to declare a winner. The arbitrary end date we had set passed weeks ago. Luke, Carlos, and I had promised not to tell the girls mostly because the secrecy made the game more exciting and we didn't want them getting any wrong ideas about our… motivations. It wasn't about them. It wasn't about feelings or relationships. It was just a stupid game.

"And now Devon's ruined it!" Luke said, throwing his hands up in the air. I couldn't tell if he was actually mad or hamming his reaction up.

I knew I had slipped up, but I insisted it wasn't a big deal. "How have I ruined it? It's been over for weeks. If I didn't say anything, you wouldn't have even remembered we were playing. What's the point of keeping it a secret if we aren't even playing now?"

Luke and Carlos disagreed, but couldn't give an answer to my question. Erica, upon hearing us argue over the foolish game, simply rolled her eyes and said little else. It was more or less how I expected her to react. Luke finally shrugged his shoulders at the cat being let out of the bag, but Carlos refused to let it go.

"You can't even keep a freaking secret. See, this is why no one talks to you!"

It was a low blow. He knew I still had insecurities around opening up to the group. I had mentioned it during some of the very rare days when we could stand to speak to each other without breaking out into a violent wrestling match or muttering passive aggressive insults under our breath. I was trying to reconnect with people and felt like I had made strides in the past few weeks with everyone except for Carlos. No matter what I said or did, he resented me. He had thrown shade at me before in efforts to fire me up, but this was the last straw and I promptly told him so.

"You know what Carlos, that's a dick thing to say, so why don't you shut the fuck up?" I said angrily. He shoved the last folded table against the others before walking away, saying nothing except for an angry huff. We had walked to the park together from Larry and Ruby's, but he didn't wait for me to put away the last few tables. We walked back to our billet home separately.

Later that night, as we passed each other in the hall getting ready for bed, Carlos threw something at me. It was his necklace that I had given him for Christmas.

"You can shove this up your ass," he hissed before marching into his room and slamming the door.

I was done. No more. I was tired of these petty fights. Nothing I did or said seemed to appease the moody Colombian. I was beginning to feel I had more or less made amends with everyone else. I was almost in a place where I could comfortably finish the program, but getting there with Carlos seemed futile now. This wasn't about having spilled the beans over that stupid competition. Hell, it wasn't even about trust. I had put in more than enough effort into trying to be friends with Carlos. If something was going to budge, it wasn't going to be me.

CHAPTER 31

June 2006. Corner Brook.

We were back in our Katimavik house, sitting lazily around on the mismatched furniture and chatting. With the milestone of our last time billeting behind us, the reality that Katimavik would be over in another month started to sink in. I was not the only one to realize that we would be experiencing a lot of our "lasts": our last hike up to the lookout in the centre of town, our last visit to the McDonald's for free ice cream, our last game of laser tag with Jordan. Everyone had their own agendas to finish before we all left and returned to our homes. Our real homes. We'd figure it all out on our own in due time, but for the time being, we tried to be present. Julie wanted to hear about each of our billeting experiences.

"Let's hear everyone's 'rose and thorns,'" she suggested, wishing to hear both the good and bad from the last two weeks. It wasn't a formal reflection exercise or anything. We simply went around to each person loitered about the living room and shared.

Rosalie started. "I loved my billet sister!" She described how the two had gone shopping and dancing together.

Tiffany followed her. "My family took me to the coast for the weekend where I met the craziest and oldest Newfie guy ever! He was my billet family's granddad. I couldn't understand a single word he said, though, but he was hilarious."

There was no denying Newfies had a unique vernacular, fulfilling every stereotype of how Canadians spoke. Every so often we would come across a resident of the province with such a thick accent, you'd swear they were acting. I had a theory that a Newfie's accent was correlated to their age and how close to the coast they lived: If you met an old timer who grew up in a small Newfoundland village right next to the coast, it was guaranteed you wouldn't understand a single word that man said, but damn, if it wouldn't be an interesting conversation and that man proved to be the most jovial Maritimer you ever had the pleasure of meeting.

The circle check on billeting eventually came around to me.

"I enjoyed Larry and Ruby. They were definitely an interesting couple and like you said Julie, surprisingly active for their age." Larry was well into his sixties but still enjoyed the occasional round of golf at the course near his house. Ruby joked he spent more time drinking there than playing. Golf might not have been her thing, but she was hardly a sedentary geriatric. She and I enjoyed some long walks around the neighbourhood and evenings sitting in the backyard while she talked about her children who lived elsewhere and had their own adventurous lives.

I paused, thinking about my "thorn." Larry and Ruby had been great. The couple had even taken me and Carlos on a few short drives, allowing us to see some picturesque places just outside of town. At their age, Larry and Ruby didn't have a sense of fleeting time, the same fear of missing out that was beginning to weigh down on the rest of us. Through no fault of their own, those trips left me with a burning desire to do more. I didn't just want to see beaches, I wanted to walk them; ocean vistas weren't enough, I wanted to get wet and splash and jump in the waves; I wanted to see what was at the top of mountains instead of just watching them pass by on the drive home. In the two weeks of billeting, I felt like I had struck a good balance between spending time with both my billets and the group. One could tell that Larry and Ruby were at the beginning stages of slowing down at their age, but it wasn't right of me to ask them to speed up for my benefit. Even if I wanted to share positive experiences with others, I couldn't rely solely on those same people to make them happen. I appreciated what the couple who had taken me in had given me. Any disappointment during my time with them was my own to bear. I wanted to say the same for my billeting partner, but simply couldn't figure that one out.

It was no secret how much Carlos and I loathed each other by that point. Julie might not have been present when the two of us broke out into our most intense fights, but I suspected she had a good idea as to how we felt about the other. I didn't think the house meeting that afternoon was the best time to point out how incredibly frustrating billeting with Carlos had been. It was pointless to beat that dead horse any longer. Any comment I had would be neither constructive nor nice, and it didn't feel necessary to spout those things in front of people, especially since the collective mood seemed noticeably positive. Carlos, however, did not share the same tact and had no problem sharing his frustrations.

"I also liked Larry and Ruby. They were an older couple, but so een-teresting. I had some good late-night chats with them," he nodded softly, looking innocently at the floor. "My thorn was I would have liked to have billeted with someone else. That was the *only* thing that ruined billeting for me I think," he concluded in the same quiet nonchalant tone.

I said nothing and made no reaction, but not for lack of feeling. I struggled to restrain myself. *Ruined? I ruined your billet experience!? Oh, fuck you. Fuck you, my friend!*

Carlos had successfully sucked the life right out of the room, just like I had tried to avoid doing. No one said anything for a few seconds until Julie broke the silence.

"Okay, well I'm glad to have you all back again. I missed you guys!"

It was a short meeting, mostly for the purpose of catching up. Having now done so, everyone dispersed from the living room. There was nothing else planned for the day which left most of us content to putter about the house, but not me. I waited until Julie was alone before I approached her. I was going to try. One. More. Time.

Trying to remain calm and civil after Carlos' comment, I asked Julie if she could mediate between the two of us. As much as I hated the guy, I couldn't help but admire Carlos' tenacity. Whenever our group managed to perform and hit a stride of shared optimism, Carlos like to throw out a rally cry of "never give up, never surrender." I couldn't tell if he still believed in the mentality he was taught at a young age, or whether he'd abandoned it and now considered the possibility of us being passable friends instead of enemies a lost cause. One thing I had taken from all the Katimavik goal-setting rigmarole was that passivity was not helpful in achieving those goals. I sure as hell wasn't ready to give up.

"Yeah, I could sense you two had some… troubles," Julie said gingerly. I gave her what I felt was just enough context so that she could understand our situation a bit more. Thankfully, she agreed to facilitate a conversation between the two of us. Carlos, surprisingly, agreed.

Later that night, Julie, Carlos, and I sat in the computer room with the door closed for privacy. Julie began.

"Carlos, you said during our billeting debriefing that you would have liked another billet partner. Can you share why?"

He grimaced as he looked at me. "Because he ruined it!" he said, exhibiting much more frustration than he had earlier. He had obviously been stewing about this as much as I had.

"How?" I demanded, firmly but calmly. "I'd like to know exactly what I did during billeting." It took great effort to refrain from raising my voice, but it was an old anger I was growing too familiar with. No matter how hard I tried, Carlos simply refused to yield and give any sort of explanation, anything that might alleviate the great mystery as to why we detested each other. I ran through my own reasons, trying to focus on specifics instead of emotions. *He's a prick. He's rude to me. He doesn't respect me. He goes out of his way to antagonize me and will actively ruin an activity for others to do so. He's selfish, saying I ruined 'his billeting,' especially in front of everyone.*

"Fuck you, you just did!" he growled at me. But Julie stepped in.

"Carlos, please. For this talk, I think we'd benefit if you two would use, 'I feel' statements. It will help provide some introspection instead of just blame." Somehow, this made Julie sound even Julie-er. But it seemed like it might work. I was glad I had asked Julie for help. A third-party mediator was exactly what we needed.

"I *feel* like he ruined billeting."

"How?" asked Julie. She also remained calm, but I could tell that if Carlos didn't elaborate then Julie would begin to share in my frustration.

He looked back at the ground. "I don't know. He just did."

My insides were doing jumping jacks of joy. *That's right asshat! How am I supposed to fix something if you won't explain yourself?*

"I'm just ..." he sighed heavily. "I'm tired of trying to be his friend." He looked at Julie, as though I was no longer sitting right across from him. "I feel like he doesn't open up with the group. He doesn't share anything. He doesn't connect with us. It's been almost nine months. I feel closer with Tiff or Val than I do with him, and they got here late. He's just… I don't care anymore." I could sympathize that our ordeal had been draining on both of us, there was no doubt about that. I spoke up.

"I feel like that's something I've been struggling with Carlos. I have tried *very* hard since we got to Corner Brook to reconnect with the group. I admit, I was very distant in Saint-Élie." I swallowed the exasperation growing quickly in my chest. "But you have thrown that in my face. 'That's why no one talks to you!' That's what you've said to me on multiple occasions." *Good. Ammo.* "How has that been constructive? How has that been helpful? I have a problem that I've been working on, and you bring that up all the time."

He retorted. "I feel like you don't listen! You never know what's going on in the group, personal or otherwise. We have to explain things to you several times because you are constantly getting mixed up. The others have said the same thing." He paused. "And because of that, I don't trust you." *Ouch.* His point struck home, but that frustration was two-sided. It was true, I didn't always know what was going on, particularly when we were in Saint-Élie. I initially chalked it up to the language barrier, but now that we were back in anglophone territory, I had no excuse. It was embarrassing to be confused so often. It left me flustered and hesitant to ask for details about excursions, or volunteering gigs, but mostly struggling to stay in the know of the constantly and ever-changing gossip of who was dating or had hooked up with whom, who was having petty squabbles and for what reason, and who was struggling with what personal demons. Maybe I missed out on learning those interpersonal skills in school or growing up in Hazelton. Maybe that's why it was so easy to leave the small town for Katimavik. I had also failed to communicate with Ashley. That friendship felt like it had survived by threads and at the cost of feeling like we missed something beautiful together. But I was not going to fail the same way here. Avoiding "drama" didn't mean I was more mature than everyone else, but by taking that route, I inadvertently ostracized myself. It was a catch 22—If I wasn't in the know or balls deep in group drama, I wasn't really involved with the group then. I didn't want to finish Katimavik as a passive spectator. I didn't like the idea of making it to the end, saying goodbye, and going home only to shrug off the last nine months and return to a life I had been so eager to leave. I was excited to return home, but I wanted to do so with more than when I had left. There was no guide for accomplishing that though. There was no quota on what to divulge to the members of my group so I felt like one of them. What exactly was I supposed to share? What deep, dark secret was I supposed to share with them so I felt like I was one of the gang, someone they could trust? How much vulnerability did I have to expose until it was deemed acceptable to these people I considered my friends? I felt like I had passed that threshold with everyone else by now. It was unspoken, but I felt content around the others, like I could be myself. For Carlos, nothing seemed good enough though.

I posed those same questions to him, but he could only shrug once again. He didn't have any more answers than I did.

Neither of us had anything else to say. We were both tired, having exhausted what we had to say without repeating ourselves. Julie presented a compromise.

"How about this: Carlos, if you can respect Devon's boundaries, maybe he can try to be a little more attentive and more vocal when it comes to group matters and let others know if he's feeling upset or misunderstanding directions and roles." That wasn't much of a stretch for me. Those were already things I was working on. "I also think it would be a good idea if you two communicated future frustrations through letters. Talking one-on-one doesn't seem to be working and I don't have to explain that I can't mediate all the time."

I liked it. Letter writing was a medium in which we could take our time, choose our words intentionally, and properly express ourselves. We both agreed and shook hands as per Julie's request before retiring for the night.

It had been a draining intervention, but an absolutely necessary one. It didn't feel as though things were fixed between me and Carlos, but there was some relief. It would be a work in progress. The two of us, and the rest of the group, would have to see what else would take place over the course of our last month to see whether Carlos and I could make amends or kill each other in the process.

We stood in what looked to be an iceless skating rink in someone's backyard. At the far end of it was a main stage, short and barely raising the dancers standing on it above the spectators. Most of us had to stand on our tippy toes to view the performances. I doubted a better viewpoint would have made much of a difference. Hell, I didn't even care that the show was being performed in a home-made skating rink, but it was the little things that could have improved the production value: There was no introduction, no program to follow, no MC or any sort of host to explain what the fuck was going on.

The first performer was a ballet dancer wearing a white skirt and beige tights. She danced in complete silence, bereft of any form of music. Off to the side of the rink, I could see there was a music system set up, but I couldn't hear any sound come of it. Were the speakers broken? How did the dancer know what to dance to? There was nothing to follow, no rhythm, no beat. Even Rosalie, with her dancer background, seemed confused. Maybe it was an artistic thing, some form of new age, post-modern ballet? Without me realizing it—perhaps due to the lack of music indicating any sort of conclusion—the dance ended. The audience applauded. I reluctantly joined them out of respect for the dancer.

The Stephenville and Deer Lake group had joined us in attending the Gros Morne Dance Festival. All three groups were in peak performing mode and had some activity or event planned for almost every day in our last month. No one seemed to mind, though, as we were getting to see a lot more of The Rock than before, and in the case of that particular day trip, some of Newfoundland's more artistic side.

The rest of the dance routine was similar to the first. Thankfully there was now music to follow, but I found it was still quiet. Each performance seemed excessively long, lasting beyond a reasonable point of enjoyment. My back started to ache after standing consistently for over an hour. I jumped at the opportunity to take part in a brief workshop where the instructors showed volunteers how to raise a dance partner in the air. It was the same move seen in Dirty Dancing, where Baby runs into Johnny's arms, using the momentum to lift her up into the air, arms and legs extended outward. I partnered with Samantha from the Stephenville group. She was nervous but excited. So was I. Samantha wasn't a large girl, but I didn't have a lot of upper body strength. I was confident I could lift her up, but uncertain if I could keep her there.

"You better not drop me, or you're in trouble, Mister!" she said with a sly smirk.

She ran into my arms and I raised her up. Barely. I tried desperately not to show the strain on my face and maintain a convincing bravado. Finally, we were told to let our partners down slowly.

"That was fun," Samantha said with a relieved grin. "We'll have to try that again sometime!"

We checked out other festival performances in the other areas. Some of us walked down a narrow path that cut through a tall field of grass, the tips of the blades standing taller than most of us. We followed wooden sticks stuck in the ground that acted as markers guiding us along. The flagging tape tied to them whipped and waved in the same coastal wind that blew through the tall grass, beckoning us with a salty maritime tune. The trail led us down a rocky bank where we gathered behind a crowd of spectators standing on a stony beach. Five minutes went by, but we couldn't see whatever it was we were supposed to be seeing. I was fascinated by the noticeable striations in the bands of metamorphic rock that jutted up from the beach, folding themselves into each other until they formed a sheer cliff. It made for a truly unique set piece.

My entrancement with the interesting geological formations was finally broken by gravelly sounds. It sounded like slow moving rocks, grinding and crushing against humming music, almost like a muffled didgeridoo, but still I saw no performers. I couldn't figure out what we were looking at until I finally saw something stir against the rocks on the beach.

It was a person. Two of them, actually. They had apparently been in front of the crowd the entire time. The two performers were camouflaged, painted head to toe in mottled tones of grey, eggshell, and other stone-like colours and patterns. From where I was standing, I couldn't even tell if they had clothes on. For all I knew, I was looking at an incredibly convincing paint job that covered their entire body, including crotch and nipples. The actors—or were they dancers?—were barely noticeable with their incredibly slow yet steady movements, crawling with what I expected was great effort over the rocks that looked exactly like them. I squinted, straining to see if there were any more invisible rock people that I had missed the first time, but there appeared to only be the two performers.

Finally, a young non-camouflaged woman stepped out in front of us. She narrated, explaining how the rock creatures were part of the myth of a local sea monster that somehow involved sea urchins and a girl on the cliffs. I could only hear bits and pieces of the story over the howling wind, made louder without grass or trees to dull its sharp whistle. The inclusion of camouflaged rock monsters alone left me intrigued by the Newfoundland lore.

It was the last day of the dance festival. Despite some of the lengthier performances, it ended earlier than we expected. Our group extended our excursion that day by spending the remainder of the evening on a beach in Deer Lake on our way back to Corner Brook. We frolicked in the local lake with our pant legs rolled up and playing in the sand. "Swimming" still wasn't allowed without sanctioned lifeguards on duty. I was musing about trail work with Erica when she reminded me the two of us didn't work that Wednesday because of the Newfoundland holiday: Orangemen's Day.

"Ya know. It's like, if ya work for the city or any other construction job where youse wear an orange vest, ya get the day off," Tony explained the next morning when we met at the sea-can container. I was skeptical of Tony, never sure if he was feeding me bullshit just to share a laugh with Shaun, so I looked it up online later that night. While it was indeed a Newfoundland and Labrador holiday, Orangemen's Day was far from what Tony had described. It was intended to commemorate the 1690 Battle of the Boyne which took place in what is now the Republic of Ireland. It was generally celebrated by those who were Protestant Irish or Scottish, of which Newfoundland had plenty. Tony didn't strike me as the patriotic or religious type. Maybe he was being sarcastic? I could never tell, but there must have been some truth to what Tony said because the rest of my group still had to go to work. Only Erica and I were allowed to stay home. I wasn't about to argue. A day off was a day off.

I used my free time that day to knock off a few items on my to-do list that had grown substantially since I started it: I wanted to send one more package home so I wasn't weighed down at the airport with Katimavik knick-knacks; I needed to sew a sweater of mine that Carlos had ripped in Quebec and promised me he would fix and—surprise—never did; I also had one particular project that I needed assistance to accomplish.

The privacy that Orangemen's Day granted me was exactly what I needed for me to go to Cyber Zone alone and undetected from curious groupmates. I wasn't interested in playing laser tag though.

Molly met me behind the welcome counter.

"What can I do for you, my son?" she asked cheerfully. "Jordan's not here, just so ya know."

"That's okay," I told her. "Maybe you can help me out…"

Julie had another 24 hours off that Friday, which left us with an extra-long PL-free weekend. Some of the group wanted to drink, others just wanted to relax. Luke, Erica, Valérie, and Rosalie left to play laser tag and go to the movies afterwards, leaving the rest of us at home.

"Who wants to driiiiiiiink?" Tiffany asked sing-songily as she emerged from her room with a bottle of vodka in hand. "Devon, you in?"

Carlos overheard. "Pft, why would he? He's a poo-see!"

And so it begins.

"Yeah, I'm in," I said with a laid-back attitude. Most of my anxiety over the Anne situation had dissipated, so I felt calmer and more comfortable with some risky behavior. It seemed like an appropriate time anyway, what with Julie being gone.

"Good. Because we're playing 20 Questions," Tiffany said.

Perfect, I thought. If Carlos kept claiming that he wanted me to get to know the group, then I'd get to know the group and the asshole could eat his words.

We gathered in Bethany and Valérie's room, a mismatched glass cup in each of our hands. It wasn't long before each of them was filled. I accepted that things were going to get heavy that night, but I was all in. Every time my cup was empty, I jiggled it in front of Bethany who had been playing bartender.

"Drunk Dey-vahn is funny!" she laughed, topping off my drink.

Drinking in the house—it was one of those little moments of naughtiness we were going to miss, among other things. A few drinks in and most of our questions focused on post-Katimavik topics: what everyone's plans were once they returned home, what we were going to miss and *not* miss about the program, and some drunken introspection on how we thought we'd changed since we'd joined.

It was my turn to ask someone a question. As drunk as I knew I was getting, I tried hard not to scowl at Carlos before I asked my question. He knew this was coming. I'd had it ready in the chAndrea since Tiffany announced the game, patiently waiting for the right time.

"So Carlos, you didn't exactly go into detail the other day, so I ask you now: How *exactly* did I ruin billeting for you?" I asked him. He wasted no time in replying, curtly shaking his head.

"I'm not answering. Tiff, go. Ask Beth a question," he deflected. Whatever boozy concoction Bethany had been slinging me all night was burning up my inhibitions quickly. Carlos wasn't getting off that easily this time.

"Just answer the fucking question, man! Here I am, getting drunk and chumming it up with you, Tiff, and Beth. I'm doing *exactly* what you wanted me to do, getting closer to everyone. Don't be a hypocrite!" I was counting on Carlos having as much pride as I had. If he was anything like me, as everyone said he was, he would not like having his integrity challenged so bluntly. I was right.

"Fuck you, *puta*! I don't have to do anything," he snapped. "You're only trying to be close to everyone because we only have a month left. You just want to feel better about yourself!" But fortunately, Tiffany and Bethany were on my side.

"Oh my God, Carlos. If you aren't going to play the game, then get out," she berated him. Bethany agreed. I didn't want to have everyone gang up on Carlos, but it was nice to have some back up for once and know that it wasn't just me that found his attitude and hypocrisy insufferable. I was drunk, but not impenetrable to his words that had sunk in. What if he was right? Was I just being selfish and acting that way for me?

Carlos was about to give another poor excuse when the door opened behind us. The rest of the group was back from the movies. Erica and Luke poked their heads into the room.

"Oh, hey guys." Once Tiffany brought the gang up to speed of what we'd gotten up to since they'd left, everyone else now wanted to join in, but Tiffany and Bethany refused. They thought it would be unfair to allow sober people to join a questioning game with participants who were already drunk.

"Especially Devon," Bethany said. I gave the crowd at the door a sloppy wink.

Voices grew louder until there were several arguments going on at once. I couldn't make heads or tails out of any of them. I helped myself to Tiffany's bottle to pour myself a drink and let things settle. It might have been overkill. Everything became a blur and it wasn't long before I passed out in my bed. I couldn't remember much of how the rest of the night unfolded but what I could recall the next morning were bits and pieces: Valérie sitting beside me, describing the movie they had seen, Rosalie crying, Erica yelling, and Luke acting pouty and sullen for some reason.

I woke up the next morning groggy and hungover, but with a satisfied grin, knowing I'd stayed out of the fights that had nothing to do with me, and that I'd put Carlos in his place.

CHAPTER 32

July 2006. Corner Brook.

As soon as I did it, I knew it was a mistake. Once the thought entered my mind, I immediately regretted it, like a cat climbing a tree, or making eye contact with a mall kiosk salesperson. There was no going back.

I started counting down.

One month left. Eight-ninths done. 30 days. Four weeks. Tick tock, Devon. Tick tock. I decided not to share this observation with anyone else. They would realize the impending countdown on their own.

It was a busy time at our work placements as much as it was at the Katimavik house. Stream and Trail staff were informed we'd soon be breaking ground for a new trail. Mini bulldozers and Cat excavators were parked in the bushier sections near Glynmill Pond. New employees had even been hired to help our crew to start cutting down trees and landscaping for the new trails. Technically, we were massively improving existing trails, which were little more than footpaths that cut through the overgrowth. There was a lot of work to be done.

I was excited for the long-term vision of more trails connecting people to the creek that fed into the large pond. The water feature was in the heart of Corner Brook. I expected it to look beautiful once the trails were complete. My enthusiasm led me to urging the group out for a walk one day to show them the preparation work Erica and I had been involved in. I was shocked to hear that most members of my group hadn't walked the scenic trails of their own accord yet. Rosalie was a surprising exception. I thought she would have abhorred walking the dirty trails and pushing past hanging branches to get through, but she had indeed explored parts of the trail on her own. She found it a gorgeous place for a stroll, reminding her of some of the walkways back in Ottawa. When I did manage to wrangle everyone to go for a walk, I showed them the massive pile of overturned earth next to the creek. They all agreed the new trails were going to be a great improvement to the city. It was too bad none of us would be around to see them finished.

"You'll just have to come back to see it, won't you, sweetie?" Jan told me the next day at work.

Jan was one of the newest employees hired to help us with the new workload. She was a woman in her mid-thirties, a motherly individual with an aged face, one with forlorn traces of deep past worries. Jan was sweet and soft spoken which was very out of place with the rest of the work crew. She also wasn't physically strong and usually relied on me, Shaun, or Tony to do heavy lifting. It made sense, but you could hear the frustration in our grunts at having to do extra labour. Jan was also an avid environmentalist, often expressing concerns for wildlife or plants whenever discussions arose regarding the new trails and further landscaping. It wasn't long before she would launch into long tirades about how our company should take better care of the trees instead of cutting them down. Once Jan learned about Katimavik and more or less what we did as volunteers, she was quick to offer suggestions as to how we should get involved with local activist groups which she herself belonged to. I quickly agreed I would look into it, even though I had no intention of doing so. The calendar for our last month was jam packed and had no room for the kinds of ideas Jan had begun to describe, but rather than explain, I just wanted the conversation to end. I realized Jan annoyed me in a similar way Jess had. There was no rhyme or reason. For all intents and purposes, Jan was a lovely person, but quickly became exhausting to listen to. I chalked my feelings up once again to a clash of personalities and kept my mouth shut so as not to upset her.

I was partnered with Jan one afternoon to move rolls of sod. They were piled onto a flatbed truck which was too large to be driven all the way down the rough trail that had been expanded into the underbrush next to it. As they were apt to do, Shaun and Terry had fucked off somewhere, leaving me and Jan to do the heavy lifting. She heaved loudly with each roll of sod she lifted onto her shoulders. I was worried she was going to fall over, but she managed to catch her balance before trudging away with it.

"So, got any big plans with your group this weekend?"

We did, actually. We were going river rafting.

It was one of the excursions I'd been working hard on my own to plan. It was the first of the three big excursions we would finish the program off with. The other two consisted of a camping trip to Gros Morne Mountain and a massive joint trip to L'Anse aux Meadows between all three groups. The Stephenville and Deer Lake participants were all jealous, which let me know I'd done well. River rafting wasn't a common activity for Katimavik groups to plan because of the inherent dangers. It was deemed too risky, so most groups didn't bother trying to convince Head Office otherwise, but I had started research early on in hopes of addressing those concerns. After several iterations of our excursion plan, Head Office finally approved it. River rafting might not have been the craziest thing to do, but to us, it felt like a dream. We still had a hard time believing it as Julie drove us down the highway following the Humber River to meet our raft guide, Kitt.

"Looks like the river is a bit high today," he told us during the required safety orientation. "That's good though, as it won't be as choppy."

Some of the girls sighed in relief. I pursed my lips in disappointment. I wanted it to be rough, wet, up and down, with plenty of splashing and squeals of glee and excitement. I knew the river wouldn't be too extreme though. When I called Kitt earlier for details during my planning of the excursion, he had explained the Humber river's relatively high safety rating compared to others in Newfoundland. The fact that it wasn't considered a dangerous river to raft on was something I highlighted in my excursion plan, a factor that likely helped us receive approval from Head Office. I wasn't going to complain, of course. Why would I? There we were, suited up with life jackets and helmets, stoked that we were doing something Katimavik participants rarely got to do.

"Alright, if everyone's ready, we can get going!"

As we floated down its gentle waters, Kitt explained some of the history of the Humber River as well as Corner Brook itself. He pointed out different geological formations as we passed them by, including the "Man in the Mountain." We were already familiar with the Corner Brook icon. Julie had pointed him out to us shortly after our arrival to Newfoundland. Having since driven past the anthropomorphic-looking cliff face on our way to various outings north of town, our group had gazed upon the old man's rocky visage many times. Kitt pointed out another face hidden amongst the rocks, however, one we were never told about.

"It's above the old man, looking downwards. Do you see it?" We squinted and tilted our heads in different ways. Only a few of us could make the second face out, or at least claimed to, anyway.

I was ecstatic when Kitt let us swim in a calmer section of the river. He was a certified lifeguard, which let us swim as per excursion policy. Not only that, we were also wearing life jackets, making it even safer to do so. I was the first to yelp with joy when I bounced off the tail end of the rubber raft into a deeper part of the Humber. That refreshing rush of cold water reminded me of home, but there wasn't a lot that didn't those days.

The rafting trip was over faster than I expected, which was surprising, considering how the high water level made our wet adventure slower and pretty uneventful. In some parts, it was almost boring. The pace wasn't enough to bother me, though, not when I knew we had done something so rare. The excursion came to a close when we passed under a bridge that crossed over into Summerside, a community on the western side of the river. As we pulled our raft ashore, Julie spoke up.

"Now, I know this will make *Devon* happy ..." I raised an eyebrow curiously. "But considering you guys are wearing lifejackets and Kitt is here, I think it's safe enough to let you guys jump off the bridge," she told us. "If you *want*," she added. "Don't feel like you have to."

Kitt concurred. "Oh yeah, people do it all the time. The river is high, so you guys will be fine!"

I inflated with exhilaration. Of course I wanted to! Much to my surprise, so did everyone else. I'd have assumed that Valérie or Rosalie would be too scared, but they were right next to me as we climbed atop the guard rail and readied ourselves to jump. The adrenaline pushed several of us to do it once more, all the while running up the grassy riverbank, giggling from the head rush of our first jump. It made me happy to have everyone try something that finished the excursion on such a high note. Swimming in rivers and bridge jumping were things I was often made fun of in my group, reckless activities that crazy small-town folk did. But now, my friends had a taste for those little joys, too.

The excitement of the day had tuckered most of us out that evening. I laid on the couch in the living room, hoping to finish a book Erica had lent me. The author, James Frey, had recently come under scrutiny for his literary forgery. After *A Million Little Pieces* was touted as a must-read by Oprah's Book Club, the author was revealed to have lied about many of the events that supposedly took place or altered the details surrounding them. Despite these controversies, I still became engrossed in the book, particularly the conclusion.

I knew little of addictions, except for my mom smoking cigarettes. What I did know, however, was that a life spent addicted to hard drugs and alcohol was a horrible experience in which people were always hurt, either directly or indirectly. Frey wasn't shy about his disdain for traditional forms of help, like support groups, professional therapists, or giving in to a higher power. I could see his point—even if those all had the potential to help you get better, didn't it still fall on you to utilize them? In the end, weren't we as individuals the ultimate catalyst in improving ourselves, regardless of the tools we choose? I didn't think it mattered what the driving force behind doing so was, whether it was guilt, pride, shame, or anywhere in between, so long as we strived for redemption. It would always come down to a choice, a choice we would have to make in order to change.

I closed the book, contemplating the cacophony of philosophies that danced in my head like fairies when Carlos walked in.

"Good job with the excursion, by the way. That was… that was a lot of fun," he said softly. "Especially the bridge jumping. I *never* did anything like that." His comment seemed genuine and made me crack a smile. That's when I noticed the pile of papers underneath his arm. They were letters, letters I had written him. "Can we talk?"

"Sure."

As part of a communications and art activity awhile back, Julie had given each of us manila file folders to decorate any way we fancied. They were meant to hold any little receipts, pieces of art, sketches, whatever things we wanted to keep as mementos. These folders also acted as an internal mail system for the house for people to leave spontaneous and anonymous notes or letters of encouragement.

Julie wanted them to be used to foster positivity in the group and as individuals. Whether it was a light-hearted joke of someone complimenting you on some obscure thing you did ("You were amazing at brushing your teeth the other night!") or a random doodle of you with a speech bubble containing some inside joke or familiar catch phrase you weren't aware you used, it was hard to deny there wasn't something oddly satisfying in finding something new in our folders. For Carlos and me, though, it was how we communicated whenever we were pissed at each other.

Our meeting with Julie had highlighted the problem between me and Carlos, but little had changed. Hashing out our beefs face-to-face wasn't working, given Carlos' stubborn refusal to elaborate in person. Julie's suggestion of communicating through letters seemed to work at first. Carlos was willing to participate. As for me, writing allowed me to take my time and effectively express myself while avoiding snapping at him, especially in front of everyone. Despite our best intentions, the letters themselves were not constructive or positive. They essentially became transcripts of our fights, hurling blame and insults and frustrations at the other. Finally at the end of my rope with the last rude letter I had received from him, I wrote Carlos that if he had anything else to say to me, he could say it to my face. It must have worked, because there he was.

I gathered my letters, having also kept the ones he'd given me. Together, somehow holding back the anger in our words, Carlos and I read the letters to each other, explaining the written jabs we had laboured over to deliver with scathing effect. Both of us knew how to push the other's buttons, but as we discovered that evening, sometimes the messages were lost in translation. There were several times we had to ask what the other meant. If Carlos proved to be anything like me, his heart was racing as much as mine was, pumping from the anxiety, the hatred, the confusion, but underneath that all, a desire for peace. The next half hour proved to be very cathartic. Like myself, Carlos had been struggling to make the most of the program with the time we had left and wanted whatever animosity between us to be resolved.

"I gotta say, *puta*, you write really, really well," he said. I ignored the insult woven into his backhanded compliment.

Carlos was impressed not only by the eloquence of my writing, but also how much I remembered about him, the seemingly unimportant and minute details he revealed about himself early in the program. In turn, I expressed the respect I had for his passions and work ethic. It felt like we were in elementary school, having been forced to end our talk by saying one nice thing about the other person. Only it wasn't forced, but by our own volition. As childish as that was, it seemed to work.

After all was said and done, there was an increasingly real sense of calm resolution between us. We felt like we were finally in a better place and hugged it out. Carlos decided to go for a walk and invited me along, but I politely declined. I had committed to calling my friends back home that night.

Once Carlos left, I grabbed the cordless phone and parked myself onto the couch. The living room was surprisingly still empty. Everyone else was oddly absent. I wasn't about to go hunting for the rest of the group, though, and dialed my calling card, having memorized the series of numbers by then.

Courtney picked up.

"So you finally made up with the foreign guy, huh? About damn time," she said bluntly. "We were getting sick of hearing about you two fighting all the time." I normally didn't share anything about relationships with Bailey and Courtney, especially personal, but I would usually vent to them about Carlos. It felt good to say something other than how annoying he had been. Even though it was something different that time, Courtney clearly wasn't interested. "But enough about your stupid squabbles, let me tell you about our bike trip!"

The two sisters had recently returned home from a bike trip. They had biked through the Rockies to Calgary to attend their cousin's wedding. It had taken them about two weeks. I was excited to hear about their experience as I hadn't spoken to them for quite some time due to how busy they'd been. I asked about the places they stopped at, the sights they saw, even the food they ate along the way. Courtney didn't go into as much detail as I would have liked, only telling me a few key events.

"And next year we're going to bike across Canada, and you're coming with us, whether you like it or not." I could never tell if Courtney was being serious with her classic dry tone. My friendship between her and her sister was built on a foundation of silliness. We never took anything too serious, which made planning things difficult sometimes. The sisters tended to go with the flow. Whereas they hated questions, I liked answers. I had found an appreciation for getting everyone on the same page, especially during Katimavik when so many things needed to be coordinated with so many people whilst volunteering or travelling. Something grand, like biking across Canada, seemed like it warranted a discussion at least, one I knew Courtney was reluctant to participate in, at least right then and there on the phone. She and Bailey had mentioned the topic once before, but they had never brought it up again and it quickly faded from my memory until that night. The premise seemed absurd, but undeniably adventurous.

"Okay, I'm in," I told her, confirming my commitment to the ludicrous idea.

"I checked the calendar, and we don't have anything planned for the rest of the day," said Julie, poking her head into the small living room several days later. "So I have a surprise for everyone. Now, I won't say what it is ..." She beamed with an air of mystery. "But there are two conditions: *Everyone* has to go, and if everyone's in, we have to leave *soon*." She explained the necessity for leaving immediately was in order to return back home before it got too dark, but refused to answer any other questions, even threatening to cancel the mysterious surprise if we asked her any more. "Oh! And you'll all need swimming gear!"

Everyone was unanimously in and quickly scattered in fits of excitement. Some of us flew downstairs to grab towels from the basement bathroom while others bolted upstairs to grab our own bathing suits. Within five minutes, we were all in the Katimavik van. There was utter silence between us until we drove past Curling, a neighbourhood of Corner Brook close to the bay.

"… So it has something to do with swimming…" I mused aloud, breaking the silence.

Julie spoke up. "Devon, if you guess anymore or even *talk* like you're guessing, we're not going." Luke punched me in the leg. I rubbed it, wincing. I shot a look back at Luke. We were already on the road. It wasn't like Julie was going to turn the van around. The silence bothered me almost as much as not knowing the damn surprise. The van was rarely ever that quiet. There was almost always someone talking. The void without that left me uneasy, but I reminded myself not to stir the pot, which I'd inadvertently been doing those days.

Carlos and I had moved past our deep-seated grudge. We no longer hated each other with a burning ferocity, but embers left us prone to the occasional wrestling match. They didn't have the same fire, though, and the matches were more fun and playful than punishing. While that conflict had more or less been settled, others took its place.

I had unintentionally arrived late for dinner and meetings several times that week, despite my best efforts. The latest incident was on a day Julie had taken over cooking from the house managers so she could make us her much-talked about walnut burgers. She assured us that despite being a vegan recipe, they were delicious. She had not been exaggerating. They were the most delicious burgers I had ever tasted. Before I started cleaning the dishes, Julie pulled me aside to talk about my repeated tardiness. Even after I explained why I had been visiting Jordan and Molly at Cyber Zone, she still wasn't happy and threatened me with a CTI if I was late one more time. I hadn't received any CTIs yet, but I didn't want to risk it and promised it wouldn't happen again.

The reason I'd been late for dinner that particular day was work related. Once our work had ended, we were expected to attend a safety meeting held at Tony's house. According to Shaun, "safety meeting" was essentially code for "staff party." Other Corner Brook Stream and Trail employees were present, including our supervisor Bret. Bethany had also recently joined us, as her placement had little work for her to do. As a couple, she and Erica were thrilled to be working together, but it also forced me to work with Jan more often.

Jan seemed to have lightened up after a few drinks at the work gathering. She wasn't as wound up by the unending social and environmental injustices going on in the world. Egged on by Shaun and Tony, she overdid it just a little and soon realized she wouldn't be able to drive home. I offered to drive Jan rather than being inconvenienced by leaving her car at Tony's. She offered me cab fare in payment of my kind deed and because I saw how late it was once I had dropped her off. I accepted and had the cab driver drop me off a block away from the house to avoid any unwanted attention. Even though I called the house to let Julie know I would be late, I was still reprimanded because of how many times I'd already been late to group functions that week. No good deed went unpunished it seemed, but sneaking leftover walnut burger bites while cleaning up made me feel a bit better.

So I kept my mouth begrudgingly shut in the van as we drove toward wherever Julie's surprise was. The silence in the van didn't just bother me, though, and proved to be too much for Julie now. Emphasizing that while there were still to be no questions, she reminded us with a lighthearted giggle that we could still talk. We didn't know where our destination was, though, or how long the drive would be. Was it just around the corner? An hour away? What span of time were we filling?

I spoke up again. Carefully.

"With Julie being all mysterious, it kind of makes me realize… we're like Scooby-Doo and the Mystery Inc. gang! Always driving somewhere in a van, getting into hijinks." Everyone turned their heads to me, curious as to what in the hell I was going on about. "Okay sure, we don't solve mysteries per se, but even that was kind of like volunteering. Think about it: Did you ever see any of them get paid?" The silence now broken, everyone began to argue that if we were to compare ourselves to the classic cartoon characters, who was which one? No one could make up their mind on whether I was the always-eating, hippy-esque Shaggy, or titular Scooby-Doo whose laugh I could do a decent impression of. Everyone agreed girly-girl Rosalie was Daphne and that Luke could pull off Fred's ascot, but no one could peg down who Velma was. We gave her to Carlos, just because.

Julie drove for another half hour or so out of town. To the east was a flat table-top mountain with no discernible peaks nor snow to be seen. Between us and the mountains was a wide valley covered in short, stunted trees, most of which were either evergreen or appeared to be stripped barkless and dry by coastal winds. I recognized the mountain scenery. Carlos and I had been this way on a short day trip with Larry and Ruby when they'd driven the two of us to Lark Harbor during billeting. I wondered if that was where Julie was taking us, but she pulled the van to the side of the road as if to answer my question.

"So, here's the deal ..."

A short hike later through the stunted landscape, then through some taller groves of trees, we arrived at Julie's secret destination. The faint trail brought us to the top of a short cliff where everyone gazed down below at the most crystalline waters any of us had ever seen. Surrounded by steep cliff edges and tall trees beyond, the pools below sparkled brilliantly with what little sun came through the foliage. Considering the stunted flora we had hiked through from the road, I noticed the vegetation around us was lush and green, making it feel like we had stumbled upon a secret fountain that might be frequented by fairies and other magical forest creatures. The water was so clear, we could see the individual colours of the rocks at the bottom of the pools, even from where we stood.

"Anna showed me this place before she had left," Julie told us. As this was a "completely off the records" excursion, Julie emphatically stressed that while we were allowed to swim, there was to be absolutely no cliff jumping, climbing, or dangerous behaviour of any sorts. She couldn't fudge her way out of this if someone got hurt. Julie looked at me firmly upon this warning and rightfully so. I was already gauging the depth of some of the pools in comparison to the heights of the nearby cliffs trying to determine if jumping off them was even viable. When I caught her stern look, I nodded, determined not to ruin it for everyone. We carefully climbed down the more manageable parts of the cliffs and made our way to the shores.

The clear water was even deeper than it looked. Diving down from the surface of the water, I could barely reach the bottom. During one dive, I spotted rocks brighter than those around them. When I surfaced, I saw I had clutched in my hand a pink shell necklace. I assumed it must have fallen off from a previous diver. As much as I wanted to believe it was a gift from Newfoundland fairy folk, I could tell it was a common jewellery piece I'd seen in alternative clothing stores. I gave it to Valérie who thought it was pretty. The unexpected treasure made the tranquilizing pool feel even more magical.

Sitting on a rock among the warm waters with my fellow groupmates, I took in the imagery of the sparkling waters and the sun casting shadows amongst the trees as it began to set behind them and eventually the Blomidon Mountain range. It was unbelievable that such a hidden gem could be in such an inconspicuous place, a short hike from the roadside. In that moment, I didn't feel like a volunteer, or like I was travelling, or that I was even a participant bound by any rules. I was just there, in a beautiful spot surrounded by friends. I didn't think the image of those sparkling waters would ever escape my memory.

After drying off, we made a small fire at the cliff top, the same spot where Julie had spoken to us.

"Final debriefing is around the corner. We don't need to discuss it in great detail tonight," she said, being mindful of the time and that we still needed to drive home. "But I want you to know what to expect. I'm willing to let you have drinks—within reason of course—and even junk food if you want." Final debriefing, she reminded us, wasn't just an excuse to break all the rules near the end of a long nine-month program, but a time intended to focus on what we were going to take from it.

Maybe that was Julie's reasoning. It was probably for the best to get those pesky distractions out of the way rather than sneaking them behind her back. After all, there would no doubt be a lot on our minds. A few drinks might help figure out exactly what that was.

CHAPTER 33

July 2006. Gros Morne National Park.

Of course the forecast called for rain.

It had been another week of intense heat that whole week. Hope against hope, I pleaded to the Maritime gods for the dry weather to remain until we returned. But every time we checked the weather reports, they said the same thing: that there would be a sudden change in precipitation. In other words, rain, rain, rain.

We readied ourselves anyway. All of us had been told about Gros Morne by coworkers, family members who had visited Newfoundland in the past, and of course our billet families. All of them emphatically told us how beautiful the park was, especially the view from the top. It was also one of our larger excursions planned so we weren't about to cancel it.

We brought three tents: one for the guys, another for the girls, and the third, smallest one for Julie, who would be sharing it with her friend Corlynne whom we agreed to let join us. We pitched camp in the rain that night at the base of the mountain. Come hell or high water, we were going to attempt the trail to the top the next morning.

Luke, Carlos, and I set up our tent quickly and with few directions spoken aloud between us, unlike the girls who were fighting and struggling with theirs. Adhering to Katimavik's rule for the separation of men's and women's living quarters meant the three of us got a tent to ourselves. The girls mocked us for having the smaller tent, but given there were only three of us rather than five, we still had extra space for comfort. This far into the program, we knew better than to point that out to the girls and instead relished the perk as we stretched out, listening to them argue amongst themselves.

Once all the tents were (eventually) pitched, everyone gathered around the fire pit. None of us were quite ready to retire to our slightly damp sleeping bags quite yet. Julie mentioned she had a surprise—she had a lot of them those days—but was hoping to have a fire going before she revealed what it was. More motivated by the desire for the trip to truly feel like camping than by Julie's hopes, I worked as best I could to birth a fire. Using some scrap paper and cardboard I found in the van for tinder, I did the best I could to get the flame from a lighter to grow into something bigger. I continued blowing at the burning edges of the flammable material, hoping the glowing embers would eventually catch the kindling around it on fire. The rain hadn't completely stopped, but it had lightened up by that point, which made things easier.

"Devon, give it up. You're never going to get that going in the rain," Rosalie pleaded, rubbing her arms to warm up.

I tsk-tsked her and continued blowing. "Little known fact, Ro," I said, carefully feeding more crumpled paper to the fire. "People from BC have unique fire-making abilities."

"What, you use gasoline?" she laughed.

"No." I looked back at her with mock seriousness. "We have *dragon breath*."

I inhaled deeply and felt my diaphragm expand slowly. I blew precisely at a promising section of paper and watched as its edges glowed brighter with an orange singe. With one more deep breath, it caught fire and quickly engulfed the neighbouring sticks around it. I continued blowing for several minutes, cautious to avoid inhaling any smoke or fumes. With each powerful breath, I raised the flames higher with a roar that grew louder and louder until it caught the illuminated eyes of everyone sitting nearby. I was as proud as I was surprised to have started the fire in the rain, but kept that to myself. Finally content that it would continue burning without my assistance, I sat on a log along with everyone else.

"Dragon breath," I whispered, winking at Rosalie. She rolled her eyes, but I caught her little smile.

"Yay! This is awesome! Thanks, Devon!" Julie clapped her hands with glee and hurried into her tent. When she returned, she was holding a brown paper bag in her hand. "I know you guys weren't *properly* screeched in Deer Lake a few weeks back because we weren't allowed rum." Luke and I looked at each other, remembering that we had recently done our own version. We quickly looked back at Julie to avert suspicion. "So I thought I'd screech you guys here. As someone from Newfoundland herself, Corlynne has agreed to help me do it."

And with a few recited lines of a classic Newfie jig and a shot each from the bottle passed around the fire, we were all screeched in. Again. *They do say the third time's a charm.* It did in fact feel a bit more traditional, even without a salty cod tongue to kiss. With a fire and now a shot of rum warming our insides, we all went to bed shortly later with silent prayers that the next day would bring drier weather for our hike up Gros Morne Mountain.

It did not.

Our spirits may not have been dampened while setting up camp, but they were a little water-logged the following morning. Most of us ate breakfast in the dry sanctuary of the Katimavik van, sitting sullenly in the seats as wet tents were packed up by those who hadn't "made" the breakfast of yogurt and granola, which really only consisted of scooping the food out into bowls. When we arrived at the base of the mountain, most of us opted for punching armholes in garbage bags as make-shift ponchos to keep the rain off us.

"Newfie rain jackets," Corlynne called them.

They seemed to do the trick. We needed every bit of perking up as we could. Our enthusiasm was low, but we decided to truck on. We were here. It wasn't like we were going to *not* hike because the conditions weren't perfect. We had even written in our itinerary report a course of action in case of "adverse weather." We knew that rain was a possibility, though, and unless it was a torrential downpour, we would simply dress appropriately and stick with our plans. Much to my dismay, "sucking it up," was not a reasonable phrase that Head Office would accept in our itinerary, even if it was indeed what we had to do.

One by one, we trudged up the muddy slopes, passing signs heeding warnings about wildlife and mountainous weather conditions as well as suggestions of suitable footwear to wear and sufficient water supplies to bring. We were prepared and had all those things. Spread between ten individuals, the weight of our supplies wasn't too encumbering.

It was an hour of uphill drudgery before we reached the first rest stop, a wooden viewing platform. In front of us lay the rest of the mountain enclosed in fog. Over a hearty but silent lunch break, Julie spoke up.

"We have a decision to make, gang," she said. If the fog didn't lift, visibility would be minimal at the top of the mountain. Not only would this mean we would miss a world-class panoramic sight, we ran the risk of potentially walking over a cliff. Julie's worries were not exaggerated. I had been warned of the same danger from Larry and Ruby and other Newfie residents. Under the worst conditions, visibility became so low that you couldn't see where you were going. Even signs posted along the trail reiterated the very real danger.

"If we're to keep going, it has to be a democratic group decision," Julie declared. "Majority rules. There can be no complaints if we don't go to the top." I hoped Julie wouldn't look at me. She didn't, even though I would have been the correct person to read disappointment from. We had heard so much about Gros Morne. It wasn't just one of our big three excursions; it was something on everyone's to-do list before we left. We *had* to make it to the top.

I thought about the decision. It didn't seem like something I would be able to shrug off easily. The goal of hiking Gros Morne had burrowed its way deep inside of me and lay there like an obstinate sliver. It couldn't just be ignored. I toyed with the repercussions if we didn't climb it, if most of the group wavered and said no. But if we didn't do it now, would we ever get the chance again? I was so excited to come to Newfoundland and here was the opportunity to experience it in what felt was one of its rawest forms: an elusive, enigmatic, yet unique piece of this country that demanded to be noticed and appreciated. Did I want that kind of regret haunting me? When would we ever come back to Gros Morne? To Newfoundland? I couldn't speak for everyone else, but I lived on the opposite side of the country. If we didn't do it today ...

This wasn't just any random hike or just another item on a list. I realized that we hadn't done anything like this as a group before. We'd done a lot together, but we hadn't climbed a mountain. There had never been such a physical and mental demand of everyone that enduring the rain, climbing steep trails, and defying the dangerous conditions asked of us. The thought of triumphing over the elements with people I'd grown close to was attractive beyond the simple justification of it being a fun excursion. I wanted to share that kind of success with everyone, even if we all felt it in our own way. If I was one of the people who refused to climb further and resulted in us descending back down the mountain, how would I feel? My decision here was not solitary. There were others to consider. Would that make a unanimous decision more meaningful or a concession more painful? No one had voiced a desire to give up yet, but that didn't mean everyone wanted to necessarily continue either. But as Julie said, it was a group decision.

I looked up at the behemoth hump, cloaked in grey fog. I could barely make out the dark patch of earth far off into the distance. Across a shallow valley was a trail that snaked up a rocky talus slope, scarring the side of the mountain we had to traverse. The fog was blowing noticeably quick past the base of the mountain. The slope rose into the distance, but not so high that I couldn't see clouds slowly roll away behind it. A few of these clouds parted to reveal a hint of blue sky. A smile crept across my face. Maybe it would all be blown away by the time we got started?

I stood up.

"I know there's a chance we may not get to see much with the fog. If anyone's going to be disappointed, it's going to be me." I looked at everyone, still sitting quietly. "But I still want to go. If enough people don't want to," I said, looking squarely at Julie, "I'll be okay with that decision and won't say anything else." I sat back down. No one said anything. The damp air around us absorbed any small noise, making it uncomfortably silent until Tiffany spoke up.

"Devon's right. Come on guys, we busted our asses this far. Let's keep going!"

Luke rose in agreement. "Aww hell, that mountain's not going to climb itself!" He sounded less enthusiastic than his words suggested, but his spirit was there. Everyone else stood up. I didn't know if the others saw the hopeful weather change I did or just went along with the momentum of the first people who spoke up, but it became unanimous—we were carrying on. Despite what Julie had said, it felt like my rally had built us up past the point for any dissent to have any effect. We all wanted to climb that motherfucker and we were going to make it happen.

It wasn't long after we started our ascent up the rocky slope that the fog subsided and we were able to see the forest below us. I wasn't sure if it was the fresh mountain air or having evaded a haunting heap of regret, but I was bounding off large rocks like a goat. I would look back to see the others gradually making their way up, taking pictures of them either exasperatedly smiling, flipping me off, or both. Our determination was greater than ever and even though most of us were quickly covered in sweat, no one complained. The final stretch to the summit took us over a path of flat stepping stones which guided us over a soft mossy part of the trail. I watched everyone step across them with great pride, exuberant in having climbed—no, conquered—Gros Morne Mountain. It was the highest mountain any of us had ever climbed.

We were rewarded with fogless views of the sparkling fjords that formed the Western Coast of that part of Newfoundland. All the sweat and muttered swearing had led us here, but we had conquered more than a mountain. Each of us had our own personal reasons that drove us forward. Whatever those were, the past frustrations and anger and worries we'd held on to were briefly swept away by a cooling wind. We may have started that climb wet and cranky, but we would leave those feelings there at the top of Gros Morne and come back with something else. Something lighter. Better.

Everyone gazed upon the fjords in reverent awe, no doubt thinking the same thing.

We were going to miss this place.

CHAPTER 34

August 2006. L'Anse aux Meadows/St. Anthony.

Two weeks. Two weeks were left. It was all I could think about. Every time the impending countdown popped into my head, I swear I could hear the ominous tick-tock of a grandfather clock off in the distance.

I didn't have time to dwell on the dreaded thought of "the end." Being occupied kept me from endless pondering, and therefore sane. That day, I was running around like everyone else. We were packing bags, moving things to the van, preparing meals, or frantically doing something or other to get ready for our final and biggest excursion of Katimavik.

Part of the intense preparations was due to the fact that the cluster would be travelling together in two Katimavik vans, not three as would have normally been expected. The Stephenville and Deer Lake groups had shrunk somewhat since we last saw them. Each had participants who recently quit, leaving just enough of us remaining to fit everyone in the cluster into two vans. Aside from making the excursion report appealing by being more financially economical and environmentally friendly, using two vans instead of three and mixing the passengers between them also brought a new excitement to things.

It had been a long time since any of the groups had a fully occupied van. Now they were filled with participants, all brimming with talk. There was rarely a minute someone wasn't sharing their eagerness to see the historical Viking villages of L'Anse aux Meadows, what they wanted to do before Katimavik was done and over with, or how they were preparing for the end of the program. Some of us still had packages to send home while others wanted to spend time with co-workers or billet families they had grown close to. Everyone was unanimous, however, in loathing the massive cleaning that was to begin shortly after we returned from our last excursion.

Head Office was moving Katimavik's Newfoundland presence to the island's east coast. Communities had expressed a great desire for volunteer groups there, especially in St. John's. As such, all three current groups, the only groups in Newfoundland at the time, had to "shut down" their respective Katimavik houses. This meant more than simply sweeping and mopping in preparation for new incoming groups. There were no more new groups coming in a rotation. As a result, Deer Lake, Stephenville, and Corner Brook Katimavik houses were to be cleaned up, cleaned out, and completely emptied of food, dishes, furniture, everything necessary to put the houses back on the market. It was a daunting workload, especially for me and Luke. We were the last pair of house managers and needed to complete the majority of cleaning before we began our final debriefing camp. I tried not to think about it and let it distract me from the epic trip we were currently on.

After a brief overnight stay at a church in Port au Choix, we carried on to St. Anthony on the northern end of the island. When planning the driving itinerary, our PLs had discouraged driving late into the night, and not necessarily because they would be the ones driving. Many Newfies warned us how moose were notorious for causing fatal motor accidents along Newfoundland roads. Whereas I thought Katimavik vans were indestructible tanks, Julie informed me how the iconic vehicles were surprisingly structurally weak, a small detail she had learned during her own training. For almost nine months, we had been driven around in flimsy metal frames on wheels. With how many participants were crammed into the vans, hitting a moose would be devastating. As such, the front passengers were emphatically given the role of "moose watcher." Their duty was to provide an additional pair of eyes to watch for any massive stray ungulates. We had also learned there was an albino moose spotted north of the island recently that week, a neat bit of news that made being lookout a bit more exciting and tolerable. Even when I wasn't on moose watch, I scanned the sides of the road vigilantly, hoping to spot the rare animal. I wanted to see it, just not up *too close.*

As we drove along Highway 430, I noticed small plots of vegetable gardens planted near the road. Every ten minutes or so we would pass by one. It was obvious that most belonged to one of the nearby houses they were planted by, but occasionally we would pass by a garden smack dab in the middle of nowhere. These odd, random patches of earth appeared to have been planted far away from any sort of populated area. They were planted mere metres away from the highway itself, but all were surrounded by some sort of fencing, some being more elaborate than others. Some fences were neat and well-constructed, artistic endeavours worthy of a second glance from a passing van filled with curious eyes. I spotted fences constructed of wooden panels with hearts or diamond shapes cut out of them with the posts adorned with painted pinwheels, and entrances designed with arched trellises covered in some sort of climbing green plant. Other fences were incredibly rustic, basic barriers that were cobbled together with visibly aged wood hastily nailed or lashed together with rotting rope. Some fences simply consisted of orange plastic netting tied to posts. It was the same kind of netting I'd seen on certain parts of the trail we were working on in Corner Brook, the kind intended to keep pedestrians out of construction sites. Every garden we passed, however, was unique in their layout, what was planted and grew, and the makeshift manner of the fence created to protect the veggies inside. I thought of them as perfect examples of the enduring and practical nature of Newfies.

As if she read my mind and possibly others in the van, Alice, the Stephenville PL who had been riding in our van, spoke up.

"Everyone's probably noticed the gardens on the side of the road." A murmur of curiosity confirmed I was not the only one who had been watching them. "Because fertile soil is rare on the island, people garden wherever they can." Participants in the van began to watch for the next garden, their existence now explained. Alice chuckled to herself. "There's a reason they call it '*the Rock*.'"

Our PL's slow and casual driving speed allowed us to take in the unique coastal views. I was surprised at how flat the highway had remained as we drove through rural communities which seemed to all have quaint names: Flower's Cove, Savage Cove, Green Island Brook, Eddie's Cove. A lot of coves, really. Each small town reminded me of the home I would be returning to soon, tiny neighbourhoods of houses, the requisite gas station, a nearby liquor store, maybe a small retailer. The paltry places might have seemed pitiful to anyone from some large metropolitan city like Vancouver or Toronto, but to the residents of that town, these tiny nodes of commerce breathed life into a town that would yield families and children who would have their own adventures and stories, memories to hold onto when those same people bravely ventured beyond the town boundary, past the next town over, maybe even managing to get off the Rock itself. Even though we drove through in the middle of the day in the summer, the communities remained eerily quiet.

Hours later, we arrived at St. Anthony, the last town north along Highway 430. The town's local Lions Club had kindly allowed us to stay in their hall for the night. A gaggle of youth poured from the vans like an unexpected clown car bringing in backpacks, tote bins, cloth shopping bags, and coolers. The last contained our supper, which several predetermined participants commenced cooking or reheating using the available kitchen. After a satisfying dinner was eaten and the dishes washed, cleaned, and stacked neatly away, a handful of participants left the hall to spend the evening exploring the small town of St. Anthony.

The large group of us wandered aimlessly this way and that until we found the shoreline. The town was small, so it didn't take long. Along the beach, we came across an odd structure. It looked like the skeletal frame of a small wooden ship. The bottom half of it was buried under the gravel. There were no sails, only ropes that connected the two wooden masts to the bow, stern, and other parts of the ship. I couldn't tell if it was a forgotten boat that had actually sunk into the ground or a display. My guess was that the structure was intended to be a sort of playground for kids to play and climb on, a tangible model of real ships to remind them of the town's maritime heritage.

"I mean, our playground had a couple of swings and a slide," I commented, envisioning myself as a majestic captain with the helm in his hands. "But this is pretty fun too."

We carried on, further exploring the shoreline until we found a wooden dock. Peering over its edge, we spotted jellyfish near the surface of the water. I had never seen jellyfish before and was surprised at how much they did in fact look and, despite the warnings from others when I poked it with a stick, feel like jelly.

Feeling rebellious with our unsupervised adventure, some participants decided to buy beer. It obviously couldn't be brought back to the Lions Club hall, so it was drank in the shadowy arch of the back exit to a large building several streets over. Regardless of Luke's assurance that no one would be caught and that everything would be fine, I politely declined to partake. This was our last big excursion and we were barely two weeks away from going home. I didn't want to risk anything that might shorten that time. Bottles emptied, we tucked the evidence politely into the corner of the covered nook and returned to the hall.

Unsurprisingly, the PLs were the first to bed, tired from a long day of driving. Most of the participants stayed up. No doubt spurred with the help of the recent illicit alcohol consumption, a game of Truth or Dare soon emerged in one of the far corners of the hall, away from PL ears. I chuckled, wondering what age that game really stopped being played. I contemplated joining but was engaged with the conversation Stephenville's Olivia and I were having.

Olivia confided aspirations to be a sex therapist. She wasn't the least bit embarrassed about her goal, instead intrigued by the intimate act in itself. She wanted to know the broader impact it had on people, how it affected their health, their relationships, even their outlooks on life. I listened intently as the petite blonde Québécoise shared what she had learned, the theories she had heard, and how she hoped to eventually attend school to pursue this passion. It wasn't much of a secret that Olivia was in an exclusive relationship with Matthieu, a boy from her own group. I wondered about the conversations the two of them must have had about the topic, whether they discussed it intelligently or became inspired by it.

I heard a voice call over to us quietly. "Dev, Olivia! Come play!" Samantha called.

Olivia resolved to go to bed, however. "I enjoyed our talk," she said, touching my shoulder softly before walking to the other end of the hall where a makeshift sleeping area was set up. I joined the others sitting in a circle on the floor.

My experience with Truth or Dare often entailed the "dare" involving an act that was disgusting, asinine, or involving a degree of nakedness. On rare occasions, it meant kissing someone. For the handful of times I'd played the game in which that happened, I always found myself struggling to hide my secret and awkward eagerness to kiss a girl if my name ever became part of the dare. They always seemed to maintain an indifferent composure, eliciting little to no reaction when the dare was voiced and after it was done, at least none that I noticed. I wasn't ugly, but I wasn't confident enough that I didn't consider myself unattractive. Maybe the idea of kissing me just didn't merit a school-girl swoon. Perhaps a well-practised poker face was better than a visible cringe. Thankfully I'd managed to avoid any sort of memories worth repressing.

I was curious if the situation would occur again. I wasn't sure if I would behave the same way I had in times past when the bottle found itself pointing at me. I was finding myself leaning towards choosing "truth" if that inevitable moment ever came, believing it to be the safer option given the current situation. As more and more participants completed their turn at the spinning whim of the empty plastic Coke bottle on the floor, I was beginning to think I wasn't the only one who had those thoughts. People lost interest in dares and soon everyone was choosing "truth." The theme did, however, remain sexual. People were asked very private, intimate questions: how many partners had they been with? Had they ever masturbated to the thought of someone in their group? Had anyone ever had sex in the Katimavik house? People were offered the respectful option to decline answering if they chose, likely out of respect and privacy in case people involved were present. I was caught up in silently observing and listening, roused after my discussion with Olivia shortly beforehand. She would regret missing out in the morning. I thought Olivia would have been in her element and learned a few things in early preparation for her unconventional career.

As we went around the circle, it became clear who was sexually experienced and who wasn't. I was surprised to learn Samantha had never even French kissed anyone before. I was oddly proud that no one in the circle passed judgement when she admitted her secret. It didn't even feel like we were playing Truth or Dare anymore. We were just strangers-turned-volunteers-turned-friends talking really. The topic just happened to be about sex. People had even stopped spinning the bottle and began sharing willingly, making the private subject seem a little more innocent than I expected. That didn't stop me from likely blushing when Stephenville's Seth—who was casually but openly gay—revealed that if he was going to have sex with anyone in the circle we all sat in, it'd be me. Not knowing what else to say, I thanked him semi-sarcastically. He winked, trying not to giggle. Samantha, who sat next to me, was asked the same question and nonchalantly gave the same answer.

"I'd say Devon as well."

I accepted the compliment in the same manner, a few degrees less sarcastic. Neither of us said anything else though and let the conversation move on, now with a new question in tow.

"Okay, if you had to have sex with any of the PLs ..."

Looking around, I realized we were actually a good-looking group. Everyone had some attractive physical quality about them—a charming smile, unblemished skin, kempt hair, alluring bosoms, enticing eyes. I couldn't help but wonder what I brought to the table.

CHAPTER 35

August 2006. Corner Brook.

Due to our return from our L'Anse aux Meadows excursion, there was no house meeting that Sunday. This left me and Luke less prepared than we'd have preferred. We were to be the last weekly house managers. After us, there was going to be a daily rotation between pairs of participants. Julie explained in no uncertain terms that Luke and I had additional chores to accomplish, chores that couldn't be passed onto the next house managers. This included deep cleaning the basement, using up as much food in the fridge as possible while still shopping for fresh ingredients, and preparing to decommission the house. There were some things that we couldn't do until the very last few days, like removing furniture or taking apart beds, but a lot of it still fell onto me and Luke. He thought I was putting too much thought into things when I started writing down everything that needed to be done, breaking down and organizing tasks according to how long I expected them to take. I disagreed. It seemed like a perfectly reasonable approach, considering how much work we had to do. I also didn't want to be stuck (or expected) to be doing all the heavy lifting like I usually was.

General cleaning always felt like an impossible task in a Katimavik house, especially ours in Corner Brook. No matter how recently someone had swept, there was always a layer of dirt or dust in the house, especially on the stairs which made the glossy varnish of the wooden steps extra slippery. It didn't help that several of us worked outdoors and couldn't help but track in that extra bit of mud or dirt. Luke and I were trying to stay on top of dust duty, but it quickly became clear that we were fighting a losing battle. Not an hour after everyone arrived home after work that week, the floor was already dirty. I almost snapped when someone accused me and Luke of not sweeping given the amount of dust on the stairwell, even though I knew damn well we had. It was at that point I knew it was a lost cause and gave up. Cleaning the light dust only gave you the illusion you were on top of things, but rarely did it stay that way.

I wanted to be as efficient as possible with our additional and mandatory chores to get them done and over with as soon as possible, but also because I had a lot of personal chores I wanted to get to. I wanted to feel like I had some semblance of control with how much was on my mind. Despite my best efforts, the crazy jumble of thoughts, to-dos, and house manager duties pulled my mind in different directions, leaving me very accident prone.

After a busy morning spent cleaning the basement, a space we had rarely used but needed to clean anyway, I tucked myself into a nook on the couch in the living room. I let a bright afternoon sunbeam warm my toes while I read a book Erica had lent me. I was trying to finish it so I could return it to her before we left. It provided a brief but welcome escape from house duties, but it must have worked too well. I had become so engrossed in the story in my hands that I forgot I left the water running in the kitchen sink to do dishes afterwards. It was a large sink that filled slowly from the faucet, even with the taps fully turned. I figured it left me a good five minutes to finish the page I was reading. Breaking my focus, I faintly heard what sounded like someone showering in the house. I thought it might have been Luke in the bathroom until he came down the stairs from the second floor and walked past the living room. But if he wasn't showering, then…

I ran back to the kitchen. The floor was completely covered in water. I quickly shut off the faucet and examined the sopping situation on my hands. And at my feet. Somehow Julie, who had been home and was finishing off a report of her own in the computer room, hadn't noticed either. Worrying she'd go into the kitchen and see the disaster I caused, I pre-emptively approached her first. Calmly.

"Julie, there's a ... surprise in the kitchen," I said sing-songily, leaning into the room from the door frame. "But I'm still working on it, so don't come in, 'kay?"

"Ooh! I love surprises!" She seemed cheerily intrigued and agreed, resuming her work.

I spent the next half hour mopping up the flooded kitchen as quickly as I could. Thankfully Luke never came into the kitchen and Julie forgot about the supposed "surprise" later that night. I never brought it up. Given how Luke and I were bollixing up a lot of house manager duties, no one was keen on surprises, especially after the last incident.

After discussing it with Luke, the two of us decided now seemed like the right time for some risky grocery shopping. This mostly consisted of shopping at a different grocery store and buying exotic fruits and vegetables that no one in the group had ever tried before. Considering we were trying to get rid of food in the house anyway, it didn't make sense to buy bulk quantities of our usual staples. Our logic was that if no one liked the new food we bought, no one ever had to eat it again. However, there was one item on our shopping list Luke and I were irrefutably required to purchase—female hygiene products.

Katimavik groups did take the purchase of these products into consideration when it came to budgeting. Even though Luke and Carlos were house managers once, the issue had never been brought up and the two of them never had to deal with buying the things. My guess was the girls had enough feminine products during that time. This was not the case with me and Luke in charge, so the girls brought it to our attention. With *specific* instructions.

"Remember, we need tampons, not pads," Rosalie told us emphatically. "Luckily all the girls in the house use the same thing, so that makes it easier on you two," she said sweetly before her tone turned menacing. "But *don't* forget them, or so help me God ..." I waited for Rosalie to giggle. She did not.

Tiffany chimed in from her bedroom, overhearing the conversation. "I will personally kick both your asses if you two screw this up!"

I circled the item on our shopping list—twice—just to be safe.

Once our shopping cart was filled with everything else on our grocery list, Luke and I stopped at the feminine product aisle. Hands on our hips, we looked up at the foreign and intimidating shelf before us.

"'Tampons. 'Super.' 'Super Plus.' 'Ultra.' 'Gentle Glide.' 'Sport'. 'Pearl'. 'Compak'. Jesus Christ!" Luke bellowed. "And then there's applicator types?"

We looked at each other with a silent panic of confusion and fear.

"I think we need a third opinion on this, Luke."

It became immediately clear that we knew absolutely fuck-all about menstruating. I whole-heartedly accepted my ignorance because I knew guessing was a dangerous game. I found the first employee I could. Thankfully it was a woman who looked to be in her early thirties. I bit the bullet and explained our situation to her. The fear of returning to the house with the wrong product unquestionably trumped any embarrassment I was having while trying to explain what business two young men had in that particular aisle.

"Let's get this straight—we *don't* know what we're doing," I told the woman. "But we have a house full of six women who need these for…" I thought about how many days were left in Katimavik. How fast did girls go through these things anyway?

The employee could see the strain in my face as I struggled to determine the quantity we might need. She shook her head, hiding a laugh. "I think what you fellas might need is the multipack."

"Multipack!" Luke and I exclaimed at the same time, exchanging glances of satisfaction. It was our best bet. Surely that would appease the girls, or at least most of them. And if not, too bad. No one could say we didn't try.

We bought the biggest box the store had and upon returning home, discreetly left it on the kitchen table like a piece of raw meat to lions. When Luke and I looked back in, shortly after people started returning home from work, we noticed the box had disappeared. None of the girls said anything, so Luke and I assumed we did well. The matter was never brought up again.

That evening, I uploaded photos from my digital camera onto an online blog I'd created. We had been doing so much in the last few weeks and amassed so many photos, so I was trying to organize them and select the best ones to showcase. I flipped through the photos from our recent excursion to L'Anse aux Meadows. It had been an interesting trip.

There was extreme fog during our visit to Norstead Village that gave a historical atmosphere to the world heritage site. We walked into recreated sod houses and interacted with historical actors dressed up in traditional Viking garb. Unlike a lot of other historical sites we had visited during Katimavik that were very protective of their assets, Norstead Village permitted us to try on the clothes and even hold and touch the recreated weapons. We had fun deciphering the value of various items that we traded at "ye olde shoppe." Having struck an amiable rapport with the blacksmith, he let us try our hands at throwing small axes at a log around the back of his building. The experience had been incredible and unanimously one of the highlights of everyone in all three groups. While the photos I rummaged through provided great memories, they could never truly capture the essence of being there.

While the photos uploaded, I casually checked my email and was surprised to find one from Linda. A few of us had kept in touch with our previous Sault Ste. Marie PL and would occasionally check in to see how she and her new participants were doing.

"Devon! So good to hear from you!" her email begun in response to the one I'd sent her months prior. I imagined Linda's joyful voice reading her message as though she was standing right beside me. Despite her admitted struggles with her current group and our reminders of the fond memories we had with her, Linda refused to admit we were her favourite bunch of kids no matter how much we cajoled her, just like a real mom. I wasn't surprised at her 'love-everyone-equally' stance. What was surprising was Linda's email, because she rarely sent them. Reading slowly through the short message, however, I could see how the sheer craziness of the story she had to tell couldn't wait. She needed to share it with me immediately.

My previous billet from Sault Ste. Marie, Andrea, had moved to the Yukon, leaving her apartment free to rent. The new renter was not only familiar with Katimavik, she had *heard* of Linda. This woman had also met Julie before. She even knew who *I* was! The new renter of my old billet was Larry and Ruby's daughter who had moved away—Anna. She and Linda instantly became best friends.

Katimavik continued to make the world a much smaller place.

Finally deviating from the momentum that seemed to take up the entire last month of Katimavik, we were thrilled for a three-day relief from work, volunteering, packing, or cleaning. Yes. It was our final 48 hours, once again combined with a holiday to make it a more gratifying 72. It felt tantamount to the "parents are away, kids will play" trope. How could it not? All our PLs were taking their days off at the same time. Although the Stephenville participants had already used their two days off, Deer Lake had not. Participants Antoine, Danica, and Krissy from that group were catching a bus Saturday and staying over. There was every expectation for drinking and shenanigans. Julie left early Saturday morning and told us she would be arriving later in the evening the day she returned, giving us even more time.

As soon as she left, the energy in the house completely flipped around. The rules changed. We were no longer participants living in a Katimavik house. We were young men and women just living side-by-side in a house together. There was no structure, or at least very little. Luke and I reminded everyone that we had finished house managing and weren't responsible for cooking for anyone. We were all to fend for ourselves. Some took that to heart. Tiffany and Bethany started drinking within five minutes of Julie walking out the front door.

"Fuck all you bitches!" Tiffany cackled. "If we have three free days, that's three free days I'm doing whatever the hell I want!"

It was a liberating attitude we all shared in our own way. So long as no one lit anything on fire or punched holes in the wall, everything was fair game. Some wanted to drink, others wanted to gorge themselves on junk food. Luke and I wanted to rent a movie that had recently come out, but Rosalie was committed to fighting us for control over the small television screen and DVD player in the living room.

"Screw that! I have all six seasons of *Sex and the City*. But you guys can join me and watch," she giggled to herself. "If you want."

We didn't. Luke and I hoped to sneak in our movie early before Rosalie dove into her TV marathon and hit up the video store as soon as it was open. Renting movies might have been a normal activity back home, but the temporary nature of Katimavik made it much less common as a participant. We didn't realize that we would have to make an account with the store in order to rent, but the cashier assured us it would only take a minute. We thought it might be awkward explaining how we had lived in Corner Brook for almost three months and were actually leaving in about a week, but our situation wasn't lost on the cashier. Once we gave our address, he recognized it.

"Oh, that's that house up on the hill there. Yeah, we've had some of your group come in here before," he told us. It must have been participants from the previous rotation. We were glad they didn't have any late charges passed onto us.

Luke and I grabbed some snacks and walked back home, eager to watch our movie. By the time we got back, Rosalie had already set up blankets and pillows in front of the TV.

"Six seasons, Devon! I've missed my girls! I need to catch up! Ooh, I love this show!"

A series about cosmopolitan women discussing relationships, clothes, and shoes had Rosalie written all over it. Luke gave up, but I wanted to have a chill afternoon, even if it wasn't watching something I wanted. I took a couch for myself while Rosalie watched "her girls" comfortably from a blanket on the floor.

As enthusiastic as we had been for a weekend of debauchery, that Saturday quickly became a relatively lazy one for everyone. Valérie joined Tiffany in drinking and maintained a steady level of drunkenness throughout the entire day; Bethany and Erica retreated to the former's room (they didn't share a bedroom. I never found out if that was an intentional decision of Julie's); and Luke decided to hang out with Jordan, accepting that we would have to watch our movie another time. In the end, a passive day was for the best. The consensus was to have a big party Sunday night, as Monday was a holiday which we planned to use for recovery, as well as cleaning up before Julie arrived later that evening. I knew I would accomplish nothing on Monday, so I decided to get a jump start on finishing some projects while everyone else did their own things. I noticed Carlos had been absent for quite some time and asked Rosalie where he was.

"Oh, he said something about the cliffs near the Walmart I think. He'd wanted to climb them for some time now," she answered without looking away from the screen. "Apparently there's a trail not far from the highway. He left this morning while you and Luke were out." Rosalie turned around now. "Weren't you saying you wanted to climb those as well?"

I had. I recalled mentioning it to Carlos while we were billeting. Larry and Ruby lived along a steep street near the upper edge of town. Not far across the highway from them were cliffs that overlooked Corner Brook. I had planned on climbing the hill that brought you to their top during billeting while I temporarily lived close to them, but it never happened. It would have been nice to do a climb with Carlos, but I still considered it a compliment that he took the same goal for himself.

Just another way we were similar, I guess.

That Sunday morning felt like our laziest ever, even for our time off. No one wanted to exert any unnecessary energy. It was squirrelled away to be unleashed that night in a final hurrah of unsupervised drunken shenanigans. As far as I could tell, everyone was still tucked away and deep in sleep, except for Rosalie who was dutifully watching her *Sex and the City* in the living room.

I brought down a Ziploc bag that had been tucked away in my belongings for nearly half a year. Inside was a large white square piece of fabric and other odd-shaped coloured pieces. It was my loose collection of pieces for my section of the quilt we had started in our fizzled sewing workshop in Sault Ste. Marie. No one had finished theirs and I doubted anyone intended to. But I kept mine, determined to one day finish it regardless of how crappily it was sewed. While I stitched away, stabbing myself with a needle, Rosalie continued to watch her show. Nearly finished my project, I was about to take a short break when I recognized a line spoken from one of the characters.

"Ro, you've watched this episode already."

She looked back at me. "What? How do you know?"

"This is the one where Carrie starts dating Mr. Big again. Samantha meets a drag queen," I explained, remembering the sequence of events. "Watch, Charlotte's going to throw a hissy fit about this guy and then they all meet up and talk about sex."

Rosalie watched the scene unfold just as I described. "Wait, have you been watching *Sex and the City*? Have you been following along?" she asked with an accusing grin on her face.

I hadn't. It had just been background noise while I played my Nintendo SP the previous night on the couch. Rosalie must have left the room and missed a few episodes and was now catching up again. She proceeded to mock me, asking if I identified more as a Carrie, Samantha, Charlotte, or Miranda. I ignored her. After snipping off the last thread, I held my quilt patch up. Alternating green squares bordered the white background. In the centre sat a brown stump with a curled leaf perched gently on top. I showed Rosalie my finished work.

"Good job, Dev!" she beamed. "You cook, you clean, you wash dishes, *and* you sew? You'll make a dashing house-husband one day!"

"Don't be so sure about the dishes. You guys never heard what happened when Luke and I were house managers, did you?"

Rosalie's eyes widened with fierce curiosity. "No, tell me!"

I proceeded to tell Rosalie how I flooded the kitchen and managed to hide it from everyone. Once I wrapped up the story, I looked back at my finished quilt piece in my hand. It seemed like an insignificant act, but in the back of my mind, it felt important. No one else had their patches. There would never be a Katimavik quilt made by our group, but I didn't care about that. We had plenty of other mementos to remind us of our nine months together. This patch was for me, a physical reminder that I was capable of seeing things through. It was practice in being true to my word, regardless of how long I had put it off. The stitching was exposed and erratic and some of the pieces sewn looser than others, but it was complete. I felt accomplished.

Several hours later that day, I found myself looking up at the cliffs from their base. As much as I enjoyed our shocking abundance of free time, I was unable to sit still for long and decided that afternoon was the time to escape the contagious lethargy of the house. I knew the way to go and walked the entire way to the edge of town, taking a few shortcuts through the trails I had become familiar with over the past three months. Once I was at the base of the cliffs, I couldn't seem to find any sort of trail head. I assumed it would have been a popular area to hike and that there might be signs indicating how to get to the top of the cliffs, but it appeared I was wrong. Still convinced there surely must have been a trail somewhere, I followed along the base until the sheer wall of rock narrowed to a point that climbing the hill became accessible. As soon as I was able to traverse upwards, I began to bushwhack my way to the top. Trailblazing like that reminded me of my childhood, not knowing what I might find as I tramped through untamed forest. The difference was that here, I had a destination. I continued to dodge thick brush as I trudged up the steep hill.

Finally, I came to the edge of the tree line which opened into a clearing that I knew would overlook the city. Before I exited the cover of their shadows cast by the August sun, I looked down at a worn footpath just metres from where I stood.

God damn it.

Despite having taken the hard way, the view was spectacular and worth the drudgery. The city of Corner Brook glowed against the rays of the sun with the sparkling waters illuminating the coastline that led to the Bay of Islands off in the distance. I could barely make out the neighbourhood where our house sat, filled with Katimavik participants ready to drink their asses off in just a few hours. I sat on a nearby rock and gazed at the city my friends and I had lived in for the past three months. My thoughts floated wistfully here and there, caught on the occasional thermal wind that gusted from the edge of the cliff just a small stone's throw away in front of me.

Would our absence be noticed when our group was gone? Would we leave an impression on the communities we lived in, or would they leave an impression on us? Were memories like footprints pressed into a landscape, naturally eroded by time? Were they worth holding onto or were they bound to inevitably fade away? At what point did one have to quit obsessing with what had taken place and just carry on to blaze fresh tracks in the world, encounter new people, and make new friends and new memories? Katimavik hadn't just been an escape from Hazelton; it had given me a different perspective, one I was still trying to articulate and understand. Things were going to be different when I went home. Maybe the town had changed. I know I certainly had. I wanted to believe it was like climbing a mountain. The hike up would always be challenging, the view might not change much, but how you felt at the top would be up to you, regardless of what you saw, because even if things appeared to be the same, what really changed was you.

I wondered if Carlos thought the same things when he was up here. We had been so alike, some days it was like seeing myself in a mirror. Maybe the reason we had such a rocky relationship was because we were truly seeing ourselves for the first time, a reflection of our insecurities as well as our own strengths. I heard people tended to flock to like-minded others, but I don't think that meant Carlos and I were set up to be best buds. He had been my foil, and as frustrating as the jackass had been, there was value in reflection between us, even if we didn't always like what we saw.

What was it about heights that made people think so damn much? I thought, snorting at the meta-irony.

I continued watching the city for a while longer and let the wind take my attention wherever it pleased. When I finally got up to leave, I took the trail down.

That night, we were going to party.

I was one of the first people up Monday morning, although it was closer to noon when I walked into the kitchen. I offered to make scrambled eggs for those who were up and awake. This made a groggy Tiffany and Valérie extremely happy, even though their grumbling and hoarse voices gave an impression otherwise. A lot of people in the house were still sleeping. Gradually, as bodies rose from the various bedrooms and the house came alive once again, everyone began to recall what had taken place the night before. The consensus: a lot.

Once everyone had eaten and sobered up a smidge, we began rounding up empties. We captured a photo of everyone in front of the colourful pile of empty booze containers that we had shaped into the Katimavik symbol. It was beautiful irony, a shimmering and sticky nod to the program that encouraged inclusive cohesion, but discouraged the social lubricant that made it happen, both of which there had been plenty of the previous night. I planned on showing the picture to Julie during our final debriefing when we knew we wouldn't get in trouble for it. We took the bags of empty bottles and gave them to the neighbours. Some of the empties rightfully belonged to them anyway, as they made a surprise appearance at the house late into the night.

I implored a final quick search for any loose bottle caps that might have escaped our thorough cleaning, lest a small piece of evidence become our undoing. Even after a hot mop of the sticky floor, we found none. Our Deer Lake guests caught the Greyhound bus and returned home. The aura of the house once again became tranquil. Luke and I even found the time to watch our movie now that Rosalie had released her grip on the TV. Part way through the film, I looked around the living room and had a disturbing realization.

"Shit!" I exclaimed. "Luke, do you know what's wrong with the living room?"

He looked around. "No, what?"

It was clean. *Too clean.* Julie would be arriving any minute. The house wasn't exactly immaculate, but I've never known a Katimavik house to be as tidy as it was right then, let alone after our 72 hours off. It would be suspicious to see everything so clean.

I ran to the kitchen and grabbed some items. Some chip crumbs on the floor here, a pillow nonchalantly tossed over there, some random papers and books left on the rug. I looked around at the props I had placed.

"Well. It's *something.*"

My timing couldn't have been any better, as Julie walked in the door.

She didn't suspect a thing.

CHAPTER 36

August 2006. Corner Brook.

The rain came down in a deluge. It had been raining for the past three days, but this storm put the rest to shame. Newfoundland's summer had been holding back most of its rain, but it was finally letting it loose. My coworkers and I were soaked through and through. None of us had bothered to wear any sort of rain jacket, though it would have proved useless anyway. I looked at Bret. I had only interacted with my supervisor a handful of times, which made his presence working alongside us that wet morning a surprise. I assumed he was filling in for employees who likely called in sick and just weren't up for working in such well-hydrated conditions. His being there made my bold request easier to ask.

"Soooo ... you think I can just call it a day?"

He smiled weakly, his resolve literally dampened. "Yeah, sure." We shook hands. He might have spent most of his time in the office, but Bret was far from a slouch and had a firm grip. "Hey, it's been good working with you, son."

I departed from the muddy trail where we stood. I was completely drenched, but singing in the rain warmed my soul as I slish-sloshed my way back home down the recently dug pathway. The trail wouldn't be open to the public for quite some time. I thought about how great it was going to look. The other established trails I walked down gave me a glimpse as to what someone could expect once it was all complete. I was proud of the paths Erica, Bethany, and I had cleared, gravelled, and tamped; the sod we had watered; the benches we had installed and painted; and the overall beautification we had contributed to Corner Brook.

It was just shy of lunchtime when I walked in the front door, sopping wet. I hoped that the house managers for the day had something hot to eat. Despite their screaming at me for dripping on the floor they had recently mopped (which I protested couldn't be helped), it was a swell last day of work.

There were lots of "lasts" in those days, which is why I suspected everyone was so emotional. They had all caught on to counting down the days, just like I had. We all had plenty going through our minds. It was difficult not to think, "That's the last load of laundry I'll do in this basement," "That's the last time I'll play laser tag with Jordan," or "That's the last time I'll go to the bar with my PL." That last one also happened to be a first for us.

"If the underage people can somehow get in, I'll turn a blind eye," Julie told us.

Julie hadn't exactly abandoned her PL responsibilities, but she and the rest of us knew damn well that Head Office wasn't sending anyone home early, not with only a few days to go until the official end of the program. The tickets were bought, the itineraries planned. Short of murdering someone, we were in the clear. We still needed to participate of course, but it made for some lenient opportunities, which Julie was game for. That night, it meant going to the bar with her group and blowing off a little steam. Best of all, the bar was really close to our house.

When examining my driver's license, the bouncer looked confused. He was likely looking for the birthday on the out-of-province ID. Whether he found it or not, he ushered me in anyway. The bouncer must have shrugged off the rest of the unique provincial IDs that followed because when I turned around, the rest of the gang was there. We had all miraculously made it inside.

It wasn't long before everyone had a drink in hand except for me. I had no desire to drink that night, which was probably for the best. We had been so busy, there had been little chance for any of us to decompress or release the emotions that had been building that week. Booze, again, served as a catalyst.

As I looked around the dark club with my dirty glass of Coke in hand, I was surprised how quickly everyone was to let loose. Spotting Tiffany kissing Carlos was certainly a surprise.

"Ah, some jerk off has been hitting on me since we got here," she later explained. I must not have noticed, but what I did observe was that she and Carlos remained committed to their apparent solution. I looked around to see what had become of the rest of my group, who were scattered about after barely an hour spent at the bar. Bethany and Erica had run off somewhere as they often did whenever they could, Rosalie was pissed at Carlos, and Luke was grousing about a drunken email he had sent to Krissy the other night.

And I somehow found myself dancing with Julie on the sticky dance floor. There hadn't been many people dancing that night, but after knocking back a few drinks, the right song must have played because she came directly to me. That, and everyone else was otherwise preoccupied. I could feel her pull me closer, readying herself to whisper a secret in my ear. Given how chaotic our innocent trip to the bar had quickly become, I was petrified of what she was going to share. Was what she was going to tell me the straw that would break the camel's back? I nervously tried to listen to what she had to say over the loud music.

"But you have to promise not to tell anyone else in the group," she insisted.

Oh God! Et tu, Julie!?

I didn't even know what I would do with the information I expected her to share. Panic overtook my body. How had I not tripped over my feet? I must have been sweating. I wanted her to just say it already.

"I think, out of everyone in the group…" she refrained for a second. "…That you would make the best Project Leader."

My stomach unswallowed itself. A wave of relief oscillated through my veins that had refused to pump blood to my brain for the last minute. If Julie had confided what I thought she was going to say, it might have been much more ... troublesome.

The song ended, and with it, our night out with Julie. We gathered ourselves and walked home, fortunately a short walk. The drunken banter surrounded me as I thought about what Julie had said.

The idea of becoming a Project Leader wasn't completely new to me. I had thought about it for quite some time, though it would be a while before I took any action in pursuing it. There was so much to do still—Canada World Youth, biking across Canada with my friends, and no doubt some other adventure after that. Those would be helpful and relatable life experiences to draw upon if I was going to help guide others during their own travel/volunteer adventure. Becoming a Katimavik Project Leader was a natural and enticing next step for me, even if it was a ways down the road. Julie's drunken, if genuine, endorsement made the potential prospect more real than ever.

I tucked the idea away somewhere deep in the back of my mind. I didn't know where I was putting it away, but I knew I'd pull it out when the time was right.

CHAPTER 37

August 2006. Channel-Port Aux Basque.

It was a quiet drive south of Corner Brook when we left the house. We drove past Stephenville on our way to our debriefing camp. There wouldn't be time for a visit to our neighbouring group. They were busy doing their own weekend of debriefing. While clusters attended Rotation Camp together, they didn't do their final debriefing one together. This time, individual groups were on their own.

Provided they met certain criteria, PLs had lots of freedom in planning the debriefing camps for their groups. Julie made it a point to keep ours secretive, including its location. Shortly after passing by two mountains that looked remarkably like a pair of breasts emerging from the earth as though a buxom giantess lay just beneath the surface, we arrived at our destination outside of Channel-Port aux Basques. Our base of operations for the next few days was a two-storied A-frame chalet that overlooked a beach with a rocky shore. It was a view that could easily be found on a postcard in a Newfoundland visitor centre.

We piled into the surprisingly spacious building, tired from the two-hour drive and anxious as to what sort of emotional demands we might experience over the next few days. And there would be a lot. This was the big one. Participants weren't being prepared for our next rotation, but for their return home. It was meant to be a time to process, to really look back over the past two hundred and seventy days and reflect on what we had done and the goals we had set, those shared or personal, achieved or still achievable. I finally felt like I had met all of mine. Katimavik had exceeded my expectations, and although it still provided its fair share of challenges and learning experiences, I was glad to have met them head on. Those challenges didn't end when the program was over though.

Reverse-culture shock was a common reaction for participants when they returned home after Katimavik. We were warned it could hit some harder than others, that we may return home and find our family, friends, and even the places we lived difficult to relate to like we once did. Many of us had changed and it was a real possibility that people might not recognize us, or vice versa. Some of us had lost weight, some had learned to cook, most of us had matured and developed some sort of healthy habit. Over the course of the next few days, all of us would figure out what else we might be bringing back. The reality was, those things might not mesh with what was waiting for us back home.

It was common to find a severe lack of motivation and accountability upon returning home when you no longer had the same structure or supports that Katimavik had ingrained into us. Participants could easily find themselves lonely despite being surrounded by old friends, friends who might not have changed, even though you had. It could be depressing when your best friends couldn't comprehend or care about the amount of tofu you had ingested that week, what a CTI was, or why the hell you wanted to start some kind of committee. They were your friends, but they weren't the ones you had worked with, planned with, played with, slept with, travelled with, and otherwise been surrounded by practically every day. Those people would no longer be there. Habits, good or bad, were easier to practise with others who practised them as well. With our fellow participants gone and no PL to keep us in line, it was easy to forgo any healthy habits we might have learned and developed in Katimavik. A decline in healthy habits made Katimavik alumni especially susceptible to depression.

The stories my brother Kyle told me corroborated those concerns. He had joined Katimavik and unfortunately never finished, but he'd heard the same warnings of what it was like to return home. Kyle was a bit cavalier in the way he described how difficult the transition was for him and even his group members who finished, prompting me to be extra cautious upon my own return home. I wondered if soldiers returning home from duty were prepared in the same way. A volunteer program spent abroad was obviously incomparable to the horrors of war, but when you got used to something, it was hard to adjust when things went "back to normal."

We all heeded this information on the situations and emotions we might experience, both then and later on. It was with these cautions that my group appropriately dubbed our last debriefing camp "Katima-detox." The name seemed befitting, not so much because we wanted to wash the program out of our system, but as a reminder that we would need to adapt to the world we would be returning to shortly, not the other way around.

Julie might have had discretion in the planning of debriefing camp, but she exercised it by delegating most of it to us. Everyone in the group was responsible for facilitating some sort of reflective activity. Rosalie's game was a good start. The heavy stuff would come later.

"We're going to play a game," she explained once we had all gathered in the chalet's living room and divided us into teams of two. "It's called *Something Touchy, Something Feely*. You two, quit laughing!"

Luke and I were trying to refrain from giggling, but we could see Rosalie was stifling a laugh herself. The purpose of her game was to look back and remember the past nine months by answering specific questions about key events that took place, a collective pop quiz for the group. With each passing question, it started to sink in just how much we had done. Everyone began to remember all those moments, big and small, planned and spontaneous, important and forgettable, or not so forgettable in some cases. Rosalie's game was fun, but it gave weight to the impending reality: The window to make more of those memories was closing. Katimavik was ending and we were going home.

Carlos was flabbergasted at the final results once the game was over.

"How in the hell did Devon and Tiff win?"

I was as surprised as he was. I had been partnered with Tiffany who hadn't joined the group until January, which meant she wasn't there for some of the events Rosalie quizzed us on. A frustrating portion of Katimavik had been my horrible attention to details, those pertaining to activities, excursions, or even relationships sometimes. As inattentive as I was when they took place, I was somehow able to recall the minutiae of things past:

"How many times did the plant get knocked over in Sault Ste. Marie?"

"What month was it when Valérie almost got crushed by ice falling through the bathroom window?"

"What was the name of the bartender in Saint-Élie?"

"When is Jordan's birthday? His *real* birthday, not his half-birthday that we celebrated?"

The winning duo of scattered-brained Devon and late-comer Tiffany was a shock to everyone. She and I relished the Newfoundland souvenir magnets Rosalie rewarded us with as our first-place prizes.

With so many workshops and debriefing activities taking place inside, the chalet quickly became cramped. Debriefing camp wasn't a vacation, but Julie did allow us to build some downtime into our schedule. We found it in a swim in the ocean one afternoon, a cold but refreshing break from the constant reflection. When we returned and everyone had changed into dry clothes, I called the group into the tiny living room. I wasn't sure if there would be a better chance to do what I had planned.

"Does everyone remember that 'You Know You're A Katima-victim When ...' website we came across in the Sault Ste. Marie?" I asked.

Everyone nodded, including Tiffany and Valérie who we had shown the website to shortly after they'd arrived and joined our group. They didn't understand the bizarre items listed at first, but it didn't take long before they were able to relate to them firsthand. I had printed the list of bullet points off and wanted to go through it with everyone and cross off all the things we've done or experienced. Having nearly completed Katimavik, I wanted to see if we had done any more of the items on that list than when we first found it.

We absolutely did. Half an hour later, we had collectively checked off nearly 90% of the list. It was incredible how different Katimavik could be for participants, yet still prompt unbelievable similarities in their experiences.

Of course, it wasn't just the things we did that made those classic Katimavik experiences. It was who you did them with, which was the focus of one of Julie's activities later that evening. We were tasked with writing letters to every individual participant in the group.

"I want you to write out any thoughts, feelings, memories, good or bad, anything that you feel the need to tell that person," she explained. "Think of it as your last chance to say those things to them."

Julie would return the letters to us later on. She encouraged us to read them when we had the chance, alone, even if it was after the program. We also didn't have to write all the letters at once, but whenever we had the chance. My letters to everyone in the group were simple to write. I'd already given those things lots of thought. I penned down fond memories, what I appreciated they brought to the group, and how I hoped to remember them after we had all gone our separate ways.

Naturally, Carlos was the exception. I had great difficulty finding the words for his letter. There was plenty to say to him, but I had no idea how to communicate it. He had been like a brother, one I hated for his adversarial nature, but respected for his determination and intelligence. Our similarities persisted even after Julie's workshop.

People had spread throughout the house to spend a dedicated hour penning their letters. Most had (or claimed to have) finished writing their letters and were relaxing for the remainder of the time Julie had given us. I knew that our last remaining days of Katimavik would not give us much opportunity to write the letters. I wanted mine done and out of the way. It was a coincidence but not a surprise when Carlos and I both walked into the tiny dining area of the chalet kitchen and took a seat at the small metal table with pen and paper in hand at the exact same time. Having lived with him for more than thirty-eight weeks and with how alike we learned the two of us were, it only seemed natural that we ended up where we did, glaring at each other from across the table.

"…You're writing my letter, aren't you?" I asked him, nodding at the paper resting in front of him.

"Yeah. And that's my letter too, isn't it?" We scowled harder at each other with the hint of a smug smirk on both of our faces. "…you bastard."

I didn't break eye contact with Carlos, but in my peripheral I could see one of the girls walk into the kitchen, catching me and Carlos locked in a Western-style shoot-out stare down. Whoever it was didn't say a word, but simply turned around and walked back to the room they came out of, no doubt wanting to avoid getting caught in the crossfire of whatever the hell was taking place right then. I wasn't sure how much time had passed, but eventually Carlos and I turned our gaze downward and proceeded to write what we had to say.

Later that evening, I grabbed a chair from the kitchen, placed it in the living room, and kicked my feet up against a windowsill. I wanted to relax for the last little bit of our free time. All the internal reflection had been mentally exhausting and I needed to close my eyes for a little bit. I popped my ear buds in and let the music from my MP3 player wash over me like the same waves I watched outside crash into the beach.

Several songs over the nine months had become group or individual favourites. The songs we sang along with in the van or danced to in the kitchen from static-filled radios glued us to the places we heard them and the people we listened to them with. Finding the names of the songs was the hard part, particularly some of the French ones we heard in Quebec. It took some internet detective work, but with Jordan and Molly's help, I was able to get all the songs I wanted, a well-balanced musical compilation of the past nine months. Our house computer wasn't capable of downloading music or burning CDs, but Jordan's was. The musical farewell gifts I made were the reason I was late to dinner and meetings so often in those last few weeks, but it was worth the risk. Everyone was ecstatic to have our own Katimavik soundtrack when I handed them out earlier that day. Even though I had previously explained to her where I'd been disappearing to and risked a CTI, Julie shot me an apologetic look when I handed her her own copy.

I closed my eyes and listened to "Move Along" by *The All-American Rejects*, one of whose songs I had included in my little musical project.

I rewound everything that had happened over the past nine months and thought about how I'd changed, what I'd seen, and even where I might be going. Memories played through my mind like a slideshow, each one denser and heavier than the last as they weaved their way into my thoughts. Did Simone regret her decision? I wondered where Daniel had ended up, and if his contrarian attitude had landed him in trouble yet? Had Victor pursued his artistic passions yet? Did Jess find the support she was looking for and deserved? Would Étienne still be painting in *Parc Mauricie* years from now? Would Jordan look up from the front counter of Cyber Zone and hope to see our smiling faces or would other customers fill that void? Would I ever run into those people again? Was everyone else thinking about those things or was it just me? The vivid reel of memories sped up faster and faster, drawing out the emotions I'd attached to them, each piling on top of each other quicker than I could process them until I thought I heard someone say my name.

My daydream bubble popped. I was back in the living room of a two-floor chalet outside of Channel-Port aux Basques, Newfoundland, along with seven other youths, several of whom were now staring at me.

I apologized, but I wasn't completely certain what for. Had I fallen asleep? Talked while dreaming? If so, what secrets had I shared?

To finish off debriefing camp, we had a bonfire. That night was about exhaling, relaxing, and letting go before moving on. We weren't going to be tethered by the duty to volunteer. There were no more Katimavik calendars or plans to adhere to. And we sure as hell didn't need to worry about whether there was enough protein in the meals cooked by house managers. There *were* no more house managers. We were still in "the program," but for all intents and purposes, we were just a bunch of people hanging out and telling stories, reminiscing. Julie drove us into town and allowed us to raid the junk food aisle of the closest grocery store. I quickly got the fire going and once everyone had a few sodium-packed hotdogs filling their stomachs and several bags of chips torn open and handed around the fire, Julie got the ball rolling by doing the same thing Linda had done six months prior.

"So I want you guys to tell me everything that went down in the house when I was gone," Julie said. "You were… an interesting group, so I *know* you have stories. Oh, and you won't get written up." Sensing some hesitation from the others, I took the reins and told Julie how our 72 hours had ended with a raucous house party.

"Oh. Well, yeah, I already knew *that!*" Julie said with a cheerful shrug.

The rest of us looked at each other nervously around the fire.

"What? How?"

"Easy. The neighbours told me," she explained.

Luke and I burst into obscenities aimed at the narcs we had apparently been living next to.

"Plus, I saw the bag of empty bottles on their porch. I mean, they party, but there was no way they drank *that much* over the weekend."

Embarrassment briefly silenced us. I knew we had cleaned up too well. But true to her word, Julie didn't punish us. Instead, she took the rebellion that night one step further and pulled out a joint. No one objected to her lighting it up, with a few participants themselves partaking in puffing and passing.

It might have been the dank smoke from Julie's weed wafting and mixing with the salty air coming off the waves off in the distance, or perhaps the mesmerizing crackle of the warm fire, but there was a serene calm that lulled us late into the night. The hours melted away as we talked about everything and nothing and munched on chips even long after we were hungry. What began as a blazing fire that night eventually died down to a gentle glow. The idea that our worries and insecurities might flutter away into nothingness like the same sparks and cinders in front of our eyes was comforting. Our concerns about tomorrow, the next day, and the day after that would fade, but until then, we were there. Some of us were more quiet than others, but we were there all the same. At the end, together.

CHAPTER 38

August 2006. Corner Brook.

Candles sat in each corner of the living room, illuminating the orange walls. In one corner was a thin grey blanket with a poster board standing upright. It was covered in assorted pictures of us, pictures by ourselves, with others, and some of the whole group. In them, we were making faces, singing, dancing, climbing trees, reading, cooking, playing in the snow, swimming, resting, but always full of life. We were happy and laughing, we were cold and exhilarated, hot and tired, we were covered in mud or sweat or some other substance, but almost all of them had us smiling in them. I noticed some of the photos were from before we even met Julie. She must have had Linda or Anne send her digital copies. Beneath the photo collage were coloured picture frames. Each contained a black and white photo of us, this time as individuals. It made the display look more like a shrine. Some photos I had never seen before, but somehow they seemed to have captured us in our most natural elements. It was hard to pin down exactly what those were, but we all seemed happy in them. This was our ceremony. Aside from the bus and airplane rides that would take us home, it would be our last official activity of Katimavik as participants.

"After this, you'll no longer be participants," said Julie, struggling to hold back a tear. One by one, she called each of us up and presented us with a certificate of completion and a sealed envelope. Inside were our reference letters from Julie and our work placements, a personalized goodbye letter, and our cheques for one thousand dollars. We had often talked about getting our cheques and what we would do with them, much like winning the lottery. The difference was that these were earned—well earned. And there they were, in our hands.

The moment seemed surreal, like it wasn't really happening. There was an air of ambiguity that we didn't care to fight anymore. The posterboard calendars were no longer on the wall, torn up and tossed into the recycling bin. The house was decommissioned. Even our beds were gone, shipped away and stored somewhere until new Katimavik houses were erected on Newfoundland's East Coast. We literally couldn't stay any longer, even if we wanted to. Julie had to remain, just a little while longer. PLs still had reports to do and other tasks which we weren't privy to and Julie never bothered to explain. But at this point, she was no longer responsible for us. And with nothing else to do, we partied once more. Though not nearly as crazy as our 72 hours, shenanigans were still plentiful.

Valérie had convinced the neighbours to come over and play for us. They set up their instruments surprisingly fast in what had previously been our living room. We never would have expected to fit two guitarists and a drummer in there, but it was quite spacious once the furniture was removed. There was just enough space for the musicians and the small group of fans, Corner Brook's soon-to-be-gone Katimavik group who was thrilled at the impromptu tribute concert. It was an honour to unexpectedly have a few songs dedicated to us. I felt guilty that we hadn't invited the guys over earlier or gotten to know them better, but rather than mope, we danced. Maybe it was the cathartic release of rocking out during an emotional time, or the surprising acoustics of the cramped room, but the garage-band quality of *The Embarrassments* was better than the sounds their muffled rehearsals had us previously believe they were capable of.

It wasn't long before the Greyhound arrived in the dreaded early morning. I was beginning to wonder if Katimavik ever chartered buses that weren't scheduled to arrive at ungodly hours. Most of the group was drunk by this point and struggled to walk up the same hill in the alley way that we had walked down three months prior. Already aboard the bus was the Stephenville group. Only, they weren't the Stephenville group anymore, just like we weren't the Corner Brook group. None of us were even technically participants anymore. Luke joked we might be considered something more like wards of Katimavik. Whatever our titles, we were back to just being individuals crammed on a bus, much like we were nine months prior. Whether we were the same people as before was something to be discussed another day. The other passengers on the bus were more or less in the same inebriated state as my now former groupmates.

A short, dark drive later, Deer Lake joined us on the bus, also with mostly drunken participants. Stepping off to help some of them with their bags, I was given a sobbing hug from their PL. Sandy looked so different as she wept, a tiny and vulnerable little thing. It was in Deer Lake that the first of our group had to leave. Luke, Bethany, and Tiffany's flights weren't departing until several hours later. They and half of the others on the bus with the same itineraries were going to wait in Deer Lake. The bus driver exhibited great patience in letting a bunch of blubbery fools say goodbye to the other bunch of blubbery fools.

Our bus drove away, slightly emptier but no less lighter. I looked out the window at the hint of daylight peeking from across the horizon. At the front of the bus, muffled cries could be heard. Unlike everyone else, I remained silent and dry faced. I felt like an asshole. Maybe it hadn't set in that I wasn't going to see Luke, Bethany, and Tiffany again. Soon it would be the rest of us departing ways. I knew I was sad. So why wasn't I crying? I had never felt such an influx of emotions: sadness, frustration, anger, fear, loneliness. It was a stew of feelings tossed haphazardly onto a plate with no cutlery and no clue what to do with it. While staring out the window added to the melodrama that played out in my head, I knew it wasn't doing anything to help with my numbing self-loathing. What did help was hearing a weeping voice shout from the front of the bus.

"Devon! Come up here, you jerk!" I heard Carlos call.

I forced myself up from my seat, stumbling past sleeping legs jutting into the bus aisle. Once I sat down next to my remaining friends who were sprawled over each other, the dam burst and I joined in their flood of tears. No one said anything though. We just cried, letting the emotion wash over us, bereft of explanation or rationale or even a witty one-liner. It was what it was. I could only imagine the poor bus driver who had to listen to the raw display just feet away from his seat.

Bags checked, plane tickets in hand, we waited in the airport terminal which was deserted that early in the morning. The peak of emotion had passed by and exhaustion from the night before was starting to settle in. It made the already empty terminals even quieter. Samantha, Erica, Carlos, and I were the first to leave. We walked in together and were welcomed by a waving Keith.

"Hi guys. You must be stoked to go home. Here."

Keith held out a box filled with water bottles. Canadian airlines now forbid over 100ml of liquids on planes, a recent policy change that we were not aware of. The bottled water was a welcome surprise as most of us were thirsty, drunk, or hungover. As Keith explained how he thought of the idea at the last minute and as his chance to say goodbye to us all, Samantha leaned over and whispered into my ear.

"Dev… do you remember what you wrote in my journal?" she said in a hush. "You know, after prom?"

It was mostly Luke's idea. Once he heard some of the girls in our group never had a high school prom, he knew he had to make their dreams come true. In the late wake of our PLs letting certain activities slide, we convinced Deer Lake and Stephenville to attend a dance night that Luke had managed to put together. He claimed to simply be a romantic, but we argued he just wanted to get laid. Whatever the reality, he made it happen and everyone enjoyed a night of dressing up and dancing to the tunes played by our good pal Jordan as DJ. It was also one of the last shared events we had before debriefing. At the end of that night, not knowing if we'd have the chance again, everyone wrote down their emails, phone numbers, and addresses. Considering how many people were drunk on the bus and in no state to start grabbing paper or pens, it was prescient that we had shared contact information at prom. I was especially grateful. Maybe it was my thrift store vest or the cologne I was sporting the night of prom, but I had been feeling confident and debonair. When Samantha asked for me to write something in her journal after everyone was danced out and ready to go back to our respective Katimavik houses, I reminded her of the revealing conversation we had in the St. Anthony's Lions Club hall. I wrote down how one day, I would teach her "Ze ways of ze French." It was pathetically cheesy, but I took a shot.

While Keith droned on about airline policies, Samantha and I quickly excused ourselves and calmly walked around the corner. Once we were out of eyeshot, we dropped our bags at the same time, embraced each other tightly and met passionately at the lips.

Mountains. God, how I missed those mountains.

I looked out the plane window at the sights below. Newfoundland had its fair share of mountains, but these were different somehow: snow covered peaks, glacier lakes, winding rivers that carved out deep valleys. The whole world below, not just the sun reflecting off snow or bodies of water, seemed to glisten in the morning sun. It felt like being welcomed back by an old friend, just like the ones I would shortly find waiting for me at the Smithers airport, waving a sassy "welcome back" sign.

It was an exhausting return home. Every so often I was overwhelmed by an unexpected well of tears, except this time I didn't have anyone to share them with. It was uncanny how nine months seemed like forever, yet as soon as I took that first step onto the retractable stairs of the plane that would take me off the Rock, it all seemed to disappear in a jolt. The people, the workplaces, the food, the adventures, the different places I'd lived and seen, all of it felt like it had taken place years ago, not the months, weeks, or for some events, even days ago which I knew to be the reality. I willed myself to recognize that that was life. Experiences and people would come and go, but if they truly were that special, I wouldn't really forget them. And because of them, I'd be a new person when I got home. Thankfully the people from Katimavik—and not just my group—had given me something to take, to use, to learn from. They were going to be part of the new me, whoever that was. I would keep that idea close to my heart, a warm reminder to give me comfort on lonely days. I didn't think people back home would understand. I couldn't describe it to them even if I tried.

With the biggest journey so far in my life behind me, I thought of the giant void I felt, the one I'd tossed question after question into, wondering what was next and where my next adventure might take me. The world was a big place. Canada alone had proven to be huge. There was so much more I still needed to see.

But one place at a time, I told myself. *For now, let's start with home.*

AFTERWORD

If I could sum up the story you just read in one word, it would be: trajectory. Sorry for wrapping it up so efficiently like that. Don't get me wrong, I still hope you read my book and didn't skip to the end for the CliffsNotes, but that's the word that comes to mind. You can debate me on that if you'd like, but you know, I wrote the damn thing.

If you've made it to this section of the book, you can tell that first year after graduating high school was a formative one for me. A certain nine-month travel volunteer program ensured that. As you are probably aware by now, Katimavik had that effect on most people, appealing to youth who were usually a little lost in their own way. Perhaps they needed to escape their hometown to see what life was like elsewhere, or maybe they wanted a chance to discover themselves without the scrutiny of the same familiar faces they grew up with present while they did so. Anyone who grew up in a small town knows what I'm talking about. Whatever the reasons for a participant joining, Katimavik meant a change.

I can now consider myself among the alumni; not only of those who completed the program—a challenge in its own right—but the fewer who have published their stories explaining exactly what that change was like for them, how it unfolded and set things up for that kind of growth to continue. If there are more of us out there who fit into this latter category, please reach out! I know from experience, Katimavik wasn't always easy to describe to people, but from what I've been told by others who I've shared drafts of this book with, I appear to have done a decent job on the matter.

Katimavik lit the fuse that would rocket me towards so many things in my future. There were times it felt like a direct course, other times like I was meandering wildly around a thick forest I thought I could competently explore just because I'd successfully hiked a few times. Whatever the mood, I was always fueled by the aspiration that I could achieve something better and gain something I hadn't had before. While it would take some time before the idea even crossed my mind, writing a book about my experience would indeed become one of those aspirations.

As most authors can attest, writing a book begins with earnest intentions which are quickly marred by the reality of, well, writing a book. It was driven of course by personal ambition of which I would find I have a lot of. Perhaps too much, which you'll find out in my other books (that ambition in action, right there). With so much introspection in preparing for this book, I realized I didn't want to merely write my story, I wanted others to know how and why I am the way I am, how I got to where I am. Another way of saying that word I mentioned: *Trajectory*. In that kind of deep, intentional reflection, we understand ourselves better. I think most of us wish to do that, and I hope people might be inspired to walk that introspective journey in their own way. I like to believe that most non-fiction strives for that goal; that by writing about our experiences, we can vicariously impart those same lessons to others, so that they might consider their own events in their lives and the role they played in contributing to developing them as a person. You know, life.

You're welcome, I guess.

The process for writing this book was more or less what you'd imagine. I first started by writing down the highlights, the best hits, the cream of the crop stories from my time in Katimavik. These were the first ones I would share with everyone back home when I returned, the ones I knew would make my friends and family laugh, gasp, cry, or sometimes to my dismay, give me looks of utter confusion or worse, disinterest. I began filling up a pad of paper with these stories, these "This one time, during Katimavik…" anecdotes, writing them down as best I could remember. As page after page began to fill, I noticed there were still gaps, missing details. I quickly realized a lot more context would be necessary, especially if I wanted to share these with a larger audience and have them relate.

I pulled out every bit of Katimavik memorabilia I had, diving into my journals, archived emails, photos, and scrap books. Doing so had the desired effect. As I walked down the proverbial memory lane, I tried to revisit my Katimavik experience and reflect on the events that took place as objectively as possible. First of all, I learned that some of the details I was convinced were accurate were in fact incorrect (keep that in mind next time you listen to that drunk guy at a party who swears his story happened exactly as he tells it). Secondly, the less pleasant memories still hurt, but I couldn't gloss over those. All of it was helpful in filling in the context for how those events and relationships came to be. Those stand-alone anecdotes no longer sufficed anymore; they became part of chapters which grew and grew, until eventually something began to emerge, tying it all together. I didn't just have a recollection of things that happened. Lo and behold, I had a story!

Don't get me wrong, that didn't make things easy. The hard part was deciding what to get rid of. As lengthy as you may have found this book, and as lascivious as some of the stories in it might seem, it's worth noting that I didn't include everything. There were indeed some things I kept out; I decided they were either irrelevant or they were discouraged by my editors. I tend to get side tracked with fluffy, extraneous details that I become convinced are necessary, a habit I would find continuing well into my adulthood. Apparently, it's quite common with creative personalities. Being concise is difficult in storytelling, whether speaking on stage or writing a book. I hope I've found a balance of that in my story and that I haven't bored you with said fluff.

But isn't that what makes a good story? Sure, the intrepid heroes got from point A to point B, but what happened in between? Who did they meet along the way? I don't want to compare myself to the likes of, say, Tolkien, but when it comes to those stories, it really *was* about the friends we made along the way, wasn't it? Even if my book lacked orcs and elves, I did mention dragons a couple of times. And as the diehard fans of the Lord of the Rings will assure you, taking shortcuts—with, like, say, giant eagles—would have lacked a certain *je ne sais quoi.* You need the extra details, the fluff, the exposition, the backstory. You need the long, drawn-out context to really get a feel for the characters in the story and their motivations, or else why the hell do you care what they do?

See? I told you being concise wasn't easy.

That's part of the process I reckon. You can see how trying to connect all those little dots can make one go a little crazy. Once you peel back the layers of what happened between a character's journey from Point A to Point B, you realize that straight line had a lot more wiggles and detours to it than you might have first realized. It's like counselling, but in book form! I can only imagine how many therapists get authors as clients.

Oh, there I go again.

Even with my due diligence, I must acknowledge that the stories within this book may not have happened 100% factually the way I have presented them. Names were changed to protect the innocent (or embarrassed); some events were shifted around in order to provide a stronger, more cohesive narrative rather than a spotty recollection of events that merely happened; and it's quite possible that my own observations could have been nothing more than speculation. I've done my best to present things as accurately as possible, while also being honest and true to the story I wanted to tell. My story. If anyone recognizes themselves within this book and have serious qualms with how I've depicted you, I'm more than happy to welcome you for a visit and discuss the difficulties of writing and publishing non-fiction. I look forward to those phone calls or messages.

I should also point out that writing a memoir is very different than writing fiction. It's not prescriptive; you don't write what you want to happen, you merely write what did. In doing so, you observe a vast difference in between who you are, the one writing; and who you were, someone who would never fathom sharing some of those stories you lived. These differences could be in the language you once used or close-minded attitudes or opinions you once held. It's a vulnerable process having to accurately portray a younger, more naïve, and yes, likely stupider version of yourself. The temptation to gloss over those embarrassing moments and paint yourself in a more positive light is real, I assure you. I must emphasize that in this book, I wrote about myself and others at a time when we were experiencing new things almost daily, and our responses or actions may not have always seemed reasonable. In that, I hope I captured the essence of a latent teenager burgeoning into a young adult accurately.

As I found myself reconnecting with my former groupmates or periodically meeting other Katimavikers throughout adulthood, we would all realize the same thing—that experience helped set the stage for something bigger. As I learned after reading Will Ferguson's *I Was a Teenage Katimavictim*, it can be eerie to find yourself part of a collective experience, even when not directly involved with those who shared it. As a seventeen-year-old, I had (and still have) a lot of ego, believing like most of us at that age, that our experiences were unique and that we should feel special, almost exceptionally, to have endured what we did. Humility eventually teaches us otherwise. I wish they taught us that in school.

Apparently publishing a book invokes similar feelings. The lows, the highs, the giddiness upon making things read the way you want them to, the hair-pulling frustration when things don't. Joining the vast community of authors and writers in the world, you quickly learn that everyone in their own right and at their own time goes through these emotions. It is not a solo experience. But when that brilliant idea of yours falls apart, you pick up the pieces, big and small, and build it back up again. And hopefully (fingers crossed) the next writing project will be a lot smoother for all those mistakes you made the first time around. And you eventually come to realize others went through the same frustrating process.

Learning, am I right?

Though those lessons unfortunately aren't always evident as they are being taught to us, hindsight has a way of peeling back the many layers and teachings that were at play during the past. Waxing nostalgic doesn't always leave you with warm, fuzzy feelings, as future readers of my books may learn. You've got to put some years behind you first before you can truly appreciate what you took from that thing you did aside from a cool story to tell your friends back home. While it doesn't help to dwell on the past, sometimes looking back can really show you how far you've come, even if you don't always know where that trajectory is taking you.

Whenever I reminisce about Katimavik, I'm always left with a glowing sense of appreciation for the opportunity that was given to me. It makes me glad that my family was supportive in me going, although I'm sure my mom and dad were simply glad to have their third child out of their house for nine months. Everyone I knew back home was happy to hear of my acceptance into Katimavik and was confident I would excel in a program that was right up my alley. They were correct.

Even today, I'm grateful not only for the people I met throughout Katimavik but also *because* of it. It truly did make the world a little bit smaller and slightly less intimidating, and in the way I think Jacques Hébert and Pierre Trudeau intended for it to do so.

I want to thank my editors Jesse Holland and Charlene Mattson. Knowing me uniquely in their own right, these two wrangled the deviating thoughts and rants my drafts had accumulated and helped me hammer out the final edits and necessary changes to produce something I was proud to publish. With a project so long in the making, one tends to develop tunnel vision. It feels amazing to see the other side.

ABOUT THE AUTHOR

Born and raised in the small northern town of Hazelton, British Columbia, Devon knew he couldn't stay put for long. After several extensive volunteer programs and even biking across Canada, Devon finally found himself ready to put some roots down. With too many creative ideas and too few outlets to express them in his hometown, he now resides in Prince George, BC, where he continues to write, perform, and get involved in his community in various ways. When he's not on stage or in a café with a coffee in hand, he's usually getting lost on his bike with a new writing project stewing in his head. *Elsewhere, Canada* is his first published novel.

Manufactured by Amazon.ca
Bolton, ON

37661285R00160